Managing Public Relations

This second edition of *Managing Public Relations* introduces students to the key concepts and practices involved in the day-to-day running of a PR operation, whether it is a company department, an independent agency, or any organized group focused on PR. The book's unique approach places the PR function within the broader context of an organization, equipping students with the essential business knowledge, perspective, and skills needed when starting out in their careers. This new edition has been updated and includes:

- Current examples and testimonials from across the globe, as well as new and updated "Executive Viewpoints."
- Expanded content on strategic planning, budgeting, and financial statements.
- Detailed commentary on topics relevant to the modern workplace, including remote management.
- Treatment of diversity, inclusion, equity, and access within PR.
- Additional content on the use of analytics, measuring return on investment (ROI), project management, toxic employees, and other topics.
- Updated online material, including an Instructor's Manual that incorporates problem-based questions, example assignments, and activities.

A highly practical and comprehensive guide, this textbook should be essential reading for advanced undergraduate and postgraduate students studying public relations management, strategic communications, and marketing management.

Peter M. Smudde, PhD, APR, is Professor and Associate Director of the School of Communication at Illinois State University, USA.

Managing Public Relations

Business Principles and Tools for Strategic Communication

SECOND EDITION

PETER M. SMUDDE

Routledge
Taylor & Francis Group

LONDON AND NEW YORK

Designed cover image: © Getty Images

Second edition published 2023
by Routledge
4 Park Square, Milton Park, Abingdon, Oxon, OX14 4RN

and by Routledge
605 Third Avenue, New York, NY 10158

Routledge is an imprint of the Taylor & Francis Group, an informa business

First edition published by Oxford University Press 2015

British Library Cataloguing-in-Publication Data
A catalogue record for this book is available from the British Library

ISBN: 978-1-032-07680-5 (hbk)
ISBN: 978-1-032-07676-8 (pbk)
ISBN: 978-1-003-20828-0 (ebk)

DOI: 10.4324/9781003208280

Typeset in Bembo
by Newgen Publishing UK

Access the Support Material: www.routledge.com/9781032076768

CONTENTS

BIOGRAPHIES FOR AUTHORS OF CHAPTERS' "EXECUTIVE VIEWPOINTS"

Felicia Blow, PhD, MBA, APR, is an award-winning leader with extensive organizational, fundraising, strategic planning, leadership, and management experience. With a 30-year career spanning work in manufacturing (Caterpillar, Inc.); waste management and environmental services (Southeastern Public Service Authority); telecommunications (Cox Communications); and higher education (Paul D. Camp and Tidewater Community Colleges), Dr. Blow currently serves as Associate Vice President for Development at the renowned historically black institution Hampton University.

At Hampton, Dr. Blow led the university's $150 million "Dream No Small Dreams II" campaign as its director. That campaign concluded in December 2019 and ultimately exceeded its goal in raising more than $166 million in support of university priorities. Among her many accomplishments, Dr. Blow led a nearly year-long strategic planning effort in 2019 to 2020 that concluded with the establishment of the Public Relations Society of America's (PRSA) first three-year Strategic Plan for Diversity & Inclusion, and served in 2020 as Co-Chair of the National Diversity & Inclusion Committee. Dr. Blow formerly served as Chair of the Universal Accreditation Board; during her leadership term, she worked to approve and initiate the APR+M (Accredited in Public Relations and Military Communication) credential which excellently positions PRSA with military organizations.

Dr. Blow is an active member of Alpha Kappa Alpha Sorority, Inc., and numerous other business, economic development, and community service organizations. She also has earned the PRSA's Accredited in Public Relations credential. Finally, Dr. Blow earned her bachelor's degree in mass media arts from Hampton University; her Master in Business Administration degree from Strayer University; and her doctorate in higher education administration from Old Dominion University.

Jillian Collins Bohr is a growth leader with a specialization in building effective new business processes for global public relations firms. Currently Director of U.S. Growth at Golin, Jillian leads new business initiatives, including leading pitch teams, analyzing growth trends, and developing best practices for the global network. Prior to joining Golin in 2018, Jillian spent several years building and growing Edelman's new business operations for the Midwest region.

Throughout her career, she has played an integral role in winning the trust and business of some of the world's largest brands and organizations during highly competitive agency reviews. Jillian holds a Bachelor of Science degree from Illinois State University, where she majored in public relations with a minor in business administration. She resides in Lemont, Illinois with her husband, Tony, and son, Jack.

Gerard "Gerry" F. Corbett, APR, Fellow of PRSA, is CEO of Redphlag, a strategic public relations firm focused on helping people and companies to define and communicate their intrinsic value. Gerry has served more than four decades in communications and technology roles with Fortune 200 firms and the National Aeronautics and Space Administration (NASA). He serves on the board of advisors of Infinite Retina and the Museum of Public Relations.

Gerry most recently was a branding instructor in the Entrepreneurship Program at the University of California at Berkeley and an adjunct professor of PR at San Jose State University. He was Chair and Chief Executive Officer of the Public Relations Society of America (PRSA) in 2012, a member of its College of Fellows, served on its board for eight years, and joined PRSA as a Public Relations Student Society of America (PRSSA) member in 1974. A native of Philadelphia, Pennsylvania, Gerry has a BA in public relations from San Jose State University and an AA degree with a major in electronics engineering from the Community College of Philadelphia.

In addition to PRSA roles, Gerry is a member of the London-based Public Relations and Communications Association; a senior member of the American Institute of Aeronautics and Astronautics; a member of the National Association of Science Writers and the San Francisco PR Roundtable. He is Past President of the International Advertising Association; and a past member of the Page Society and the National Investor Relations Institute.

Jennifer Detweiler is Director of Employee Communications at Expedia Group, a travel tech company. She leads people and culture communications, reaching more than 18,000 employees worldwide. Before joining Expedia Group, Jennifer worked at Aon, a global professional services firm, and was responsible for internal and executive communications for its Health and Retirement Solutions practices. Jennifer has ten years of experience in internal communication, serving in both in-house and agency roles, focusing on organizational change, communication strategy, storytelling, and executive communication.

Prior to joining Aon, Jennifer worked for Edelman, a global public relations firm, where she consulted for clients including Hewlett-Packard, Jazz Pharmaceuticals, Baxalta, Barilla, and PayPal. Her work has been recognized by industry-leading award programs such as the IABC Gold Quill Award, the PRSA Chicago Skyline Award, and the Ragan Employee Communications Award. Jennifer graduated *magna cum laude* from Illinois State University with a Bachelor of Science degree in public relations. She also holds a Master of Science degree in communication from Illinois State University.

Ulrike Haugen is Executive Vice President and Chief Communications Officer of the DNV Group in Oslo, Norway. She is a member of DNV's Executive Committee with Responsibility for Communications, Public Affairs and Sustainability, reporting directly to the Group President and CEO. She is also President of the German–Norwegian

Chamber of Commerce. Ulrike has more than 20 years' extensive communications, marketing, sustainability, and business development experience within international corporations with positions in Norway, the UK, Germany, and Italy. She has worked in the maritime, energy, and legal sectors and holds a German law degree from the University of Bonn and an MBA from the London South Bank University.

Jessamyn Katz is President of Heyman Associates, a premier communications executive search firm that serves the areas of corporate communications, public relations, public affairs, and related fields. As leader of the firm, Jessamyn sets standards for client work and manages major national and global searches. After nearly a decade in New York, she built the firm's West Coast presence and has developed particularly close relationships across that technology-heavy region. She also partners on worldwide initiatives with colleagues in Europe and Asia.

Jessamyn has led searches to fill myriad executive-level roles in strategic communications, investor relations, marketing, and other specialties within those functions. She advises clients across sectors, with an emphasis on technology, healthcare, financial services, nonprofits, and higher education. She is also an active member of the Arthur W. Page Society's Page Up association and is on the Institute for Public Relations (IPR) Board of Trustees.

Jessamyn developed a taste for PR while still in college through internships at Abernathy MacGregor and Burson-Marsteller and knew she wanted to develop her career around people who build brands and preserve their reputations. With nearly 14 years of experience in the function of communications—with increased exposure to marketing over time—she's a credible counselor to clients and candidates and keeps a close watch on where these functions are heading.

Jessamyn is a *cum laude* graduate of Bucknell University with a bachelor's degree in psychology and education. Having lived in Texas, Switzerland, and California, she approaches work and life with a broad worldview. Her Papillon Olivia doesn't make a very good foreign language practice partner, though, so her German and Spanish are a bit rusty. She travels whenever she can and is a devoted fan of SoulCycle.

Tina McCorkindale, PhD, APR, is President and CEO of the Institute for Public Relations. She taught as a professor for 15 years and has more than ten years of experience working in corporate communication and analytics. She is a member of the Page Society, The Seminar, the Commission for Public Relations Education Steering Committee, the AMEC (International Association for Measurement and Evaluation of Communication) Academic Advisory Board, the California State University Dean's Advisory Council in Communication, and the University of Oregon Strategic Communication Leadership Network. She frequently gives presentations and publishes in academic journals and industry publications about the current and future state of the public relations and communication industry. In 2019, she was selected as one of

40 national leaders to participate in the 91st Joint Civilian Orientation Conference, the most prestigious public outreach and full immersion program in the Department of Defense.

McCorkindale serves on the board of several industry groups and two academic journals. She is the recipient of the 2017 PRSA David Ferguson Award, was inducted into the *PR News* Measurement Hall of Fame, and received the 2020 PRSA Puget Sound Professional of the Year award. McCorkindale received her bachelor's degree in journalism with a minor in marketing from the University of Southern Mississippi, a master's degree in public and corporate communication from the University of South Alabama, and her PhD in communication from the University of Miami. She lives with her family, dogs, and chickens in Seattle, Washington.

Gary Myers is Founder and Former President of MorganMyers, a communications counseling firm serving national and global clients in the agricultural and food industries "from pasture to plate." His firm's work is frequently recognized with Silver Anvils from PRSA. In addition to his leadership at MorganMyers, Gary is Past Chair of PRSA's Counselors Academy. His agency was one of the founding members of The Council of Public Relations Firms, with Gary serving as Board Treasurer in that trade association's early years. Gary is a recipient of the Agricultural Relations Council's Founders Award and has been inducted into the ARC Hall of Fame.

After retiring from MorganMyers, Gary taught a variety of communications courses for the University of Wisconsin-Whitewater, and the capstone campaigns course for West Virginia University's master's degree in Integrated Communications. He currently consults with agency owners from time to time on agency management issues.

Cheryl I. Procter-Rogers, APR, PRSA Fellow, MCC, is an award-winning public relations and business strategist and executive coach. She provides individual coaching and thought leadership in areas such as leadership and career transitions, leadership growth, and transformational leadership.

Prior to that, she served as a senior consultant and executive coach for her firm, A Step Ahead PR Consulting and Coaching. She developed and implemented strategies and counseled clients in the areas of crisis and executive communications, strategic planning, change management, leadership effectiveness and business strategy. She conducted media training and facilitated board retreats. Cheryl has been an executive coach to more than 700 C-Suite executives over more than 25 years.

For more than 40 years, Cheryl has worked with an impressive portfolio of executives and Fortune 100 companies as an executive for DePaul University, Home Box Office (HBO), Nielsen Marketing Research, and Golden State Mutual. As a consultant and coach, she has worked with Coca-Cola, Nissan, Allstate, McDonald's, McCain Foods, the former Valparaiso Law School, Sigma Gamma Rho Sorority, and the Magellan Corporation.

She was the 2006 National President and CEO of the Public Relations Society of America (PRSA), the profession's premier organization with more than 30,000 members. She remains the youngest person inducted into its College of Fellows with more than 350 members. She is PRSA's 2011 Gold Anvil recipient, the Society's highest award presented to one professional each year whose work significantly advances the profession and sets high standards for the practice of public relations.

Cheryl has authored more than 100 articles, contributed to a dozen public relations and coaching books, and is frequently interviewed and quoted in the media. She was selected as one of the top 20 Best Executive Coaches in Chicago and is one of more than 1,300 people in the world who holds an International Coaching Federation Master Certified Coach (MCC) credential. She currently serves on the editorial board of *Choice*, a magazine for professional coaches and is Secretary/Treasurer for the International Coaching Federation's Global Enterprise Board.

She earned her bachelor's degree from Bradley University, an MBA from Keller Graduate School of Management, and a master's degree in Leadership and Change Management from DePaul University.

Elliot S. Schreiber, PhD, has moved successfully in and out of the corporate, academic, and consulting worlds during a 45-year career. He has been in sales, corporate strategy, marketing, and corporate communication, advancing rapidly to become the most senior marketing and communications executive at three global corporations. He has taught at several universities in Canada and the USA, has run an international management consulting firm, and has been a consultant to major corporations, associations, and nonprofits. He is recognized as one of the most knowledgeable and experienced experts in the fields of brand, reputation and risk management, and governance. He is the author of *The Yin & Yang of Reputation Management: Eight Principles for Strategic Stakeholder Value Creation and Risk Management*, and co-author of *Achieving the Execution Edge: 20 Essential Questions Corporate Directors Need to Get Answered about Strategy Execution*. He is a graduate of the University of Delaware and received his PhD from Penn State University. He holds both Canadian and U.S. citizenship.

Tiara M. Tucker, MS, is a trailblazer and multiple award–winning PR and communications strategist, speaker, coach, community advocate, social justice and mental health activist. Tiara is the visionary founder and CEO of Tiara PR Network, LLC, her boutique communications firm supporting and connecting clients and communities, and of Speak That! Movement, Inc., her women–led nonprofit organization equipping and empowering professional women in business. Tiara served as the 2022 Vice President of Diversity & Inclusion for the Dallas chapter of the Public Relations Society of America (PRSA).

Tiara has almost two decades of noteworthy experience with a Fortune 50 company, specializing in public affairs, corporate responsibility, communication strategy, executive-level support, event planning/hosting, philanthropy, nonprofit portfolio management, and associate/community engagement. Outside of Corporate America, she has been the creator, executive producer, MC, host, moderator, and keynote speaker for a variety of platforms and organizations over the years.

In 2021, Tiara was featured in *Black Enterprise* as one of "10 Amazing Black Women Making Moves Right Now." In the same year, she was honored as a "40 under 40" by the PRSA Dallas chapter. In 2022, Tiara became the inaugural recipient of Illinois State University's Andrew Purnell Jr. Trailblazer Award, which recognizes alumni courageously making a positive change. She has been featured in *Sheen Magazine* as "The Woman Helping Change Lives One Person at a Time." Tiara has also been featured on the Bravo TV Network in an episode of *The Real Housewives of Potomac*.

To expand her education beyond her BS and MS degrees from Illinois State University, she has attained a Certificate in Mindfulness; a Certificate in Life Coaching; a Certificate in Diversity, Equity and Inclusion in the Workplace; and aced a Nonprofit Leadership and Community Engagement graduate course at Harvard University, where she was later invited back by two Harvard professors to be a guest lecturer.

INTRODUCTION

CHAPTER OUTLINE

The idea of running a public relations (PR) operation, whether it is a company department, an independent agency, or any organized group focused on PR, is a highly advanced one. Wherever it is housed, the business and practice of public relations is an advanced, strategic, and highly collaborative process. To prepare people for careers in public relations, PR curricula across colleges and universities offer courses from an introduction to the field and profession to developing specific kinds of PR discourse, to analyzing PR cases, to the planning of campaigns. In fact, the Commission on Public Relations Education (CPRE, 2018) specifies that undergraduate PR programs (at a minimum) comprise five courses: an introduction to PR, research methods, writing, campaigns (case studies), and internships. Interestingly, a course that would build a fundamental understanding of the "business side" of public relations is missing. However, the report of the CPRE's 2021 summit with public relations leaders in industry *and* academia found that

> students need to get more comfortable with research, data and analytics *as well as "the language of business."* If students are going to contribute to strategic decision-making they need to access resources that will help them develop understanding and capability in these areas.
>
> (CPRE, 2021, p. 7, emphasis added)

This point about graduates of PR programs needing to have familiarity with business concepts and practices is vital to their and their employers' success. For many, many years, organizational executives have complained that newly hired public relations professionals (i.e., PR program graduates) generally do not know enough about business operations and strategy (see Arthur W. Page Society, 2007). These reasons are at the core of this book and the reason why it is so necessary for PR students to have a course in managing public relations that integrates these concepts, principles, and practices.

DOI: 10.4324/9781003208280-1

LEARNING THE BUSINESS CONTEXT FOR PUBLIC RELATIONS

Public relations programs at colleges and universities typically require their students to cap off their major with a course on campaign design and development. The substance of such a course is, indeed, valuable because it brings together lessons learned about the what, how, and why of public relations in a systematic approach to public communication. To think, however, that campaign design and development is precisely or even sufficiently analogous to understanding what a manager or an executive in charge of a whole public relations operation—an agency or a nonagency's department (including nonprofit, nongovernmental, and governmental organizations)—must do is shortsighted at best.

Indeed, with today's economic and business environments and those of the foreseeable future, a campaigns course is woefully insufficient as the only capstone to a PR major: it typically lacks a kind of business focus that organizational leaders need their employees to possess. *Not only must public relations professionals be expert communicators for any purpose and in any medium, they also must be competent business people.* And that business competence must at least begin at the advanced undergraduate level and not be learned haphazardly on the job.

Yes, public relations graduates must know how to develop and lead campaigns, but, more important, they must understand the day-to-day matters of what it takes to run a PR operation. After all, students who graduate with an acute awareness of how they will be managed *and* how their work fits into a larger strategic picture for an organization, even down to the profit-and-loss statements and resource allocations, will be far more valuable and valued than those who are just bright technicians.

Although double majoring in public relations and business or even majoring in PR and minoring in business (or vice versa) may be alternative solutions to educating PR students about the business dimensions of public relations, for many students, these alternatives are not possible or are out of reach. Many students come to public relations after trying business programs, which means they have divorced themselves from that arena to join one that is assumed to be related and (perhaps) easier or more suited to them. Many other students never consider business because they are more interested in the technical and (I daresay) the "sexy" (i.e., socially alluring and exciting) aspects of public relations that include events, celebrities, interviews, and other things. Other students integrate public relations with another field, such as theater, biology, or athletics, because they sense a synergy between the two fields that would serve them well as a communicator, for example, in a fine arts organization, a biotechnology company, or a sports team or sports equipment manufacturer.

What is missing in all of these approaches is a focus on the fundamentals of business, management, leadership, and operational areas that precisely matter to the effective running of a public relations group on a daily basis. This book could not begin to replace the formal study of business and management, but it can and does place business, management, leadership, and basic operations squarely in the public relations field for new professionals. Accordingly, this book's purpose is to introduce to undergraduates on PR programs (and early-career PR pros) selected key concepts and practices involved in the running of a PR operation in any organization.

WHY *THIS* BOOK?

This second edition of *Managing Public Relations: Business Principles and Tools for Strategic Communication*, originally published in 2015, is a direct outgrowth from these observations about public relations education and my unique combination of industry and academic experiences gained over a 36-year career. I held an executive-level position in charge of public relations, worked in corporations, worked in an agency, was a consultant, and am a university professor with a strong record of effective teaching and research publication. This book combines scholarship and best practices for students and professors.

This textbook brings together practice, research, and theory. Most important, this textbook is very much meant to prepare students for their professional careers and all the pragmatic business-oriented matters for handling ambiguous situations of varying types and scales. Accordingly, then, this book does *not* present a theory of or for managing public relations, because that is not its purpose. This book, necessarily based on the pragmatic nature of business, focuses on principles and practices that are required of and employed by organizational executives in their running of public relations operations; only then, as matters require, are relevant conceptual or theoretical perspectives employed to substantiate the what with the why of the business side of public relations. Very importantly, this book's preference for pragmatism is supported by recent research that shows public relations professionals tend to rely greatly on and sharpen their practical knowledge, skills, and abilities and not rely much on theory, all of which is contrary to what many academics believe (see Claeys & Opgenhaffen, 2016; Cornelissen, 2000; Hayes et al., 2019; Hocke-Mirzashvili & Hickerson, 2014; Paskin, 2013).

In this way this book will be of great value to those embarking on their public relations careers because they will have a sensitivity to and sensibility about essential management matters in the successful running of a PR operation. In other words, readers will know how they will be managed so they can perform better than they would without this foreknowledge, and readers will be better positioned to grow in their careers as they obtain opportunities for advancement.

For a class using this textbook, students need to assume to the best of their abilities the mindset of a public relations executive, and the substance of the course is to help them achieve that mindset more and more every day. The biggest challenge lies in getting students to not think like students and think like professionals—like their future bosses and colleagues think, most of whom were trained and are experienced in business. It is essential that public relations professionals understand the business needs and expectations of their colleagues, and academic programs in public relations can benefit greatly by training students in business thinking by using this book and the course material available for it.

The first edition was the first textbook ever to cover the combination of topics needed for this nontraditional course. This second edition is still the only textbook on managing public relations suited for higher education curricula. Even so, there are other books addressing matters of public relations management that cluster in three groups: (1) highly academic books, (2) practice-area-focused textbooks, and (3) big-picture management books.

The highly academic books rely on theory so heavily that PR professionals are scarcely familiar with the literature cited; more important, they are too heavily academic in their content to be usable, useful, and used by practitioners.

The practice-area-focused textbooks break down public relations into the staid categories of media relations, consumer relations, investor relations, etc., but do not connect these things to the larger business picture and strategy. They reflect a kind of silo approach to public relations practice. Moreover, these textbooks are more focused on campaign management than the overall successful management of a whole public relations operation on a daily basis.

The big-picture management books are the closest to this book because they are the only ones that address many of the day-to-day matters of running a public relations operation. Some are either too old or are too focused on either just corporate or just agency operations or just one process approach—exemplifying more the corporate–agency split than the others. Others have been recently published that frame their content in terms of being "MBA based" and applicable in PR. The choice certain books make to address public relations mostly in agency organizations seems based on the prominence (i.e., "sex appeal") of PR firms and consultants, even though corporate PR operations are dominant in the field. The older books do not address matters of overall business strategy and, especially, the measurement of business performance against the strategy that management requires today; however, the newer books do.

All three groups of books miss the mark for what today's (and tomorrow's) public relations students must understand about how successful PR operations work in both corporate and agency organizations. The first two groups of textbooks treat the subject of PR management by focusing on the more popular, "sexy stuff" of public relations at the expense of connecting the dots among the daily, regular business matters that must be addressed to keep the public relations function a valuable and valued part of any organization.

Managing Public Relations uniquely addresses the pragmatic, day-to-day management matters for public relations executives in both corporate or "nonagency" settings (broadly conceived and inclusive of for-profit, nonprofit, institutional, nongovernmental, and governmental organizations) and agency PR operations, while at the same time, it connects the dots between practice and theory. In other words, this book is about leading and managing public relations operations. In addition, this book addresses the use of objectives to manage public relations resources and offers approaches for proactive and reactive situations with a variety of stakeholders.

WHERE AND WHEN THIS BOOK WOULD BEST WORK

Managing Public Relations is meant for a new, nontraditional approach to a capstone course in public relations that is more focused on the day-to-day matters of running a PR operation than matters for devising individual communication campaigns. The point of the book is that public relations functions in a much bigger business picture than is covered in any other course, and PR students/graduates must be introduced to that and apply tools for PR business so they can add the greatest value to their employers or clients.

Managing Public Relations breaks into a fragmented market for advanced public relations textbooks for academic audiences. The book is most useful for upper-division college/university courses in public relations, where students are completing their undergraduate work in PR, are required to take a course in the management of public relations, and are seeking their first jobs in the field after graduation. This book could also be used in a traditional campaigns course to particularly ensure that matters of daily business operations frame how it is that campaigns can be developed at all, making that traditional course richer and more valuable. Graduate students, too, would find this book useful for its revelations about the business and operations of public relations.

Students would obtain the knowledge they need to begin their careers on a better footing than those without education in the management practices of public relations. Professors who teach, research, and serve in public relations education would have a textbook that enables them to address the most salient matters for the effective management of a public relations function in any organization. Additionally, the book would also serve well as a ready resource for practitioners wanting guidance about fundamental matters of running PR operations. Overall, then, *Managing Public Relations* insightfully and uniquely bridges theory with practice for its target readers, and it does so purposefully, leaning toward the pragmatic matters of operations management.

WHAT IS IN THIS BOOK AND ITS SUPPORTING MATERIAL?

Managing Public Relations touches on aspects of the field that emanate from its theory and research foundation and does so to springboard into the salient matters about running a public relations operation. Again, this book does not present a theory of PR management; nor does it cover the full range of theories about public relations because students would have covered them in previous, prerequisite courses. This textbook, in its second edition, addresses the running of a public relations operation that includes agency and nonagency worlds simultaneously, demonstrating the greater degree of similarity than difference among the places and ways PR is employed organizationally.

The unique features and strengths for readers of this updated textbook include:

- Revisions in all chapters (some more than others) to present new and additional material that, in the present milieux, would prove pertinent and actionable in and for any public relations operation.
- Reorganization of all chapters so that they flow in a better, more logical way that helps students' learning.
- Initial outlines of each chapter's contents, so readers see how they will progress.
- Graphics that illuminate selected topics, so readers obtain additional insight into matters addressed in the text.
- Lists of key words and concepts, so readers can focus on and use ideas more effectively during and after reading. Key words are in bold in the text so they can be found and understood in context.
- Lists of sources and recommended readings at the end of each chapter, so readers may continue their learning and, if desired, build their libraries on important matters for managing public relations.
- Direct application of current, foundational research from the public relations field and business concepts and approaches common to leaders of public relations functions. This application gives readers the most contemporary understanding of the theory, demands, and methods for effective management of public relations operations.
- Concise recapitulations of selected foundational concepts and principles of public relations that should be familiar, remembered, and, most important, applied anew within the bigger context of top management's demands for successful PR in any organization.
- "Day-to-day" connections between an organization's overall strategic plan and how public relations, like all other organizational functions, must devise and enact

its own plan to help the overall organization achieve success, which demonstrate the specific things executives and their departments must do as contributors to the overall business.

- Explanations and examples of current management practices and technologies, which bring to bear an ample range of scenarios on readers' need to "see" how they work. The chapters' content and design allow individual instructors to (a) apply their own knowledge and experiences to build upon that content (plus an instructor's manual); and (b) take the class in directions that fulfill students' learning interests.
- First-person testimonials from actual PR executives representing corporate and agency worlds—"Executive Viewpoints"—that examine matters germane to the chapters' principles, methods, and tools, making them all the more "real" to readers as they realize how they work and why.
- Supplemental material for instructors to provide them with guidance and ideas for class discussions, activities, assignments, and course planning. Other instructor-focused material includes a dedicated website for this book hosted by Routledge.

Readers will find that this textbook does not focus on particular tactics of public relations. Doing so would not be in line with the book's purpose and thesis. As will be addressed in Chapter 5 and Appendix A, strategies (i.e., categories of tactics) and tactics (i.e., specific PR actions) will be given as examples in the context of the bigger strategic planning picture. So, because these aspects of strategic planning are already covered specifically in PR writing texts and courses, there is no need to cover them in further depth. Similarly, research methods, including those used for social media analytics, are covered well in other texts that specifically address them; therefore, they are not covered in depth in this book. In these ways, the context of running the business of PR operations is kept in sharp focus, even addressing issues relating to the future direction of the PR field and PR practice and management.

The pressures for excellence in all facets and all phases of one's career, beginning at an entry level, require at least a basic understanding at the undergraduate level of business matters that enable specific PR operations to do what they do and do it successfully—adding value to an organization. This book, over the long term of a reader's career, should also serve as an important reference source for all things related to the business side of public relations. Students, then, truly ought to keep and use this book as they embark on and sail the sea of their careers.

REFERENCES

Arthur W. Page Society. (2007). *The authentic enterprise: Relationships, values and the evolution of corporate communications.* Author. Available online: https://knowledge.page.org/wp-content/uploads/2019/02/Download_Report.pdf.

Claeys, A-S., & Opgenhaffen, M. (2016). Why practitioners do (not) apply crisis communication theory in practice. *Journal of Public Relations Research, 28,* 232–247.

Commission on Public Relations Education (CPRE). (2018). *Fast forward: Foundations + future state. Educators + practitioners: 2017 report on undergraduate education.* Author. Retrieved from www.commissionpred.org/commission-reports/fast-forward-foundations-future-state-educators-practitioners/.

Commission on Public Relations Education (CPRE). (2021). *Industry/educator summit report.* Author. Retrieved from www.commissionpred.org/wp-content/uploads/2022/03/CPRE-2021-Summit-Report-Final.pdf.

Cornelissen, J. P. (2000). Toward an understanding of the use of academic theories in public relations practice. *Public Relations Review, 26,* 315–326.

Hayes, R. A., Robertson, S. L., & Seys, A. N. (2019, March). Does our research matter to the profession? Perspectives of practitioners on academic research. Paper presented at the International Public Relations Research Conference, Orlando, FL.

Hocke-Mirzashvili, T. M., & Hickerson, C. (2014). U.S. public relations educators' identification and perception of the discipline. *Public Relations Review, 40,* 100–106.

Paskin, D. (2013). Attitudes and perceptions of public relations professionals towards graduating students' skills. *Public Relations Review, 39,* 251–253.

1

CHAPTER 1
LEADERSHIP AND MANAGEMENT IN PUBLIC RELATIONS: TWO SIDES OF THE SAME COIN

CHAPTER OUTLINE

How great is public relations? Very! In fact, public relations is a valuable and valued organizational function, especially among top organizational leaders. According to the most recent Generally Accepted Practices *GAP VIII* report from the University of Southern California's Annenberg School for Journalism and Communication (2014), "About 40% [of the senior-level communication professionals surveyed] report that PR/Com actively participates in corporate strategic planning, while over 45% view this as [a] grey area" (p. 17); nearly 60% of survey respondents said that C-Suite executives take public relations recommendations seriously, while almost 32% also see it as a grey area (p. 18). Additionally, public relations is seen in the C-Suite as a valuable contributor to financial success (p. 19).

This great value that public relations has garnered over the years has not been easily achieved. Since the first public relations positions were officially created more than a century ago, professionals have had a long uphill battle to gain respect and, most importantly, to make links to organizational performance beyond the number of news

DOI: 10.4324/9781003208280-2

stories produced in a given period of time. It is, therefore, incumbent on public relations as a field, and public relations professionals individually, to continuously improve PR's perceived and real value to organizations and society.

This chapter takes the first step into the arena of managing public relations operations as a valued and valuable part of any organization. The key here is that public relations management is dependent on effective leadership that, in turn, informs management practices. To this end, this chapter presents a historical view of public relations, explains how it is defined, and what operational areas it includes. This historical context relates and builds up to perspectives of leadership, management, and followership that are crucial in the work environment. Important components of the discussion are models of public relations that guide practice, the current state of leadership in public relations, and lessons to be learned from job postings asking for public relations leaders.

HISTORY'S REVELATIONS

We know much about the historical evolution of the practice of public relations over the past century and beyond (see, for example, Cheney & Vibbert, 1987; Cutlip, 1994, 1995, 1997; Cutlip et al., 1994; Ewen, 1996). The formal practice of "public relations" does not emerge until 1889, when Westinghouse competed with Edison General Electric over the establishment of alternating electrical current over direct current, and Westinghouse created the first formal public relations position (Cutlip, 1995, p. 202; Cutlip et al., 1994, p. 98). Until this point, the responsibilities that eventually came to be associated with public relations were referred to under terms like "publicity," "promotional activity," and "press agent," all of which were closely associated with coverage of corporate activity in the press. The term and function of "public relations" then were still fairly new, but not without a heavy load of semantic baggage, as PR "became institutionalized in the large public agencies that arose to meet several environmental challenges [of social order (labor unions), political order (Roosevelt's New Deal), economic order (the Great Depression), and technological order (radio and 'mass culture')]" (Cheney & Vibbert, 1987, p. 169).

Public relations and those who have practiced it are seen through a negative lens that seems based on negative first impressions. As Grunig and Hunt (1984) put it,

> in its early development, public relations was equated with persuasion and/ or propaganda [i.e., a secular approach to "propagating the faith" about an organization]. Most people still have that concept of public relations today, explaining the common suspicion, mistrust, and even fear of it.
>
> (Grunig & Hunt, 1984, p. 21)

For example, growing out from the labor movements in the early 1900s, primarily in the steel, oil, meat-packing, and railroad industries, and fertilized by muckraking journalistic practices about what was going on, both business and government alike adopted aggressive practices of public communication and defense (Cutlip, 1997, p. 23). So in the eyes of business and government leaders, public relations was seen as an essential means to combat hostility and court public favor; but in the eyes of the public, it was seen as a way to manipulate people's thinking about issues. Contemporary social critics continue to claim that the ideal of "free and robust debate" that is at the heart of our culture is in grave danger of being "seriously imbalanced by the large, money-stuffed war chests and armies of skilled communicators that the powerful special interests can put into the field of debate" (Cutlip, 1995, pp. 280–281).

From William Henry Vanderbilt's 1882 statement, "'the public be damned'" (Cutlip, 1995, p. 188), to today's sense and reference from terms like "spin" and "spinmeisters," negative views of public relations have long guided people's thinking about the profession and public relations professionals. At worst, public relations suffers from a poor image—an unscrupulous endeavor of wordsmithing or shameless image-mongering. Such negative views are supported by examples such as Facebook's mishandling and dismissiveness of whistleblower Frances Haugen, a Facebook data scientist, who showed how the company develops and applies data algorithms that will ensure enormous profits but at the cost of harming people and undermining society (see Timberg, 2021). But cases like Johnson & Johnson's superb management of the Tylenol tampering (see Rehak, 2002) and numerous excellent product launches and other campaigns (e.g., annual PRSA Silver Anvil winners and the International Association of Business Communicators' (IABC) Gold Quill winners) show that there are far more positive and ethical examples of public relations.

DEFINING THE FIELD

Remember, too, that other professional fields, like accounting, law, engineering, and medicine, have had their share of examples ranging from troubling and imprudent behaviors to triumphant and stellar professionalism. Even in the face of these troubles and triumphs, people have been able to understand these other fields better than public relations. Indeed, throughout public relations' history it has not been as well defined and easily understood as those other fields. The principal reason seems to be that over the preceding 100-plus years, public relations' importance has grown and grown in so many different ways with innovative means of communication that it looked as if it was one thing *and* many things at once. So, depending on one's view (not necessarily those definitions expressed in scholarship and textbooks), public relations was simply a matter of engaging in media relations to obtain news-media coverage. Another definition could express public relations as a matter of orchestrating beneficial relationships with publics. Still other definitions could focus on functional matters of informing people, cultivating attitudes, or inspiring particular behaviors. The multiplicity of definitions about PR has made it more difficult to understand than other fields that are comparatively easier to define and more widely or intuitively understood because of their reliance on mathematics, science, and, especially, centuries of tradition.

Various efforts to define public relations have been made, most frequently within the scholarship about the field. Recognizing this difficulty of identity for the profession, the Public Relations Society of America (PRSA) has sustained a focused effort over the years to define public relations. Although the PRSA had had its own definition since 1982, the organization sought to build consensus about a definition by involving PR professionals, and the scope of the definition includes all practice areas of public relations. The result of the PRSA's work was this definition: "Public relations is a strategic communication process that builds mutually beneficial relationships between organizations and their publics" (2022, para. 3).

PURVIEW OF OPERATIONS

As the profession evolved, so too did its purview of operations. In this way public relations came to subsume much more than any single category of communication, like media relations. Public relations came to be the central authority on matters relating to the ethical use of language and symbols to inspire cooperation between organizations and their publics. Practice areas that may have once belonged to one functional unit, like employee communications to human resources or investor relations to finance and accounting, were placed under the public relations umbrella. Communication expertise was the key, and operational efficiencies and added value to an organization were the benefits.

Public relations, then, includes multiple areas, many known well and some not known much at all: media relations, employee relations, retiree relations, government relations, analyst relations, investor/shareholder relations, dealer/retailer relations, community relations, event planning, digital and social media communication, and others. It seems funny in this list that any audience that could be identified and joined with the word "relations" qualifies as a practice area. But that is okay because public relations is fundamentally a matter of inspiring cooperation between organizations and their various audiences as much as is practicable, depending on an organization and its purposes. Table 1.1 shows PR's "core budgetary responsibilities," which means that PR has more than 50% of the control over the budget for any listed activity, as found through the *GAP VIII* report (Annenberg School, 2014, p. 57). Notice that this list presents, on the one hand, a kind of prioritization of essential public relations work (also called "practice areas") for virtually any organization of any kind; and, on the other hand, a revelation about how much PR can be tied to other organizational functions, like marketing and human resources.

The general approaches taken in any practice area and the overall operations of public relations can be understood in terms of Grunig and Hunt's (1984) models of public relations, which are shown in Table 1.2. Indeed, their **models of PR** are especially

Table 1.1 Core responsibilities based on PR's control over budget

Activity	Control (%)
Media relations	92.8
Corporate communication/reputation (other than advertising)	85.0
Crisis management	83.0
Social media participation	81.3
Social media monitoring	79.0
Executive communication	76.4
Measurement and evaluation of communication effectiveness	73.2
Social media measurement	72.0
Corporate external website	71.5
Employee/internal communications	70.0
Corporate image (logo usage, etc.)	67.1
Issues management	66.0
Community relations	65.4
Marketing PR/product PR	64.8
Public affairs	59.4
Advertising-corporate image, issues	58.8
Multimedia production	53.6

Source: Based on Annenberg School (2014)

helpful in capturing salient matters of management, especially resource allocations. Based on both the history and contemporary practice of public relations, these models provide us with a good starting point to dig into the soil of managing PR.

As Table 1.2 shows, public relations models progress from simple, one-way (linear, monologic), organization-focused communication to complex, two-way (recursive, dialogic), all-party focused communication. Indeed, from a management perspective, these models explain why certain communication choices are made. The linear models are the simplest compared to the two-way models. The linear models can be conducted with minimal resources an organization has available to get the word out and not interact with any members of target audiences. The publicity/press agentry model, for example, allows for "hosing out" as much information as possible without regard to audience reception, and the public information model only applies already-known audience concerns during development. The recursive models, however, require more resources because of the interaction between an organization and its publics. The two-way asymmetrical (2WA) model favors an organization and is less resource intensive than the two-way symmetrical (2WS) model, which favors all publics equally. All models could and should employ methods to measure effectiveness and value for the investment after a communication effort is completed; we will touch on this topic in Chapter 6.

Table 1.2 Public relations models and their usability

Model	Purpose	Research	Communication flow	Preference	Practiced
Publicity/press agentry	Propaganda; truth not essential	None or little	Linear (source to receiver)	3rd	1st
Public information	Information dissemination; truth important	Little; focused on secondary audience studies	Linear (source to receiver)	4th	2nd
Two-way asymmetrical	Scientific persuasion; truth essential	Formative and primary studies to evaluate reactions and attitudes prior to official release	Single-cycle recursive, unbalanced effects (source to receiver to source [feedback])	1st	4th
Two-way symmetrical	Mutual understanding; truth essential	Formative and summative primary studies to evaluate understanding	Continuously recursive, balanced effects (source to receiver to source and back again [dialogic])	2nd	3rd

Sources: Grunig & Grunig (1992); Hunt & Grunig (1994)

One way to think of the 2WA model is that it is the public information model on the steroids of primary research for audience feedback. The reason 2WA is more complex than the public information model, but less complex than 2WS, is that the 2WA model only requires one primary-research cycle between an organization and representatives of its target audiences, thus favoring the organization in the process by using a single-cycle recursive process to obtain feedback that would be used to improve any aspects of the communication effort. That single cycle of interaction between an organization and audience representatives is enough to obtain sufficient and authoritative feedback about messages, symbols, media, and other facets of a planned communication effort before it is formally rolled out to all audience members. The continuously recursive 2WS model requires dynamic, ongoing, and built-in dialogic channels in an entire communication effort. Those channels both (1) facilitate dialog between an organization and its publics; and (2) measure communication effectiveness and value for the investment. Such symmetry necessarily requires thorough and expensive arrays of the resources of time, people, technology, facilities, and others to make it work 24/7 for anyone who wants to use the 2WS model.

Most important for all four models, these resource-allocation matters reveal why in the two righthand columns of Table 1.2 there is such a pronounced difference between what public relations professionals prefer to use and what they actually practice. Simply put, PR professionals greatly value the ideal of dialogic communication and would easily want to engage in it every time, but the daily press of business and the constraints on resources make dialogic communication something best applied to projects with the time, people, facilities, technology, and money to monitor, make sense of, report on, and submit recommendations from the continuous cycles of communication between an organization and its publics. The dominant practice, then, for public relations professionals is not dialogic but, rather, monologic, as the typical small staffs of corporate communication groups make do with the limited resources they have and communicate *to* audiences more than *with* them.

There is a fifth model—the *contingency* model—that allows for combinations of the other models of public relations to be employed in ways that best suit communication needs and resource availability, especially within the context of campaigns. For example, the contingency model works as an organizing framework for an entire public relations operation, because such an operation can work solely as one model and then shift to another model as business needs dictate. On a more complex level, the contingency model can explain how a company launching a product may design a two-phase PR campaign. The first phase could be publicity to pique people's interest in a new product and do so in ways that evoke mystery and curiosity along with major benefits of ownership. The second phase could involve a two-way asymmetrical model as the company engages in primary research to test messages, symbols, media, and other facets of the remainder of the campaign on one or more representative samples of target audiences so that the final communication effort is as effective as possible when all its components are ultimately rolled out.

Another example of the contingency model would be the handling of **disruptive situations**, such as **crises**, **public tragedies**, **issues**, or **incidents**. But remember that not everything is a "crisis" (see Hayes & Smudde, 2015). A disruptive situation may feel like a crisis because of the heightened internal attention and resources given to it, and there may be some public visibility; however, the key to whatever the disruption is depends on its characteristics. These kinds of disruptions require allocation of resources in ways that are commensurate with the situations they involve (Hayes & Smudde, 2015; Hayes et al., 2017; Smudde, 2001).

- An *organizational crisis* is "a specific, unexpected, and nonroutine event or series of events that create high levels of uncertainty and simultaneously present an organization with both opportunities for and threats to its high-priority goals"

(Ulmer et al., 2015, p. 8). These emergencies are likely the result of mistakes, oversights, or system deficiencies.

- *Intentional crises* are events "that are initiated by intentional acts designed to harm an organization" (Ulmer et al., 2015, p. 10). Examples of intentional crises are terrorism, sabotage, workplace violence, poor employee relationships, poor risk management, hostile takeovers, and unethical leadership.
- *Unintentional crises* are "unforeseeable or unavoidable" (Ulmer et al., 2015, p. 12) events that harm an organization. Examples are natural disasters, disease outbreaks, technical interactions, product failure, and economic downturns.
- *Public tragedies* are disruptive, large-scale, and catastrophic events affecting people directly and indirectly. People personally identify with the victims, circumstances, and consequences. A collective approach to coping that technology enables is to facilitate mourning, grief, and support (Hayes et al., 2017).
- An *issue* is a matter that arises unexpectedly from someone or some group that argues for its importance and demands that something be done (Crable & Vibbert, 1985; Smudde, 2001, 2011). Issues develop methodically over time through public argumentation between an organization and those who brought the issue to public importance plus interested stakeholders or sympathizers until it is resolved.
- *Incidents* are particularly isolated matters of importance that arise fairly commonly in organizations and are resolved within the operational area in which they occurred (perhaps with the assistance of one or more other areas or an external service specialist like a plumber, electrician, or someone from the same or another department) within a very short time span (often within the same day). Examples of incidents would include computer crashes, copier breakdowns, absent employees, assembly line tooling malfunction, transportation problems, customer complaints, and water leaks (see Coombs, 2012; Hayes & Smudde, 2015).

Among these disruptive situations, you will notice there is a progression from crises to incidents that shows decreasing levels of disruption (highest to lowest) that command immediate responses and resource allocations that fit the circumstances. Among these six types of emergency situations, the incident is the simplest and the most common, which means that contingency plans and resource allocations are easier to muster and manage. In contrast, for the remaining five types, what begins as one disruption can beget another and still another. For example, Hurricane Katrina in 2005 devastated the Gulf Coast region encompassing Louisiana, Mississippi, and Alabama. Katrina obviously was a disaster when it happened. But before Katrina hit, it technically was an issue of public safety because civic leaders knew the limitations of the levee system and escape routes and knew that they were not ready for a hurricane of Katrina's magnitude. After Katrina, organizational crises arose for the Federal Emergency Management Agency (FEMA), New Orleans and other affected cities, and the states in that region.

In terms of Grunig and Hunt's public relations models and resource management, the kind of disruptive situation can dictate the type of PR model that applies (if at all) and, subsequently, resource allocations. Figure 1.1 shows that effective contingency

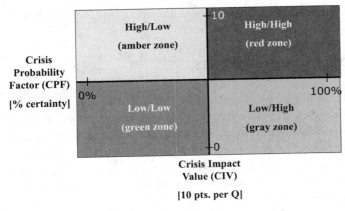

Figure 1.1 Disruptive situation risk-planning grid
Source: Fink (1986, p. 45)

planning efforts must examine risk to an organization in terms of (1) the probability of any emergency with (2) its degree of impact on an organization (Fink, 1986; Ulmer et al., 2015). In this way, public relations and organizational leaders must, to the best of their ability, articulate how certain resources must be allocated, including the most effective and efficient model for communicating with publics. The most dominant communication during disruptions likely would be one way (linear, monologic), which is either press agentry and/or public information. There is little time to incorporate two–way (recursive, dialogic) communication until such time that a dominant model of dialogic communication makes sense. In the case of issues, because the time span from inception to resolution is typically much longer than it is for crises of any sort, a dialogic model may be in effect from the beginning.

Key to the effective application of any model of and all available resources for public relations is leadership. Two concepts directly related to leadership are management and followership, and all three concepts are our next stop.

SIMILARITIES AND DIFFERENCES BETWEEN LEADERSHIP AND MANAGEMENT

The literature about leaders and leadership as well as managers and management is vast, and this small section on these intertwined subjects is only meant to be a usable and useful introduction to selected concepts that would prove generally valuable in the running of a public relations operation. Important, too, is the relationship between leadership and management. Also important is the relationship between leaders and managers with followers, knowing, too, that leaders and managers will also be followers. Both skill sets are essential for effectiveness in public relations, although it is rare that any one person may be truly "excellent" in both. The balance of this chapter explores the interrelationship between leadership and management, including interactions with followers.

LEADERSHIP DEFINITION AND APPROACHES

When we think of leadership, we think of what it takes to ensure that people work well together on something in which they all have a stake. *Leaders without followers are alone, and followers without leaders are lost.* Leadership, then, necessarily involves followers and is an enabler of group success or failure, balancing task and relationship matters along the way. More specifically defined, "leadership is human (symbolic) communication which modifies the attitudes and behaviors of others in order to meet shared group goals and needs" (Johnson & Hackman, 2018, p. 12).

Someone's performance as a leader is founded on several dimensions. The first is personal character, which concerns one's ethos—who someone is, what someone stands for, how someone presents themself verbally and nonverbally, how other people think about and respond to someone, and the personality someone exudes. The second is situations, which are occasions someone handles well or not and can define that person as a good or bad leader. Third is the nature of the task, which dictates the kinds of expertise needed to handle it and reveals the level of competence someone has with it. Finally, there are the relationships among group members, which should be nurtured in ways that inspire attitudes and behaviors that result in desired outcomes. Interestingly, a leader's unique role in a group allows for some behaviors that differ from those of all other members if, and only if, those behaviors provide direction and uphold group norms.

James Kouzes and Barry Posner have perhaps studied leadership more than anyone and have produced important and insightful work over many years about leaders and leadership. In their book, *The Leadership Challenge* (2017), they show the results of findings from their long-term and international studies of leadership, which included respondents from six continents (Africa, North America, South America, Asia, Europe, and Australia), with the majority from the USA. Figure 1.2 lists in ranked order the characteristics people admire most in effective leaders (pp. 28–31). Most important in their findings are the first four characteristics (those in bold italics in Figure 1.2) of most-admired leaders, the characteristics that consistently received more than 60% of respondents' selections. In fact, those top four characteristics are keys to *credibility*, which Kouzes and Posner show to be the foundation of effective leadership. In other words, focusing on and doing well with the four top characteristics solidifies one's credibility and ensures that all other characteristics fall into place for effective leadership.

Leadership can also be examined in finer levels of detail, all of which are helpful to understanding what it takes to lead a public relations function. Also, remember that leadership is a function of communication, as stated in the definition of leadership given above. Accordingly, three levels of detail are leader *communication styles*, leadership

• *Honest*	• Cooperative
• *Competent*	• Ambitious
• *Inspiring*	• Caring
• *Forward-looking*	• Determined
• Intelligent	• Courageous
• Broad-minded	• Loyal
• Dependable	• Imaginative
• Supportive	• Mature
• Fair-minded	• Self-controlled
• Straightforward	• Independent

Figure 1.2 Characteristics of most-admired leaders
Source: Adapted from Kouzes and Pozner (2017, pp. 28–31)

orientations, and leader *types.* Leader *communication styles,* as Johnson and Hackman (2018) explain, can be best understood in three categories that hinge on certain attitudes and behavior patterns.

LEADER COMMUNICATION STYLES

The first level of detail about leadership is **communication styles**, of which there are three. Leaders with an *authoritarian* communication style are those who want complete control ("my way or the highway"). They are leaders who selfishly dictate that something will be done according to their own wishes and no other way. In contrast to this negative, malevolent kind of authoritarian leader, there is a positive, benevolent form. A benevolent authoritarian leader engages in reasoned explanation about why things must be done in the manner they demand so that others understand. Leaders who use a *democratic* communication style are those who seek consensus ("everyone must have a say"). These leaders actively pursue people's views and feedback, then consensually weigh the pros and cons of alternatives to reach a mutually agreed–upon decision. Leaders using a *laissez-faire* communication style are those who keep a distance ("leave them alone") from followers. This communication style takes two forms: a positive form and a negative form. The positive form of a *laissez-faire* communication style is enacted by a leader who functions as a sage guide who is available to group members for direction and advice, while also giving them the freedom and authority to explore and solve problems. The negative form of a *laissez-faire* communication style is enacted by a leader who functions as a disinterested party, abdicating responsibility to the group and letting it struggle with interpretations, procedures, direction, and all other matters until the final products of the group are in.

LEADERSHIP ORIENTATIONS

As leadership and followership concern people getting things done and working well together, there are two very basic orientations leaders can have about working in groups of any size. Each orientation can employ any of the communication styles and is largely one-dimensional, which can be risky when someone only practices one orientation without appropriate attention to the other. Indeed, the two orientations are effectively opposite ends of a spectrum, with blends of each to varying degrees between them.

The first **leadership orientation** is *task-focused*. These leaders are primarily if not solely concerned with getting a job done well, done on time, and done according to specifications and expectations. (Followers, too, can be task- focused.) They are fastidious or even dogmatic about adhering to project parameters. The second leadership orientation is *relationship-focused*. These leaders are primarily if not solely concerned with people working well together. To these leaders, group chemistry and team spirit are vital to success, and any work can only be completed with such strong, collegial interpersonal relationships. (Followers, too, can be relationship-focused.) Again, these two orientations are opposite ends of a spectrum of what is really needed, which is a favorable balance of task focus *and* relationship focus, which can vary depending on the needs in a situation for a group (i.e., sometimes more focus on relationships, at other times more focus on the task, but never without some attention to the other orientation).

In reality, however, both of these orientations imply and rely on the other, because to get a job done well, on time, and on spec means people must get along. And having people who work together means they should have complementary backgrounds (i.e., knowledge, skills, abilities, and experiences), genuine interest in each other and harmonious personalities, and produce successful results. But leaders who are overly task-focused would undermine group morale from too much work and not enough personal recognition, support, or "play." Similarly, leaders who are too relationship-focused would spell doom for group productivity, as group members see they are expected to excel at socializing and getting along with one another more than producing great work. Leadership, then, means recognizing when and how to achieve a favorable balance between task and relationship needs when times demand more attention to work than relationships and vice versa. Additionally, leader communication styles need to be applied appropriately to get work done with people who work well together.

LEADERSHIP TYPES

At the third level of detail about leadership is the types or "views" of leaders. **Leadership types** concern characteristics of leaders that cluster in eight categories. The *traits* view concerns how well leaders exhibit effective interpersonal behaviors, cognitive/intellectual abilities, personality, motivation to perform, and experience/knowledge in areas required of them in their positions. *Situational* leaders are adaptive to group, individual, and environmental demands, which means they have a kind of intelligence to size up and respond well to what is going on in context. *Functional* leaders are those who, as we saw in the **leadership communication styles**, play particular roles when needed, such as applying a task, relationship, or individual focus to reestablish a better balance within the group so it can reach its goals. *Relational* leaders are those who rely on a combination of hierarchical and social positions between themselves and others to move people to action and meet group goals.

Transactional leaders represent the traditional form of leadership that uses formal authority to procure resources and inspire followers' involvement, commitment, and productivity. In relation to Maslow's (1987 [1954]) hierarchy of needs (see Figure 1.3), transactional leaders enable group members' lower-order needs, beginning with physiological needs, then safety and security, then love and belonging. Transactional leaders, then, may be thought of as stereotypical managers. In contrast, *transformational* leaders are those who are visionary, address and go beyond transactional leadership, and enable people to become more than they are by appealing to self-esteem and self-actualization needs, especially through empowerment strategies. Figure 1.3 shows that transformational leaders must also be transactional leaders (i.e., good managers), but transactional leaders do not necessarily have to be transformational leaders.

Servant leaders are those who focus on others' needs first and thereby see themselves as stewards of both the organization and its people, including customers. Servant leaders see followers as partners and distribute rewards fairly, which fosters an equitable and just environment in which to work. *Charismatic* leaders are seen as especially gifted leaders who possess and exude self-confidence and competence; they tend to be extraordinary orators, linking symbolic myths and group goals effectively. Charismatic leaders usually arise at just the right time when a group is facing dire consequences and needs a highly

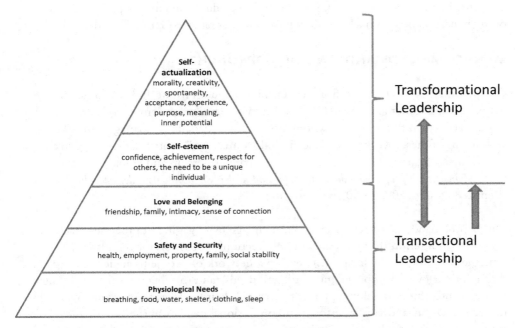

Figure 1.3 Maslow's hierarchy of needs
Source: Adapted from Maslow (1987 [1954], pp. 98–104)

inspirational, visionary, influential, and enthusiastic leader. Both servant and charismatic leaders are, in a sense, more advanced transformational leaders.

Two additional leadership types are authentic leaders and love-based leaders. In many ways, these perspectives are related to both transformational and servant leaders. *Authentic* leadership is based on the idea that a leader should make the most of the person they are. Like servant and transformational leaders, authentic leaders are interested in serving others, empowering them, and making a difference in the bigger picture. Authentic leaders, then, are tuned into their natural abilities and inabilities, their strengths and shortcomings, and they rely on their abilities and their strengths to not only overcome their inabilities and shortcomings, but they also are genuine, ethical, compassionate, purposeful, and values-driven in guiding people in achieving objectives and becoming better versions of themselves in the process (see George, 2003).

Love-based leadership begins with the idea that the inherent dignity of people deserves love—*agape* love (i.e., willing the good of another as other)—in all human pursuits. Love-based leaders possess an emotional connection with an organization's vision, mission, and vales. These leaders act out of love of people *and* out of the love of what they do for people through their work, leisure, and anything in between. In this way, love-based leaders follow a very steady emotional compass that guides them in their relationships, responsibilities, and responses to circumstances. Even tough circumstances can call for "tough love" when someone is in need of a firm response to improper behaviors or poor results. In this way, like transformational, servant, and authentic leaders, love-based leaders are most interested in others achieving peak performance individually and in groups through the overt application of love in all they do with and for people (see Czarnecki, 2010).

MANAGEMENT DEFINITION AND APPROACHES

On the other side of the coin from leadership is **management**. Indeed, someone may be both a leader and a manager. But the two terms cause some confusion. One word that is often thought of as synonymous with leadership is "management." The verb forms of these two words, "to lead" and "to manage," contribute to this thinking but need clarification. One useful way to compare leadership and management is this: "*Managers are people who do things right and leaders are people who do the right thing*" (Bennis & Nanus, 2003, p. 20, emphasis in original).

On the one hand, *leaders* seek and produce change by engaging in processes that (1) create an **agenda** through establishing direction with vision for the future and strategies for producing change; (2) develop a network of people to achieve the agenda through their own example (align words and deeds); and (3) obtain results according to the agenda through helping people to channel their energies to overcome obstacles, realize the vision, and satisfy personal and professional needs. On the other hand, *managers* seek and produce predictability and order by engaging in processes that (1) create an agenda through planning and budgeting; (2) develop a network of people to achieve the agenda through organizing and staffing; and (3) obtain results according to the agenda through monitoring and controlling operations and problem solving (Johnson & Hackman, 2018, pp. 13–14).

Managing, simply put, involves systematic and ethical ways of directing people, allocating resources, and getting things done according to defined strategic objectives, including ingenuity and innovations along the way that can make processes, outputs, and customer experiences better than expected. The literature about managing and management is enormous, and this section, like the preceding one on leadership, has a decidedly sharp focus. Indeed, this short section introduces you to the basic concepts of management that will continue to be applied throughout the rest of this book as they bear on the running of a public relations function.

Peter Drucker, the celebrated and acknowledged guru of the management field, explained that being an effective manager is learnable and has three equally important tasks that must be performed to be successful: (1) "[establishing] the specific purpose and mission of the institution, whether business, enterprise, hospital, or university"; (2) "making work productive and the worker achieving"; and (3) "managing social impacts and social responsibilities" (1993 [1973], p. 40). Drucker is responsible for articulating a highly recognized concept: "management by objectives" (**MBO**). The key in MBO is for a manager *and* each follower (also called a "subordinate") to work together and define particular objectives that are in tune with the strategic plan, can be achieved within a definitive span of time, and add value to the operation (Drucker, 2006 [1954], 1993 [1973]). Once the objectives are defined, the manager and employee structure a system to monitor and measure an employee's progress toward meeting those objectives. That system ensures that the employee's performance is on track and feedback is given and, if performance is not on track, corrective action can be made sooner rather than later. We will cover performance management in more detail in Chapter 6 and other management matters for public relations throughout this book.

In the grand scheme of things, as Drucker (2006 [1967]) observes, "Effectiveness is what executives are being paid for, whether they work as managers who are responsible for the performance of others as well as their own, or as individual professional contributors responsible for their own performance only" (pp. ix–x). For Drucker, the substance of an effective executive is found in **eight practices** he defined in 2004 (rendered in Table 1.3), after a consulting career of more than 65 years.

Notice how the eight rules cluster into three categories of benefits for the executive and, thereby, for subordinates and the organization. The benefits proceed from the foundational practices that enable learning as much as is practicable, from taking action on that knowledge, and then from making sure everyone is committed to and involved with achieving the desired results. To these eight practices Drucker (2006 [1967]) adds one that he considers so vital that he called it a rule: "Listen first, speak last" (p. 63). His point is that all these practices can be undermined by people who allow their "personalities, strengths, weaknesses, values, and beliefs" to get in the way of anything individuals and the group need and want to accomplish.

Table 1.3 Drucker's eight practices of effective executives and their benefits

Practices	Benefits
Asked, "What needs to be done?"	Obtain needed knowledge
Asked, "What is right for the enterprise?"	
Developed action plans	Convert knowledge into action
Took responsibility for decisions	
Took responsibility for communicating	
Focused on opportunities rather than problems	
Ran productive meetings	Fostered organizational responsibility and accountability
Thought and said "we" rather than "I"	

Source: Adapted from Drucker (2004)

Discipline is absolutely essential, Drucker argues, and these eight practices and the overarching rule to listen make up a solid recipe for enacting that requisite discipline for realizing management and organizational success. Discipline guides managerial decision-making, which concerns (1) identifying a situation as generic or an exception, (2) defining the parameters of possible solutions, (3) describing the ideal solution no matter what constraints or concessions must be made, (4) devising an action plan to carry out the chosen solution, and (5) measuring the validity and effectiveness of the decision in the real-world context (Drucker, 2001, pp. 242–243). In many ways, the practices of management apply exceptionally well to the most effective types and styles of leadership. No leader or manager can exist without followers. The key is how well effective leaders and managers work *with* followers/subordinates and vice versa.

FOLLOWERS

A leader without followers is alone, and followers without a leader are lost. The literature about followers and followership is broad, but sadly, some of that literature about followers examines followers from a leadership perspective, making it biased in that regard and eschewing the truer nature of followership and effectiveness of followers. Even so, there is a solid foundation of followership-focused literature that provides great insight into the characteristics and types of followers, both of which are important for followers and leaders to know

Generally speaking, as Johnson and Hackman (2018) explain, there are three very basic categories of followers. The first is *best* because these followers think for themselves and take the initiative. The second category is *worst* because these followers must be told what to do, how, and when, and they need constant supervision. The third and final category of followers is *typical* because they take direction well and complete work according to stated expectations. With a more specific assessment of followers, Kellerman (2008) provides us with a view that identifies five levels of engagement of followers with leaders. Kellerman's five **types of followers** can be appropriately placed within Johnson and Hackman's three basic categories of followers.

- *Isolates* are completely detached, including from knowledge about and responsiveness to leaders and what is going on to fulfill a mission. If invited, these followers can provide healthy skepticism.
- *Bystanders* are observant of what is going on but do not participate very much, if at all, effectively adopting a neutral stance on everything and, thereby, giving tacit support for leaders and what is done. These followers can be engaged by giving specific invitations to do so in ways that play to their strengths or areas of expertise.
- *Participants* are engaged in some way, including favorable attitudes toward leaders and making contributions to the cause. Because of their involvement in things, these followers can contribute well, for example, when asked to assess pros and cons, risks and benefits.
- *Activists* have strong feelings about their leaders and the mission in which they are engaged, contributing great amounts of time and effort to the cause, even if that means changing processes, policies, plans, leadership, etc. These followers are solid self-starters and willing to identify challenges on their own and take on new challenges as they are required.
- *Diehards* have the greatest degree of passion, dedication, and loyalty to the group, its leaders, and the mission in which all are engaged, including being willing to give their lives to the cause that consumes them to ensure success. These followers possess a very deep passion for the cause and the organization, making them especially predisposed for doing whatever it takes for success.

Leaders have the special challenge to determine effective ways to involve each type of follower, and Kelley (1998) explains followers according to their levels of independent, critical–analytical thinking, and engagement to achieve success. Kelley's approach can be applied together with Kellerman's to add useful detail. For Kelley, *alienated* followers are highly independent, disillusioned, and interested in fighting rather than serving. These followers can provide healthy skepticism, if invited. *Conformist* followers are committed to group goals, rarely express their own ideas out of fear, and agree with a leader's view ("yes people"). These followers can, however, offer valuable alternative viewpoints when invited or challenged to do so. *Pragmatist* followers are moderately independent and engaged people who cope well with uncertainty but are unlikely to be promoted to jobs with greater responsibility and authority. These followers can contribute well when asked to assess pros and cons, risks and benefits. *Passive* followers project little original thought or commitment, rely heavily on supervision, meet minimal expectations, and may possess a small skill set or suffer from repeated defeats by authoritarian leaders. These followers can be engaged by giving specific invitations to do so in ways that play to their strengths or areas of expertise. *Exemplary* followers are critical thinkers and active participants who contribute innovative ideas and go above and beyond expectations. These followers are always willing and responsive to engagement challenges. According to Kelley (1992, 1998), these followers add value to an organization, weave effective webs of relationships, and cultivate a courageous conscience.

One type of exemplary follower is *servant* followers, which is the complement to servant leaders. Servant followers are a counterpart to servant leaders. Importantly, servant followers are people who want to remain followers instead of becoming leaders, which reduces destructive competition and conflict and keeps the focus on organizational goals. Servant followers assume that leaders seek the best for the organization and work to assist the leader with their work, which helps the team as well (Johnson & Hackman, 2018, p. 391). Another type of exemplary follower is *courageous* followers, who place the organization, its purpose, and its values as supremely important, well above the role of a leader. In this way, then, courageous followers accept higher levels of risk than other followers. Courageous followers take responsibility for themselves and the organization, and these followers reflect well on themselves and how they can personally improve in any way that helps the organization. Courageous followers will take the initiative to change the organizational culture through challenges to its rules, assumptions, and procedures (Johnson & Hackman, 2018, pp. 391–394).

Leaders should carefully observe followers' characteristics so that the leaders have a sound sensibility about each person's motivations, attitudes, knowledge/expertise, skills, work ethic, and so on that can help or hinder individual *and* group performance. Followers (and other organizational leaders) should likewise carefully observe leaders' characteristics so that the followers (and other leaders) can accurately assess and effectively work with each other. An effective leader looks after their followers, and effective followers look after each other and their leader. In followers' relationships with leaders, followers must present solutions when pointing out problems to leaders. Executives are pressed for time, operate at 35,000 feet (10,668 meters) above the action, are focused on decision-making, and want perspective and recommendations for problems, not mere lists of problems. If someone is going to identify a problem, that person must also recommend one or more solutions, with a recommendation for one solution among others, if multiple solutions are offered. This approach helps executives in taking action while showing that followers are invested in making progress in getting the work done.

In sum, if you think about it, as long as leadership and management are two sides of the same coin, followership is the middle and the edge that make up the whole coin. Hallmarks of effective leader–follower dynamics parallel Lonergan's (1990) "transcendental imperatives" for human relationships: attentiveness (i.e., being alert to what is going on and listening carefully to others), intelligence (i.e., recognizing to what one pays attention, recognizing patterns, and making good sense of things), reasonableness, (i.e., weighing the products of one's understanding and arriving at good judgment), responsibility (i.e., owning up to one's thoughts, attitudes, and actions to then apply or improve them in practical ways), and charity (i.e., love what you do, do what you love, and do what you do out of love). With this general background about the nature of leaders, managers, and followers, the next step is to examine the specific principles and practices for effective leadership in public relations.

RUNNING MEETINGS

Bringing people together to focus on a defined project or some kind of opportunity requires skill in attending to both task and relationship matters—and doing so in a way that respects people's time. Meetings, then, are a very important opportunity for leaders to lead and for followers to follow, and both can fulfill either role. Although there are many very practical sources about how to run meetings effectively, there are some very basic aspects of **running effective meetings** that are well worth covering.

A meeting is called for selected people to attend because they have some stake in the matter of the meeting and can contribute to its business fruitfully. In this way, any work related to or specifically for a meeting must be completed before the meeting, especially if what must be done is to become familiar with the subject(s) for the meeting. However, meetings can be called for people to perform particular work tasks, and in this case, there may be things that each person has to do in preparation for doing the expected work during the meeting.

With the exception of "work meetings," where the purpose is for members to complete one or more specific tasks together, any meeting generally must fulfill defined purposes, which typically are to report on progress and results, determine gaps to fill or generate ideas, make decisions or obtain approvals for actions, and identify next steps and give task assignments with deadlines. These purposes can be addressed well with an agenda that is set, shared, and followed. Sometimes, depending on the "personality" of the group to be involved in a meeting, time limits for each agenda item and/or for the whole meeting must be defined. To make sure that the content of a meeting is documented, someone must record what was said and done for each agenda item during the meeting. This record must accurately and concisely document all discussion and any decisions. Instrumental in the running of good meetings is effective leadership, management, and followership as explained previously.

CHARACTERISTICS OF EFFECTIVE PUBLIC RELATIONS LEADERS

Among the many topics addressed in the literature about public relations, leadership historically has not been well covered. In recent years, however, more investigations about the nature and practice of leadership in public relations have been conducted and published. Indeed, the first release of findings from the most comprehensive study of leadership in public relations was *Cross-Cultural Study of Leadership in Public Relations and Communication Management* (Berger et al., 2012), as the study addresses multiple dimensions of leadership and is truly global in scope. The Cross-Cultural Study—the fullest presentation of its findings are in Berger and Meng (2014)—also identified the ten most pressing issues for public relations leaders (Figure 1.4). The study stands as the source of the great insights about leadership for the profession. The study also fits our focus well for the leading of public relations functions.

Given all that leaders in public relations are and do, they are "sense-makers" who

> must be convincing representatives of their organizations with individuals and groups outside the organization, while at the same time convincingly representing the interests of those outside groups and individuals to executives inside their organization. They must possess vast flows of information and opportunities while at the same time converting this 'bigness' of information to the 'smallness' of messages—140-character expressions and 6-second brand messages. They must be authentic as individuals even as they serve as proxies for the values and the practices of their organizations.
>
> (Berger & Meng, 2014, pp. 311–312)

At the core of the Cross-Cultural Study is the idea of "excellent" (i.e., "ideal") leadership in public relations. Guiding the Cross-Cultural Study was this definition:

> Excellent leadership in public relations is a dynamic process that encompasses a complex mix of individual skills and personal attributes, values, and behaviors that consistently produces ethical and effective communication practice. Such practice fuels and guides successful communication teams, helps organizations achieve their goals, and legitimizes organizations in society.
>
> (Meng et al., 2012, p. 24)

This definition of excellent leadership in PR reflects the topics we covered in this chapter about leadership and followership. Based on this definition, the researchers

---

1. Dealing with the speed and volume of information flow
2. Being prepared to effectively deal with crises that may arise
3. Managing the digital revolution and rise of social media
4. Improving the measurement of communication effectiveness
5. Improving employee engagement and commitment in the workplace
6. Dealing with growing demands for transparency of communications
7. Finding, developing, and retaining highly talented communication professionals
8. Meeting increasing demands for corporate social responsibility
9. Meeting communication needs in diverse cultures and globalizing markets
10. Improving the image of the profession

Figure 1.4 The ten big issues for public relations leaders
Source: Berger and Meng (2014, p. 44)

identified a number of components of excellent leadership and tested them. Indeed, the study's findings "are consistent with those in traditional managerial leadership research" (Meng et al., 2012, p. 32). A usable and potent model of excellent leadership in public relations, blending Meng (2012) and Berger and Meng (2014), is shown in Figure 1.5.

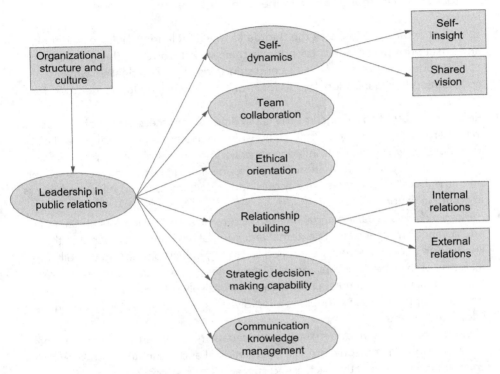

Figure 1.5 The model of excellent leadership in public relations
Sources: Berger and Meng (2014, p. 45); Meng and Berger (2013); Berger (2012)

In this model, originally articulated by Meng (2012) and tested and developed as part of the Cross-Cultural Study, there are six components to excellent leadership in public relations, shown in the six ovals stacked in the center. A seventh component is the rectangle in the upper left, which reflects the effect individual organizations have on how people perform their public relations functions. The components complement one another and make up a cohesive and balanced structure for understanding **excellence in PR leadership**. The Cross-Cultural Study showed that this model is valid for public relations practiced in other nations as well as the United States (Berger & Meng, 2014; Berger et al., 2012; Meng & Berger, 2013). The components of the model are defined as follows by Meng (2012, pp. 337–338):

- *Self-dynamics*—Concerns the degree to which a leader lives up to expected characteristics of most-admired leaders (see Figure 1.2). This component relies on leaders understanding themselves (e.g., strengths, weaknesses, etc.) and "present[ing] traits such as high self-confidence, emotional maturity, initiative, and stress tolerance."

- *Team collaboration*—Concerns the intensity of collaboration and, thereby, the cohesiveness that is fostered among those on the PR team. The PR leader's role here is to "create a climate of trust and flexibility within the team, facilitate positive interdependence among team members, and between team members and leaders."

- *Ethical orientation*—Concerns the degree to which PR leaders believe in, uphold, and enact principles of ethical conduct in their work. Involved in this component of the model is adherence to values and standards of professionalism while contributing to organizational goals for strong performance plus doing good for others.

- *Relationship building*—Concerns the capabilities and successfulness of PR leaders in building networks of beneficial relationships for both the organization and its stakeholders, which affect its influence and performance. Relationship building through "interaction, information exchange, and linkage between an organization and its publics" is key to resource acquisition and allocation, and it fosters success in communication.

- *Strategic decision-making capability*—Concerns how well PR leaders understand and balance an organization's external and internal environments such that the knowledge about these can be applied to strategic decision-making as well as all facets of the organization's communication needs. Particularly important are leaders' abilities "to stimulate new ideas, persuasively sell new ideas to higher-ups, and improve responsiveness in a rapidly changing, complex environment and information market."

- *Communication knowledge management capability*—Concerns "the process of gaining, applying and converting public relation[s] and communication knowledge and expertise into effective tactics and strategies." This component of PR leadership focuses on educating people about public relations' importance, value, and contributions to organizational effectiveness.

- *Organizational structure and culture*—Concerns the degree to which a PR leader may be "excellent." More particularly, "leadership style in an organization is not only determined by the organization's legitimating principles and values but also largely moderated by the social structure and cultural norms within the society [in which] it operates."

Earlier studies of leadership in public relations made important findings on not only the types of leaders of PR operations, but also the more effective type that seems to be most successful. In her survey of public relations leaders, Jin (2010) found that four leadership types occur among them: transactional, transformational, democratic, and situational. Of those four, transformational was determined to be characteristic of the best for successful leaders. As she says, "The findings reflect the trend of participative management and the balance between task and relationship skills of public relations managers…. Stronger transformational leadership is more likely to emerge among more empathetic leaders [and] bring more confidence among employees" (p. 174). This conclusion supports Werder and Holtzhausen's (2009) study of public relations leaders, where "inclusive leadership style was a significant predictor of transformational leadership style, which supports the importance of collaboration, shared decision making, and participative practices in effecting change in public relations environments" (p. 424). Management by objectives, then, can be all the more successful in a PR operation, strengthening the team's overall performance and ensuring individual team members' success.

Leaders must be competent in other ways beyond those covered so far. The dimension of **emotional competence** has emerged as an important and especially telling characteristic of public relations (and other) leaders. Jin's (2010) study explored this characteristic in detail. Indeed, her study revealed five important features of emotionally competent PR leaders:

1. PR leaders must be empathetic, a core trait that drives PR leaders' accurate assessment of employees' emotions and helps them to address those emotions with sensitivity and understanding.
2. PR leaders should be flexible in decision-making power sharing and be strategic in the power-sharing negotiation process at the same time.
3. PR leaders should be very experienced in motivating and maintaining optimism at the workplace by creating experience of enthusiasm and excitement among employees.
4. PR leaders should know how to take accommodative actions and express their accommodation when confronted by disagreeing employees if resolving the disagreement will lead to task efficiency.
5. PR leaders should enhance their skills of negotiation and influence-gaining when communicating their disagreements with top management in decision-making conflicts.

This last point about abilities to negotiate with and influence others is especially pronounced for leaders. In fact, one's emotional competence must be exercised ethically for one's self and others. That is, emotional competence must be used for good and not evil—not using emotions and emotional appeals for manipulative purposes (Kilduff et al., 2010; also see Alexander, 2011; Grant, 2014). At this point, persuasion is a vital tool in a leader's toolbox. Effectiveness in persuasion is more about establishing common ground than getting one's way. Ethically, persuasion also must avoid deception, while one must also be on guard to identify deception. As we have already seen, leaders must balance matters of tasks and relationships, but they must also do so with an acute sense of the larger context surrounding a situation and those involved. That larger context is defined by the organization's strategic plan plus its overall history of operations, participation in a particular industry, and adherence to legal, community, and other expectations. Public relations leaders work among other leaders, all of whom need and want to achieve certain things on their respective agendas—presumably in tune with the organization's strategic plan.

Because of the natural **boundary-spanning** business of public relations, PR leaders may be among the most adept at building relationships and working well with those in an organization's **"dominant coalition"** (Grunig, 1992), which "is that inner circle of organizational members, often executives, who hold the greatest power. They make strategic choices, allocate resources, influence organizational values, and shape organizational ideologies" (Berger, 2007, p. 223). Public relations leaders, as we saw at the beginning of this chapter, are increasingly becoming part of organizations' dominant coalitions, which means PR leaders are increasingly involved in strategy development, resource allocations, values shaping, and ideology. In many ways today and beyond, public relations leaders (and the PR professionals who work with them) perform a highly valuable function of conscience *plus* communication expertise *plus* business savvy that is vital to organizational success at every level.

MANAGING ACROSS GENERATIONS

Employee engagement in public relations necessarily spans multiple generations, each with much to offer the others. The matter of managing not only younger generations of workers but also mixed generations of workers has risen to prominence, with good reason: people work later in life as more and more new workers join the ranks, especially in professional fields like public relations (see Deal, 2007; Martin & Tulgan, 2006).

Generational differences on a broad social scale have been a popular topic of analysis at least since "baby boomers" noticed significant differences in the way they grew up compared to their next cohort, "generation X." More recently, analyses have expanded to address the subsequent generation, referred to as "generation Y" (a.k.a. "millennials" or the "net generation"). The generation after this is (what else?) "generation Z" (a.k.a. the "new silent generation").

At a basic level, the generational differences in the workplace revolve around values. Generational analyses about workers' values provide insights not so much about differences in kind but in degree. These analyses confirm that values about work, leisure, professionalism, reward, and punishment matter to everyone. The key seems to be expectations for living up to these values as all generations of workers negotiate them with each other, starting with employee handbooks and branching out to workplace interpersonal interactions. Most particularly, as Deal (2007) demonstrates, all generations share common ground, but the challenge is establishing it in the best ways that work for people (i.e., know your audience).

In public relations, many budding professionals come from colleges and universities as interns and recent graduates. They collaborate with and, most of all, learn from seasoned professionals in all stages in their careers. Therefore, having both sensitivity to and sensibilities about generational differences is important to successful leadership, followership, and operational success. The essentials for effective leadership in PR, as given in this chapter and especially in the previous section, are necessary to effectively manage public relations.

The managing of public relations operations relies on the competence, work ethic, and character of leaders *and* followers. Never in the profession's history has this statement not been true. In those vastly abundant times of successful and ethical communication, public relations professionals show well that they are expert and moral beings who use language and symbols to inspire cooperation between organizations and their publics. In the next chapter we will look at the similarities and differences between public relations practiced in corporate settings (i.e., for-profit, nonprofit/institutional, and nongovernmental organizations) and in agency settings (i.e., businesses specifically focused on providing PR expertise for corporate clients).

EXECUTIVE VIEWPOINT

Leadership in the Public Relations Field

Dr. Felicia Blow, APR

This is truly an exciting time to be considering leadership in the field of public relations. As a new professional considering post-graduation opportunities, thinking "now" about the type of leader you wish to become is critical. If your long-term career goal is to be named a C-suite executive of a major corporation, your decision and professional exposures likely will be far different than if you wish to lead a boutique, sole proprietor PR agency. Building your "leadership toolkit" is a very wise thing to do.

A key point that must be understood is that leadership can be thankless, lonely, and requires a dedicated and focused professional. Additionally, leadership requires the capacity and ability to paint a shared vision and to guide your organization to success.

For my doctoral dissertation, I conducted intensive analysis on the leadership style that best describes the type of leader I aspired to be early on in my career. The best descriptor for my leadership aims is "transformational." Transformational leaders "shake things up." Transformational leaders move organizations to greatness. They tend to be change agents. Transformational leaders also have a strong work ethic, believe in accountability, are innovators, are courageous, and deliver results.

From the vantage point of results-driven leadership, excellence is largely measured by one's effectiveness as evidenced through organizational performance. In that regard, I am truly a "results-oriented" leader. A results-oriented leader is one who tends to be decisive and is confident in taking charge. They are focused, logical, and organized. They are task-orientated and set high expectations for themselves and those around them. They also are ethical—with a very high degree of integrity—and are empathetic.

As students, you are learning about historical figures who are models in leadership excellence. Individuals such as Edward Bernays (1891–1995) is one such leader often referred to as "the father of public relations," one who pushed boundaries and created innovations. Others include Ivy Lee (1877–1934), Betsy Plank (1924–2010), and Arthur Page (1883–1960). But there are "hidden PR figures" who also are standard bearers for our profession. They include individuals such as African-American leader Ofield Dukes (1932–2021), and Don Padilla (1921–1992) who were innovators, creating lasting change in our profession. These PR pioneers searched for opportunities to innovate, grow, and improve. They exemplify truly great leaders who have created motivating, purpose-driven visions.

As you consider your leadership journey consider these points of view:

- **Be adaptable.**
  I have worked in a wide variety of industries, working with and leading teams in the manufacturing, waste management, environmental services, telecommunications, two-year higher education, and four-year higher education arenas. Each of these transitions helped me to grow and expand as a leader.

- **Choose volunteer leadership opportunities that give you the opportunity to lead, learn, and grow.**
  I have held many local, regional, and national Board of Directors leadership roles (including Chair) for organizations such as the Public Relations Society of America (PRSA), the Chamber of Commerce, academic organizations, and many others.
- **Learn as many aspects of the PR and communications profession as you can.**
  In my leadership journey, the disciplines I have led include employee relations, fundraising and development, media relations, digital communications, government affairs, graphic design, crisis management, and many other areas.
- **Start out small if need be to gain the skills needed for leadership.**
  Over my career, I have led very small teams of one to two persons to very large PR teams of 20 full- and part-time persons or more, as well as indirect leadership of boards and entire professional organizations.
- **Remember that leadership is situational.**
  A good leader modifies their style to the situation and the individual, while not compromising on the results and/or expectations and outcomes.
- **Do not be afraid to fail.**
  In my career, I have had great opportunities and a multitude of leadership successes. I also have had great challenges and have experienced abject failure. I have had people leadership success in that I have coached, nurtured, motivated, and led my groups to major triumphs. I also have had difficulties in engaging with teams to support and be inspired by a shared vision. In all of these experiences, there is one thing that is consistent: you cannot lead a team if you are afraid to innovate and try new things.
- **Never stop learning.**
  Learning is "lifelong." Learn a new skill set. Gain a degree. I secured my bachelor's degree in 1988. I earned my MBA in 2010. I earned my PhD in 2021. At each phase of my life, I chose to take another degree that would accelerate my career. Perhaps your decision will be in music, a foreign language, or computers. Continue to sharpen your mind. Never stop learning something new.

Finally, as a "people leader," you must remember that you are not brought to an organization to make friends. You are there to do a job. This fact does not give you license to "act a fool" (as my mother would say). It does, however, set strict expectations to fulfill your role in the overall organization's success.

In conclusion, recognize that as a future leader, you will be challenged. Your vision will be criticized. You may even be ostracized due to the decisions made. However, as good leaders, you must not be deterred nor distracted. In closing, as shared earlier, leadership can be lonely, and thankless, but it is also incredibly rewarding.

KEY WORDS

Communication styles	Incidents
Leadership communication styles	Eight practices of managers/ executives
Leadership orientations	Follower types
Leadership types	MBO
Management	Running effective meetings
Models of PR	Agenda
Disruptive situations	Excellent PR leadership model
Crises	Emotional competence
Public tragedies	Boundary spanning
Issues	Dominant coalition

REFERENCES

Alexander, R. (2011, April). The dark side of emotional intelligence. *Management Today*, 46–50.

Annenberg School for Journalism & Communication, Strategic Communication & Public Relations Center. (2014). *GAP VIII: Eighth communication and public relations generally accepted practices study (Q4 2013 data)*. University of Southern California Annenberg Center on Communication Leadership. Available online: http://ascjweb.org/gapstudy/.

Bennis, W., & Nanus, B. (2003). *Leaders: The strategies for taking charge* (2nd ed.). Harper Business Books.

Berger, B. (2007). Public relations and organizational power. In E. L. Toth (Ed.), *The future of excellence in public relations and communication management* (pp. 221–234). Lawrence Erlbaum Associates.

Berger, B. (2012). *Key themes and findings: The cross-cultural study of leadership in public relations and communication management*. The Plank Center for Leadership in Public Relations. Available online: http://plankcenter.ua.edu/the-summit/.

Berger, B., Zerfass, A., Reber, B., Meng, J., Jin, Y., Petersone, B., … Herrera, M. (2012, November 1). Cross-cultural study of leadership in public relations and communication management. Presentation made at The Plank Center Leadership Summit in Chicago, IL. Available online: http://plankcenter.ua.edu/the-summit/.

Berger, B. K., & Meng, J. (Eds.) (2014). *Public relations leaders as sensemakers: A global study of leadership in public relations and communication management.* Routledge.

Cheney, G., & Vibbert, S. L. (1987). Corporate discourse: Public relations and issue management. In F. M. Jablin, L. L. Putnam, K. H. Roberts, & L. W. Porter (Eds.), *Handbook of organizational communications: An interdisciplinary perspective* (pp. 165–194). Sage.

Coombs, W. T. (2012). *Ongoing crisis communication: Planning, managing and responding* (3rd ed.). Sage.

Crable, R. E., & Vibbert, S. L. (1985). Managing issues and influencing public policy. *Public Relations Review, 11,* 3–16.

Cutlip, S. M. (1994). *The unseen power: Public relations, a history.* Lawrence Erlbaum.

Cutlip, S. M. (1995). *Public relations history: From the 17th to the 20th century, the antecedents.* Lawrence Erlbaum.

Cutlip, S. M. (1997). The unseen power: A brief history of public relations. In C. L. Caywood (Ed.), *The handbook of strategic public relations and integrated communications* (pp. 15–33). McGraw-Hill.

Cutlip, S. M., Center, A. H., & Broom, G. M. (1994). *Effective public relations* (7th ed.). Prentice Hall.

Czarnecki, G. (2010). *Lead with love: 10 principles every leader needs to maximize potential and achieve peak performance.* Milton Rae Press/Morgan James Publishing.

Deal, J. J. (2007). *Retiring the generation gap: How employees young and old can find common ground.* Jossey-Bass/John Wiley & Sons.

Drucker, P. F. (1993). *Management: Tasks, responsibilities, practices.* HarperBusiness. (Original work published 1973.)

Drucker, P. F. (2001). Effective decisions. In P. F. Drucker, *The essential Drucker: The best of sixty years of Peter Drucker's essential writings on management* (pp. 241–260). HarperCollins.

Drucker, P. F. (2004, June). What makes an effective executive? *Harvard Business Review, 82*(6), 58–63.

Drucker, P. F. (2006). *The effective executive.* HarperCollins. (Original work published 1967.)

Drucker, P. F. (2006). *The practice of management.* Harper & Row. (Original work published 1954.)

Ewen, S. (1996). *PR! A social history of spin.* Basic Books.

Fink, S. (1986). *Crisis management: Planning for the inevitable.* AMACOM.

George, B. (2003). *Authentic leadership: Rediscovering the secrets to creating lasting value.* Jossey-Bass.

Grant, A. (2014, January 2). The dark side of emotional intelligence. *The Atlantic.* Available online: www.theatlantic.com/health/archive/ 2014/01/the-dark-side-of-emotional-intelligence/ 282720/.

Grunig, J. (1992). Communication, public relations, and effective organizations. In J. Grunig (Ed.), *Excellence in public relations and communication management* (pp. 1–30). Lawrence Erlbaum Associates.

Grunig, J. E., & Grunig, L. A. (1992). Models of public relations and communication. In J. E. Grunig (Ed.), *Excellence in public relations and communication management* (pp. 285–325). Lawrence Erlbaum Associates.

Grunig, J. E., & Hunt, T. (1984). *Managing public relations*. Holt, Rinehart & Winston.

Hayes, R. A., & Smudde, P. M. (2015). The Incident: Not just another organizational disruption. *Journal of Public Relations Research, 27*, 416–430.

Hayes, R. A., Waddell, J. C., & Smudde, P. M. (2017). Our thoughts and prayers are with the victims: Explicating the public tragedy as a public relations challenge. *Public Relations Inquiry, 6*(3), 253–274.

Hunt, T., & Grunig, J. E. (1994). *Public relations techniques*. Harcourt Brace.

Jin, Y. (2010). Emotional leadership as a key dimension of public relations leadership: A national survey of public relations leaders. *Journal of Public Relations Research, 22*(2), 159–181.

Johnson, C. E., & Hackman, M. Z. (2018). *Leadership: A communication perspective* (7th ed.). Waveland Press.

Kellerman, B. (2008). *Followership: How followers are creating change and changing leaders*. Harvard Business School Press.

Kelley, R. (1992). *The power of followership: How to create leaders that people want to follow and followers who lead themselves*. Doubleday/ Currency.

Kelley, R. (1998). Followership in a leadership world. In. L. C. Speard (Ed.), *Insights on leadership: Service, stewardship, spirit, and servant-leadership* (pp. 170–184). Wiley.

Kilduff, M., Chiaburu, D. S., & Menges, J. I. (2010). Strategic use of emotional intelligence in organizational settings: Exploring the dark side. *Research in Organizational Behavior, 30*, 129–152.

Kouzes, J. M., & Posner, B. Z. (2017). *The leadership challenge: How to make extraordinary things happen in organizations* (6th ed.). John Wiley & Sons.

Lonergan, B. (1990). *Method in theology* (2nd ed.). University of Toronto Press. (Original work published 1973.)

Martin, C. A., & Tulgan, B. (2006). *Managing the generation mix: From urgency to opportunity* (2nd ed). AHD Press Inc.

Maslow A. M. (1987). *Motivation and personality* (3rd ed.). Pearson. (Original work published 1954.)

Meng, J. (2012). Strategic leadership in public relations: An integrated conceptual framework. *Public Relations Review, 38*, 336–338.

Meng, J., & Berger, B. (2013). An integrated model of excellent leadership in public relations: Dimensions, measurement, and validation. *Journal of Public Relations Research, 25*(2), 141–167.

Meng, J., & Berger, B. K. (2014). Research design and methods. In B. K. Berger & J. Meng (Eds.), *Public relations leaders as sensemakers: A global study of leadership in public relations and communication management* (pp. 38–54). Routledge.

Meng, J., Berger, B. K., Gower, K. K., & Heyman, W. C. (2012). A test of excellent leadership in public relations: Key qualities, valuable sources, and distinctive leadership perceptions. *Journal of Public Relations Research, 24*(1), 18–36.

Public Relations Society of America (PRSA). (2022). About public relations. Retrieved from www.prsa.org/about/all-about-pr.

Rehak, J. (2002, March 23). Tylenol made a hero of Johnson & Johnson: The recall that started them all. *The New York Times*. Available online: www.nytimes.com/2002/03/23/your-money/IHT-tylenol-made-a-hero-of-johnson-johnson-the-recall-that-started.html

Smudde, P. M. (2001). Issue or crisis: A rose by any other name. *Public Relations Quarterly, 46*(4), 34–36.

Smudde, P. M. (2011). *Public relations as dramatistic organizing: A case study bridging theory and practice.* Hampton Press.

Timberg, C. (2021, October 22). New whistleblower claims Facebook allowed hate, illegal activity to go unchecked. *The Washington Post.* Available online: www.washingtonpost.com/technology/2021/10/22/facebook-new-whistleblower-complaint/.

Ulmer, R. R., Seeger, M. W., & Sellnow, T. L. (2015). *Effective crisis communication: Moving from crisis to opportunity* (3rd ed.). Sage.

Werder, K. P., & Holtzhausen, D. (2009). An analysis of the influence of public relations department leadership style on public relations strategy use and effectiveness. *Journal of Public Relations Research, 21*(4), 404–427.

RECOMMENDED READING

Clampitt, P. G. (2010). *Communicating for managerial effectiveness* (4th ed.). Sage Publications.

Drucker, P. F. (2001). *The essential Drucker: The best of sixty years of Peter Drucker's essential writings on management.* Collins Business Essentials.

Gregory, A., & Willis, P. (2013). *Strategic public relations leadership.* Routledge.

Kelley, R. (1992). *The power of followership.* Currency.

Kouzes, J. M., & Pozner, B. Z. (2006). *A leader's legacy.* John Wiley & Sons.

Levine, A., & Dean, D. R. (2012). *Generation on a tightrope: Portrait of today's college student.* Jossey-Bass/John Wiley & Sons.

Maxwell, J. C. (1999). *The 21 indispensable qualities of a leader: Becoming the person others will want to follow.* Thomas Nelson.

Maxwell, J. C. (2007). *The 21 irrefutable laws of leadership: Follow them and people will follow you* (revised & updated ed.). Thomas Nelson.

Selden, B. (2008). *What to do when you become the boss: How new managers become successful managers.* Outskirts Press.

Sutton, R. I. (2007). *The no asshole rule: Building a civilized workplace and surviving one that isn't.* Business Plus.

Twenge, J. M. (2006). *Generation me: Why today's young Americans are more confident, assertive, entitled—and more miserable than ever before.* Free Press.

Twenge, J. M. (2017). *iGen: Why today's super-connected kids are growing up less rebellious, more tolerant, less happy—and completely unprepared for adulthood (and what that means for the rest of us).* Atria Books.

2

CHAPTER 2
TEAM MANAGEMENT

CHAPTER OUTLINE

Group work in any profession is not only inevitable, it is a certainty. Even sole practitioners, like freelance writers, graphic artists, and others, must work with and within groups of people on projects and programs. To be sure, much of the work that groups do is done task-by-task by individuals on their own or perhaps in smaller work teams of fellow group members. Nevertheless, the work of each group member, whether done alone or with others, contributes to the overall success (or failure) of the larger group. Individuals contribute through collaboration, for better and for worse. Always remember that teams share in victory and defeat! The whole is truly greater than the sum of its parts, and every part matters. The weakest link in the chain determines the chain's strength.

To build upon and complement the preceding chapter on leadership, management, and followership, this chapter is focused on the team side of public relations management. To this end two topics are examined. The first covers the characteristics of highly effective teams, based on long-term and broad-based studies. Principles such as leadership, ethics, strategy, and performance intersect and are extended in this discussion. The second topic concerns external experts known as freelancers, consultants, and vendors, who may be hired to help a PR team as *ad hoc* team members. The discussion reveals why such experts should be considered, on what grounds they should be hired, why they might be fired, and how the size of external experts' organizations can matter.

DOI: 10.4324/9781003208280-3

TRAITS OF TOP-PERFORMING GROUPS

Much research and advice about effective teams and teamwork abounds on the Internet, in libraries and booksellers, and through seminars, workshops, and other venues. Chapter 1 examined details about effective leadership, management, and followership that also apply to teamwork so that teams of any size and sort can be as successful as possible. For our purposes in public relations, and without going into the rich details about small-group dynamics, at least two fundamental questions about teams dominate: (1) What are the traits of effective teams? and (2) On what grounds do effective teams thrive? Two particular long-range and broad-based studies completed by Frank LaFasto and Carl Larson (LaFasto & Larson, 2001; Larson & LaFasto, 1989) answer these questions. In their first study, Larson and LaFasto (1989) identified and studied 32 highly effective teams over a three-year period to discover what the characteristics were that made them so successful. Teams ranged from the crew of a U.S. Navy aircraft carrier to a McDonald's product-development team, from surgical teams to a championship football team. The results of research clearly showed **eight common traits of highly effective teams**:

- *Clear, elevating goal*—The team has a defined, single reason and purpose for existing, and it both focuses members' work and inspires members to embrace something greater than they are individually and collectively.
- *Results-driven structure*—The team is organized and operates in ways that most effectively and efficiently channel efforts and resources to realize objectives that will yield solid performance and determine ultimate success.
- *Competent team members*—The team is made up of intellectually, emotionally, pragmatically, and interpersonally smart people who know what, how, when, and why to do the right things in the context of the elevating goal and do what it takes to get the job done well.
- *Unified commitment*—The team's members identify with the team, are deeply involved, and are unwavering in their dedication to the team's cause and their willingness to expend whatever effort it takes to succeed.
- *Collaborative climate*—The team members establish a work ethic among all members that encourages everyone to work well together and seek input or feedback, test ideas, and confront challenges because more minds are better than one.
- *Standards of excellence*—The team develops and upholds expectations for individual performance, handling responsibilities, and being accountable for outcomes.
- *External support and recognition*—The team enjoys the genuine commitment to and resource allocations for its cause from the larger organization, including the celebration of milestone achievements and reward structures tied to performance.
- *Principled leadership*—The team is led by someone who places the team's needs before their own. The leader is visionary and communicates that vision vividly

and in terms that inspire members to embrace it to change things for the better. The leader also enables members to become the best people they can be by unleashing their creativity. Leaders also nurture new leaders.

Each of these traits is made all the more potent when coupled with LaFasto and Larson's (2001) follow-up study. Indeed, this second study is the culmination of their work over a 15-year period that included data gathered from more than 6,000 members and leaders of all kinds of teams in many arenas of human activity, including industry and private and public organizations. Effective team members, according to the researchers, possess **two categories of instrumental factors** among them: (1) *working knowledge*, which is based on the relevance, depth, and breadth of experience plus acute problem-solving abilities; and (2) *teamwork*, which depends on openness (being candid, honest, inviting), supportiveness (helping others succeed), action orientation (being self-motivated to act and encouraging others to take action), and personal style (being positive, enthusiastic, confident, fun to work with). The results of this very long-term study showed that the most effective teams thrive on the following **five dynamics**:

- *Collaborative members*—Team members like working together and want to collaborate so that each person and the group achieve success at all levels in all things.
- *Positive relationships among members*—Team members get along well with each other in ways that foster candid communication which strengthens relationships, enhances productivity, and makes a difference at the micro and macro levels.
- *Productive problem solving*—The team follows a structured approach to solving problems that is focused, inviting, and communicative so that the physical, mental, and spiritual (i.e., *esprit de corps*) energies expended, although draining, are fulfilling and lead to making the best decisions possible.
- *Leadership that encourages group achievement*—Team leaders consistently define and focus on the elevating goal, ensure a collaborative climate, build confidence, demonstrate technical know-how, set priorities, and manage performance.
- *Organizational environment that truly supports collaboration and teamwork*—The team's work environment enables clarity, confidence, and commitment toward performance expectations, outputs, and ultimate goal achievement through sound management practices, effective operating structure and processes, and effective operating systems geared toward performance standards.

In many ways the cohesiveness of group members is a common thread that runs throughout these insights about effective teams. Indeed, **cohesiveness** is a counterpart to collaboration, which predominates in Larson and LaFasto's work. Cohesiveness, as explained by Hogg (1992), is key in several ways. It attracts members of a group and results in a "feel" for the group. Members look forward to interacting with the group, feel loyalty to the group, and wish to contribute to its projects. Cohesiveness, then, is an important source of motivation and a factor that enlivens discussions with members who come prepared. Cohesiveness emerges from feelings members have for one another, rewards members' experience in interactions with one another, builds value that members attach to the assignments the group undertakes, and cements members' expectations that their work will be supported and rewarded by the organization.

Differences among team members would ultimately affect team management. Very much in tune with the material in Chapter 1, leaders are instrumental in promoting cohesiveness in teams by developing a group identity, building group traditions, stressing the value of teamwork, recognizing good work by members, helping set attainable goals, providing group rewards, keeping psychologically close to members, treating people with respect, and bringing the team back on track if needed. What leaders and their groups do is not done in some willy-nilly fashion but, rather, is framed by an appropriate and effective structure.

GROUP STRUCTURE

Communication is the glue for effective groups in every way. As Larson and LaFasto's work showed, group structure must facilitate group productivity and, thereby, success. Group structures are created in response to a group's reason for existing so that its task can be handled best and expected results obtained. The structure that a group employs determines individual involvement through communication by virtue of one's place in the structure. In this way, group structure and communication structure are essentially one and the same.

Two basic communication structures are centralized and decentralized formats (DeVito, 2009). **Centralized structures** put someone, usually the leader, at the center of all group communication. Any and all communication from within or from without must go through the leader. Group members may not communicate with another member except through the leader. There are several advantages of a centralized structure:

- It is most efficient when solving simple problems, especially when time is of the essence, taking advantage of strict divisions of labor.
- Fewer messages are communicated.
- There are few changes in communication or answers to inquiries.
- The central person is the most satisfied and has high morale.
- The central person is motivated to be the leader (having keys to information).

At the same time there are two major disadvantages. One is the presence of low morale among group members because they are not involved except when the leader communicates with them. The other disadvantage is that communication interactions among other members are limited. So member dissatisfaction is largely a function of limited information about the big picture and other details of what is going on.

The second communication structure is decentralized. This kind of structure is largely democratic and allows for communication among all members equally or with some limited restriction, such as people being permitted only to communicate when their turns come up in a sequence. The advantages to **decentralized structures** are:

- They solve complex problems with fewer errors, especially when time is not at a premium, taking advantage of open divisions of labor.
- There is high group satisfaction, morale, and motivation.
- There are more opportunities to make friends (talk to everyone).
- They are more effective at generating creative solutions to problems (freely express ideas, etc.).

There are two important disadvantages to decentralized structures. First, the problem-solving process for complex matters is often slow. This first disadvantage derives from the second—that having more communication opportunities among all members means more time is needed to entertain, evaluate, and decide on issues. When situations call for swift decisions when time is of the essence (e.g., a disruptive situation like a crisis), a decentralized structure very well may not be the best one and a centralized structure should be employed.

When people work together in teams using "computer-mediated communication technologies to work interdependently across space, time and organizational boundaries" (Berry, 2011, p. 211), they are operating as a **virtual team**. Virtual teams' members can be located across the office as much as across the world. The term "virtual team" is a bit of a misnomer, because the team is real, but it is "virtual" because members meet and work using digital channels for communication, such as video applications like Zoom, Webex Meetings, Microsoft Teams, FaceTime, and others. So they may never meet physically in the same place. Nevertheless, communication structures in virtual teams can be centralized or decentralized, depending on their purpose and the constraints they face.

Virtual teams share many of the challenges and traits of traditional teams, but the management of teams is all the more demanding because people can do what they need and want to do with much greater independence than in teams meeting face-to-face (Berry, 2011). Effective virtual team management, then, relies on stronger-than-usual knowledge and understanding of the group dynamics and accountability explained in this book, so that both task and relationship dimensions are attended to well at all times. (See the "Executive Viewpoint" by Jennifer Detweiler at the end of this chapter.) Effective leadership also requires a savvy use of the team's communication channels because, after all, knowing the audience and their perspective is as critical as it is in a face-to-face situation.

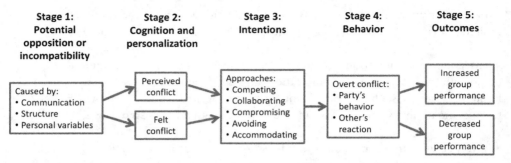

Figure 2.1 Conflict process model
Source: Robbins and Judge (2008, p. 487)

CONFLICT

No matter what structure a group uses, and no matter how well a team may be led and managed, conflict can emerge. **Conflict** occurs when there is a clash between at least two people or parties who perceive each other as negatively affecting something the other cares about (Robbins & Judge, 2008). Viewing conflict as a process makes it manageable, which is a valuable perspective for a team leader. The process, as explained by Robbins and Judge (2008), consists of **five stages**, shown in Figure 2.1.

In stage 1, certain factors contribute to the emergence of conflict between one person and another. Communication concerns the meaning attached to intentional and unintentional messages of any kind. Structure refers to the multiple variables that exist within the context of the work environment of the people in conflict. Personal variables involve personality types and the emotional competence of the people involved.

In stage 2, the conditions that gave rise to a possible conflict become real at a perceived level (i.e., when observed) and/or at a felt level (i.e., when emotions are evoked). This stage is the one where conflict is defined and emotions predominate and fuel the conflict process.

Stage 3 concerns the decisions people make to act in certain ways. The decisions are focused on the intentions that one party believes are behind the conflict. Two dimensions of intentions interact: *cooperativeness* (i.e., other focus) and *assertiveness* (i.e., self-focus). Handling a conflict in this stage can be done by identifying certain intentions that appear to be at play:

- *Competing* ("I win, you lose"; low cooperative and high assertive)
- *Collaborating* ("Let's work together"; high assertive and cooperative)
- *Avoiding* ("Ignore it and it will go away"; low cooperative and assertive)

- *Accommodating* ("All right, we'll do it your way"; low assertive and high cooperative)
- *Compromising* ("We all get much of what we wanted"; equally cooperative and assertive)

Stage 4 is the implementation stage for the intention-based solution to the conflict reached in stage 3. Stage 4 involves the statements, actions, and reactions of those in conflict during implementation. The interaction between those in conflict may be *functional* (i.e., controlled behaviors, like discussion, negotiation, and argument) or *dysfunctional* (i.e., destructive behaviors, like threats, walkouts, riots, wars). Note that dysfunction is possible at any time and is counterproductive for group performance. If there is too little conflict, more conflict should be injected to spark creativity; if there is too much conflict, a resolution ought to be reached so that performance is not lost.

In stage 5, the results of the conflict resolution implemented in stage 4 are counted. When conflict sparks curiosity, inspires creativity, enables a strong problem-solving environment, and mitigates groupthink, functional outcomes are very likely. **Functional outcomes** are those that enhance personal or group performance. When conflict spurs discontent, fuels confrontation, dissolves relationships, and destroys group cohesion, dysfunctional outcomes are highly likely. **Dysfunctional outcomes** undermine individual or group performance. Although conflict is often perceived as only bad, when it is managed well for a highly effective team, conflict can be a force for good, especially to drive innovation.

CREATIVITY

Strictly speaking, **creativity** concerns the creation of something from something else. A potter uses clay to make a vase. An engineer designs a bridge using steel and concrete. A public relations professional produces a campaign using language, symbols, people, and media. Creativity, then, implies a process of making something. Everyone is creative, and people are creative in ways that others may not be. The challenge for leaders is how best to unleash team members' creativity. Creativity often comes organically, as it does spontaneously when someone is addressing an immediate challenge. But creativity also can be experienced on demand, as it would during "creativity sessions" called by a leader to have team members meet to come up with big ideas for a client. In the public relations profession, people are highly creative and, as we saw in Chapter 1, thrive on leaders who enable them to make the most of their creativity. So a basic understanding of creativity can be valuable for PR leaders and followers.

The study of the process of creativity began "about 400 years ago [when] scientists discovered that our brain, not our heart, was responsible for our intellectual activity" (Green, 1999, p. 26). Over the last century, especially the latter half, many attempts at defining the creativity process have yielded some fairly common characteristics.

The incongruity of what is going on with what needs to happen, as is the case in trying to strategize how to rebuild an organization's damaged image, is fertile ground for creativity. Another way to think of it is *cognitive dissonance* (Festinger, 1957), where there is a kind of harmony or consistency or congruity that needs to be established but is not and needs a means to achieve it. Again, creativity is the key—a means to make order out of chaos.

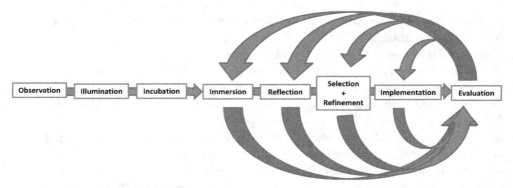

Figure 2.2 Model of creativity as a process

In PR a creative solution may seek to establish dissonance within a public (e.g., a need in people's lives is not being met when they thought it was) because there is a great way to achieve harmony in their lives (e.g., meet the need with the thing ethically prescribed in targeted messages). Within the context of public relations practice, Figure 2.2 is my model of the creative process that reflects other attempts at modeling it, complements this chapter's content, and is consistent with the overall approach of this book about public relations management.

The **creativity process** is both linear and recursive. It is linear in that it proceeds along eight sequential **steps** because people tend to work one step at a time. The process also is recursive because, at later stages in the process, someone may go back to and through certain prior steps while still moving the project forward in time toward its completion. This combination of linearity and recursiveness accommodates the way the human mind works, especially while solving problems. As long as "necessity is the mother of invention"—of creativity—problem solving is at the heart of creativity.

In Figure 2.2, the creativity process begins with *observation*, which is the identifying of something interesting, perhaps a problem, opportunity, or whatever. Upon that observation, *illumination* occurs, which is the "Aha!" moment of inspiration when the observed thing is seen in a new light. Upon the illumination or idea, *incubation* involves defining and thinking about the thing/idea and the new "take" on it for its possibilities, limitations, etc. To make the most of the experience and idea thus far, *immersion* takes place, which involves playing with the idea in various ways, from studying/planning to drafting/prototyping of possible solutions/approaches. Next is *reflection*, which features further thinking about and redefining of the thing/idea and possible alternatives and considerations about what could be added or subtracted, augmented or diminished. At this point, a two-part step of *selection and refinement* (i.e., to choose and to refine a thing/idea) focuses on choosing the best thing/idea from among alternatives and refining the chosen thing/idea as much as is practicable to its final state. With the thing/idea in a workable form, *implementation* involves creating the final version of the thing/idea for its purpose. After the thing/idea has been implemented, it must undergo *evaluation* to determine how good the thing/idea is in any way and make any needed improvements. During the process, it is important to note that the process's steps can fast-forward or – backward to other steps to tend to matters that need attention. A brainstorming session highlights the first few steps quite plainly, and the creativity process builds upon such brainstorming.

Having ideas in the first place can be a major challenge. If you have ever experienced "writer's block," you have experienced the struggle. Kohr (2012) prescribes a usable way to have at your disposal a font of creativity from which you can "connect the dots" from one insight to another that can, in turn, spur ideas to act on. For communication professionals, the prescription is this: always be curious, define what you want to achieve or solve, throw out old prejudices and assumptions, gather relevant and pertinent information about your own purpose, know for whom your idea is meant to add value, record your own thoughts about your thinking, examine competing organizations for what they are and do, examine organizations in other markets and industries for interesting things they are and do, research trends in society and among your organization's customers, learn from work done in other fields and disciplines for what they espouse, and involve others with whom you can advance ideas.

What has proven to be instrumental in inspiring creativity among people is using a mix of communication channels with team members (Thatcher & Brown, 2010). In fact, a mindful mix of communication channels (face-to-face as well as mediated) that works well with team members—collectively and, especially, individually—serves to bolster self-esteem as a way to also inspire creativity. When it comes to managing creativity among professionals, Thatcher and Brown (2010) argue,

> For teams made up of individuals with high self-esteem and high levels of social category diversity, managers should monitor team communications to ensure that there is not too much face-to-face communication. [And] even if creativity is not formally encouraged or a job requirement, managers can provide an organizational environment that is open to new ideas.
>
> (Thatcher & Brown, 2010, p. 298)

From a management perspective, the creativity process should be a gold mine of opportunity and innovation. Everyone has the opportunity to be creative, especially those assigned a task to solve a problem or capitalize on an opportunity. A transformational leader, for example, could best facilitate an environment conducive to creativity among staff members at all times. To spark more and more innovative ideas, a leader could, for example, encourage people to think like a child—to think without the limits amassed through growing up into adulthood—about a situation or problem, especially during brainstorming sessions. Doing so can release ideas that might not be allowed if a more mature, adult attitude prevailed. Critical-analytical thinking would be saved for the later stages in the creativity process. When managing a team for creativity, Florida and Goodnight (2005, p. 126) argue that **three principles** should be the guide:

1. Help employees do their best work by keeping them intellectually engaged and by removing distractions.
2. Make managers responsible for sparking creativity and eliminate arbitrary distinctions between "suits" (i.e., leaders/managers) and "creatives" (i.e., followers/employees).
3. Engage customers as creative partners so you can deliver superior products.

Key to these principles is the idea that "creative capital is not just a collection of individuals' ideas, but a product of interaction" (p. 126). In other words, the nature, makeup, structure, and processes of highly effective teams enable them to release their creativity in value-added ways. Sutton (2003) researched effective management practices that facilitated innovation and found that unusual approaches ("**weird rules**") to viewing situations can be at least as effective, if not more so, than conventional approaches. To this end, Sutton (p. 97) prescribes a series of ideas to manage creativity in teams facing certain situations; his prescription is shown in Table 2.1.

The idea of "outside-the-box thinking" is a call for creativity that is a widely expressed mantra in organizations and society at large. We must, however, be careful to recognize that we can think outside the box if, and only if, we know what box we are dealing with in the first place. Not that the original box should constrain our creativity but, rather, we must learn from and know what we have—we must discern whether or not and to what degree constraints still must be accommodated. This is the realm of effectively managing creativity. Sutton (2003), like Florida and Goodnight (2005), found that creativity needs a management approach that does more amplifying than squelching of innovation. As Sutton put it, "Managing for creativity, I've discovered, means taking most of what we know about management and standing it on its head" (p. 96).

An important point in all this is that to do the right thing means having the best environment and people to do it, and sometimes those things need to experience conflict. Creativity, then, is fueled by conflict in many ways (e.g., conventional versus weird, old versus new, known versus unknown, proven versus untested), which is framed by attitudes about one being thought of as better than another, even though either may achieve desired results. In this context, then, a better term for conflict might be "cognitive dissonance" (Festinger, 1957). The issue, however, is how to achieve even better results.

Table 2.1 Weird rules for managing creativity

Situations	Conventional ideas that work	Weird ideas that work
Decide to do something that will probably ...	succeed, then convince yourself and everyone else that success is certain.	fail then convince yourself and everyone else that success is certain.
Reward ...	success; punish failure and inaction.	success and failure; punish inaction.
Seek out ...	and be attentive to people who will evaluate and endorse the work.	ways to avoid, distract, and bore customers, critics, and anyone who just wants to talk about money.
Think of some ...	sound or practical things to do, and plan to do them.	ridiculous or impractical things to do, and plan to do them.
Find some happy people ...	and make sure they don't fight.	and get them to fight.
Hire ...	"fast learners" (of the organizational code).	"slow learners" (of the organizational code).
Hire ...	people who make you feel comfortable, whom you like.	people who make you uncomfortable, even those you dislike.
Hire ...	people you (probably) do need.	people you (probably) don't need.
Take our past successes ...	and replicate them.	and forget them.
Use job interviews ...	to screen candidates and, especially, to recruit new employees.	to get new ideas, not to screen candidates.
Ignore people ...	who have never solved the exact problem you face.	who have solved the exact problem you face.
Encourage people ...	to pay attention to and obey their bosses and peers.	to ignore and defy their bosses and peers.
Summary	Efficiency indicates effectiveness in the implementation and use of proven ideas.	Creative companies and teams are inefficient (and often annoying) places to work.

Source: Sutton (2003, p. 97)

The key is to unleash creativity to view and solve problems in unusual and effective ways. Unleashing creativity can work well when the leadership and management approaches, especially those explained in Chapter 1 as the most effective in the PR profession, genuinely foster innovation for the greater good. Creativity, as it has been addressed thus far, has been treated from inside an organization. But it can be fueled from the outside through the hiring of external experts in particular fields.

PROJECT MANAGEMENT

Teams of people come together for many reasons, and probably the biggest reason is to solve a problem or confront an opportunity. As we have seen, teams exist to fulfill a singular purpose (a *vision* of an ultimate outcome), and many times that vision is realized through a project of some kind. The need for a project and a team of people to address a problem or opportunity often can originate from one or more top organizational leaders, whose support is essential to the team's existence and, especially, the value contribution of the work done on the project. Because of the great prominence of teams and projects that need managing in any business, the literature available about effective project management is enormous. Using a highly potent and informative guide from Harvard Business School (2004), this short section will only summarize salient issues on the subject of project managementas a process.

The first thing to know is that a **project** comprises particular and pertinent work that will yield specifically defined results within a given period of time. Certain people are part of a project team because they possess specialized knowledge, skills, abilities, and experiences that apply to the project and the team's purpose. With the resources of people, time, material, services, and others, **project management** concerns the allocation, application, and measurement of those resources to complete the project within its timeframe. *Effective project management* means that team members share a healthy and supportive attitude toward each other and their unifying purpose, work is done well, and work is completed on time to realize the project's vision, making wise use of resources, minimizing risks, and ultimately delivering on objectives at expected or better-than-expected levels.

With this understanding, we know that projects can be of any type, size, scope, and duration. Very important, too, is that projects have a lifespan and must be managed as a process. Processes must be flexible as much as they are definitive, because processes are for people (with varying attitudes, presumably mostly positive) to work together and be successful. Some people will enjoy the process and experience, and others may merely tolerate it so they can do what they must and move on. This reality calls upon the topics of this chapter as well as the topics of effective leadership and followership in Chapter 1 that are so vital to project and project-team success. The **project management process** (see Figure 2.3) is fairly simple and proceeds along four phases of (1) defining and organizing, (2) planning, (3) execution, and (4) closure.

The first phase of the project management process comprises two parts. The first part is *defining* a project's objectives clearly and thoroughly, including the timeframe in which the project will begin and end so that the project's vision can be realized. Key defining

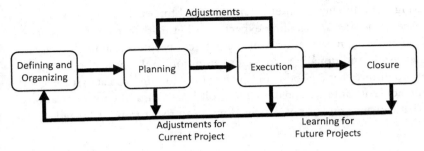

Figure 2.3 Project management process model
Source: Harvard Business School (2004, p. 3)

factors are the true need and purpose of the project, the people who see the problem/ opportunity as one worth addressing, the stakeholders in the outcome of the project and their goals, and criteria for determining success/failure. The second part is *organizing* the right people (many or all of whom were involved in defining the project) and initial necessary resources according to the project's vision and the stated objectives so work can begin. The conversations around what the project is and what it is supposed to achieve can vary in length, depth, and tenor among the people involved in this phase. Indeed, the organizing in this phase encompasses clarifications about expectations (individual and group), resources, stakeholders, and other factors (including handling adversity, interpersonal conflict, collaboration, and communication), all of which are necessary so the team understands the parameters for working well together to realize the project's vision, fulfill the objectives, and deliver solid results.

The second phase encompasses *planning* the project based on the results from the first phase. The objectives determine the parameters for what can be done (strategies) and with what (tactics/tasks) so that the project's vision can be realized. Each objective is developed with one or more strategies; and then, specific tactics or tasks are tied directly to each strategy to show what goes with what in terms of how results will be measured and achieved. Assignments of project team members will be made for working on tactics/tasks within a needed timeframe. Workloads among team members must be scrutinized so that any work fits people's areas of expertise and workloads are assigned fairly. Importantly, team dynamics must be monitored and addressed, such as matters of adversity, interpersonal conflict, collaboration, and communication. During this phase a project's feasibility (i.e., the probability that it can be completed well and on time as expected) would be addressed, perhaps confirming that it is feasible or it is not, in which case the project may need to be reconsidered, redefined, and reorganized. Additional resources may be requested, and planned resources may be reallocated as needed.

The third phase of the project management process involves *executing* the plan developed in the second phase. At this point the project has all its components and resources in place and ready to be deployed. The effective management of the project's execution involves making sure everyone is doing well (e.g., motivated people, negotiating the influence of internal and external forces, decision-making) and all resources and energies are yielding expected or better-than-expected results. During execution, periodic measurements of the project's progress against the stated objectives are necessary. Additionally, paying close attention to the project team's morale will help to ensure that a good team spirit is functioning as a catalyst for good work. Addressing adversity, interpersonal conflict, collaboration, and communication are all matters that can arise and, if not managed well, can result in poor (or failed) performance.

The fourth and final phase in the process is *closure*. Like anything, projects have an end, which means operations on executing the plan cease. It also means that the project team looks back over the project to assess how well it went and what was achieved. All measurements of effectiveness taken against the objectives are tallied, analyzed, and reported in detail. Lessons about what worked well and what did not and what could be done better next time are all documented. Team members also should talk about the personal side of working together and what contributed to making the experience valuable and what made it troublesome. After all the "loose ends" are tied up, the project is complete and the team disbands.

Project management, as shown in Figure 2.3 and as summarized, appears at first to be purely linear, but it is really recursive. Experiences in business (and other matters of life) are very rarely so straightforward. Although the process has a definite starting and ending point, people may go back and forth among the phases to adopt and adapt to new aspects of a project that pertain to other phases and the requisite concerns and work of them. There are good project and project-team experiences, and there are bad ones too. The best personal approach to working on a project team is to always do your best, do not take things personally, follow through on your promises and commitments, do not make assumptions about people and things without having actual and credible information, and listen carefully and actively while testing ideas and information (see Ruiz & Mills, 1997; M. Ruiz, J. Ruiz, & Mills, 2010).

FREELANCERS, CONSULTANTS, AND VENDORS

Public relations work is multifaceted. Programs and projects can often involve people from outside an organization because they have very special and needed capabilities and expertise. Think of it this way: when someone is ill, they go to a medical professional. When someone needs financial advice, they go to a financial advisor. When someone requires legal advice, they talk with an attorney. When someone wants personal advice, they ask for help from a qualified person, such as a parent or sibling, trusted friend, or priest. These situations are analogous to those found in organizations (generally) and particularly in public relations (specifically).

Leaders of operating units in organizations often need or want the help of experts in particular areas—to join their teams on a temporary basis to help with something important. The primary objective in seeking and hiring the help of external experts is to add value to an organization in very specific ways. As you might imagine, an expert's performance in their duties will be measured in appropriate ways so that value can be determined definitively, especially if an expert may be used again or, perhaps, recommended to others seeking similar help. Having an outside expert can reap many benefits, especially as there would be a mix of internal knowledge and experience about an organization blended with external knowledge and experience based on multiple organizations' successes (and failures). A systematic search of some kind should be applied to find and hire the most appropriate freelancer, consultant, or vendor.

In public relations, like other professions, there is a wide range of external experts who practice their crafts—writing, planning, advising about and managing crises, organizing events, producing displays and exhibits, printing, designing communications, analyzing digital and traditional media, conducting quantitative and qualitative research, coaching executives, and so on. These professionals mesh well with existing PR teams and can be grouped into three commonly used categories of freelancers, consultants, and vendors.

FREELANCERS

The first category is **freelancers**. "Freelance" is a term that comes from medieval times, when a knight was released by his lord from exclusive allegiance to that lord—the knight was free to use his lance and sword in causes to help defend or fight for other lords; thus the term, "freelance." In today's terms, freelancers are people who, similarly, are free to work for whom they wish with the knowledge, skills, abilities, tools, and experiences they possess. For the communication field, these experts are independent contractors who very often are sole proprietors (i.e., they work for themselves). Freelancers are highly skilled in specific areas, such as writing, visual design, event planning, photography, digital media design and content, and others. Freelancers charge for their work by the hour or by project, providing details about their rates or estimates for projects to clients. Of the two methods of charging for services, hourly rates may be preferred because they are seen as the fairest accounting of the work that was done (Kopelman et al., 1995). Other rates, such as word count in the case of writing for periodicals, are common (see Boyd et al., 1997; Brewer, 2013; Yudkin, 1988).

CONSULTANTS

The second category of external experts is **consultants**. These experts can be independent (sole proprietors) or incorporated (agencies), and there are numerous books and other resources about effective consulting. Simply put, consultants add value to their clients in many ways, similar to freelancers, but with greater access to resources (largely their own) to do their work because they have both the breadth and the depth of knowledge, skills, abilities, tools, and experience for the communication field. A consultant's value lies in their "intervening in a system to stop some destructive human process and to improve the ability of the organization to function" (DeWine, 2001, p. 23). Consultants bring the best of both worlds (internal and external) and can fulfill a number of roles, including provider or technical expert, investigator, advocate, prescriber, teacher or stimulator, change agent, and colleague/collaborator/reflector (Gayeski, 1993, pp. 181–183). The consultation process includes identifying problems or the deeper nature of a problem already identified, conceiving of solutions or actions to take, implementing a solution or action, and following up to ensure successful implementation and addressing areas for added attention (DeWine, 2001, p. 31).

There are many reasons to hire consultants. Obvious ones include strategic reasons—they provide good service, meet deadlines, keep promises, do thorough work, and pay attention to details (e.g., tasks/outputs and billing). Consultants typically have a solid track record of and a strong reputation for good performance for a variety of clients, and they may charge more for their work than freelancers but be competitive with PR agencies. More specifically, consultants can (Beard, 2001, p. 129):

- Provide a second opinion on strategy
- Implement programs
- Fill experience and capability gaps
- Provide overseas resource
- Advise about special situations
- Provide access to contacts
- Do research
- Meet workload peaks
- Support subsidiary operations
- Reinforce issues to management.

While there are reasons to hire consultants, there may be reasons to fire them. Firing a consultant may be based on, for example, lack of preparation, poor listening, losing touch with a client, using a competitor's product/service, failing to service the account properly, not paying enough attention to client–consultant "chemistry," and poor political savviness within the client's organization (Lukaszewski, 2003). Consultants can charge for their work on an hourly, project, or retainer basis.

VENDORS

The third category of external experts is **vendors**. These experts are providers of specialized products and services. Examples include printers, videographers, graphic designers, web hosts and programmers, digital/social media creators or analysts, exhibit makers, caterers, providers of promotional items, animal handlers, decorators, etc. Vendors may be hired as subcontractors to agencies, freelancers, or consultants to fulfill work required under a contract with those primary providers. Client approval of a vendor hired by an agency, freelancer, or consultant may or may not be necessary. As a matter of fair disclosure and honesty, it would be best for those primary providers to explain the need for and decision to subcontract work to a vendor. Cost, timing, and other issues would need to be defined as proper and appropriate under the contract between a client and its external expert.

SIZE MATTERS

For all the reasons there may be to hire an external expert of any type, the aspect of size is important to consider. There are advantages and disadvantages to hiring large and small firms. Table 2.2 shows some of the advantages, and Table 2.3 shows some of the disadvantages.

No matter what size of firm an organization hires, learning about the client in all respects will be an issue. The question is, then, how well *and* how fast can external experts learn and then apply that learning competently in work that must be done. It is interesting to notice in comparisons between the **pros and cons** of large and small firms that size can be both a strength and a weakness for each. On this point, size matters not in terms of the scale of a firm's operations, but rather in terms of other essential dimensions that make up the reasons for hiring a firm of any sort. The three dimensions of quality, service, and price (like three legs of a stool) work together to support a firm's case for being in business and building its business with satisfied (even enthusiastic) clients.

Table 2.2 Advantages to hiring large and small firms

Large firms	Small firms
• Many resources & wide range of services	• Selected resources & narrow range of services
• Strong reputation	• Focused customer attention
• Extensive experience/expertise	• Specialized experience/expertise
• Industry staying power	• Swift response
• Huge network	

Table 2.3 Disadvantages to hiring large and small firms

Large firms	Small firms
• Size	• Size
• Bureaucratic slowness	• Specialization and resource limitations
• One of many clients	• Small client network
• Billings-driven	• Business-building critical (billings-driven)
• Not using full range of services	• Subcontracting very possible
• Cost	

EXECUTIVE VIEWPOINT

How Teamwork Changed during the Pandemic

Jennifer Detweiler, Director, Employee Communications, Expedia Group

As an employee communications leader at a global company, I've had a front-row seat for watching the world of work change over the last few years. While many human resources professionals have used the term "future of work" for decades, the pandemic forced us to confront that reality sooner than we thought and changed our perceptions of work forever.

As this chapter discussed, teamwork has always played a significant role in companies' success. Rarely in the professional world do you ever work alone. You're always part of a team—working toward a shared goal and seeking to fulfill a company's mission and purpose.

When the pandemic hit, most employees transitioned to working from home overnight, and companies had to find new ways to drive engagement and productivity among teams. So, what happened?

1. **Teamwork became more inclusive**. In some ways, the pandemic was an equalizer of the employee experience. Suddenly, most employees were collaborating over screens instead of some people being in a conference room and others being virtual. It allowed more people to have a voice in meetings and created a shared experience that all teams could bond over.

2. **Technology enabled teams to stay in constant communication**. Imagine if the pandemic had hit before we had access to technology like Zoom, Microsoft Teams, OneDrive, and Slack. It would have been much harder to do our jobs remotely. Thanks to technology, those communication tools became critical for teams to stay in touch and make progress on projects in the pandemic. This allowed work to continue. It also blurred the lines between work and home, with many professionals putting in more hours at work since it was harder to shut off when your office was the kitchen table or a desk in your living room.

3. **Team engagement went virtual**. For a team to succeed, members must feel committed to one another and enjoy working together. While it's hard to foster engagement and genuine connection over screens, many companies and managers tried, scheduling virtual events from happy hours to check-ins to town halls.

Suddenly teams were meeting over screens more than ever—but was it effective? According to Eric Garton and Michael Mankins' (2020) article in *Harvard Business Review*, companies with higher productivity pre-pandemic saw a 5% to 8% increase in productivity in 2020. And companies with less productivity pre-pandemic saw a 3% to 6% further decline.

According to Garton and Mankins, the organizations that were productive pre-pandemic used this as an opportunity to become even more so. Eliminating commute times meant more time for focused work. It also removed the physical boundaries of teams and allowed top talent across the company to come together virtually to solve an organization's biggest challenges. And it enabled those organizations to source talent from everywhere—focusing less on where someone is based and more on the value they can add to the company.

While productivity thrived in some organizations and teams, companies struggled to keep employees engaged. Employees were stressed and dealing with new challenges, such as homeschooling children or caring for sick loved ones. Finding creative ways to support employees' well-being became more critical than ever.

At Expedia Group, we experimented with several tactics to address this, including:

- Well-being webinars
- No-meeting days
- Additional paid time off
- Creative programming—my favorite being Storytime, where employees volunteered to read stories to Expedians' kids over Zoom, giving parents a much-needed break.

We used surveys and participation rates to determine what worked well and what didn't, and some tactics were more popular than others. However, none of them felt like a true replacement for in-person connection and collaboration. When it came time to decide the future of work, with employee input, we landed on a hybrid approach, giving both opportunities to connect in person and the flexibility to work from home part of the time.

When it was safe to do so, we transitioned to hybrid work and reunited in offices. While it's exciting having teams back together, hybrid working brings a host of new challenges—how do you make remote team members feel included and connected, when is the best time to come together as teams in-person versus working at home, etc.? These are challenges we'll have to work through in the foreseeable future.

Whether a company has chosen a remote, hybrid, or entirely in-person approach, we can all agree on one thing—we're not going back to the way things were. How we work has changed forever. It's on us as communication professionals to support leaders and organizations in this new world. While it'll be challenging, it'll also be rewarding and fun. We get to determine the future of teamwork—together.

REFERENCE

Garton, E., & Mankins, M. (2020, December 1). The pandemic is widening a corporate productivity gap. *Harvard Business Review*. Available online: https://hbr.org/2020/12/the-pandemic-is-widening-a-corporate-productivity-gap

KEY WORDS

Eight traits of highly effective teams

Two categories of instrumental factors of effective teams' members

Five dynamics used by highly effective teams

Cohesiveness

Centralized structure

Decentralized structure

Virtual team

Conflict

Five stages of conflict

Functional outcomes

Dysfunctional outcomes

Creativity

Creativity process steps

Three principles to manage creativity

Weird rules for creativity

Projects

Project management

Project management process

Freelancers

Consultants

Vendors

Pros and cons of firm size

REFERENCES

Beard, M. (2001). *Running a public relations department* (2nd ed.). Kogan Page.

Berry, G. R. (2011). Enhancing effectiveness on virtual teams: Understanding why traditional team skills are insufficient. *Journal of Business Communication, 48*(2), 186–206.

Boyd, A. L., Clark, T., Blocksom, P, & Gilbert, J. (Eds.) (1997). *Writer's Digest handbook of making money freelance writing.* Writer's Digest Books.

Brewer, R. L. (Ed.) (2013). *2014 writer's market.* Writer's Digest Books/F+W Media.

DeVito, J. A. (2009). *Human communication: The basic course* (11th ed.). Pearson Education.

DeWine, S. (2001). *The consultant's craft: Improving organizational communication* (2nd ed.). Bedford/St. Martin's.

Festinger, L. (1957). *A theory of cognitive dissonance.* Stanford University Press.

Florida, R., & Goodnight, J. (2005, July/August). Managing for creativity. *Harvard Business Review,* 124–131.

Gayeski, D. (1993). *Corporate communications management: The renaissance communicator in information-age organizations*. Focal Press.

Green, A. (1999). *Creativity in public relations*. Kogan Page.

Harvard Business School. (2004). *Managing projects large and small: Fundamental skills for delivering on budget and on time*. Harvard Business School Press.

Hogg, M. A. (1992). *The social psychology of group cohesiveness: From attraction to social identity*. Prentice-Hall.

Kohr, M. (2012). Creativity: Powering integrated marketing communication ideas. In C. L. Caywood (Ed.), *The handbook of strategic public relations and integrated marketing communication* (2nd ed., pp. 737–750). McGraw-Hill.

Kopelman, A., Shagas, K., & Levine, J. (1995). *National Writers Union guide to freelance rates and standard practice*. National Writers Union.

LaFasto, F. M. J., & Larson, C. E. (2001). *When teams work best: 6,000 team members and leaders tell what it takes to succeed*. Sage.

Larson, C. E., & LaFasto, F. M. J. (1989). *Teamwork: What must go right/what can go wrong*. Sage.

Lukaszewski, J. (2003, March 19). Effective consulting: Getting those you advise to listen to and act on your advice. Presentation at the PRSA Southeastern Wisconsin Professional Development Conference, Milwaukee, WI.

Robbins, S. P., & Judge, T. A. (2008). Conflict and negotiation. In *Organizational behavior* (13th ed., pp. 482–515). Pearson Education.

Ruiz, M. A., & Mills, J. (1997). *The four agreements: A practical guide to personal freedom*. Amber-Allen Publishing.

Ruiz, M. A., Ruiz, J. L., & Mills, J. (2010). *The fifth agreement: A practical guide to self-mastery*. Amber-Allen Publishing.

Sutton, R. I. (2003, September). The weird rules of creativity. *Harvard Business Review*, 94–103.

Thatcher, S. M. B., & Brown, S. A. (2010). Individual creativity in teams: The importance of communication media mix. *Decision Support Systems, 49*, 290–300.

Yudkin, M. (1988). *Freelance writing for magazines and newspapers: Breaking in without selling out*. Harper & Row.

RECOMMENDED READING

Adams, J. L. (1986). *Conceptual blockbusting: A guide to better ideas* (3rd ed.). AddisonWesley.

Bowen, S. A., Rawlins, B., & Martin, T. (2010). *An overview of the public relations function*. Business Expert Press.

Callen, B. (2010). *Manager's guide to marketing, advertising, and publicity*. McGraw-Hill.

Cooperrider, D. L., & Whitney, D. (2005). *Appreciative inquiry: A positive revolution in change*. Berrett-Koehler Publishers.

3

CHAPTER 3
PROFESSIONALISM, ETHICS, AND LAW: THE GOOD PERSON REPRESENTING AN ORGANIZATION WELL

CHAPTER OUTLINE

Public relations has suffered from a bad reputation for virtually all of its history, as we saw in Chapter 1. That bad reputation is based on rather convenient arguments that cite limited and selected examples of unethical or unlawful public relations to say that the entire profession is inherently evil. Because of this kind of card-stacking against public relations, misunderstandings about the profession and negative stereotypes prevail. Sadly, then, the unethical or unlawful behavior of one PR professional can adversely affect everyone as people can often find it easier to point out the bad because it is not supposed to happen, whereas good things are expected and, therefore, are not noteworthy. Such a negative orientation is highly skewed and unreasonable. As we will see in this chapter, public relations operates in many of the grey areas of ethics and

DOI: 10.4324/9781003208280-4

law, but clarity about ethics and the law with clients and our own organizations not only mitigates any problems, but it also substantiates the overwhelming efficacy of the profession.

PROFESSIONALISM

Thanks to the hard work of professionals and scholars the world over, public relations' image and reputation as a vital, ethical, and valuable organizational and social function have improved greatly (see Coombs & Holladay, 2007; Edwards & Hodges, 2011; Fawkes, 2015; L'Etang, 2012 [2004]; Taylor, 2010). Key to improving PR's image and reputation is **professionalism**. Professionalism in public relations is the sum of many components that have withstood the test of time and include at least the following (Keane, 1974; Pieczka & L'Etang, 2001):

- *Body of knowledge and self-assessment*—A field-specific body of knowledge with unique theory presents and systemizes concepts, terminology, principles, and assumptions that, in turn, may be applied in rigorous methodologies to analyze and synthesize whole cases and particular phenomena of public relations so we can know how to evaluate the practice for what works and why, what is trending, and how the profession is evolving.
- *Ethics code and enforcement/integrity*—A definitive set of principles guides practitioners' decision-making and behavior within the field, including provisions for ensuring that practitioners know, enact, and enforce the code of ethics so that the profession's integrity is sustained.
- *Specialized training/education*—A general approach to teaching and learning about public relations functions as a framework for a full range of education/ training content in dedicated resources (e.g., vocational reading, higher education courses, conference seminars, individual workshops) offered through various credible institutions and organizations focused on public relations.
- *Entry qualifications, performance standards, certification, and independence*—A basic set of expectations (largely documented and proffered by professional organizations) directs people to what is important in order to break into a public relations career, exercise great discipline in the discharge of their duties at all times, thrive and advance in their career and the field, demonstrate and maintain competence, and exercise autonomy to apply their expertise in PR to "do the right thing" without fear of reprisal or the distraction of second-guessing by others, especially management and clients.
- *Occupational interests and organizational support*—A consistent positive attitude toward the PR profession prevails within individual organizations and among other organizations that value public relations' contributions to business and society. That attitude is sparked by organizations dedicated to the advancement of the PR profession, such as the Public Relations Society of America (PRSA), the International Association for Business Communicators (IABC), the Global Alliance for Public

Relations and Communication Management (GA), and the International Public Relations Association (IPRA).

- *Social legitimacy quest and legal recognition*—A strong record of useful and important contributions from the public relations field demonstrates a significant role in the social and civic factors of everyday life, particularly as practitioners work ethically to improve the *status quo* and adhere to legal and regulatory requirements.
- *Social responsibility*—A sensitivity to and sensibility about what matters in the public interest and the social consequences of particular actions enable practitioners to balance the needs of their organizations with the needs of the public on the full range of issues, from the mundane to the controversial.

Fundamentally, public relations requires a high degree of professionalism among all practitioners at every level, and this professionalism involves doing the right thing in the right way at the right time for the right people for the right reasons. Because of the evolution of the field of public relations, including all its practices, tools, methods, and principles, the profession also has evolved. Nevertheless, the components of professionalism for the public relations field serve as a good foundation on which to build our understanding of two vital matters: ethics and the law.

ETHICS

In the public relations field, there are ample resources on ethics. From the PRSA's website to individual books and journal articles, the knowledge base about public relations ethics is well established. Indeed, ethics is covered in public relations curricula at colleges and universities. So, the objective here is not to chronicle that enormous knowledge base, but rather to explore ethics generally and make connections with public relations specifically, especially in terms of the management of PR operations of any kind.

BUILDING UP TO ETHICS

Ethics derive from morals and values and not the other way around, as shown in Figure 3.1. That is, **values** are the origin of the hierarchy that builds up to ethics,

Figure 3.1 Hierarchy building toward ethics
Source: Smudde (2011, p. 155)

comprising a shared, intersubjectively developed system of beliefs and mores that govern choices about good/bad, virtue/vice, desirable/undesirable, etc. Values make up the basis for judgment and action and can be applied by individuals and through group consensus. Values, then, are the foundation of a society and, thereby, the basis for morals. **Morals** are standards of personal behavior, obligations, or duties that are based on a hierarchy of values (religious and/or secular) of right and wrong. Morals benefit others, perhaps contrary to self-interest, and, in turn, are the locus of the development of ethical principles. **Ethics** are comprised of social rules, usually codified formally for everyone in a community, and govern individual and group character, conduct, and consequences. The relationships among values, morals, and ethics can be traced within the context of a culture (see Boehm, 2012). In terms of professionalism, at an elementary level, values, morals, and ethics together concern what a situation is, how it relates to other situations, what principles guide people and their actions, and what ought to be done and why— all these matters are germane to public relations.

ETHICS ORIENTATIONS AND REASONING

Two great areas of ethics philosophy concern universal and situational ethics, and these two areas often clash in the practice of public relations. The reason for the clash is that people often rely on experience and rules to guide present and future actions, and the orientation about applying experience and rules in matters of judgment and action can differ enough to cause problems in ethical decision-making. For the first ethics area, *universal ethics* involves the study and application of specific ethical principles to all relevant cases equally. The principle of universality is at play here: "if one judges that X is right or good, then one is committed to judging that anything exactly like X, or like X in relevant respects, is right or good" (Frankena, 1973, p. 25). In public relations, for example, a universal principle of ethics is truth-telling, which means the truth must be told every time, including times when there is insufficient information to share.

The second ethics area, *situational ethics*, involves the study and application of ethics principles on a case-by-case basis. This area of ethics is also referred to as *ethical relativism* or **relativism**. Frankena (1973, p. 109) explains three kinds of relativism:

- *Descriptive relativism:* "the basic ethical beliefs of different people and societies are different and even conflicting."
- *Meta-ethical relativism:* "there is no objectively valid, rational way of justifying one [ethical judgment] against another; consequently, two conflicting basic judgments may be equally valid."
- *Normative relativism:* what is right or good for one individual or society is not right or good for another, even if the situations involved are similar, meaning not merely that what is thought right or good by one is not thought right or good by another (this is just descriptive relativism over again), but that what is really right or good in the one case is not so in another.

It is important to recognize that, for each of these three kinds of relativism, neither one serves as the basis for any of the other ones. Of the three kinds, normative relativism is most germane to public relations practice because it can reflect something of professionals' ethical decision-making. For example, the whole truth about an organization's newly launched product would be shared in media relations efforts, but selected truthful matters about the same organization's role in a controversy may be shared through similar media relations to protect corporate interests that may be relevant in a lawsuit to be heard in a court of law. Relativism of any kind, then, is dangerous because it allows for multiple degrees of variation in ethical thinking in every case, calling into question what truly is ethical. *If anything in any situation can be rationalized as ethical, ethics is meaningless.* This point means that universal ethics has far more potency and applicability than people might acknowledge.

Helping us to make the best ethical decisions are other particular areas of ethics philosophy. Curtin and Boynton (2001) provide us with one of the most usable treatments of ethics philosophy for decision-making in public relations, because they explain "the philosophical principles underlying ethics and relate them to models of public relations practice to demonstrate how form and function mutually inform public relations ethics" (p. 411). Table 3.1 (the first of three tables derived from Curtin and

Table 3.1 Ethics orientations and reasoning

Orientation	Types of reasoning	Problems/criticisms
Teleology—"emphasizes outcomes; the ends justify the means. Ethical actions are those that result in the greatest good."	*Restricted teleology*—calculates consequences for a particular group or person.	Calculations are subjective at best and often unreliable (e.g., value of human life), so such a pseudo-mathematical approach oversimplifies the intellectual rigor necessary to make sound decisions.
	Utilitarianism—stresses consequences to society as a whole; seeks the greatest good for the greatest number.	Knowing any consequences in advance is inherently difficult (see restricted teleology), and looking at short-term consequences can often be short-sighted.
Deontology—"good consequences are not in and of themselves sufficient to guarantee good actions; some acts must be done regardless of their consequences."	*Rule deontology*—follow rules when making ethical decisions (e.g., the Golden Rule, the Ten Commandments, Kant's categorical imperative, professional codes of conduct).	Sometimes correct actions have disastrous consequences.

(continued)

Table 3.1 Cont.

Orientation	Types of reasoning	Problems/criticisms
	Act deontology— weigh both acts and consequences to determine ethical action; rely on rigorous applications of concepts like duty, justice, rights, etc. (e.g., distributive justice).	Inherently difficult to apply and results can often degenerate into *ethical relativism*, where every situation is approached individually (perhaps to rationalize inappropriate behavior) and no consistent guidelines are applied from case to case.
Axiology—values and virtues form the basis for good action.	*Aristotle's Golden Mean*—determine the most appropriate middle ground (i.e., virtue) between two extremes (i.e., vices) within a given context.	Can be reduced to a mere mathematical "average" between two extremes, which grossly oversimplifies the rigor required.
	Egoism—engage in enlightened self-interest so that what one does is good for others as well as good for oneself.	The basic motive for action may be purely selfish and masked by a justification for the action's goodness for others.
	Ethical advocacy—harness the power of persuasion for ethical ends, provided that the persuasion conforms to criteria for evaluation, priority, sensitivity, confidentiality, veracity, reversibility, validity, visibility, respect, and consent (Gower, 2018).	People can still use persuasion intentionally or unintentionally in unethical ways (e.g., logical fallacies or fabricated facts) or for unethical reasons or impure motives.

Source: Based on Curtin and Boynton (2001)

Boynton's work) summarizes specific ethics orientations/theories, the types of reasoning that are instrumental in each, and the pros and cons to them. The series of three tables (Table 3.1 through Table 3.3), then, present a usable way to account for the details of ethical decision-making and action which you have encountered in your studies of PR.

In Table 3.1, the first of the three tables, the fundamental philosophical and intellectual foundations to ethical reasoning in any field are presented in the left-hand column and are essential to the rest of their examination of public relations ethics in the successive, remaining columns. (Note that the orientation of axiology in this table is an addition to Curtin and Boynton's original material, and axiology [i.e., the study or philosophy of values] is included in the subsequent tables to similarly extend Curtin and Boynton's treatment of ethics.) Ultimately, effective decision-making that results in fair and just action reflects the concerns for ethics—that public relations leaders (and their staffs) know how to make the right choices to do the right things at the right times for the right people and for the right reasons.

Table 3.2 summarizes Curtin and Boynton's (2001) explanations about the levels, stages, principles, and reasoning in ethical decision-making that mesh with Grunig and Hunt's (1984) models of public relations that we covered in Chapter 1. In this table, we achieve a finer level of detail in ethical decision-making in PR that begins with a kind of attitude about ethics (i.e., "level"; from basic to advanced) and proceeds rather systematically through certain numbered stages of thinking that square with one's level of ethical thinking. Depending on one's stage of ethical thinking, particular principles that rely on a dominant form of reasoning reflect the demands of a specific PR model.

Table 3.3 summarizes Curtin and Boynton's explanations about the biggest picture of ethical decision-making by blending type of (i.e., school of thought about) PR ethics, what it means for PR practice, the kind of reasoning that is involved, the stage of ethical decision-making anchored in Table 3.2, and the problems with each orientation shown by row. In this table, which adds the type of "communitarianism" to Curtin and Boynton's work, we can trace in even greater detail how a given school of ethical decision-making applies precisely in public relations as governed by certain kinds of reasoning through certain stages of ethical thinking. Notable, too, in the table are the problematic concerns shown for each type/school of ethical decision-making.

A particularly useful tool for ethical decision-making is a code of ethics, which falls into the category of rule deontological ethics. The material in Tables 3.1 through 3.3 is essential to understand because it is the foundation of ethics codes. Ethics codes have their origin in, as Figure 3.1 shows, particular values and then make associations with related actions. There are many examples of ethics codes, including international codes (e.g., United Nations Declaration on the Rights of Indigenous Peoples), societal codes (e.g., the Ten Commandments), professional codes (e.g., PRSA's, IABC's, GA's, or IPRA's codes of ethics), organizational codes (e.g., statements of values and ethics in employee handbooks), and the personal beliefs every person holds. Like anything, codes of ethics have advantages and disadvantages, and Table 3.4 lays out some of them.

Table 3.2 Ethical decision-making stages and PR models

Level	Stage	Principles	Reasoning	PR model
Preconventional (focus on self-interest)	**1.** Fear of reprisal from overlings	Personal goals; situation consequences; emotional reactions	Restricted teleological focus on outcomes	Propaganda; press agentry
	2. Exploit situations for personal gain	Manipulation & deception; short-term rewards sought		
Conventional (conformity to commonly accepted expectations & standards)	**3.** Promote group interests	Place goals of & benefits to group above all else	• Teleological focus on benefits of actions to group • Axiological focus on values	Public information (journalist-in-residence); two-way asymmetrical
	4. Obey letter of the law	Reliance on written codes as legitimate authority	Rule deontological focus on group-held principles for behavior	
Postconventional (personal autonomy & critical reflection)	**5.** Social concern	Societal consequences outweigh client benefits	Utilitarianism	Two-way symmetrical
	6. Situational ethics	Societal benefits based on universal principles of equality, justice, fairness, etc.	Act deontology (categorical imperative)	

Source: Based on Curtin and Boynton (2001)

Table 3.3 PR ethics models and decision-making

Type	Definition for PR practice	Reasoning	Stage	Problems
Coorientation	Achieve convergence between organization & publics; journalistic standards prevail (media relations)	Teleological	3	Journalistic norms condemn PR as inherently unethical
Advocacy (social responsibility & persuasion)	Advocate position of organizations persuasively; ideas compete in free market of ideas (democratic); guard against deliberate deception, etc.; be organization's conscience	Teleological	3, 4	Ends not necessarily in best interest of all but of organization; conflicts of ethical interests among persons, organization, publics, society; potentially more powerful voice from those who can afford PR
Professionalism	Ethics codes, accreditation, licensing; influence of professional associations	• Rule deontology • Axiology	4	Unenforceable & vague codes; accreditation is not necessary & sufficient; cultural differences undermine universality of codes; promotes image of professionalism
Game Theory	Decision-making calculations of situations' dimensions and probable outcomes; cost-benefit analysis; subjective assigning of numerical values; "what if" analyses of all players	Teleological	2, 3, 5	Nearly impossible to know outcomes in advance; values are arbitrary; unethical behavior may be allowed; focused on client primarily; possible reduction to gamesmanship
Corporate Responsibility	Organization doing good (corporate philanthropy, corporate citizenship) helps bottom line—cost-benefit analysis	Restrictive teleology (enlightened self-interest)	3	Relies on self-regulation; motivation not always clear; difficult to achieve without more organizational power for PR

(continued)

Table 3.3 Cont.

Type	Definition for PR practice	Reasoning	Stage	Problems
	Follow principles that publics are stakeholders & treated as ends in themselves—obligations to rights of internal & external publics plus balance interests between them (issue management)	Act deontology (social contract theory)	6	
Structural/Functional Approach	Division between technicians (advocates) and PR managers (advisers); strategic goal achievement (systems theory)	Rule deontological (RD); teleological (T), if incomplete codes	3, 4	Technician = advocate implies organizational loyalty & ethical conflicts (RD→T); managers allowed more autonomy with higher status & ethical leeway/freedom (T→RD)
Accommodation/ Discursive Approach	Emphasizes relational aspects (technical, partisan & mutual values); process of communication = place of ethics; ensure possibility of & enactment through collaborative decision-making; unethical clients will not like/engage in process	Utilitarianism	3, 5	Why use rules when persuasive communication solves; systematic approach goes back to S/F approach; ethics is privileged to powerful professionals
Contingency Theory	Weigh internal & external factors to determine best PR practice; employ four-step framework	Act deontology (situational ethics)	6	Difficult to apply consistently; danger of reduction to ethical relativism; rationalize inappropriate behavior
Communitarianism	Places great emphasis on an organization's responsibilities to society/ communities of operation	Utilitarianism (greatest good for the community is good for organization)	5	Relies on relativistic thinking; can put an organization into a dilemma when good is contrary or irrelevant to an organization's mission, values, etc.

Source: Based on Curtin and Boynton (2001)

Table 3.4 Ethics codes' pros and cons

Advantages	Disadvantages
• To increase public confidence • To avoid increased government regulation (indeed, many codes were developed for this reason) • To improve internal operations/ standardize behavior • To respond to transgressions	• Having a code doesn't necessarily translate into credibility • Codes are written by those who are most likely to follow them • Codes can be written as broadly or as narrowly as members desire • If voluntary, not everyone has to belong to the professional organization • Not all codes are enforceable • Unless meaningful dialog takes place, the "code" becomes an empty "god term"

Source: Courtright (1996)

Being mindful of the advantages and disadvantages helps practitioners at all levels to understand the benefits and limitations of having a documented set of standards for expected behaviors. Perhaps most important to understanding the importance of ethics codes is the complementary roles they play. As Brinkmann (2002) explains, all ethics codes are values-based, written standards meant to guide practice in a profession or industry. Ethics codes, he argues, are established to mitigate moral conflict, establish professional standards, ensure professional morality, and promote a moral climate in which work is performed. Additionally, ethics codes are mostly voluntary while some are involuntary. For example, to be a member of professional organizations, including the PRSA and the IABC, one may be required to sign a pledge to uphold the organization's ethics code, which includes upholding that code in one's own work as well as making sure others uphold the code too. In this way a member would behave unethically if they did not report another member (or perhaps a member of the profession but not the professional organization's member) who acted in a way that breaks the ethics code or pertinent laws.

All the philosophical and theoretical foundations for ethics are essential for people to both think and act ethically. The ethics principles covered thus far would be fruitless if there were no ways to enact them to make sound ethical decisions.

RESOLVING ETHICAL DILEMMAS

Arguably, everything someone does has an ethical dimension. In the field of public relations, anything done to inspire cooperation between an organization and its publics is inherently and unequivocally wrapped in ethics issues. This principle means that ethics is ever-present and, therefore, paramount every step of the way, from the conception of a PR effort through its execution and measurement (Smudde, 2005). When ethical dilemmas of any magnitude arise, they require appropriate levels of rigor in resolving them. The question is this: what approach can be used to **resolve ethical dilemmas**, especially in the workplace?

Among the various methods and models for ethical decision-making available, the PRSA prescribes its *Ethical Decision-Making Guide* (Fitzpatrick, n.d., p. 1) as a tool for day-to-day application. The process covers six sequential steps:

1. "Define the specific ethical issue and/or conflict."
2. "Identify internal and external factors that may influence the decision."
3. "Identify key values" from a code of ethics (e.g., the PRSA's values of advocacy, honesty, expertise, independence, loyalty, and fairness).
4. "Identify the parties who will be affected by the decision and define the public relations professional's obligation to each."
5. "Select ethical principles [from a code of ethics] to guide the decision-making process."
6. "Make a decision and justify it."

Important actions after this process are monitoring results so you know how well your decision worked and why, and retaining information about the whole case so that it may be used at some future point, if necessary. The six steps in the *Ethical Decision-Making Guide* can be visualized in Figure 3.2, which is known as the "Potter Box," named after Dr. Ralph Potter of Harvard Divinity School, who created it as a model for ethical decision-making (see Christians et al., 2001). The most notable difference between the two is that the *Guide* adds a step between the boxes about values and ethical principles to identify affected parties and the obligation a PR pro has to each.

At the message level, Baker and Martinson's (2001) TARES test is another useful rule deontological approach that can help immensely to ensure that any given public

Figure 3.2 The Potter Box
Source: Christians et al. (2001, p. 6)

relations discourse avoids unethical and unlawful problems. The test, as Gower (2018) presents it, is as follows:

- *Truthfulness of the message.* Does the communication provide the audience with sufficient information to make an informed decision on the issue?
- *Authenticity of the persuader.* What is the communicator's motive? Will someone other than the communicator benefit from the message?
- *Respect for the persuadee.* Does the message treat the public with respect and as human beings?
- *Equity of the appeal.* Does the communication take advantage of a public's vulnerability?
- *Social responsibility for the common good.* Does the message serve the larger public good?

(Gower, 2018, p. 19)

Because of its particular focus on messages, the TARES test is especially useful during the entire process for developing public relations discourse—from conception to writing to reviews/approvals to editing/revising to final publication. TARES, then, gives practitioners a way to test the very content of their work as they develop it so that it balances ethics issues for both an organization and its publics. Between a code of ethics and the TARES test, there is a strong complementarity because the former helps practitioners account for the bigger picture of public relations as a social good while the latter helps practitioners focus on the smaller aspects of very specific public relations discourse that are part of the big picture.

Ethics is central to public relations. Those who lead and manage a public relations operation hold the key to enabling staff to perform ethically in all respects. More specifically, as Lee and Cheng (2011) show, PR professionals learn best about ethics from leaders who live by and educate their staffs about personal and professional ethical decision-making, behaviors, and standards. Such learning by example about ethics is more effective than focused workplace ethics initiatives (Lee & Cheng, 2012) that lack rewards for ethical behavior and focus on merely completing structured study programs. So, the ethics tools covered in this section are highly usable and useful, and they must be used by any PR practitioner at any level. If ethics is one side of the coin of professionalism, law would be the other side. The two disciplines are essential for practitioners to know and use.

LAW

The counterpart of ethics is the **law**. The two disciplines are interrelated. Successful PR managers are effective decision-makers on ethical and legal issues. Public relations managers are, then, instrumental in making sure that ethical and legal matters are systematically and properly addressed throughout the PR function, especially so that PR technicians enact those principles well in public relations material. The most successful public relations professionals are those who proactively forge relationships with legal counsel sooner rather than later during a disruptive situation. So before we examine particular matters of the law that pertain to public relations management, we must briefly explore the relationship between law and ethics.

BUILDING A SYSTEM OF LAWS

Generally speaking, laws "are the principles that structure the relationships between government and the governed and among the people within a society" (M. G. Parkinson & L. M. Parkinson, 2006, p. 2). Given how societies evolve, and without going into great detail because of space limitations, at some point a system to manage everyone's individual and shared interests will be needed, resulting in a governing structure for a society. That governing structure includes a system for encoding various sanctions on behavior (i.e., laws), resolving disputes that arise among people and groups in a community, and imposing consequences on those who break any law. Because people in a community have come together for a variety of reasons with shared values, perhaps the most important being matters of mutual interests and benefits to living and working together in one society, the common ground of values and morals evolves into principles of ethics and, ultimately, a system of laws. So extending the scheme and analysis for Figure 3.1, law derives from ethics, which is shown in Figure 3.3.

This hierarchy only demonstrates how, similar to the construction of buildings, one element must necessarily be built upon another that is strong and robust enough to support the elements to come thereafter. This construction, then, is why values are the foundation for a community on which to further refine particular principles that guide individual and group actions and decision-making through increasing and necessary levels of complexity. Law is at the top of the hierarchy not because it is best or most

Figure 3.3 Hierarchy building toward law
Source: Model extended from that in Smudde (2011)

important (no element is better than another), but because law is the necessary capstone to the effective functioning of a community that has already encoded and enacted so much of the common ground its people share through the supporting structures of ethics, morals, and, most especially, values. As elements of the hierarchy may undergo change when communities evolve, the structures above (and perhaps below) them may require commensurate change, similar to the renovation of an old house so that it can be more structurally sound, better to live in, and longer lasting while still being recognized for what it always has been.

With this perspective on the big picture of law, we can begin exploring selected topics that are important for public relations managers as they lead PR operations. Admittedly, the preceding perspective on how laws emerge and sustain communities is simplistic, but it is useful for our purposes. In addition, there are ample resources that cover the great depth and breadth of knowledge about the law that cannot be covered in this volume. Indeed, public relations leaders ought to have and use at least one volume that addresses the law and public relations (e.g., Carter et al., 1993; Gower, 2012, 2018; Moore et al., 2011; M. G. Parkinson & L. M. Parkinson, 2006, 2008). Nevertheless, within the context of managing a public relations operation, this section summarizes the matters of cooperation between PR and legal staffs, the First Amendment to the U.S. Constitution, particular areas of law relevant to public relations practice, and federal regulatory bodies whose jurisdictions affect public relations.

COOPERATION BETWEEN PUBLIC RELATIONS AND LEGAL STAFFS

When they are working together on the same side, lawyers and public relations professionals share the same interest in an organization's well-being and the effects on stakeholders. So neither professional wants an organization to be subject to legal scrutiny or have to go to court. Beyond this common ground, there are important differences. Lawyers and public relations professionals come at problems from different perspectives, as Table 3.5 shows. Lawyers have as their ultimate venue of concern courts of law, where disputes are contested and decided according to applicable laws. Public relations professionals are ultimately concerned about the court of public opinion, where any matter can be contested at any time by any means and according to any argumentative purpose. Again, PR managers are instrumental in good ethical and legal decision-making, especially with the sound counsel of attorneys and the critical-analytical skills of PR technicians.

Table 3.5 Lawyer–PR differences

	Main venue	Approach
Lawyers	Court of law	Say "No comment"
PR pros	Court of public opinion	Say something reasonable & credible

Because of the dynamics and demands of each venue, lawyers and PR professionals have different approaches to handling incidents publicly. Lawyers are concerned that whatever may be said by company officials could and would be used against them in a court of law. With the proliferation of social media and personal video technology, misstatements can cast a long, dark shadow over an organization in many ways for a long time, from a given situation or case to corporate image and reputation. Saying "No comment" is often assumed to be (rightly or wrongly) a sign that something bigger is going on, and it is only a matter of time until we all find out. Public relations professionals are sensitive to the need to not say something inappropriate, but are also sensitive to the need of publics for some kind of statement, even if it is to say that nothing can be said at the time because of certain restrictions (and state them), but more information will be forthcoming as circumstances allow. In this way both legal and ethical matters are upheld for everyone concerned.

At this point it is important to recognize that many lawyers are amenable to public relations concerns and cognizant of the risks of not commenting and of commenting. Indeed, lawyers are naturally very interested in cooperating with public relations and all other operational areas of an organization. Generally speaking, lawyers provide great value to public relations because of their specialized perspective on communication in the corporate and social spheres. In this way, the cooperation that lawyers seek with public relations professionals can be built in a few simple and potent ways.

- *Understand the law*—Have a basic knowledge of what lawyers do and, most especially, the kinds of laws and legal matters that are relevant to public relations efforts of any scope. Such knowledge can serve you well while you plan actions, develop material, and share discourse with stakeholders.
- *Critically analyze situations*—Thoroughly examine any situation for both its upside and its downside on the company, primarily, and its stakeholders, secondarily. Also find any case examples that may apply so you can learn from them and apply any lessons to your situation. Such analysis would reveal the range of salient matters about the impacts of a situation on stakeholders and knowing when to seek counsel from a legal professional.
- *Explain objectives, strategies, and tactics*—Know precisely what you want from a situation on public relations grounds (i.e., effects on awareness, attitude, action), how you are going to do it, and what specific actions you will take. Such an explanation will present the complete picture of what is sought for and from stakeholders through an organized public relations effort of any scope.

Instrumental in this **cooperation between lawyers and public relations professionals** is dialog about these matters at the outset of any public relations work. So involve lawyers early, and throughout any PR effort, to make sure an organization follows the law and upholds ethics principles. Lawyers are argumentative by nature and profession, and your ability to present your case matters because you need to reach a decision about what would work best, take action on that decision, and evaluate how well the action fulfilled expectations. In situations that have progressed to the level of legal action in a court of law, a public relations professional's counsel is very important so that stakeholders are informed to the extent that is allowed by legal strategy for defense and, if applicable, restrictions given by the court or stated in an applicable law.

FIRST AMENDMENT

The keystone to public relations practice is the **First Amendment** of the U.S. Constitution. It presents five specific freedoms (numbered in the text below) that are also general in their individual scopes:

> Congress shall make no law respecting [1] the establishment of religion, or prohibiting the free exercise thereof; or abridging the freedom of [2] speech, or of [3] the press; or [4] the right of the people peaceably to assemble, and [5] to petition the Government for a redress of grievances.
> (https://constitution.congress.gov/constitution/amendment-1/)

The focus of the First Amendment is protecting individuals from government while expressing their opinions publicly (see Zompetti et al., 2013). Matters concerning protections for individuals from organizations or protections for organizations from government are contested matters. Indeed, the question about whether and to what degree organizations have freedom of speech is primary. The answer is yes and no.

Organizations may or may not have protections for free speech, depending on who the target public is, what a message's intent is, and how courts have ruled in related cases. In instances when there is imminent danger to people or property, there must be reason or "just cause" to forbid certain kinds of speech, such as threats and phony calls for help. Very generally, courts have ruled that organizations can speak on their own behalf and be protected under the First Amendment if, and only if, the content of their speech can be protected regardless of speaker. So the issue of free speech for organizations is not that they are protected like individual citizens, but rather that as long as what an organization says can be protected under the First Amendment, it must be protected. Indeed, decisions about freedom of speech for organizations are made through the judicial process and are the substance of case law, which includes decisions made in courts of law on individual cases; we will address this topic shortly. The central factor in such decisions is whether an organization has engaged in political speech or commercial speech, each of which has different levels of protection.

Not all speech is equal, and under the First Amendment, different degrees of protection are afforded to different kinds of speech. Figure 3.4 illustrates the degrees of speech protection. *Political speech* is the most protected because, after all, political speech was instrumental in the founding of the United States of America as the original 13 colonies sought separation from Great Britain and fought a revolution for it. Political speech concerns all matters and manners of commentary about our government and issues of the day in any respect as part of the normal course of democracy. *Artistic speech*

Figure 3.4 Degrees of speech protection under the First Amendment

concerns the creative expression of ideas using language and symbols for aesthetic purposes, such as creative work done in literature, fine arts, performing arts, and so on, and it can include graffiti and street performances too. *Commercial speech* concerns the use of language and symbols for the purpose of inspiring economic transactions in the marketplace, and examples include advertisements, direct marketing, public relations, online content, and others. In case law, commercial speech is usually considered the least protected form of speech, with clear Supreme Court guidance on justifying governmental regulation and control through the "commercial speech doctrine" from the *Central Hudson Gas & Electric* case and the ruling on the *Citizens United* case (see Table 3.6).

Of the **three kinds of speech**, public relations (and advertising and related speech fields) falls largely into the category of commercial speech but can cross over into political speech. Public relations discourse may concern matters of products and services, and it may address matters of social and political issues. Courts have been reluctant to limit corporate political speech; however, court decisions/case law limitations have been placed on "buying" candidates (e.g., support and/or votes on certain regulatory matters) and protections of shareholders—from "compelled" speech that requires or forces adherence to and advancement of a particular thesis (e.g., to "toe the line" on an organization's stance regardless of one's own view). Historically, courts treated commercial speech as "unprotected" by the First Amendment, although limited protection has been afforded in recent case law. Guidance on free speech protections relies on **case law**, especially "tests" developed in court rulings. As a result, commercial speech is (at most) a grey area of speech protection because of the varying factors of audience, purpose, and especially decisions in cases tried and decided in courts of law.

Table 3.6 presents a summary of selected cases on political and commercial speech that matter to public relations. It must be noted that there are many cases that concern legal dimensions for public relations, and the cases here represent a small but solid sample of case law applicable to PR. Any volume on public relations law can serve to add detail to these selected cases and present information about other cases. What is important about the selected cases in Table 3.6 is that they provide a useful overview of the guidance about and "tests" for free speech protection that affect public relations practice. Additionally, matters of commercial speech are regulated by particular agencies of the federal government, most prominently the Federal Trade Commission. Table 3.7 lists federal agencies that have

Table 3.6 Selected free-speech cases bearing on public relations

Case name and year	Central issue	Decision	Impact on PR
Virginia State Board of Pharmacists v. Virginia Consumer Council (1976)	It was illegal in Virginia for pharmacies to advertise prices for prescription drugs, which was under the purview of the VCC for oversight and enforcement.	The court ruled that there cannot be limits on pharmacies' right to provide the public with information about prescriptions, including pricing.	Allows for broader range of topics that facilitate marketplace transactions on regulated products; in this case, prescription drugs.
First National Bank of Boston v. Belloti (1978)	Paid-for, corporate speech affects voting outcome, which FNBB engaged in when it campaigned for a particular ballot measure that was in the company's and its industry's best interests.	The court ruled that contributions are permissible for the political process and campaigns in the voters' interests, as long as there is no requirement for employees/ members to vote a particular way.	Broadens opportunities for organizations, particularly for-profit companies, to assert their positions on ballot measures, candidates, etc.
Central Hudson Gas & Electric v. Public Service Commission of New York (1980)	The original law banned electricity utilities' advertising, which CHG&E engaged in when it advertised energy conservation tips.	The court ruled that advertising that promotes services for power conservation must not be limited because the issue has greater relevance in the public interest.	The decision presents a four-part test for First Amendment violations of government regulations on commercial speech: 1. Is the expression protected? It must be lawful and not misleading. 2. Is the asserted government interest substantial? 3. Does the regulation advance the government interest asserted? 4. Is the regulation more extensive than necessary to serve government interest?

(continued)

Table 3.6 Cont.

Case name and year	Central issue	Decision	Impact on PR
Kasky v. Nike (2003)	There are limits on corporate communication about corporate social responsibility policies, initiatives, and performance, and Nike was accused of false statements about its use of substandard labor practices in the manufacturing of its athletic shoes.	The case was settled out of court without a ruling, and Nike agreed to make a $1.5 million contribution to the Fair Labor Association. The U.S. Supreme Court avoided hearing the case on appeal.	Without a court decision, the case provides little guidance about commercial speech freedoms, but it does suggest avenues for legal risk organizations should guard against.
Citizens United v. Federal Elections Commission (2008)	The case concerned two precedents in campaign finance law and the regulation of paid-for speech by organizations, especially nonprofit, advocacy organizations and labor unions. Citizens United argued that it had the right to air a documentary film about Hillary Rodham Clinton and to air advertisements about the film during the presidential primary season.	The Supreme Court ruled in a 5 to 4 decision that Citizens United engaged in political speech that was protected, and there could be no prohibitions or restrictions on organizations' independent expenditures supporting candidates for office.	The Supreme Court's ruling gives the strongest First Amendment protection of corporate speech about public issues. Nevertheless, communication professionals, especially those involved in political activities about issues or candidates, must have a good knowledge of federal and state regulations on campaign contributions.

Table 3.7 Particular federal regulatory structures relevant to public relations

Agency	Summary
Federal Communication Commission (FCC)	• Regulates interstate and international communications by radio, television, wire, satellite, cable, phone, and Internet in all 50 states, the District of Columbia, and U.S. territories. • Established by the Communications Act of 1934 and operates as an independent U.S. government agency overseen by Congress. • Committed to being a responsive, efficient, and effective agency capable of facing the technological and economic opportunities of the new millennium.
Federal Election Commission (FEC)	• Federal law prohibits the use of corporate resources to influence the outcome of an election. • Political Action Committees (PACs) are used to support candidates and political parties. • SuperPACs are groups that support and promote particular social changes.
Federal Trade Commission (FTC)	• Created in 1914 to prevent unfair methods of competition in commerce as part of the battle to "bust the trusts." • Especially involved in overseeing/enforcing truth in advertising. • Only federal agency with both consumer protection and competition jurisdiction in broad sectors of the economy.
Food and Drug Administration (FDA)	• Purpose is "to protect, promote and enhance the health of the American people." • For commercial speech, the primary concern is advertisements for the food system and pharmaceuticals, including direct-to-consumer ads and video news releases.
Foreign Agents Registration Act (FARA)	• Individuals who represent foreign governments must register and report to the State Department.
Freedom of Information Act (FOIA)	• Guarantees individuals access to government records. • Media can also make FOIA requests. • Ongoing challenge for government public information officers. • Can also be a problem for government contractors.
Securities and Exchange Commission (SEC)	• Established in 1934 to protect investors and ensure that securities markets are fair and honest. Monitors financial affairs of publicly traded companies. Seeks to prohibit fraud, market manipulation, and insider trading. • Core principle is that investors should be able to make decisions based on timely and accurate information. • Key concepts are *materiality* (i.e., information that would lead a "prudent person" to make an investment decision) and *disclosure* (i.e., material information must be broadly disseminated as soon as it is known). • Sarbanes–Oxley Act requires tracking and control of internal and external financial reporting accuracy, including compliance among corporate leaders.

jurisdiction over particular areas of law, including industry practices and punishments for illegal actions. The text in this table comes from the respective agencies' websites.

PARTICULAR AREAS OF LAW

Remember that old saying, "Sticks and stones may break my bones, but words will never hurt me"? Under the law, however, words can inflict harm of various kinds and degrees. In addition, there is the need to protect certain instances of language and symbol use from being misused or usurped without the author's or originator's consent. **Six particular areas of the law** address matters of harm and ownership that are important in public relations: privacy, defamation of character, copyright, trademark, contracts, and fraud. Table 3.8 summarizes the salient points relating to these areas.

Table 3.8 Legal areas pertaining to public relations practice

Area	Definition/description	Key points
Contracts	Legally enforceable promises between two or more parties about something legal and of value to all	Parties to contracts can be organizations or persons who are of age (at least 18 years old) and sound mind. Contracts may be written or oral, and the former is strongest to enforce. Sufficient evidence of agreement is essential for enforcement of any contract. Breach of contract occurs when a party does not fulfill its duty under the agreement.
Copyright	Immediate protection for an originator's expression of ideas, concepts, or principles made in any fixed form	Protection generally lasts the life of the author plus 70 years, expiring on December 31 of the final year. Some copyrights last longer. Formal filing for copyright is not required. Intellectual property falls under this area of law. The doctrine of "fair use" is key, and so is the Digital Millennium Copyright Act.
Defamation of Character	Injury to a person's, organization's, product's, or service's reputation	Defamation may be defined as libel or slander, depending on particular state law. Individuals or organizations that are defamed

Table 3.8 Cont.

Area	Definition/description	Key points
		must prove defamatory content, publication, identification, damage, and fault. For public figures or officials, the element of fault must rise to a standard of actual malice.
Fraud	Intentionally misrepresenting facts, lying about something, or concealing information for the purpose of personal, financial, or other material gain for one's self or one's organization. The intent of fraud is to induce another person to act upon it and, in turn, suffer legal injury.	Injured parties can be entitled to certain remedies based on the nature of the situation (e.g., several times the amount of financial gain the guilty organization sought). Contracts that are based on fraudulent information would be immediately void.
Privacy	The right to be left alone and free from unwanted public scrutiny	Four torts ("wrongs") of privacy are intrusion, false light, publication of private facts, and appropriation.
Trademarks	Protection of a word, phrase, logo, symbol, color, sound, smell, packaging, or other distinguishing characteristic associated with a particular product or service. The use must be specific to a class of goods, distinctive, and avoid confusion in the marketplace.	Three levels of trademark are service mark (^{SM}), trademark (^{TM}), and registered trademark (®). Formal registration is not required for a trademark or service mark, but is strongly recommended. Trademark registration lasts as long as the mark is used in commerce and must be renewed periodically.

PRIVACY

Under the U.S. Constitution, *privacy* is not specifically guaranteed, but it is inferred from the Fourth Amendment's protection from illegal search and seizure and protection for withholding personal information from public view. Privacy is basically the right to be left alone and free from unwanted publicity. The legal basis for privacy has been developed through state laws and decisions in court cases about invasions of privacy. Court cases amount to civil lawsuits of an individual versus another individual, or a company versus a company, or an individual versus a company, where the state is the arbitrator. In these civil suits one of four *torts* ("wrongs") would be the focus. The first tort is *intrusion*, which is the improper and intentional invasion of someone's (including an organization's) physical seclusion or private affairs. Cases of paparazzi using high-powered cameras on public property to take photographs of celebrities in their own homes or property qualify as intrusion.

The second tort is *false light*, which is a distortion, fabrication, or fictionalization of someone's (or an organization's) physical presence/appearance. For example, a dentist who publishes a newsletter for their services with a photo of a patient showing lovely, straight, and white teeth also includes "before" and "after" photos of teeth. While the "after" photo is actually the patient's teeth, the "before" photo shows grossly uncared-for teeth that are not the patient's teeth. The patient can sue for false light and very probably win because dental records can easily show the difference.

The third tort of privacy is *publication of private facts*, which involves the disclosure of true personal information that may be embarrassing or offensive. Unveiling a list of someone's prescription drugs and any claims about a medical condition without permission on social media would be an example of this tort. For an organization, the publication of a plan to market a product or service would also be an example because such plans are confidential to the organization.

The fourth and final privacy tort is *appropriation*, which is the use of someone's (or an organization's) name, voice, or likeness without consent. Organizations are especially vigilant about the use of their brands so that they are not used without permission or misused when permitted to be used. Examples involve brand names on clothing on television programs that must be blacked-out because they were not granted permission to be shown. Other examples include celebrities whose likenesses are used to promote a company, product, or service without permission, and those celebrities can seek damages for that illegal use of their likenesses. When any person is portrayed in commercial speech, photo, video, or any public medium, model releases are essential whether a person is paid or not, as in the case of employees being photographed for company brochures, websites, and annual reports.

DEFAMATION OF CHARACTER

An individual's or an organization's reputation, including the reputation of a brand, product, or service, can be harmed—"defamed"—through *libel* (i.e., written defamation) or *slander* (i.e., spoken defamation). For individuals, defamation of character centers on the concept of "actual malice," which means that the perpetrator of defamatory statements intentionally wanted to harm a person's reputation; or "negligence," which involves carelessness with private or privileged matters instead of exercising the care expected of a reasonable person acting prudently. Public officials (i.e., people with a significant level of public responsible for policy making), public figures/ celebrities, and ordinary citizens can suffer from defamation of character. Organizations may be defamed through libel presented in any medium of communication, written, visual/video, or audio. For organizations to prove defamation through libel, they must establish what the precise content of the defamation is, show how the content was published and possibly republished, show that the organization or any of its assets was clearly identified, demonstrate damage to the organization through false or errant content, and assert that the perpetrator is at fault for all the preceding conditions.

COPYRIGHT

Intellectual property is protected under copyright law. For an individual or an organization, a work of any kind and content is immediately protected under copyright law from the moment it is put into fixed form in writing, video, photography, audio, drawing, painting, or another medium. Individuals and organizations may file for a formal copyright through the Library of Congress, and forms with instructions are available online. An author or originator of a work may assert copyright protection by saying, "Copyright," and/or © along with the year and the name of the copyright holder (e.g., © 2023 Peter M. Smudde). Copyright protection lasts the life of the author/originator plus 70 years, expiring December 31 of the final year. After a work's copyright expires, the work becomes part of the "public domain." But some copyrights can be extended to legally protect them under the Copyright Term Extension Act.

Under copyright law, only the expression of ideas, concepts, or principles can be protected, not the raw ideas themselves. So, for example, no one can copyright public relations, but anyone may copyright their views of and approaches for public relations. Interestingly, U.S. government documents cannot be copyrighted because they are owned by all U.S. citizens and are provided for their use. Cases of copyright infringement concern whether someone or an organization either misused all or part of a copyrighted work (e.g., plagiarism or violations of "fair use") or caused sufficient confusion in the minds of people so as to make one work appear like the original article (e.g., "knockoffs" of Coach handbags, or an advertisement that shows one product in a similar way to that by which another manufacturer previously advertised it).

The use of copyrighted works is fairly straightforward and requires adherence to several basic points, although the specifics of the law are much more thorough and must be consulted. To use a copyrighted work, an individual or organization must secure the owner's permission. Once permission is secured there may be royalties to pay. However, under the "fair use" doctrine, copyrighted material can be used in limited ways according to the purpose, the amount of the work used, any profit that may be gained through the work's use, and whether it is a parody of the original because these are unique works themselves, created to be *distorted imitations* of original works to purposefully comment on them. Moreover, creators of parodies are not required to obtain permission from copyright holders. In fair use cases, however, the original source of a work should be cited, and bibliographic approaches like those from the American Psychological Association (APA) and Modern Languages Association (MLA) offer standards for giving credit to original sources. In the case of stock photos, for which there may or may not be royalties to pay depending on the provider, sufficient credit may be given by merely stating the source of a photo.

In the digital age the issue of copyright protection is a vital part of the law that public relations professionals must know. The Digital Millennium Copyright Act was passed in 1998 to address the unauthorized copying of software, music, videos, and other content (whether digital or not) into digital form onto other media than their originals. The Act establishes rules for downloading and sharing files, as well as outlawing attempts to circumvent antipiracy measures and outlawing code-breaking devices.

TRADEMARK

Under trademark law, a trademark protects a word, phrase, logo, symbol, color, sound, smell, packaging, or other distinguishing characteristic associated with a specific product or service. A trademark, then, is a name (a "mark") applied to a product to differentiate it from others in a similar class of goods (e.g., the name of one line of shoes, say "FastDash," in a company's full line of all the shoes it offers for sale against all other shoemakers' shoes). Not to be confused with *trade names*, which are the names of organizations that offer products and services, trademarks make goods and services distinctive to avoid confusion in the marketplace. There are three levels of trademark: *trademark* (™), which denotes a physical good or product distinct from all others of its kind or class; *service mark* (ˢᴹ), which is used to denote the delivery of a service instead of a physical product; and *registered trademark* (®), which denotes that a product or service has secured formal protection through trademark registration with the U.S. Patent and Trademark Office or a state's Secretary of State's Office.

The first two kinds of trademark exist from their first use (i.e., placing the mark on a product or service on a regular basis and not abandoning its use on future goods or services) and do not have to be registered; however, the third kind is the best approach to ensure the strongest legal protection. For example, FastDash athletic shoes would be FastDash™ before registration and FastDash® after registration. The same would be true for a service before and after registration. Registered trademarks must be registered with the U.S. Patent and Trademark Office or a state's Secretary of State's Office to prove ownership and use of the mark, last for as long as the mark is in use, and must be renewed periodically. Before a mark is used as a trademark or service mark, a search should be conducted for whether the mark is already in use to ensure there is no infringement.

CONTRACTS

Contracts are legally enforceable promises (i.e., an offer is extended and then, after negotiation, agreement is reached; if no agreement, no contract) between two or more parties about something of value to all of them and the legal means by which to fulfill the promises. Parties to contracts can be organizations or persons who are of age (at least 18 years old) and sound mind. Contracts may be written or oral, and the former is strongest to enforce. No matter what kind of contract is used, sufficient evidence of agreement is essential for enforcement of any contract. During the course of a contract, the performance of all parties matters so that the terms of the agreement are properly upheld. If the terms are only partially upheld by one or more parties, the parties are said to be in *breach of contract* and the other parties may seek remedies, up to and including a lawsuit. Because of the great complexity of contract law, it is best to secure legal counsel when drafting, negotiating, and executing any contract.

FRAUD

Fraud is intentionally misrepresenting facts, lying about something, or concealing information for the purpose of personal, financial, or other material gain for one's self or one's organization. In the PR profession, practitioners are in possession of many kinds of information of varying levels of importance to both an organization and its publics. Certain regulations administered by various governmental agencies address what information can be withheld and what cannot. For example, under securities law, organizations must disclose any "material" information that would be important to investors when deciding to buy, sell, or hold shares of stock, bond issues, or other similar financial instruments. If an organization does not disclose material information, or if it discloses erroneous information for the purpose of influencing the capital markets, that organization commits fraud. In contrast, however, organizations do not have to disclose their marketing plans because to do so would compromise the organization's competitive position by making public its business ambitions against its competitors and for its target customers. In another example, if an organization enters into a contract of any kind (e.g., hiring an agency to help its PR efforts), but does not fully disclose or does not provide truthful information that is material to the contract (e.g., the organization has filed for bankruptcy and payment for services may be difficult), that also is fraud.

Fraud invalidates any contracts, and the injured party(ies) would be entitled to certain remedies that fit the situation and the financial gain that the guilty organization sought. In the end, PR pros must always be on guard against efforts to be anything less than truthful and lawful, and a code of ethics specifically from a professional organization for public relations can be most useful in guiding one's conduct. Knowingly providing false or misleading information in any organizational communication is fraud.

GOVERNING CONCEPTS

Public relations professionals have the duty and responsibility to, as the Roman orator Cicero might say, always be "the Good person speaking well" on an organization's behalf for applicable publics. We know there are more good people than bad in the world, and the bad ones are most successful at capturing our attention, especially through mass media, because what they do is not what is expected—what is expected is goodness, not badness. The complexity of the law and ethics, as well as how they intertwine with professionalism, must not deter public relations professionals from continually learning about them and applying them. While it may seem to be a lot of work to abide by the many laws of the land, the strict ethics standards for the profession, and the high expectations for everyone in the PR field, two governing concepts could make that work easier: love and discipline.

When we approach our lives, work, and relationships through **love**—*agape* love—we make connections with the greater good and truth that each person seeks and shares for one's self and, most importantly, for others. When we think of love in this sense, it is the "perfect communion between persons" (Burke, 1970 [1961], p. 30). Love "is the principle not only of micro-relationships (with friends, family members, or within small groups), but also of macro-relationships (social, economic, and political ones)" (Benedict, 2009, p. 8). Love requires good judgment. It may mean saying no and disappointing someone. It may mean giving a harsh truth about something when that truth is not what someone wants to hear. It may also mean celebrating success or mourning loss. **Discipline**, too, is key as it is instrumental in keeping focus on the myriad things that inundate our senses and sensibilities. Discipline is developed through practical training about public relations and the day-to-day duties, responsibilities, and expectations we have as professional communicators. Discipline also comes from the rules and norms we follow in our daily lives, which in all respects both enable and lead us in every experience (Anderson & Englehardt, 2001).

In any situation for public relations professionals, love relies on thoughtfulness, ethics, discipline, and foresight; and love is expressed at least through honesty, tactfulness, courtesy, and sensitivity to others. These aspects are key character traits and hallmarks of professionalism among good public relations counselors, who act justly on the sound basis of knowledge, skills, and abilities. In a tiny nutshell, maintain your own ethics and lawfulness through honesty in relationships, opinion, identity, and self; by using accurate and truthful information; by engaging in prompt correction of errors; and by revealing conflicts of interest. So, in the end, we PR professionals truly and always apply values, morals, ethics, and laws to do the right thing in the right way at the right time for the right people for the right reasons.

EXECUTIVE VIEWPOINT

Commandments for Powerful PR Performance

Gerard F. Corbett, APR, Fellow of PRSA, Redphlag

The U.S. today is in a critical stage of concern, consternation, conflict, and calculated misinformation. One needs only study and analyze the state of information and misinformation that is permeating pseudo and legitimate news sources to get a sense of the consequences that can arise and influence behaviors pro and con. Just pick up a copy of *The Washington Post, The New York Times,* or *The Wall Street Journal* to sense the dilemma we all face as concerned citizens of our republic.

As public relations professionals in this age of real-time, all-the-time, 24-by-7 news, we have an obligation to counsel clients and managements on behaviors that are moral, just, objective, and sincere. The bottom line is that we are in a time where "doing the right thing" is our avenue out of this malaise of mis-, mal- and fake information. Public relations has the mantle to lead this charge, and time is of the essence. To be successful, PR professionals at corporations must evolve the position in ways that engender the best and appropriate behaviors of always doing the right thing.

In many ways, public relations professionals are both the moral compass and the conscience of their organizations. The following are ten recommended commandments that underpin optimum and ethical public relations outcomes.

1. Public relations professionals today and moving forward are activists seeking to engage, enlighten, and energize an organization's many stakeholders. They are not only dedicated gatekeepers or distributors of information from their companies to the media and the public. Moving forward their purview ought to include paid and owned media to assure consistency and coherence.
2. Public relations professionals advocate not just for their organizations but also for their organization's constituents, stakeholders, and naysayers, which adds the important role of presenting the stakeholders' interests and views to management.
3. Public relations professionals serve as strategic content developers and storytellers, helping their organizations formulate key messages that are resonant, respectful, and responsible based on corporate culture, the nature of the organization, and the needs of all of the organization's constituents.
4. Public relations professionals help and even lead an organization in building mutual trust by encouraging transparency and integrity throughout the organization and being willing to take on relevant tough issues to build that trust.
5. Public relations professionals are counselors who actively advise and guide organizations in honestly and truthfully communicating and behaving in the best interests of society and constituents, such as customers, employees, shareholders, and the communities in which they operate.
6. Public relations professionals are enablers and connectors, helping organizations stay grounded, stay compassionate, and stay sensitive to the needs and desires of their communities.
7. Public relations professionals are the conscience and moral compass of the organization, being ever vigilant to ensure that the organization is consistently, collaboratively, and cohesively "doing the right thing" always for all of the organization's constituents.
8. Public relations professionals must be bold, courageous, creative, and willing to put a stake in the ground in convincing senior managements to implement policies and processes that can engender trust universally without regard to politics and subjective preferences or agendas.
9. Public relations professionals consistently stay abreast of and even ahead of the state of the art from a communications, technology, and social norms standpoint.
10. Public relations professionals are educators, mentors, role models, and consummate leaders not afraid to learn, fail, and pioneer.

Bolstering these commandments, one only needs to examine actions by many organizations that have not done the right thing and stand as examples of poor and unethical or questionably ethical public relations. The following two examples come to mind.

- The International Olympic Committee gave itself a black eye by allowing the return to the 2022 Beijing Olympic competition of a young "Russian Olympic Committee" "figure skating" member despite her having tested positive for a banned substance that improves heart performance. The right thing would have been to validate the ban, setting a crucial example that doping will not be tolerated. The final blow came when the young skater performed negatively in her final run, pushing her to fourth place. Blame can be found on many sides. The net effect, though, is that the International Olympic Committee and, indeed, the Olympics have suffered measurably in reputation decline. Commandments 2, 4, and 7 are not in the makeup of any parties involved, including the IOC, Russia, and China, each of whom selfishly focused on their own interests.
- Timely enough, the public relations industry suffered a stain on its reputation as a result of solid investigative journalism by Keith Kelly of *Crain's New York*. The CEO of 5WPR purchased and operated a supposed industry news site known as Everything-PR. The site was operated in secrecy by the CEO; it promoted itself as a legitimate industry news site when it was not and, instead, was promoting false stories about competitors of E-PR and its clients. The impact of this situation will likely be felt for many years. The ultimate resolution of this matter is yet to be seen, but clearly it is counter to "Doing the Right Thing." In fact, this masquerade violates at least four commandments: 4, 5, 7, and 10. A review of each tells the tale.

Taken together, these two examples and the ten commandments of optimal and ethical public relations reinforce the great importance of not only effective, honest, and relevant public relations, but, most important, the supreme centrality of the moral, ethical, and authentic character of public relations that the people in the PR profession must be and achieve at all times. Decision-making about what to say, to whom to say it, why to say it, how to say it, when and where to say it must weigh moral and ethical principles against a situation and values that pertain from all those involved so that, as this chapter said, "the right thing is done in the right way for the right people for the right reasons in the right way at the right time."

KEY WORDS

Professionalism	Deontology
Values	Axiology
Morals	Resolving ethical dilemmas
Ethics	Law
Relativism	PR–attorney relationship
Teleology	First Amendment

Three speech types covered by the First Amendment	**Love**
Case law	**Discipline**
Six areas of law for PR	

REFERENCES

Anderson, J. A., & Englehardt, E. E. (2001). *The organizational self and ethical conduct: Sunlit virtue and shadowed resistance.* Harcourt College Publishers.

Baker, S., & Martinson, D. L. (2001). The TARES test: Five principles for ethical persuasion. *Journal of Mass Media Ethics, 16*(2/3), 148–175.

Benedict XVI (2009). *Charity in truth.* Ignatius Press.

Boehm, C. (2012). *Moral origins: The evolution of virtue, altruism and shame.* Basic Books/Perseus Books Group.

Brinkmann, J. (2002). Business and marketing ethics as professional ethics: Concepts, approaches and typologies. *Journal of Business Ethics, 41*, 159–177.

Burke, K. (1970). *The rhetoric of religion: Studies in logology.* University of California Press. (Original work published 1961.)

Carter, T. B., Franklin, M. A., & Wright, J. B. (1993). *The First Amendment and the fifth estate: Regulation of electronic mass media* (3rd ed.). The Foundation Press.

Christians, C. G., Fackler, M. B., Rotzoll, K. B., & McKee, K. B. (2001). *Media ethics: Cases and moral reasoning* (6th ed.). Allyn & Bacon.

Coombs, W. T., & Holladay, S. J. (2007). *It's not just PR: Public relations in society.* Blackwell.

Courtright, J. L. (1996). An ethics code postmortem: The National Religious Broadcasters' EFICOM. *Journal of Mass Media Ethics, 11*(4), 223–235.

Curtin, P. A., & Boynton, L. A. (2001). Ethics in public relations: Theory and practice. In R. L. Heath (Ed.), *Handbook of public relations* (pp. 411–422). Sage.

Edwards, L., & Hodges, C. E. (Eds.) (2011). *Public relations, society and culture: Theoretical and empirical explorations.* Routledge.

Fawkes, J. (2015). *Public relations ethics and professionalism: The shadow of excellence.* Routledge.

Fitzpatrick, K. R. (n.d.). *Ethical decision-making guide helps resolve ethical dilemmas.* Retrieved from www.prsa.org/docs/default-source/about/ethics/ethics-case-stud ies/ethics-case-study-ethical-desision-making-guide.pdf.

Frankena, W. K. (1973). *Ethics: Foundations of philosophy series* (2nd ed.). Prentice-Hall.

Gower, K. K. (2012). Public relations law. In C. L. Caywood (Ed.), *The handbook of strategic public relations and integrated marketing communications* (2nd ed., pp. 57–69). McGraw-Hill.

Gower, K. K. (2018). *Legal and ethical considerations for public relations* (3rd ed.). Waveland Press.

Grunig, J. E., & Hunt, T. (1984). *Managing public relations.* Holt, Rinehart & Winston.

Keane, J. G. (1974). On professionalism in advertising. *Journal of Advertising, 3*(4), 6–12.

L'Etang, J. (2012). Public relations and democracy: Historical reflections and implications. In S. M. Oliver (Ed.), *Handbook of corporate communication and public relations: Pure and applied* (pp. 342–353). Routledge. (Original work published 2004.)

Lee, S. T., & Cheng, I-H. (2011). Characteristics and dimensions of ethical leadership in public relations. *Journal of Public Relations Research, 23*(1), 46–74.

Lee, S. T., & Cheng, I-H. (2012). Ethics management in public relations: Practitioner conceptualizations of ethical leadership, knowledge, training and compliance. *Journal of Mass Media Ethics, 27*, 80–96.

Moore, R. L., Maye, C., & Collins, E. L. (2011). *Advertising and public relations law* (2nd ed.). Routledge.

Parkinson, M. G., & Parkinson, L. M. (2006). *Law for advertising, broadcasting, journalism, and public relations: A comprehensive text for students and practitioners.* Lawrence Erlbaum Associates.

Parkinson, M. G., & Parkinson, L. M. (2008). *Public relations law: A supplemental text.* Lawrence Erlbaum Associates.

Pieczka, M., & L'Etang, J. (2001). Public relations and the question of professionalism. In R. L. Heath (Ed.), *Handbook of public relations* (pp. 223–235). Sage.

Smudde, P. M. (2005). Blogging, ethics and public relations: A proactive and dialogic approach. *Public Relations Quarterly, 50*(3), 34–38.

Smudde, P. M. (2011). Focus on ethics and public relations practice in a university classroom. *Communication Teacher, 25*(3), 154–158.

Taylor, M. (2010). Public relations in the enactment of civil society. In R. L. Heath (Ed.), *The SAGE handbook of public relations* (pp. 5–15). Sage Publications.

Zompetti, J. P., Moore, M. A., Smudde, P. M., & Hunt, S. K. (2013). The right to peaceable assembly and social movements: The role of "occupying" space as a way to speak. In N. S. Lind (Ed.), *First Amendment rights: An encyclopedia* (Vol. 2, pp. 237–256). ABC-CLIO.

RECOMMENDED READING

Bivins, T. (2004). *Mixed media: Moral distinctions in advertising, public relations, and journalism.* Lawrence Erlbaum Associates.

Brunner, B., & Hickerson, C. (2018). *Cases in public relations: Translating ethics into action.* Oxford University Press.

Fitzpatrick, K., & Bronstein, C. (2006). *Ethics in public relations: Responsible advocacy.* Sage.

Haggerty, J. F. (2003). *In the court of public opinion: Winning your case with public relations.* John Wiley and Sons.

Luttrell, R., & Ward, J. (2018). *A practical guide to ethics in public relations.* Rowman & Littlefield.

Martin, D., & Wright, D. K. (2016). *Public relations ethics: How to practice PR without losing your soul.* Business Expert Press.

Moore, R. L., Maye,.C., & Collins, E. L. (2011). *Advertising and public relations law* (2nd ed.). Routledge.

Sieb, P., & Fitzpatrick, K. (1995). *Public relations ethics.* Harcourt Brace College Publishers.

4

CHAPTER 4
DISTINCTIONS BETWEEN AGENCY AND NONAGENCY OPERATIONS

CHAPTER OUTLINE

Public relations is truly a growth industry. One of the most interesting and promising facts about the public relations profession is that, according to the U.S. Bureau of Labor Statistics annual report, *Occupational Outlook Handbook*, the job outlook continues to grow by double digits every year. Indeed, the 2022 *Handbook* (Bureau of Labor Statistics, 2022a, 2022b) shows that the job outlook for the period 2020 to 2030 shows a "faster than average" rate (for all occupations) of 13% for "public relations and fundraising managers" and a "faster than average" rate of 11% for "public relations specialists."

So the overall picture for the public relations profession looks very good, and it should. Almost any kind of organization needs or will need to inspire cooperation between itself and its publics through systematic communication efforts. Many organizations have their own public relations operation or someone who handles it (e.g., an attorney, chief executive, or founder), while others do not. In any case, it is very possible that outside firms—public relations agencies—would be invited to "bid" on the PR work an organization needs (see Chapter 10).

In the public relations industry, there are two arenas of practice: agency and nonagency. Importantly, public relations practiced in agency and nonagency ("corporate") arenas are more similar than different. This chapter briefly summarizes the salient matters about agency and corporate PR that are most prominent among PR leaders and new hires. (More detailed treatments are rare, but a very good one to turn to is Wilcox et al.'s [2013] chapter in the book, *Think Public Relations*.) This chapter also addresses parallel topics for both corporate and agency public relations so that similarities (they share the same topics) and differences (they approach those topics uniquely) can be explored. Additionally, this chapter looks into data about corporate and agency public relations leadership positions through job postings for executives.

DOI: 10.4324/9781003208280-5

NONAGENCY ("CORPORATE") PUBLIC RELATIONS OPERATIONS

The "corporate" arena of public relations includes a variety of organization types. The reason is simple: they differ significantly from agencies, which are in the business of serving clients, including other agencies. The players in the nonagency ("corporate") arena of public relations, then, include for-profit companies/corporations, nonprofit/ institutional organizations (e.g., public universities, religious organizations, hospitals, organizations complying with the 501[c]3 provision in the U.S. tax code, some professional organizations, many civic/community groups, philanthropic organizations, political action groups complying with the 501[c]4 provision in the U.S. tax code), governments and affiliated bodies (e.g., departments of transportation; health and human services; secretaries of state, etc.), and nongovernmental organizations (e.g., local and national, domestic and international; private educational institutions, the Roman Catholic Church, Amnesty International, Doctors Without Borders).

Public relations practiced in the nonagency arena is considered "**in house**." This designation refers to the fact that organizations of these types almost always have a communications department of some sort under some suitable name (e.g., public relations, corporate communication, strategic communications, public affairs), and that department or group does the internal *and* external communication with an organization's publics. That communication can encompass all or most of the core practice areas of public relations, such as media relations, employee relations/internal communications, government relations, investor relations, community relations, and so on. Additional communication work, including social media, advertising, website content, executive and board of directors' communication, and others can also be included, depending on the needs and structure of an organization.

Within the corporate context, a public relations department is viewed as an internal resource of experts about all matters of communication. It is important, then, to recognize that those working in a **nonagency ("corporate") PR** department are being paid to be the best communicators in and communication counselors for the organization. The various practice areas in public relations, as touched on above and in Chapter 1, require competent technicians and managers. In fact, in the U.S. PR industry the number of people employed in technician-level jobs is 272,300 and the number of people employed in management-level jobs is 89,000 (Bureau of Labor Statistics, 2022a, 2022b). The many and varied communication needs an organization can have means that the experts in the PR department must be well equipped and well positioned to handle them. (If a communication opportunity is large or diverse enough, an agency may be called in to help, and we will address this point later in this chapter.) For corporate contexts, it is useful to think of an organization's various operational groups as internal customers of the PR department. Communication, as Jensen (1995) argues, is "a core competency" (p. 15), which means that public relations (alternatively called "corporate communication" in many organizations; it is also called "public affairs" in governmental organizations) is "an enabler that makes all people skills and competencies effective. It is a **core enabling competence** for any company that wants to implement the plans and strategies it's designed" (p. 17, emphasis added).

Any organization operates according to some plan for how it does its business. Such a plan covers the entire organization and specifies particular objectives that the whole organization seeks to achieve. In this way organizational plans are strategic in nature because they define what, how much, when, by whom, and for whom things will get done in the big picture. Each operating unit, like a public relations department, must have its own strategic operating plan to show what parts of the organizational plan the department will specifically support with defined objectives of its own. We will address strategic plans in more detail in Chapter 5. At this point, though, it is important to recognize how an organization's separate operating units work together for the greater good of the organization. It is equally important to recognize for our purposes that the PR operation supports—enables—the work of other operating units. In this way, other operating units in an organization stand as internal clients to the PR department, and the department executive is responsible for ensuring that those clients' needs can be met successfully every time.

For example, if an organization has a research and development department, where great innovations are conceived, designed, and implemented into prototypes, top management and the public relations department may want to call attention to particular innovations. Such "calling attention" could involve developing a campaign that celebrates the specific advances and reflects important values of the organization, its customers, and other pertinent publics. Another example would be benefits changes. The human resources department would work with the PR department to make the best communication effort possible among employees and, perhaps, retirees, who are usually considered "family" like employees because they worked there, care about and feel connected with the company, and are collecting a pension from the company.

Nonagency public relations officials work with their organizations' top management and the management of operational areas, such as research and development, manufacturing, legal staff, human resources, finance and accounting, sales, and marketing. Instrumental in these working relationships are the subject matter experts in operational areas who give credible, technical information and guidance about subjects being addressed in communication efforts. Much technical information, ranging from organizational performance to product specifications and beyond, is required for accurate, complete, and timely information that would be communicated in any manner with any public. For example, when an organization must disclose information about its financial performance, PR officials will involve not only the chief financial officer (CFO) but also others who work for the CFO, such as the treasurer and designated corporate accountants who assemble performance data for the required public reports. Another example would be organizations that are announcing a new product or a new innovation for an existing product. PR officials would work very closely with the lead product engineer and product-line manager plus particular experts on any components or systems as needed. The idea is to obtain the most accurate and complete information that can be communicated in the chosen media that will fulfill strategic objectives.

The reputation of the corporate PR operation and its staff must be impeccable. Competence in communication is primary for all PR professionals. Competence as a leader and manager is essential for the executive in charge of the public relations function. Having a strong reputation among all other operating units and top organizational management is an everyday responsibility for the PR executive and the PR staff. Ample research and profession-specific literature have documented the fundamental skills that public relations professionals are expected to have, especially as times and technology change. (Chapter 11 covers such skill sets.) Generally speaking, those skills fall into the categories of writing, interpersonal communication, ethics, knowledge of the business, strategic thinking, project management, meticulous attention to detail while keeping an eye on the big picture, technical command of communication channels (traditional and electronic), measurement and evaluation (analytics), and taking the initiative or being proactive. **Internal reputation**, then, is a function of doing good work, being good coworkers, and being good stewards of the organization's image, reputation, objectives, particular market offerings, and overall business.

From an outside perspective, a corporate public relations group also can have a strong reputation. In this way, other organizations of any type in any industry would think of a particular company's PR operation as a standout example among all others. This kind of **external reputation** for a nonagency PR function can be facilitated through the leader publishing articles, giving speeches or presentations about the profession, serving in professional organizations (e.g., Public Relations Society of America, International Association of Business Communicators, and Arthur W. Page Society), providing case examples of the organization's successes or "best practices" in public relations, and through other outlets. Winning prestigious awards, especially at a national or international level, can also enhance the reputation of a corporate public relations department.

One's successfulness in a corporate PR setting would be the basis for career advancement. Often career advancement for those working in corporate PR at any level is typically achieved through promotions to positions of greater responsibility, higher authority, and bigger challenges, but finding a better job elsewhere (corporate or agency) works well too. Public relations people tend to be among the most well-connected people in business, so leads about job openings can be shared easily and quickly by word-of-mouth, including text messages, e-mail, and social media. We will look into this area of career advancement in Chapter 11.

WHAT ARE NGOS?

The term "non-governmental organization," or **NGO**, came into currency in 1945 because of the need for the UN [United Nations] to differentiate in its Charter between participation rights for intergovernmental specialized agencies and those for international private organizations. At the UN, virtually all types of private bodies can be recognized as NGOs. They only have to be independent from government control, not seeking to challenge governments either as a political party or by a narrow focus on human rights, non-profit-making and non-criminal.

The structures of NGOs vary considerably. They can be global hierarchies, with either a relatively strong central authority or a more loose federal arrangement. Alternatively, they may be based in a single country and operate transnationally. With the improvement in communications, more locally based groups, referred to as grass-roots organizations or community based organizations, have become active at the national or even the global level. Increasingly this occurs through the formation of coalitions. There are international umbrella NGOs, providing an institutional structure for different NGOs that do not share a common identity. There are also looser issue-based networks and ad hoc caucuses, lobbying at UN conferences. ...

At times NGOs are contrasted with social movements. Much as proponents of social movements may wish to see movements as being more progressive and more dynamic than NGOs, this is a false dichotomy. NGOs are components of social movements. Similarly, civil society is the broader concept to cover all social activity by individuals, groups and movements. It remains a matter of contention whether civil society also covers all economic activity. Usually, society is seen as being composed of three sectors: government, the private sector and civil society, excluding businesses.

NGOs are so diverse and so controversial that it is not possible to support, or be opposed to, all NGOs. They may claim to be the voice of the people and to have greater legitimacy than governments, but this can only be a plausible claim under authoritarian governments. However, their role as participants in democratic debate does not depend upon any claim to representative legitimacy.

Source: Willetts (2012; reprinted with permission)

AGENCY PUBLIC RELATIONS OPERATIONS

The "agency" arena of public relations comprises only one type of organization: business firms of various sizes that provide any other organization with the specific expertise and resources to solve particular communication problems. The players in the agency arena operate on a full range of dimensions: one or a handful of people to hundreds of employees, local to global offices, and general to specialty foci. Agencies are in the business of serving other organizations, called "clients," so an active part of their operation rests in finding new clients as well as identifying new opportunities with existing clients. In this way, organizations in the corporate ("nonagency") arena of PR could be clients in the agency arena, and agencies sometimes serve other agencies when projects are large enough to warrant the extra outside help. Those who work in agencies are said to be working on the "agency side," while those who work for companies or other organizations are said to be working on the "client side."

According to Dmitry Diment of IBISWorld (2021), public relations firms in the United States experienced growth and contraction between 2016 and 2021, with the global COVID-19 pandemic taking much of the blame for the recent contraction. Rather than typical mass-media communication efforts, direct online communication with target audiences, using digital media channels, were used in greater measure to demonstrate companies' value and benefits to audiences and customers. In this way, the power of digital media (especially social media) that can be measured well with data analytics has proven highly potent for PR agencies to use for their clients. Data analytics concerning customers (current and potential) has also proven highly beneficial to PR agencies, as they can perform deeper data analyses about their clients, clients' customers, markets, influencers, and other factors through customer relationship management (CRM) systems.

Because agencies seek business opportunities from other organizations, they are outside of those organizations and, consequently, are referred to under the terms of **"outsourcing"** or "out-of-house" or "outside" firms. Agencies can encompass as much or as little of the universe of public relations as they wish, and they may include other areas like advertising, marketing, and technical communication. Essentially all the core practice areas that could be employed in the corporate arena can be handled in the agency arena, and agencies can specialize in any one of them, up to all of them. Supporting areas, such as graphic design, Internet and digital communication, and measurement/evaluation can be included together with the core practice areas or handled individually as an agency's sole business.

Those agencies that focus on individual practice areas are called "boutique" agencies. For example, Reputation Partners Public Relations, located in Chicago, is exclusively focused on "enhancing, protecting and rebuilding corporate reputations" by being expert in subjects that pose much risk and benefit to organizations: public relations, issue and crisis management, marketing, labor communications, employee and labor communications, corporate social responsibility and sustainability, digital and social media, and financial communication (Reputation Partners, 2022). Other agencies may focus on specific kinds of businesses or industries. For example, MorganMyers, a prominent public relations firm near Milwaukee, has served clients chiefly in the food and agriculture industries, from farm cooperatives and manufacturers to retailers and industry trade groups.

Viewed as external experts, agencies possess and provide the essential and needed expertise that clients need. Any independent business or organization can be a potential client for an agency. In this way, too, individual consultants, who operate as sole practitioners, also can offer organizations the needed expertise, and consultants will have a network of other specialists, from graphic artists and printers to event planners and video production houses. Consultants can be brought in to help agencies or corporate PR clients, as covered in Chapter 2.

Because an agency may serve a wide variety of clients, working in an agency requires a lot of flexibility and discipline. Most importantly, an agency serves any client as if it is the only one the agency has, even though the client knows otherwise. (We will cover client-centered communication in Chapter 8.) After all, the client hired the agency because it demonstrated an appropriate and definitive track record of success, expertise, and resourcefulness that impressed the client more than other agencies. Any track record of success is testimony to an agency's ability to serve many clients on many projects and programs at once because the staff *knows* the clients' businesses very well—maybe even better than the clients. (How agencies build their businesses will be examined in Chapters 9 and 10.) **Agency PR** professionals serve multiple clients by working on multiple client teams, so mindful focus plus disciplined and diligent work on each client's jobs are vital. The flexibility to shift to new demands for any one client at any one time is also vital. The best way to ensure that focus and progress on any client are not lost is to know yourself well and manage your own time and projects meticulously. That focus and progress requires much reading, writing, discussions, and other work to provide clients with excellent public relations and excellent service on the accounts.

The starting point for any public relations work is deep knowledge about any client's strategic plan at the organizational level (the big picture for the client) and the operating level (the specific picture of the client's business's parts, beginning with PR). Interestingly, agency personnel are often viewed by their clients' executives as replaceable because, in the corporate realm, those organizations tend to have more loyalty to their in-house experts. Consequently, agency personnel must truly know the client's industry and not rely on the client for education about its industry. It is also vital to have additional deep knowledge about a client itself, such as its history (i.e., from its founding to the present plus its performance record, especially from the last five to ten years), target market(s) and market positioning, recent news, reputation and image, community involvement, awards, litigation, regulatory environment, certifications, and other dimensions. Knowledge about a client in these areas provides necessary background to explain how and why a client is the way it is today, and what it wants to and can be in the future according to its strategic plan. Again, we will examine strategic plans in more detail in Chapter 5.

This deep client knowledge is also essential for agency professionals to possess and apply when working with clients' management. As we covered in the section about corporate public relations, there are potentially many levels of leaders in a client's organization who may be involved in a PR project or program, from top executives to operational leaders to subject matter experts. You will be working with people at various hierarchical levels with exceptional degrees of experience and knowledge, and interpersonal skillfulness and credibility in your work are essential. It is a matter of both professionalism and relationships. We focused more on professionalism in Chapter 3, will focus on client communication in Chapter 8, and will cover social skills in Chapter 11. For now, it is important to recognize that being *genuinely* respectful, honest, credible, and forthright with anyone makes up the basis for good client interactions that fuel your good work.

Because agencies live and die by the clients they serve and how well they serve those clients, a reputation for good work hangs in the balance. That reputation spreads exclusively externally because of the nature of agency business. People talk about the good, the bad, and the ugly of agencies that have served them and others. Rumors about ineffective agencies can truly harm their businesses just as the reputations of stellar agencies truly help to build their businesses. Agencies with good reputations tend to attract better and more employees as well as better and more clients.

So the quality of work, character of people, and track record for success for any agency are the biggest factors in the spreading of reputations. Similar to corporate PR operations, agencies can greatly enhance their reputations externally by their leaders publishing articles, books, or book chapters about matters that are key to their agencies' business and the practice of good, ethical public relations. Those same leaders can also give important speeches, presentations, or seminars that educate, inspire, and challenge the state of the public relations business. While the agency leaders gain notoriety for themselves, they also bring great recognition to their agencies, which is a strong combination for building agency image and reputation.

As an agency's reputation improves and grows, it gets associated with its employees who have been integral in that success. Career advancement in agencies is typically achieved through promotions within the firm but also by finding opportunities for advancement with other firms. Sometimes clients will be so impressed with a member of an agency's team that they want to hire that person full-time for their public relations department. Note, however, that the contractual agreement between an agency and a client may expressly forbid clients from actively seeking to hire ("poaching") agency employees. The reverse of this situation is different. An agency employee working on a client's account, however, may ask a client if they would be interested and willing to hire that agency employee, making sure there is ample documentation which shows that the agency employeeinitiated interest about such an opportunity. Overall, the extensive networks that public relations people have are instrumental in their getting leads about job openings. Again, we will look more into career advancement in Chapter 11.

WHAT JOB DESCRIPTIONS CAN TELL US

Although it might not be obvious, job postings for management-level employees are a great place to find what organizations want in their leaders. More specifically, job postings for public relations leaders in the corporate and agency arenas specify particular qualities and professional backgrounds that are sought for executive-level positions. Many online resources are available to find such job postings. In addition, there are many companies that specialize in searching for executives in particular industries—they go by terms like "executive search firms" or "headhunters." Remember, too, that word-of-mouth communication about open leadership (and other) positions can be especially valuable, because the people passing the word along to you likely have the information before many other people do and may believe you are especially well suited for the job. (We will cover career paths in public relations in Chapter 11.)

Research about the public relations profession has defined two basic roles: technician and manager (Dozier, 1992). Simply put, the **technician role** focuses on the development of public relations material of many types for particular purposes, such as writing and campaign design. Technicians include interns, assistant account executives, account executives, senior account executives, communications coordinators, and supervisory and middle-management employees. The **manager role**, in contrast, focuses on matters including strategic planning, business development, resource allocations, and staff development. Managers are organizational leaders/executives with titles like director, executive director, assistant vice president, vice president, senior vice president, executive vice president, chief communication officer, principal, partner, or president.

It is very important to note that even though the word "executive" formally occurs in a low-level technician position (usually at agencies), it is not an actual executive-level position. Technicians are not necessarily required to possess leadership abilities, but they are expected to be excellent users of language in any medium, observant, creative, and very well organized. In other words, technicians are either traditional or exemplary followers. Notice, too, that the concept of manager subsumes what we addressed in Chapter 1 about concepts of both leadership and management, and the role of manager assumes that someone also is a highly competent technician who can do the job when required. In other words, the most effective managers are transformational leaders who are also emotionally competent, as we saw in Chapter 1. Of the two basic roles in public relations, we are primarily focused in this book on the manager role and leave matters pertaining to the technician role to sources about public relations writing and campaign design. In cursory reviews of a large number of U.S. job postings collected by my students in PR management courses, certain patterns emerged and have remained consistent for PR leaders in nonagency and agency arenas (see Table 4.1).

Table 4.1 Some dominant characteristics for nonagency versus agency management/ executive positions

Nonagency	Agency
• Master's degree preferred (especially MBA) but bachelor's degree acceptable	• Bachelor's degree
• 7–15 years of experience (10 years and over is most common) and proven track record of success, especially in leadership and corporate strategy	• 7–10 years of experience and proven track record of success, especially in leadership
• Superior writing and interpersonal communication skills	• Very strong public speaking and writing skills
• May ask for agency experience	• Focused on and highly skilled at pitching and bringing in new clients
• Previous managerial and supervising roles are desired	• Varied experiences in both agency and corporate PR desired
• Experience in the corporation's industry is needed	• Able to handle a high-stress workload
• Competent in all areas of public relations techniques, especially social media and measurement/evaluation	• Focused on teamwork and team building
• Relationships with established networks are essential	• Competent in all areas of public relations techniques, especially social media and measurement/evaluation
• Able to promote the organization, especially brand and image	• Able to think creatively and come up with sound ideas quickly and efficiently
• Experience with planning, budgeting, and human-resources matters	• Experience with planning, budgeting, forecasting, and personnel development
• Median pay: $119,860 per year ($57.62 per hour)*	
• Number of management jobs: 89,000*	

Note: *Bureau of Labor Statistics (2022a)

Any review of job openings for any position in public relations reveals a certain consistency across organizations and industries. The reason is that public relations is the common denominator for all job postings, and the variations from one job to the next will be based on how an organization operates, has operated, and plans to operate over time in its given industry and its target markets therein. For example, a global corporation that produces fiber-optic cable, a domestic company offering post–disaster clean-up services, a communications agency with several offices across the country, and a local faith-based nonprofit organization that helps the elderly would all need public relations leaders who are expert public relations technicians *and*, most important, are experienced in matters of business that include (at least) strategy, performance management, budgeting and forecasting, personnel, communication law, and ethics.

Individually, however, those same companies need leaders who have specialized knowledge, skills, and experience that suit their respective businesses. Someone with a great deal of local **nonprofit PR** background may not be suited for a leadership position at a multinational manufacturing company. But someone with a great deal of agency PR experience that included serving many clients successfully over the years in particular industries could make a move to a corporate PR department, especially if the person's experiences were in related industries. The opposite of that could be done as well, as a long-term corporate PR leader has a successful track record plus deep knowledge of an industry and its various players in the market.

Every public relations professional must know how public relations fits into the bigger picture of any organization's mix of activities that are devoted to promoting it and its offerings (e.g., marketing, advertising, direct mail, customer service)—including situations where an organization is using multiple agencies and has multiple programs underway. Such knowledge, based on a solid understanding of the similarities and differences between agency and nonagency PR operations, is valuable in doing ethical and legal work, developing sound strategic plans, managing the many resources needed for successful communications, making solid decisions while leading an engaged PR team, and building that team's reputation and track record.

EXECUTIVE VIEWPOINT

Intersecting Worlds of Corporate and Agency PR

Cheryl I. Procter-Rogers, Senior Consultant,
A Step Ahead PR Consulting and Coaching

When asked by public relations and marketing students whether they should pursue opportunities in an agency or a corporation, I respond with, "It depends." The truth is it doesn't matter if you work for a corporation, nonprofit, government office or agency. What does matter is that you find a place where you can hone the essential skills and acquire the management experience you need to be successful in any arena.

Early in my career I thought titles were really important until I began my public relations job search. It was a daunting experience then and it's even more so today. Now, there can be 100 or more titles describing the same function in corporations. Somehow though, the PR agency world has gotten it right and the titles are relatively consistent from agency to agency. My regional director title at HBO could be equivalent to a vice president title elsewhere or manager at yet another corporation. I stick with senior consultant with my consulting practice as it seems to be a title everyone gets. When a PR manager recruits and hires for an in-house department, it is critical to have an understanding of the misconceptions titles sometimes create. It is very important for a supervisor or manager in an agency to have these same insights as they build relationships with their client contacts.

My first PR job was in the public relations department of a national insurance company. There were three of us, a vice president, a secretary, and me. What I gained in experience and knowledge in six short months could not be duplicated in a department of 30 or even in an agency.

When you work alone or with a small staff like we had, you do the writing, editing, photography, media pitching, production, social media, designing, and the implementation of various programs. You also serve as an advisor to top management, all before lunch! After lunch, you train others on how best to represent the company, manage internal and external events, and manage budgets.

When you manage a large staff, you spend more time in planning, managing the team, and advising. The most successful managers in a corporation or agency are generalists and have either performed many of the functions they manage or have an intimate knowledge of the various roles. Also, knowing how and when to use research and how to interpret data are essential for both.

When I was excluded from important meetings or sidelined during business discussions at the insurance company, I quietly questioned why. Finally, I asked the president and learned that it was because they were talking about the *business*, which to them, had nothing to do with public relations. I quickly immersed myself in learning to read and understand financial statements and the business of insurance. This new vocabulary and understanding elevated me in the eyes of management and, I'm confident, led to many promotions. Having an acumen for business has served me well in all corporate and consulting roles I've been in since then.

While working in both agency and corporate arenas, I found there are certain aspects of the two areas that are very different:

- *Demonstrate value*—In-house, you are often given a longer time for producing results, which is quite the opposite in the agency world, where the clock is ticking as billable hours mount.
- *Day-to-day*—In-house, you are part of the management team. You gain an intimate knowledge of the company because you are there to hear the gossip and give advice accordingly. You're there spotting possible PR opportunities and moving fast to head off trouble. As a consultant, you are strictly in an advisory role and are often called upon for special projects. The agency performs alone or in tandem with in-house staff. The consultant can't duplicate the loyalty, understanding, and attention provided by an effective in-house staff person.
- *Resources*—Depending on the size of the department, an outside agency can bring greater depth and experience to solve problems or take advantage of opportunities.
- *Objectivity*—For in-house teams, personal relationships can cloud judgment and make it harder to say no or challenge traditions. It's easy to get stuck. Agency consultants come to the relationship with fewer biases and are often more objective, bringing a fresh perspective.

Here are life lessons I pass on to you:

- Know how to read a balance sheet and income statement; understand the business of your employer or client. It will accelerate your opportunities to be included in important discussions.
- Build your business acumen through self-study or an additional degree.
- Challenge yourself by taking courses or studying topics outside your core area of communications and marketing.
- A different way to build credibility within an organization and expand your network is by working across the organization. Seek out opportunities to meet with executives in different departments. During these discussions, you may find projects where your expertise could be valuable. Here's a chance for you to stand out and step up!!!
- Trust is critical to your success. Having both people and communication skills can impact how quickly you are able to establish trust. Ineffective communications can result in misunderstandings that can lead to missed deadlines, projects that don't match with expectations, and other issues. Those with great people and communication skills help influence their credibility as a leader, friend, spouse, and parent.

Finally, just like individuals, agencies and corporations have personalities and preferences too. When considering a career opportunity, I encourage you to connect with your passion for our profession and seek environments that support your continued growth and development!

KEY WORDS

Nonagency ("corporate") PR	**In-house**
Agency PR	**Outsourcing**
NGO	**External reputation**
Core enabling competence	**Technician role**
Internal reputation	**Manager role**

REFERENCES

Bureau of Labor Statistics. (2022a). Public relations and fundraising managers. In *Occupational outlook handbook*. U.S. Department of Labor. Available online: www.bls.gov/ooh/management/public-relations-managers.htm.

Bureau of Labor Statistics. (2022b). Public relations specialists. In *Occupational outlook handbook*. U.S. Department of Labor. Available online: www.bls.gov/ooh/media-and-communication/public-relations-specialists.htm.

Diment, D. (2021, November). *Public relations firms in the US*. US Industry (NAICS) Report 54182. IBISWorld. Available online: https://my.ibisworld.com/us/en/industry/54182/industry-outlook.

Dozier, D. M. (1992). The organizational roles of communications and public relations practitioners. In J. E. Grunig (Ed.), *Excellence in public relations and communication management* (pp. 327–355). Lawrence Erlbaum Associates.

Jensen, B. (1995, August). Are we necessary? The case for dismantling corporate communication. *IABC Communication World*, 14–18, 30.

Reputation Partners Public Relations. (2022). *Capabilities: Overview of our services*. Author. Available online: https://reputationpartners.com/capabilities/.

Wilcox, D. L., Cameron, G. T., Reber, B. H., & Shin, J-H. (2013). Today's practice: Departments and firms. In *Think public relations* (pp. 69–87). Pearson.

Willetts, P. (2012). What is a non-governmental organization? *UNESCO encyclopaedia of life support systems*. City University of London. Available online: www.staff.city.ac.uk/p.willetts/CS-NTWKS/NGO-ART.HTM.

RECOMMENDED READING

Actis, R. G. (2006). *Management's last frontier: A communications system to focus and sustain a culture of achievement.* Pearson Custom Publishing.

Beard, M. (2001). *Running a public relations department* (2nd ed.). Kogan Page.

Dickinson, D. (2003). *The new account manager.* The Copy Shop.

Edelman, R. (2001). *Inside the minds: The art of public relations: Industry visionaries reveal the secrets to successful public relations.* Aspatore Books.

Maister, D. H. (1993). *Managing the professional service firm.* Free Press.

5

CHAPTER 5
OPERATIONS TOOLS I: STRATEGIC PLANS AND FINANCIAL MATTERS

CHAPTER OUTLINE

No organizational function is an island. For public relations, a strategic approach should not be developed in isolation from other functional areas in an organization, especially if PR's focus is an annual plan for corporate publicity or a concentrated promotional effort, like a product launch. Public relations works among other operating areas of an organization. Marketing, finance, legal, human resources, research and development,

DOI: 10.4324/9781003208280-6

sales, and manufacturing areas could all be affected by and benefit from public relations. These functions may deserve to be included in the PR plan in some way, depending on the business needs and the company's overall strategic plan.

For example, marketing's promotional advertising could be timed with editorial placements in publications. Financial performance should be echoed in relevant press releases, company backgrounders, and conversations with influential people in the media or among industry analysts. Legal staff should review PR discourse before it is released and may require management of legal issues. Human resources may require certain employee communications about new benefits plans or other internal programs or policies. Research and development may have created a breakthrough technology that works more simply, cheaply, and effectively than anything available. Sales would need published articles and success stories about the company and its customers. And manufacturing would look to PR to publicize major product or service achievements that affect the company, its customers, and the competition.

These kinds of organizational needs show how deeply public relations can penetrate an organization. Even going a step further, public relations can help corporate leaders reach out to their publics by communicating what they and the organization stand for in the market and society. An overall strategic communications program would integrate PR with executives and other corporate functions to build stronger relationships with an organization's internal and external publics on whom success depends. Through such planned integration, public relations practitioners can anticipate corporate or policy issues that may gain importance and account for them in the formal communication plan.

Top management has high expectations for public relations and wants it to succeed. That success must be on business terms—adding value as a strategically core organizational function. Along with the concepts from the previous chapters, particular "tools" for effective management of a public relations operation, like any organizational unit, are essential. This chapter is the first of two that present and explain selected and fundamental operations tools. In this chapter we will cover strategic plans, finance, time management, and billing. Chapter 6 will include tools for managing **performance** and personnel.

STRATEGIC PLANS

Plans are to organizations as hymnals are to choirs. Hymnals, ranging from complex pieces like Handel's *Messiah* to grade school performances, show the words and music for a choir of many people who sing various parts—sopranos, altos, tenors, baritones, and basses. Without the hymnals, choir members would not know exactly what to sing and when and how. For an organization, its plan is its hymnal, including the information about what its parts are expected to do, when, and how much. An organizational plan, then, is the one document that presents what everyone in an organization is working toward during a given period of time, usually a calendar or fiscal year.

PLANNING PROCESS

Any organization is comprised of various parts. Figure 5.1 shows how the most basic parts interrelate, from the primary and largest element of the organization itself, to the next level of operating units (i.e., departments or divisions), to project teams, to the smallest and most integral element of individual employees. The bigger an organization, the potentially more numerous the layers, but these four layers work well for our purposes. Along with all operating units in an organization, public relations works *with* management within a single system for what Anthony (1988) calls the processes of strategic planning, management control, and task control.

The name for that system is the "corporate performance management" (CPM) system, and it and its processes are owned by management and can involve employees at many levels. (Another, older term for CPM systems is "business information systems.") A **CPM system** employs defined methods, metrics, processes, and systems to measure performance that are needed to monitor and manage that performance. So a CPM system turns strategically focused data into usable information that is necessary for reporting results, assessing operational plans, and making decisions.

In a CPM system, **strategic planning** takes key management initiatives and supports top-down and bottom-up planning processes. This two-way planning process allows for checks and balances among the various views of what can and must be done among an organization's operating units. Fundamentally, strategic planning involves deciding on an organization's goals and the strategies based on an accurate, complete, and honest

Figure 5.1 Basic organizational parts or layers

situation analysis; then deciding how best to attain them through setting objectives, budgeting, and/or rolling forecasts. (Budgets and forecasts will be treated later in this chapter.) **Management control** is a process that supports planning by providing organizational insight, communication, and focus. It involves managers influencing other organizational members to enact the strategies by monitoring plan performance, supporting the analysis of alternatives, and taking corrective action. **Task control** involves making sure that specific tasks are carried out efficiently and effectively. It is tactics- or transaction-focused, encompasses the literal results sought in the strategic planning process, and is measured according to the management control process.

This CPM system for strategic planning, management control, and task control leverages organizational knowledge and insight by blending these processes into a single, synchronous, and ongoing system to better implement strategies, strengthen decision-making, and make management at all levels more effective (see Ariyachandra & Frolick, 2008; M. Bourne & P. Bourne, 2011; Buytendijk et al., 2004; Scheer et al., 2006). The system's process is typically engaged annually, and any **project** or **contingency planning** would follow a similar path, being in sync with the organization's overall strategic plan and the PR function's strategic operating plan. Indeed, when time is especially of the essence, public relations leaders' strategic thinking is internalized and supported by extensive experience and knowledge of what works and what may not. Strategic thinking in such situations involves a compressed process covering most or all elements of a strategic plan, resulting in efficient and effective management decision-making that is in tune with the organization's bigger strategic picture.

It is interesting that the starting point for the strategic planning process is really the end point—top management determines what it wants the organization ultimately to be and achieve (i.e., the vision and objectives); then it begins the process to figure out how the organization will get there. The strategic planning process, then, is primarily dialogic among leaders and staff in all operating units. As Figure 5.2 shows, developing the strategic plan (i.e., "planning efforts") is a top-down process that begins with top management as it thoroughly analyzes the organization's situation in all respects and then sets the course for the company. Operating activity (including budgeting) is a

Figure 5.2 Strategic planning process model
Source: Smudde (2011, p. 148)

bottom-up process at the tactical, operational level with managers and employees who have the responsibility, expertise, and experience with day-to-day demands. These people perform a kind of "reality check" on management's strategic course, which can propel the company forward. During the bottom-up process, operational units examine management's objectives, decide what is doable and what is not, and allocate resources (i.e., proposing to add, subtract, or realign resources) to ensure success. In turn, management works with operations to fine-tune the plan by aligning needs and wants at all levels.

Key assumptions about the organization's current and anticipated future environments are also noted and understood by all parties. Both processes *together* result in a complete view of the business from all perspectives and focused on one vision for the company (also see Drucker, 1994; Mintzberg, 2007; Robert, 1997, 2006). It may take some time to consistently demonstrate the value of public relations before others embrace its value contribution. The planning, budgeting, forecasting, consolidating of performance data, analyzing of performance data, and reporting on results can and must work in public relations' favor.

This whole top-down and bottom-up process can take some time to complete, and it is contingent on an organization's culture and systems. In the end, the result is (1) a single strategic **organizational plan** for the entire organization; and (2) individual strategic **operating plans** for each organizational area, such as those mentioned in this chapter's introduction. Operational plans, budgets, and forecasts must all "roll up" to the organizational plan, budget, and forecast. Such an approach ensures that everyone everywhere in the organization is working toward the same ends and they all understand how everyone else will help them get there. All sections of the plans are the same, but the content differs because each operational area has its own plan to fulfill the expectations specified in the organizational plan.

What it is important to recognize is that an organizational plan specifies how operational units will contribute to the organization's overall success; however, those specifications at the organizational level are not sufficiently detailed to run any given operating unit. That deficiency in an organizational plan means there must be more specific plans at the operational level to provide people with the detail they need to do the work in their parts of the business that will fulfill overall, organizational objectives. In other words, plans for individual projects or programs must directly roll up to the operational plans to which they are aligned, not the overall organizational plan. So there is a hierarchy for plans that is essential to understand because each plan builds upon or, more appropriately, rolls up (and down) to another.

Figure 5.3 shows the nested relationship for strategic plans, with the principal one being the organizational plan and a series of subordinate, even "nested," plans needed for an organization's various operational and tactical demands. Certain plans are developed annually while others are developed as needed, and one is generated once. All of them

Plan Type (Most encompassing to least)	Defining Characteristics
1. Organizational	The primary plan with the broadest scope because it concerns the whole organization; it is the foundation for all other plans; produced annually, assessed frequently, and revised when needed.
2. Operational	The plan for an organizational business/operating unit (e.g., department); has specific scope to fulfill particular organizational objectives through that unit because of its unique contribution to the organization; produced annually, assessed frequently, and revised when needed.
3. Project/Program	A plan that targets a specific effort that fulfills one or more objectives in the operational plan; produced as needed ("ad hoc") and assessed during and after implementation.
4. Contingency	A plan meticulously developed within an operation's bailiwick to address disruptive situations (i.e., any kind of unanticipated disruptive situation) in definitive ways so that those matters can be resolved effectively and efficiently and in tune with the organizational plan and the organization's image and reputation; the scope may range from an operational unit to the organization as a whole; produced once and assessed and revised at least annually, possibly through drills or simulations.
5. Personal/Position	A plan with a scope of an individual to guide someone's performance in a given job or position, potentially including career aims; produced annually, assessed periodically, and revised as needed to accommodate operational and job changes.

Figure 5.3 The "nesting" relationship and fit among plans

are assessed and updated/revised on a regular basis, depending on contextual factors. It may help to think of the relationship or the fit among these plans into one another like Ukrainian nesting dolls, with the outermost doll being the organizational plan and the innermost doll being the personal/position plan. This conceptualization is consistent with that shown in Figure 5.1 as well.

There is one major caveat: strategic plans go out of date essentially as soon as they are finalized and approved (see Drucker, 1994). The reason is because the process to develop a plan rests on information about an organization's enacted environment, which is really a snapshot in time—at the time it is taken. Certain assumptions also were made about the future. This dynamic does not mean that planning is a useless exercise—far from it! An organizational plan is needed to ensure everyone knows for what they are working (i.e., the choir must have a hymnal). Operational plans are essential so that people in a particular unit know more precisely what they are doing that will fit into the bigger scope of the organization's plan. Moreover, because things change quickly inside and outside an organization, all aspects of any strategic plan (at the organizational or operational levels or both) must be flexible enough to accommodate change and still achieve success. Public relations' inherent boundary-spanning capabilities become more potent and important to an organization in this regard.

PLAN CONTENT

Any plan is meant to be usable, useful, and most of all, used. Notice that the context so far has been organizational and operational plans, *not* campaign or project plans, which we will address shortly and in the larger organizational context. A strategic plan must contain sufficiently detailed information that enables people at any level in an organization, especially those with managerial/supervisory responsibilities, to direct organizational resources to fulfill specific objectives over a given period of time. *The most important thing to remember about a strategic plan is that you are creating a "business case," where each section requires argumentative explanation and defense within any context the organization faces.*

The key parts (but not the only parts) of an organizational plan, as indicated by the process model in Figure 5.2, are the company's vision, mission, situation analysis, objectives, strategies, and tactics. But there is more to a plan than those matters. A full example and explanation of an entire strategic plan and its contents are given in Appendix A, and you must examine it carefully in addition to this chapter. Figure 5.4 outlines the basic contents of a strategic plan at any level (i.e., organizational to personal), where certain parts may be added or subtracted as needed. In fact, when all these features are presented in writing in a formal plan, they can be formatted in such a way that the information is organized and actionable—even to the point to show which objectives apply to which parts of the budget and vice versa. Other aspects would be required (e.g., situation analysis, critical success factors, key performance indicators,

- **Executive summary** (very concise summary of the plan's content, focusing on the problem, the solution, and anticipated results; write last)
- **Business definition** (a very short statement about what the organization's business is, for whom, and how it does business; this content may be optional)
- **Vision** (concisely say a long-term future state for the organization)
- **Mission** (concisely say why an organization exists and how it does its business)
- **Value proposition** (specify the unique differentiator/idea and the compelling proof points for that differentiation/idea; functions also as the supreme *key message platform* for the organization)
- **Situation analysis** (a concise, concrete, and thorough description of the state of affairs the organization faces, including accounting for internal and external factors that may affect success; a.k.a. problem/opportunity analysis)
- **Audiences/stakeholders** (internal and external and why they are vital)

Present together in a table. {
- **Objectives** (big-picture accomplishments sought; must include effect sought, measurable amount of the effect sought [goal], audience targeted, and deadline; should include benchmark for goal)
- **Strategies** (statements that systematize tactics toward one or more objectives and goals; organizational strategies become operational objectives)
- **Tactics** (specific actions to be taken to meet/exceed goals and fulfill objectives)
}

- **Critical success factors** (things/events that could help or hurt success; why is knowing these things valuable)
- **Key performance indicators** (milestone measurements taken along the way to track progress toward goals; why is knowing these things valuable)
- **Timeline** (overall and by phase; relate to objectives/goals and metrics)
- **Budget and resources** (give data as specifically as possible; explain what's needed and why; return on investment [ROI] and value-added for the change are key)
- **Evaluation method** (*post hoc* measurements and analysis of outputs, outtakes, outcomes, and outgrowths)
- **Appendices** (any additional evidence or documentation specifically needed to support sections of the plan)
- **References** (list of sources used in any of the plan's content)

Figure 5.4 Basic plan parts (see Appendix A)
Source: Smudde and Courtright (2012)

budget, timeline, evaluation methods), which also are presented in Appendix A, and will be addressed later on in this chapter as they pertain to public relations.

BASIC ORGANIZATIONAL BACKGROUND

The starting points for a strategic plan are the basic matters for understanding an organization—what it is and why it exists. Often these matters begin with a "definition of the business" for an organization, no matter what kind it is, but this statement may be optional for a given organization because leaders know it well. A *business definition* must be specific to what the business is that an organization conducts, for whom, and in what ways. A concise statement of this sort often can be found in existing, current documentation about an organization, so it can be used to maintain consistency of messages.

Other matters about an organization also are essential to specifically state in a plan in appropriate terms, namely:

- what an organization (or a project or program) wants to be and achieve in the future (**vision**);
- what an organization does and offers in its daily business that adds value to customers/clients/stakeholders (**mission**);
- what the compelling matters are that differentiate it from all other organizations that compete with it somehow (**value proposition**).

Note that a vision statement is necessarily focused on the future—what an organization (or project or program) ought to be and achieve; and it must be concisely written as such and usually as a single sentence. A mission statement is focused on the present state of operations and should be written concisely to express that state of being. A value proposition is focused on customer/client interests or needs that only can be met by a specific organization and is written with particular concise details about the big idea and the proof points that support it. See section 1.0 in Appendix A for further explanation.

Additional background about an organization's *structure* is needed to explain and show the hierarchical structure of who reports to whom by position and level. This structure must be explained—why it is the way it is and who in it most matters for the plan's implementation and success. Organizational structure is often based on how an organization came into being. So *history and culture* also may be necessary (see section 1.6 in Appendix A) to explain the organization's overall context to ensure that it is understood and, particularly, applied in later sections as needed, especially the situation analysis. In fact, an organization's culture is instrumental in the organization's execution of its business and enactment of a strategic plan.

Culture is born of an organization's history and is learned and perpetuated among its members through values, rules, norms, stories, policies, procedures, discourse, symbols, rites, rituals, and so on. Values are particularly important because they articulate the most important things (intellectually, emotionally, and behaviorally) for and about an organization; the things that are the true foundation for why it exists at all, does what it does in the ways it does them, and wants to continue to exist and evolve for the better. Culture, then, is both the process and product of humans working and being together.

In organizations, as Keyton (2011) explains it, culture is characterized by several things. Organizational culture is shared by a defined group (of any size) of people who all embrace and enact it. It is made up of multiple elements simultaneously, and those elements are artifacts, values, and assumptions. Data sources to learn about and document an organization's culture can be written and unwritten, and they include slogans, philosophies, and value statements; the type of people in an organization; symbols, stories, and heroes; and rituals, rites, and routines (Clampitt, 2010). All these cultural elements together combine into a lens through which group members view and interact with the world around them. The elements also work together as a system, where one element is not more important than the others but, rather, they inform one another through human action.

For a strategic plan, then, a sufficient understanding and concise documentation of organizational culture can provide critical information and insights about motivations and predictions about why an organization is what it is, does what it does, and may do or not do what it needs to do to be more successful in the ways it wants and needs to be. Such insight would also be useful in anticipating people's attitudes about and responses to a strategic plan and whether it may be implemented or not. See Appendix A for additional details about these basic matters of an organization's background that need to be in a plan, including laying out a plan's content from beginning to end.

SITUATION ANALYSIS

Because a strategic plan is very timebound, the environment ("situation") that the organization faces must be explained. So a key part of effective planning and any strategic plan is a *situation analysis*. The content of this part of a plan sets the context—why the organization is in the position it is in—and, most especially, points to what the organization can do to improve itself. The section comprises five parts: (1) formally defining the situation, (2) spelling out who the stakeholders are, (3) identifying and evaluating the competition, (4) presenting the results of a SWOT analysis (of an organization's **s**trengths, **w**eaknesses, **o**pportunities, and **t**hreats), and (5) finally arguing for the market position the organization occupies.

All sections of the situation analysis are very important, and a simple, potent, and common approach to it is a **SWOT** analysis. (Three other environmental-scanning methods—gap analysis, force-field analysis, and order restoration—are presented in

Chapter 9 and are applied to market analysis. Please go to Chapter 9 now to learn about them.) A SWOT analysis relies on a two-step process of (1) brainstorming about the current internal factors that are *strengths* and *weaknesses* for the organization; and then (2) analyzing those internal factors in terms of known and expected external (a) *opportunities* to capitalize on strengths, achieve successes, and minimize or eliminate weaknesses plus (b) *threats* of any kind that may hurt the organization to any degree or become obstacles to overcome. (See section 2.4 in Appendix A.)

An effective SWOT analysis does not stop at just filling out the strengths, weaknesses, opportunities, and threats. An effective SWOT analysis must examine the data in each of the four parts for their implications (i.e., what they mean to the organization in terms of attributes, like importance, scope, influence, etc.). It then presents possible action items that can address the data in each of the four parts (e.g., doing something specific to capitalize on every stated strength, minimize or eliminate a weakness, pursue an opportunity, and avoid any foreseeable threat). A four-column, multirow table, like the one in Appendix A, should be prepared and can be used most effectively for any organization. The information and insight gained through a complete situation analysis (shown in section 2.0 in Appendix A) is enormously valuable for discerning an organization's target publics and stakeholders, competition, and market position, but it all is especially vital for laying the foundation of a strategic plan's core: objectives, strategies, and tactics.

CORE PLAN SECTION AND ITS CONTENT

The core of a strategic plan—because all other sections of a plan apply directly into it—concerns specific information about *what to do, how,* and *with what.* Again, make sure you carefully read the example of an entire strategic plan and its contents in Appendix A. In more specific terms for the core of a strategic plan, Figure 5.5 presents a kind of formula for presenting any single objective, its strategy(ies), and its tactic(s) all at once so they can be visually tied to one another from left to right and vice versa. Figure 5.6 shows how to apply Figure 5.5 with a mundane but pertinent example, including a

Objectives (EGAD)	Strategies	Tactics
Effect+Goal+Audience+Deadline 1. Awareness/Understanding 2. Attitude/Emotions 3. Action/Behaviors 4. Output/Discourse (*Benchmark*: Point of comparison for each objective given for **each** objective.) (*Rationale*: Why the goal in **each** objective is reasonable.)	The broad category(ies) of work that would be done that covers the tactics listed per category. (*Apply Hayes et al., 2013.*)	• Activity 1 • Activity 2 ... • Activity n

Figure 5.5 Formula presentation of core plan content

VISION: Have fully stocked food stores for the home		
Objectives (EGAD)	**Strategies**	**Tactics**
Must replenish 40% of our food on hand by month's end. (*Benchmark*: Known needs for this time of year.) (*Rationale*: The present food store is 60% capacity and the gap must be made up to reach 100%.)	1. Hunting 2. Fishing 3. Grocery shopping 4. Gardening	1a. Deer season 1b. Turkey season 1c. Other game as allowed by season 2. Fish area rivers and lakes 3. Go to grocery store 4a. Grow favorite veggies (lettuce, garlic, shallots, cherry tomatoes, snap peas, broccoli, green beans, sweet peppers, jalapeño peppers, beets, carrots, and cabbage) 4b. Preserve veggies for out-of-season eating

Figure 5.6 Fleshed-out example of core plan content in service to a vision

specific vision for what the objective, strategies, and tactics are geared to. A thorough situation analysis using a robust environmental–scanning method (one method will be explained in the "The Plan on the Whole" subsection below; also see Chapter 9 and Appendix A) is key to the development of a plan, particularly its core. Each column effectively poses three key questions and the answers to those questions:

1. What must we achieve in support of the vision? (objective)
2. How categorically will we achieve it? (strategies)
3. What specifically will we do? (tactics)

As you look at Figure 5.5 (also see Appendix A) you can read *from left to right* what needs to be done to move us closer to realizing our vision (objective), how things will be done (strategies), and what actions will be specifically taken (tactics). And you can read the table *from right to left*: what specifically will be done (tactics) is part of how the objective will be achieved (strategies), and these elements will achieve the ultimate outcome that is desired (objective). This approach is a true part-to-whole presentation of the plan's core content.

With this very general orientation to the core components of a plan, we must examine each part for what they are, how they work, and why they are needed to work as they do.

OBJECTIVES
Objectives state, in a single sentence, the high–level results (**effects**) an organization wants to achieve by a certain measurable amount (**goal**) for a particular public or stakeholder group (**audience**) over a defined period of time (**deadline**). (**EGAD** is a

mnemonic way to remember these four essential elements of a well-formed objective.) Note that, depending on an organization's preference, the words "objective" and "goal" may be interchanged, but do not let this terminological problem get in the way of your understanding and work. Furthermore, organizations may call a long-term or broad-based objective a "goal" or "overall goal" instead of a "vision," while anything else is an "objective." Again, do not let that stand in your way of understanding what is sought and doing your work. Either way, objectives must address matters that will, indeed, help move an organization closer to realizing its vision while simultaneously contributing to the mission.

Objectives for a strategic plan are statements about the big-picture accomplishments sought that move an organization closer to realizing its vision, which translate into the plan's value within the situational context for your organization. In very general terms, as much treatment of the topic argues, objectives ought to be SMART: simple, measurable, attainable, relevant, and timely. This general approach is good, but for us it is insufficient because it lacks the kind of specificity we need. In this way, objectives written in EGAD form are SMART but also more definitive and effective, as we will see.

Objectives written in EGAD form must only specify *one* effect that will be sought and directly measured against a *goal* for the amount of the effect sought thatmatters to a particular *audience* by a particular *date*. Objectives can be written as one of **four types** that seek to achieve one specific effect:

- *Awareness*—concerns a degree of change or impact sought in knowledge, information, or understanding (guiding metaphor is the *head*).
- *Attitude*—concerns a change or impact sought in degree or kind of opinion, belief, or emotional buy-in (guiding metaphor is the *heart*).
- *Action*—concerns a change or impact sought in degree or kind of behavior or task taken or not (guiding metaphor is the *hands* [and feet]).
- *Output*—concerns the creation of tangible forms of discourse (verbal, nonverbal, symbolic), from documents to events (guiding metaphor is *stuff*).

Because an objective must focus on one and only one effect, any objective that seeks more than one effect (e.g., "Increase awareness and sales of product X by year's end") is ineffective and must be broken into multiple objectives—one for each effect and following the EGAD formula plus a benchmark for each. So specific objectives are more meaningful than general ones. An objective can be written to specify results over any span of time, from creating particular outputs (e.g., press releases, meetings with news organizations' editors, receptions for corporate celebrations) to achieving long-term outgrowths (e.g., awareness gains, attitude changes, behavior modifications). The dates for realizing objectives are essential to knowing when results are expected.

Additionally, always state a **benchmark** (i.e., the point of comparison from prior experience, secondary research, or another source) for the goal within or after an objective. And always give a *rationale* for the stated goal to establish why that goal is reasonable and attainable. Without a benchmark, there is no context and, therefore, no way to know if a goal is either reasonable or achievable. The rationale is necessary to give further context about why the goal is reasonable and attainable—as a way to answer questions about the goal's pertinence before they are asked. Maintaining the clarity of what is what within any EGAD objective and its relational parts (i.e., benchmark, strategy[ies], and tactic[s]) is essential for proper and accurate measurements of success. Examine Figure 5.4 and section 3.1 in Appendix A for examples of presenting an objective with its benchmark and rationale.

Objectives' benchmarks must be stated simply and clearly and be well documented. Any organization that has been around for a year or more ought to have some, but if not, especially because it is brand new, benchmarks can be identified by finding out how competitors have performed or by researching published cases or examples of what organizations have done in similar situations. This is why a thoroughly researched situation analysis is so useful. You also must do research to find out if any benchmarks can be identified (even though they are not specifically for your organization) through case studies, best practices, news/journal articles, market or industry reports, local/regional/national chambers of commerce, etc. If after all that work you still do not have any benchmarks, you may state that, because there are no prior data, this first-time pursuit of an objective will establish a benchmark for the future. *Do not* use this last point as a cop-out for not doing the work to find benchmarks!

Objectives guide all milestone measurements of success (see section 3.3 in Appendix A) and the final, overall evaluation (see section 3.6 in Appendix A). All final measurements must be compared to the benchmarks. Here are some examples of proper EGAD objectives with benchmarks and rationales:

- Increase customer awareness about UltraExtreme Diapers by 27% by November 1 2023. (Benchmark: 52% customer awareness in 2022. Rationale: 27% lift in awareness would yield a level of 79% customer awareness, which is on par with our main competitors.)
- Establish 7% market share in the enterprise software segment by December 31 2023. (Benchmark: 6% market share in 2022. Rationale: The new-product roll-out and estimated customer demand for it projects that at least a 1% lift in market share is possible.)
- Install new, more effective production-management system for all business units by the end of the third quarter. (Benchmark: previous quarter's and historic trend of system efficiency has leveled off and is beginning to decline. Rationale: the existing system is outdated and in need of replacement.)

Note in these objectives that the *goal* is included in the objective—it is the G in EGAD. Also note that just because percentages are used in two of the three examples that only percentages are usable—they are not. Use whole numbers or other measurable units whenever it works best, such as a target number of attendees for an event, not a percentage increase of attendees from the previous year. Additionally, note that in each objective a *benchmark* and a *rationale* is given and stated simply, as they should have been addressed at some length in the situation analysis section. This approach for writing and presenting objectives is much more effective for readability and understanding because all four elements—effect, goal, audience, and deadline (EGAD)—are presented in a single statement. (See section 3.1 in Appendix A.) An alternative approach some organizations use is to separate goals from objectives, but this approach is not user-friendly and not recommended. The "unified" approach to writing objectives given here is much more efficient and effective, so no separate section about goals is needed.

STRATEGIES

Strategies specify the steps toward achieving desired results by identifying categories of activities (i.e., tactics) that apply to one or more objectives. One strategy may help fulfill more than one objective, making it an efficient means for realizing outcomes. For example, strategies can be media relations, events, social media, internal publications, interpersonal communication, and so on. Notice that embedded in each strategy is a wide range of tactics (see the next bullet list). For example, Mastodon, Facebook, LinkedIn, Instagram, TikTok, and others are the tactics of a social media strategy. Additionally, strategies can be approaches for inspiring cooperation through messages. In this vein, strategies include sharing the most salient information, inspiring groups to influence others, leaning on sources' inherent credibility, the force of verbal and nonverbal cues, and choosing channels that pique audience's interests, foster two-way communication, and invite audiences to participate. (See Appendix A and Chapter 7 for additional details.)

Strategies are categories of tactics. Each strategy must be directly linked to the objective(s) it supports. The reasons to employ strategies must be evident in the SWOT analysis (mentioned in the next subsection) and, possibly, other parts of a situation analysis (see section 2.0 in Appendix A). Strategy statements systematize tactics toward one or more objectives. Strategies, then, state simply, directly, and conceptually how any objective will be achieved by establishing categories for tactics. Strategies may be broad or narrow in scope, depending on the objectives and the target audiences. (See Figures 5.4 and 5.5.) The most effective strategies are usually those that can be used to achieve more than one objective. The following list (Hayes et al., 2013) shows basic categories of tactics that allow for several ways to convey messages that inspire cooperation between an organization and its publics:

- *Salient information*—Provide varying levels of information to different target publics depending upon their information needs.

- *Group influence*—Use existing groups to endorse and deliver the message to the target public.
- *Source credibility*—The character, ethos, and audience perceptions of a source and its expertise, believability, trustworthiness, and other personal factors are impeccable.
- *Opinion leaders*—Influencers; spokespersons; endorsements from members of the target public; third-party implied endorsement by or of the media.
- *Verbal cues*—Effective and consistent use of clear language and cohesive organization of content to convey intended meaning appropriate for the audience in all messages, slogans, themes, etc.
- *Nonverbal cues*—Effective and consistent use of images, mood, gestures, logos, colors, locations, atmosphere, etc. to convey intended meaning.
- *Selective exposure*—Place messages in vehicles/channels that the target public is likely to accept and use. Two basic channel strategies are:
  - *Interactive versus noninteractive media*—Use media that are interactive with the target public. Or use media that remind the target public of the message but require no interaction.
  - *Interpersonal versus mass media*—Engage the target public on an individual, personal level. Rely on the mass media to deliver messages to the target public.
- *Two-way communication*—Design tactics that enable the target public to communicate with the client.
- *Audience participation*—Engage the target public in activities that facilitate delivery of the message.

Writing strategy statements involves beginning with an objective. Then think generally about what you would do to fulfill it, and state the category from the list above. To each strategy you use for an objective, directly tie tactics that fit it (see Figure 5.4 and section 3.1 in Appendix A).

TACTICS

Tactics are the very specific forms of discourse you create or activities you will do that (1) fit within the strategy(ies) statement(s) given to support an objective and (2) achieve the stated objective(s) associated with them. When choosing tactics, it is vitally important that PR professionals *know*—because of thorough audience research—that target publics will, indeed, like them and use them. Because tactics could fit one or more strategies and more than one objective, simply list the same tactic any time it applies to a strategy that relates directly to it and a given objective. Sample tactics include any mobile phone apps, any social medium, press releases, news conferences, media interviews, annual reports, websites, trade shows, and any of the other PR discourse types shown in Figure 5.7 (also see Chapter 7 and Appendix A).

Tactics concern specifically how you will uphold each of your strategies to, ultimately, fulfill a given objective. Remember that public relations encompasses multiple

Advertisements	Magazines	Press releases
Advertorials	Matte releases	Public service announcements (PSA)
Annual reports	Media advisories	Satellite media tours (SMT)
Articles	Meetings	Social media (each specific one)
Audio news releases	Mobile phone apps	Speeches
Backgrounders	Newsletters	Tip sheets
Biographical statements	Photo news releases	Video news programs
Brochures/pamphlets	Pitch calls	Video news releases
Case studies	Pitch letters	Weblogs (blogs)
Fact sheets	Podcasts	Websites
Flyers	Posters	White papers
Frequently asked questions (FAQ)	Prepared statements	Wikis
Interviews	Press conferences	Written correspondence
Issue reports	Press kits	

Figure 5.7 Public relations discourse genres—Example tactics of PR

practice areas that focus on communication with particular publics that may or may not be stakeholders. Those PR practice areas can include media relations, employee communication, community relations, financial/investor relations, and others. Tactics, then, would very often be specific to a practice area and used strategically for pertinent audiences. For example, in media relations, the **PESO model** (i.e., paid, earned, shared, and owned media channels) would likely guide strategic planning for producing, disseminating, monitoring, and measuring messages to external publics in the best media to raise awareness about, shift attitudes on, and inspire action regarding some news (see Freberg, 2021). Also, for example, employee relations might use wholly internal channels to inspire employees to understand what is going on with an organizational change, embrace it emotionally, and act on it appropriately.

In tune with a stated strategy for a specific objective, tactics include the people, discourse types, or technology you will use; for example, reporters, face-to-face meetings, or wire service. A plan ought to mix and match analog, digital, and experiential tactics based on solid research (e.g., brand personality, medium/channel characteristics, and audience research) about the opportunity in all respects. Tools may be written, spoken, or visual means to facilitate communication between an organization and its audiences. Tactics also include actions you want to take or plan to happen. Example tactics are to get reporters to run a personal finance story about a new corporate bond; write a press release to announce an important corporate achievement, a unique perspective on the business or market, or other appropriate "newsworthy" subject; hold "briefings" between senior management and frontline supervisors about organizational changes. Still other tactics include the ways to get done what you need to meet an objective. For example, make a pitch to reporters that they may interview the CFO for a personal finance story on a new corporate bond; upload an electronic file via the Internet to wire service for distribution; have small-group, face-to-face meetings between senior managers and supervisors as part of an organizational-change program.

THE PLAN THUS FAR

An organizational plan, again, is the foundation or basis for all other plans shown in Figure 5.3 that an organization may need. Just as everyone in a choir must use a hymnal to sing their parts well and in sync, so everyone in an organization must work toward the same objectives. And like a choir, when certain members sing while others do not, each part of an organization will work differently to fulfill organizational objectives. For example, an organizational objective (applying the EGAD formula), "to achieve the number-one or number-two position (benchmark of Y) in all the markets it serves by the end of the calendar year," would require the work of people in research and development (R&D), manufacturing, public relations, and sales. But other organizational areas, like finance and accounting, human resources, and legal staff may not have much of a role to play or any role at all.

Notice a pattern developing here: a plan and its associated objectives begs the question, "How?" At the organizational level, the example objective—to establish a position as number one or number two in the markets the company serves—needs to indicate which operating units would play a role, and that is part of the feedback during the planning process shown in Figure 5.2. At the operating level for PR, the objective to lift customers' perceptions by a quantifiable amount would be addressed by certain strategies (e.g., media relations, customer-interaction campaigns, and advertising) that entail particular tactics (e.g., press conferences and editorial meetings; product trials; product placements, print and online ads, and Facebook).

So, according to the nesting relationship among plans described for Figure 5.3, an objective in the organizational plan must be assessed for its applicability to any and every operating unit. If an operating unit determines that it has responsibility and accountability for achieving any organizational objectives, that unit must address them in its own operating plan so that it is clear what strategies, tactics, and resources would be applied over time to achieve success. For example, in an operating plan for public relations, one objective that should help the organization establish itself as number one or number two in the markets it serves would be (using the EGAD formula), "to improve customers' perceptions of product quality by X% (benchmark of Y with a rationale for X) by the end of the second quarter in the calendar year."

All the parts of a strategic plan must fall within the scope of the company's **mission**, which is a statement about what business the company is in and how it applies resources to get the company closer to realizing its *vision*, which is the ultimate state of being a company wants to reach and stems from a thorough understanding of an organization's state of affairs and capabilities to attain that ultimate state of being. Figure 5.2 shows how these features in the process of strategic planning relate to one another. Appendix A shows a template for a complete strategic plan, including explanations about and examples for each section, including these given here. To ensure that the plan is working and, ultimately, is successful (or not), performance against the objectives must be determined and reported.

PERFORMANCE AND REPORTING MATTERS

Throughout the development and enactment of any plan of any type, organizational leaders and their staffs must monitor the larger economic and social environment for anything that may or will positively or negatively affect the organization's path to success. In a real sense, a strategic plan represents an ideal path to success. Figure 5.8 shows a visual comparison between the ideal path of a strategic plan and the probable, actual path for enacting a plan. The ideal path assumes a reasonably steady state of affairs. But remember that a plan goes out of date as soon as it is approved because it is based on information about the past, present, and future gathered and applied at a particular point in time. And that information about the future is the most tenuous, no matter how well defended it is, because many assumptions also go along with the predictions about the future. As Figure 5.8 shows, in reality many variables can and do change, which requires one or two or many alterations in the course toward the same target for success. Such variables could include changes in regulation, new competitors, mergers and acquisitions, emergency situations, and so on.

From vision and internal culture to local communities and broad markets, the data about operations, competitors, regulations, customers, and many other aspects must be followed to ensure that any plan is still on target, and if it is not, adjustments/revisions to it may be required, including the creation of a whole new plan if absolutely necessary. Information and analysis about critical success factors (CSFs) play an important role in (1) analyzing past performance and projecting ongoing performance in comparison to the situation analysis; and especially, (2) reporting on performance for better and for worse and recommending courses of action. Indeed, periodic reporting is required, and the schedule for reporting on a plan's performance will be dictated by management's needs for information. We will address **performance measurement**, **performance management**, and **performance reporting** in greater detail in Chapter 6. At this

Figure 5.8 Path comparisons between the ideal and probable actual paths of a strategic plan

point, however, we must look more deeply into the sections of a plan that are perhaps the most focused on performance measurements. (See Appendix A for additional details for all parts of a plan, including measurement.)

OBJECTIVES

As we have already seen, objectives are the primary points on which success (or failure) is measured and determined. No other aspects of the plan attract this supreme level of scrutiny, although other plan parts would be scrutinized on their own terms when a plan is successful or not. Required in any plan are performance targets—the goals specified within every EGAD objective. Those goals can be of any kind, such as financial, market, knowledge, attitude, behavior, outputs, outtakes, outcomes, outgrowths, and so on. As we have seen, fulfilling any objective is made possible through the stated strategies and their associated tactics. Attaining, exceeding, or missing any performance target is an indication of success or failure. As we already saw, objectives must follow the EGAD approach and specify one *and only one* effect that can be directly measured to evaluate performance within a given time period.

Because objectives are supremely important for measuring performance, there must be an accounting for as many factors that may act on it for better and for worse, and these are called "critical success factors." Also, to ensure that a plan is on track, measurements against the objectives must be taken periodically, and these are called "key performance indicators." Then, showing what it will take to enact the objectives are a budget and a timeline.

CRITICAL SUCCESS FACTORS

Whenever you would like to accomplish something of any type or scope, you probably imagine things that can help and hurt your ability realize that accomplishment. In strategic planning, the same principle is at play. You can and must imagine and document the kinds of things, events, circumstances, or whatever that could help or hinder success in enacting a plan. These factors that matter critically to success or failure to a strategic plan are called "**critical success factors**" (**CSFs**). The results of a thorough environmental-scanning method (e.g., SWOT) would be instrumental in identifying many of the CSFs that matter to a plan.

To make sure you have considered what can contribute to or undermine the success of your strategic plan, you must show what those things can be (positive *and* negative) when trying to meet your objectives. Those factors can come from several directions. More specifically, CFSs can be accounted for as follows and tied to each objective (see section 3.2 in Appendix A):

- *Opportunities*—occasions where an organization can capitalize on the situation to garner support and build its image.

- *Barriers*—include, but are not limited to, ideological, attitudinal, or social opposition to or legal, regulatory, or institutional restrictions on an organization doing what it believes it should to solve a problem or manage a situation.
- *Environment (internal and external)*—business issues command attention and fuel communication. For example, low profitability undermines a company's and its leaders' credibility; product problems and failures damage a company's reputation; third parties are reluctant to endorse a company; a merger or acquisition diverts attention to organizational changes.
- *Resources*—staff, technologies, facilities, funding, and other support required to fulfill communication objectives should be sufficient; such resources may be supplemented by knowledgeable and experienced outside resources to take on intensive special projects when required.

The table for CSFs that is presented in Appendix A allows for specificity in all four of these categories, as any number of examples may pertain in each category (column) for each objective (row). Additional explanation about the overall collection of CSFs may be needed to emphasize important "take aways" from them and what the collection means for successfully enacting the plan.

KEY PERFORMANCE INDICATORS

It is never a good idea to wait until after a plan or project is completed to determine whether it was successful or not. Waiting until the end wastes many opportunities to check on progress along the way, just as road signs give you an indication of where you are when driving to some destination. You must frequently determine the progress toward realizing objectives. Checking progress allows you to make any corrections, avoid obstacles, or capitalize on opportunities. **Key performance indicators** (**KPIs**) are a collection of important *formative* measurements of performance. Each formative measurement of the effect sought in a given objective is called a "leading indicator" for progress—it is a performance measurement of an objective that is taken periodically to show the degree to which the enactment of a plan is on track or not for that objective.

Note that measuring against any objective means precise, direct measurements of the effect sought. For example, if you have an objective that measures increased awareness of something and you only measure a publication's circulation or webpage hits, you have *not* measured awareness. All you have measured is the number of times a story was published or a webpage was clicked on; you have not measured whether people are *truly* more aware of your message. You must use a research method that will yield the data you need, probably a "pre-post" design that measures people's awareness of something before new messages go out and people's awareness of that same thing some time after new messages go out. For output objectives, you need only measure whether or not the thing that was to be produced (e.g., press kit, news conference, customer event) was produced when it was supposed to or not (and on budget). You may also want to use secondary measurements about effects of the output, such as people's opinions or, if the output is an article by an organization's executive, the reach and spread of the piece.

KPIs must be divided up reasonably over time so that the goals, as stated in the objectives, are realized by the end of the timeline. Any leading indicator must be tied to the respective objective it is measuring and take measurements at predetermined intervals of time leading up to the culmination of the plan (see section 3.3 in Appendix A). If possible, KPIs should be shown in comparison to benchmarks for a similar period. All KPIs must also ultimately build up to the final, overall evaluation measurements for the entire plan as stated in the objectives.

BUDGET

Also required in a plan is a **budget**, which measures performance based on resource allocations, especially in terms of money. A budget not only shows anticipated income and expenses, it also must include an analysis. Key questions to answer in a budget analysis are:

- What are the assumptions behind the data and resource allocations?
- What do you need to especially point out about the big picture of the budget?
- What are important relationships among items in the budget?
- Why is this budget reasonable and accurate as an allocation of resources to implement the plan?
- How will the results from achieving the objectives bring a **return on investment (ROI)** of the resources being allocated to this plan?

You must show estimated costs and note the sources/vendors for those costs in your budget spreadsheet. You must also keep records of the estimates you got in case someone wants to see them or has a question. Your budget must be detailed for all the components of each tactic. For example, if you want to produce a brochure, what will be the particular costs for writing, designing, printing (including paper), mailing, and evaluating it? Additionally, you may also want to show the budget for time along with each monetary cost. If you do this, make sure it is consistent with your timeline.

Again, budgeting is not only something concerned with money going out and coming in. Budgeting concerns the bigger picture of how resources—the primary resource being money—are allocated across all operational needs to fulfill a strategic plan. Other resources include people, time, facilities, technology, machinery, equipment, and so on. When money is allocated, it is often tied to these other resources (and vice versa), such as when salary and benefits are applied to people, rent and utilities are applied to facilities, and time is applied to the depreciating value of buildings, machinery, and equipment. A PR leader is supremely responsible for all budgeting matters and must make sure all budgets are on track by helping managers understand what is expected and reviewing budgets and actual expenses for accuracy and explanations. More information about budgets will be presented in the next section. These issues now lead us into the realm of basic financial responsibilities for public relations leaders, who are often without a background in finance and accounting.

TIMELINE

Time is also an essential performance measure, as time is a vital resource to manage. Presenting a **timeline** necessarily requires an explanation of the work to be done over time and why time would be used as planned. An explanation of the timeline, especially "pressure points" (i.e., when tasks overlap and resources may be stretched) and interrelationships among planned activities, is also absolutely necessary. Key questions to answer when explaining the timeline are:

- Can the program be done in the time allotted?
- Can the results be achieved in the time allotted?
- How will intersecting or concurrent activities affect the project, and what must be done or kept in mind to manage them well?
- What contingencies can be made if any time is lost?

Any plan needs a timeline, and it should be in the form of a *Gantt chart* (see Figure 5.9) or another visual method to show the span of time for all activities at once. A straight list of dates and actions can work well if it is very short, but even then, a chart would be much better because its content will be easier to understand because of the visualization of the span of activities over time. In a Gantt chart, such as Figure 5.9, you must show the detail for every tactic under each objective (using the same color family, the light-colored rows of cells are for each tactic, and they are beneath the darkest-colored cells to show they are associated with the objective). A strategic plan must be in sync with the organization's fiscal or calendar year. Figure 5.9 shows a fiscal year, beginning December 1.

FINAL EVALUATION

Always remember that the objectives guide all measurements of success, including KPIs and the final, overall evaluation. KPIs, as *formative* measures of performance, build toward holistic or *summative* measures when a strategic plan is completed—they define overall success/failure for the whole plan—against the objectives and compared to the benchmarks. Evaluations are *post hoc* measurements and methods for analysis of:

- **outputs** (i.e., PR discourse and tactics employed per any objective)
- **outtakes** (i.e., publics' immediate or short-term responses to tactics and messages)
- **outcomes** (i.e., publics' responses to tactics and messages over a "medium term")
- **outgrowths** (i.e., publics' responses that have lasted over a long term and indicate that the cumulative effect sought was or was not established) (see Lindenmann, 2006).

Figure 5.9 Example Gantt chart

Research methods of quantitative and qualitative designs are essential, and all final evaluation measurements must be linked to the stated objectives. Accordingly, the final evaluation approach for a strategic plan must give basic statements about what method would be used to measure each objective. Some key questions to answer when designing your measurement scheme are:

- How will you measure the success of reaching the plan's objectives?
- How have the critical success factors affected the plan's success?
- What have your leading indicators told you?
- Can you create a means for continuous feedback from your target audiences?
- Did the target audiences receive the messages?
- What was the reach and spread of any print, broadcast, or digital media coverage?
- How was the organization portrayed in media reports?
- What do people think about the organization now as compared to their opinions before the plan was implemented?
- Did the plan fall within budget and were the resources sufficient?
- What unforeseen circumstances affected the plan's success?

Final measurements are the culmination of what the KPIs measured along the way. Use the findings from the final evaluation to create future evaluations and communication plans. Finally, take the opportunity to note ways to improve things along the way and at the end of the project.

For the final evaluation, compile the data, analyze the results, and report on the findings. Also state your conclusions and propose ways to act. Use this report to help you create future evaluations and communication plans. Finally, you should take the opportunity to note lessons learned plus ways to improve things along the way and at the end of the project. Your postmortem analysis should address how to do things better next time, including alternative methods, discourse, channels, and so on.

FINANCE AND ACCOUNTING MATTERS

By now it should be very apparent that mathematics is a critical skill for public relations professionals, at least because of the need for measuring performance on financial and nonfinancial grounds. The financial health of a public relations function, just like all operating units in an organization, is usually something that public relations students do not learn unless they are minors or double-majors in some area of business, such as accounting or finance. Indeed, certain aspects related to finance are addressed in the previous section about strategic planning. Although the realm of information about *finance* (i.e., managing an organization's financial resources) and *accounting* (i.e., recording and reporting on financial transactions) is vast, there are certain topics that are perhaps the predominant ones that public relations managers rely on most on a daily basis.

To obtain a full appreciation for all the dimensions of finance and accounting, it would be best to take one or more courses in them, including a course in managerial accounting. Short of taking such courses, you may want to dive into the subjects on your own through books and other sources like those by Schoffner et al. (2011), Siciliano (2015), and Fields (2016). In this brief section we will focus on two selected topics: (1) **core financial statements** and (2) budgets and **forecasts**. In fact, these particular topics are especially potent when agencies research potential and current clients, and they are critical when corporations research other organizations for partnerships, competitive positions, acquisitions, or other business insights. Additionally, these topics are vital to seeing and connecting public relations performance both for itself and for a whole organization.

THE FOUR CORE FINANCIAL STATEMENTS

Any organization must keep track of its financial performance. Accounting is a discipline that is especially focused on that effort. Depending on how an organization is organized, its accounting records must reflect that organization, while at the same time upholding Generally Accepted Accounting Principles (GAAP), which are the rules for financial reporting for all organizations. These rules are developed by the accounting profession along with input from the U.S. government. The GAAP rules, then, serve as the framework for producing readable and usable information about any organization's performance and management's effectiveness in running the organization. The accurate and timely recording of financial and other performance data is, therefore, vital to protecting an organization's assets through effective management control and task control. Financial performance data are available to managers and top leaders for "slicing and dicing" in any way possible so they can see how strong or weak any part of the operation is at any time. In fact, a CPM system would allow managers to "drill down" to ever-greater depths of detail in performance data (e.g., projects and budgets) that pertain to the parts of the business for which they are individually responsible.

Standardized reports are used to show an organization's actions in terms of the kinds of financial transactions that account for them. In this way, these reports present information at the highest possible level as they cover a whole organization. These reports are prepared on a regular basis (e.g., monthly, quarterly, annually) so that management and stakeholders have the most timely, complete, and accurate information about organizational performance. Those standard reports are called **financial statements**, and they are of **four types** (Rich et al., 2010):

- *Balance sheet*—reports the assets (i.e., resources) an organization owns and its liabilities (i.e., claims that others, including investors/stockholders, have on those assets) at a stated point in time. The data for assets and liabilities must equal each other and, therefore, are said to be "in balance." If they do not, there is a fundamental accounting error somewhere. When reading a balance sheet, notice what the assets and liabilities are as well as how they are accounted for. Different classifications of assets and liabilities can be reported, and a balance sheet indicates how much an organization owns and how much others have a claim on any parts of the organization. Be sure to read the footnotes to line items because they give additional detail.

- *Income statement*—reports how well an organization has performed in terms of revenue, expenses, and income over a given time period. The simplest form of this financial statement (i.e., *single-step* income statement) fundamentally shows whether or not an organization is operating at a profit (i.e., net income) when revenue from all sources exceeds expenses or at a loss (i.e., net loss) when expenses exceed revenues. For *multi-step* income statements, three subtotals are important to note (Rich et al., 2010):
  1. *Gross margin (gross profit/loss)*, which is "the difference between net sales and the cost of sales (or cost of goods sold)" (p. 19) and shows the initial profit made from selling a product or providing a service.
  2. *Income (loss) from operations*, which is "the difference between gross margin and operating expenses" (p. 19) and shows how much an organization spends to sell goods or provide services as well as run the organization.
  3. *Net income (loss)*, which is "the difference between income from operations and any nonoperating revenues and expenses" (p. 19) and shows the "bottom line" as to whether an organization made (or lost) money in its operations.

  When reading any income statement, look at the subcategories of revenues and expenses and how the data are shown with specific line items that consolidate a lot of data about sources of revenue or expense. Footnotes to line items give additional detail, and you must read them too.

- *Cash flows*—reports on the flow of cash into and out from an organization during a period of time. Line items will show sources of income and outflow. Cash flow indicates an organization's creditworthiness because it is an indication of its ability to pay its bills. This ability to immediately pay debts is also referred to as *liquidity*. When reading a statement of cash flows, look at whether or not the final total is positive or negative and to what degree it is positive or negative for the period of time indicated. The more positive an organization's cash flow, the better. Make sure you read the footnotes to line items because of the additional detail given.

- *Retained earnings*—reports the amount of an organization's income that was kept for the business and how much was distributed to organization owners/investors during a period of time. When reading a retained earnings statement, look at how much income an organization earns but does not distribute to investors in the form of dividends. The amount of income kept for the business indicates how much organizational management plans to invest into the company for future growth. As always, footnotes to line items give additional detail, so be sure to read them.

These four financial statements answer key questions about how well an organization is performing *overall* compared to recent previous periods of its history, what economic resources an organization has and who has claims on them, and where the organization obtained its cash and where its cash went (Rich et al., 2010). The preparation of financial statements is part of the larger accounting cycle *during* a period of reporting (i.e., analyzing transactions, journalizing transactions, and posting transactions to the general ledger) and *at the end of* a period of reporting (i.e., preparing a trial balance of accounts, adjusting the accounts, preparing financial statements, and closing the accounts) (Rich et al., 2010).

Reading the financial statements is an important skill to develop as a manager because you need to know where in an organization's big picture your operation has its stake and what it contributes (see Berman et al., 2006; Ittelson, 2009). A particularly important section of financial statements that must be read is the "management discussion and analysis," also referred to as "MD&A." This section is the official narrative explanation about what the organization experienced and why, including financial data to demonstrate it. Again, the organization's structure will be helpful in finding into what line items in any financial statement public relations and other operating areas fit.

Where would public relations fit in? Very often PR work will be covered in the income statement in line items labeled with terms like "promotional activities" or "marketing." Remember that these line items consolidate a lot of data into standard, GAAP categorizations that make the complexity of financial information understandable to people without them having to know the deep details about every operating unit and every project or program it handled. As a leader of a core operation to an organization, you should be able to understand how and where public relations affects revenue and margins. You should also be able to help employees find how their work shows up in these statements and what these statements say about the strength and viability of the organization and the competence of its top leaders.

BUDGETS AND FORECASTS

Much of the deeper detail beneath these financial statements is found in the more pragmatic financial tools of budgets and forecasts, which are typically administered by managers (ranging from operational leaders to project team leaders) with the help of their staff members. Although we addressed budgets earlier in this chapter, there are additional, important matters to cover.

Budgets are anticipated, periodic patterns for income and expense over a given period (usually one year but it can be longer or shorter) for a particular organizational operation to an individual program or project in that operation. Budgets actually reflect an organization's true priorities and whether or not it lives up to them according to its values, vision, mission, and value proposition. The lines/rows in a budget spreadsheet are the "accounts" or "cost centers," depending on how an organization wants to refer to them. Budgeting "conservatively" is a preferred approach that calls on managers to be truly realistic about expected income and expenses—to not overpromise and underdeliver.

There are two kinds of budgets: **administrative** and **functional**. The first concerns a whole operational function, like that of public relations, and the second concerns individual projects or programs. Both kinds of budgets are tied to strategic plans commensurate with their level of activity. Administrative budgets usually span a 12-month period (a calendar or fiscal year) and cover planned operational expenses, including wages and salaries, benefits, rent of the business facility, telecommunications, postage, printing, and so on. These items are typically based on historical use, which serves as a starting point for expected future expenses. Functional budgets could span any length of time necessary to complete a project or program and make the clearest ties between results and resources allocated to realizing the plan for a given project or program. Key to functional budgets are *direct costs* for necessary material, supplies, and services (i.e., costs from outside companies engaged in the project/program) and *indirect costs* (i.e., items from the administrative budget and out-of-pocket expenses). Billable hours would be included also and broken out as a separate category in the functional budget for an agency.

A related financial tool to budgets is **forecasts**, which are very short-term views (i.e., days, weeks, months) of anticipated patterns of income only and are especially useful in tracking trends, such as sales. Forecasts have the advantage of being more flexible compared to budgets because the short span of time is more easily accommodated, but that short time span can also be a disadvantage for forecasts because the horizon for planning and action is always so short. Forecasts are also solely focused on income and not expense, but that focus on income enables managers to identify trends right away. Budgets, however, have an advantage of keeping an eye on the long term and the bigger picture of income *and* expense while also having the flexibility to accommodate changes as needed. Forecasts can be especially useful in public relations to indicate periods of time when an organization may not expect much income and promotional work could be planned in advance of such periods to shore up demand and, thereby, sales. Budgets and forecasts, then, are very potent tools for planning and executing public relations work that should be used in tandem whenever possible.

In either case, budgets and forecasts are kept as confidential information within an organization (i.e., they are not shared publicly). Most important, budgets and forecasts must always be compared to **actuals**, which are the data about real income and expense accounted for at specific times during a reporting period that a budget or forecast covers. Comparisons between budgets/forecasts and actuals provide managers with key information about how well plans are being enacted with resources that were allocated and anticipated. Reports about budgets/forecasts versus actuals should be generated and analyzed regularly—in sync with the reporting cycle for the financial statements. Just like the relationship among the various levels of plans, budgets and forecasts must roll up to the successively higher levels of budgets and forecasts. Being "on budget" is good and expected. Being "under budget" could be great, provided there was no loss in expected results and quality. And being "over budget" can be very bad, and there must be compelling and defensible reasons for it.

THE BUDGET PROCESS

The top leader in an operational area of an organization, such as the vice president of public relations, is responsible for developing and managing that area's budget—and does so with the help of managers of the various activities in that operation who have direct responsibility for particular parts of the overall PR budget. An organization's finance and accounting (F&A) department orchestrates the entire budgeting and accounting process, providing the framework and rules for creating budgets and forecasts in the way the organization needs them. This orchestration is essential because each operational area's budget and forecast must roll up to the organization's total budget, forecast, and other financial statements as needed. F&A, along with top management and the legal staff, is responsible for making sure that all financial reporting is in compliance with applicable rules and laws.

Creating a budget or forecast is a relatively straightforward process, and individual organizations have particular procedures and requirements for budgeting and forecasting that must be followed. Generally speaking, when a past budget for the same or similar need of any scale was previously created and is available, it can be used as the basis for determining what income and expenses would be expected under the associated plan to meet that need. If additional money or resources are needed beyond what was used in the prior budget, or if money and resources are needed for new initiatives, a manager must make a formal **budget request** that stipulates (a) what is needed and by when, (b) why it is needed, including the expected value that will be added, and (c) how much it will cost and through which provider. If there is no prior budget, the process goes on with as much documentation of anticipated financial impacts as possible. For forecasts, trend data about past and anticipated future revenue are used along with information about economic and market performance and direction.

The tactical elements of a plan dictate what should be listed as the income and, more likely for public relations, the expenses. Data must be gathered about every aspect of every tactic in the plan that covers costs in terms of time, money, people, equipment, technology, suppliers/vendors, and so on. Include items like postage, mileage, labor, overhead, and 10% for unforeseen expenses. These data then are broken down into categories (i.e., cost centers) based on the objectives they serve in the plan and are presented in a spreadsheet with the categories and line-item detail for each income and expense.

BUSINESS CYCLES AND BUDGETING

Organizations experience something called "**business cycles**," which are the increases and decreases in demand for their offerings (i.e., products or services) over a period of time. Figure 5.10 shows a graph of a hypothetical business cycle, where the middle of the year is the period of least sales activity for the organization. The more an organization's business cycle shows great demand, the more an organization stands to

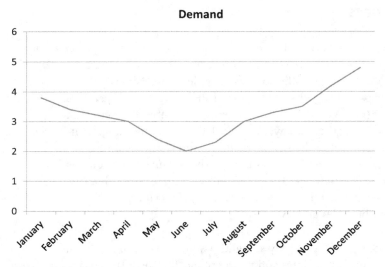

Figure 5.10 Business cycle curve for sales activity

gain in revenue. Conversely, the more a business cycle shows reduction in demand, the less an organization will see in revenue and it may even see a loss. One such cycle is based on replacing products after their useful lifespans. For very durable products that are used for many years, that cycle can be very long because the products do not need frequent replacement. An example of this is metal stamping machines for car fenders and hoods. Those machines can operate for many years, and only the molds and dies need to be replaced when a car design change is made. Less durable products, like socks, need replacement more frequently. Another cycle is seasonal, which includes industries like agriculture (i.e., the growing season), education (i.e., the academic year), and retail stores (i.e., holiday shopping) that have very predictable periods of great activity.

Because each organization faces its own business cycle, whatever and however long that cycle may be, organizational leaders must know and understand it so they can lead their operations in ways that make the most of the ebbs and flows of business and the revenue that goes with it. In particular, operational leaders, including those in PR, must use knowledge about business cycles to anticipate when during a year activity and the costs associated with it may be best undertaken. Forecasts can be instrumental in this regard. As we will see in Chapter 9, it is possible to plan for the rise and fall of business cycles so that the highs are not so high and, most important, the lows are not so low, which manages revenue flow as evenly as possible over time.

Throughout the process of preparing any financial reports or proposals, be sure to keep all documentation about all aspects of the budget, forecasts, actuals, and other data for future reference and, perhaps, defense in case there are questions or problems with the final budget document. Such documentation would include estimates from outside companies to provide goods or services that would fulfill any stated objective. Other documentation may be in the form of internal reports from other operational areas that are working with or have some bearing on public relations efforts under a given plan. Bottom line: the results of the plan must justify the costs for doing the work.

TIME MANAGEMENT

"Time is money" is an old saying that rings true all the time in virtually any business pursuit. Because time is a vital resource among many, it must be effectively managed. The best way to begin thinking about managing time is at the individual level of one's self. How does someone manage their time? Are they successful? Where can they improve? These are important, basic questions that require detailed answers. Personal time-management methods that someone may use to organize their daily work are essential, especially if such methods sort someone's daily "to-do list" in terms of both importance and urgency.

The more important and urgent something is, the more it must be done before the other tasks on the list. If other tasks are added during the day, the list needs revision. More important, on an operational basis, **timesheets** are very useful tools for gaining insight about time management. Insight about time management can be gained through timesheets not only at the individual level. When aggregated across an entire public relations operation, timesheets yield valuable data that are useful in two ways:

1. Calculating how much it would cost to do certain work of any scope, from writing a press release to campaign planning and execution.
2. Determining areas of inefficiency where work can and must be improved measurably while upholding high standards for quality.

Timesheets require a level of detail that many new PR employees detest because logging time spent on each project seems like true drudgery. Frankly, it is more fun to do the work on a project than to log the details of time and other resources and decisions of that work. However, timesheets are absolutely essential: they document what was done, how much was done, and how long it took, for what reasons, and by whom at every level (from intern to chief executive). Timesheets come in many different forms and formats, from sophisticated and secure online systems to spreadsheets or paper logsheets. Timesheets also are necessary in making sure you get paid for the work you do.

Fundamental components of timesheets are employee name, client, project name, activity completed, and time used for that activity. The time someone spends on work must be stated specifically and accurately, categorized appropriately (e.g., by client and/or project), and shown clearly to the nearest tenth of an hour (i.e., six minutes is one tenth of an hour). This means that tenths of an hour occur in multiples of six: 6, 12, 18, 24, 30, 36, 42, 48, 54, and 60. Rounding 50 minutes to the nearest tenth of an hour would be 48, or 0.8 of an hour. Note that 15 and 45 minutes can still be listed as 0.25 and 0.75 of an hour, respectively, but may be rounded up to 0.3 or 0.8, respectively. Timesheets must be filled in as someone completes their work on any project. Depending on the system formatting, a timesheet may display data-entry lines for the day the work was done or for a whole week, including weekends and holidays.

The more someone uses timesheets, the more aware of their work habits and efficiency they become. This result is a very good thing because everyone needs to know how they work and how long it could take to complete any assignment, and having the data helps in making such estimates. From a manager's point of view, data from timesheets are valuable to see how efficient public relations staff members are individually and collectively. Moreover, timesheet data are valuable as the basis on which to make estimates about what it will take to do one kind of job or another, and for agencies to bill clients for work completed under contract. Managers, then, must meticulously review each employee's timesheets against the projects to which they are assigned to ensure that budget limits are not exceeded. Timesheets are not just something used in agencies. Corporate PR operations use them to measure productivity but not for billing.

In the end, then, a system for time management that is both simple and powerful for individuals and management is necessary for an effective and efficient PR operation. Time management should and must be a value-added activity for doing public relations work because it is an essential way to document the business of PR professionals that shows contributions from the individual level to the operational level.

BILLING

Turning time into money is the realm of billing. Accounting for this matter about resource allocations used to bring a plan to fruition also is in the realm of billing. **Billing**, then, is the documentation of all costs that have gone into completing work on another party's behalf. People's salaries and benefits (i.e., compensation), operational expenses for the physical presence and equipment of a PR function, and the expenses incurred for particular programs or projects are all translated into billing statements, also called **invoices**. Whether at an agency or a nonagency PR operation, all work by staff members can be translated into a fair and competitive hourly rate. Hourly rates are much more common for agencies than for corporate organizations, but rates can be useful in determining relative costs for projects and programs that become useful in budgeting corporate PR operations. That rate also depends on external factors that, at a minimum, compare to the rates of other similar operations in the local or regional market. Rates for staff members and leaders are calculated similarly, but the rates are not the same. Agencies typically have a **rate card** that specifically shows what hourly rate is applied to the work its employees do based on their job titles. The difference between the rates of staffers and leaders is based on compensation matters that reflect the greater range of knowledge and experience of leaders over staffers, so the hourly rate for leaders is higher than that for staffers.

Note that the billing process, when viewed as a big picture, begins with estimates. When someone asks a public relations group to "**bid**" on a job, that means that person wants an estimate of what it will take to do the work they specify. (We will address these specifications, called "requests for proposals," in Chapter 10.) Estimates are not mere guesses, but rather, well-researched and defensible statements about the expected resource allocations that will be needed to complete a job. Those resources include, of course, time, money, and material, including mark-ups (to be addressed shortly). The value of timesheets and solid experience and knowledge now come into play. An estimate, then, includes a statement about the job requested (i.e., a mini-plan) and a breakdown of the amount of time and material needed to complete the job and the costs for personnel and material. Past and potential efficiencies must also be part of the work to develop an estimate.

If the estimate is accepted and a contract for the job is executed, work on the job begins. As the job progresses, all time and material costs are logged and documented (i.e., timesheets, receipts, and progress reports). When an agency purchases material for a job or employs the help of others as a subcontractor in the work for a client, it has an immediate liability to pay for that material and that subcontractor. To cover the cost for those payments before the agency's client pays the bill for the work the agency did, the agency may **mark up** its costs for the material or subcontractor by a percentage that covers the interest for having paid the subcontractor before the client paid the agency. A mark-up of 15% to 18% for out-of-pocket expenses is common in the public relations business. Mark-ups are understood and must be reasonable and defensible, and they may be negotiated, as a client may ask an agency to provide services "at cost," which means to not charge a mark-up.

Agency work may be billed in one of three ways, which is defined in the contract between an agency and its client: (1) hourly, (2) project, or (3) retainer. **Hourly billing** is the simple invoicing for the time and material used for completing work for the client. This approach to billing is the most common, and it is considered as the fairest because it is a true item-by-item accounting of what was done as it was done. **Project billing** involves invoicing for an entire project once it has been completed. Project billing is based on a client's acceptance of a holistic and comprehensive proposal for completing a wide range of work (e.g., a PR campaign or publication project) that includes all costs that will be accounted for in one invoice. **Retainer billing** involves a contractual relationship between a client and an agency that, for the same fee paid monthly or so, covers any and all work, no matter how much or how little work is necessary. This form of billing can be the riskiest for both client and agency because the cycle of business activity may be very high for a period of time, but later on very low. Forecasting becomes key in this billing approach. In theory, the retainer approach should balance for both parties over the course of a year, but very close scrutiny to budgets and results is absolutely necessary to make sure one is not losing money and resources. Because retainers are so open-ended in terms of the scope and volume of work that may be done, they can be renegotiated if cycles warrant higher or lower fees paid for the respective amount of work forecasted. Hourly and project billing are unlikely to be renegotiated because they are contractual obligations. Negotiation of any contract is best handled before signing, as Chapter 3 suggested and Chapter 10 will show.

One or more **invoices** for the job, depending on the terms of the contract and the duration of the job, show what was done, how much was done, and at what cost. Applicable taxes must be computed and included as well. Costs are itemized simply but thoroughly so that it is readily apparent how the work relates to the original agreement. A formal invoice is prepared and sent, thereby formally presenting a request for payment for work completed. Invoices, over time, function not only as proof of what was done and how much it cost, but they also function as benchmarks for future planning and budgeting. And when invoices are coupled with the full range of performance reporting about a given program or project, they function as points of comparison that may be used to weigh the merits of the same or competing organizations that may be considered for other jobs in the future.

Public relations involves the measured and ethical use of language and symbols to inspire cooperation between an organization and its publics. A key phrase is "measured and ethical," which refers to a strategic bias to the practice of public relations, not merely or only tactics. It also implies literally the application of methods of measuring performance and success. Strategy and the process of strategic thinking, as covered in this chapter and extended in Chapter 6, can be viewed as a systematic, forward-looking approach for a situation that, given certain parameters (e.g., knowledge, experience, research, timing, budget, resources, enacted environment), defines what must be achieved, how achievements will be made, and why the approach can be determined successful or not.

EXECUTIVE VIEWPOINT

A 158-Year-Old Company Lives Its Purpose and Puts Energy Transition at the Center of Its Corporate Strategy and Public Relations Efforts

Ulrike Haugen, Executive Vice President and Chief Communications Officer, DNV Group

Det Norske Veritas (DNV), which is focused on assurance and risk management, particularly in the maritime and energy systems industries, was founded in Oslo, Norway in 1864. At that time the Norwegian shipping industry was experiencing rapid growth and an international market for marine insurance was needed. The Titanic disaster in 1912 brought safety at sea to the forefront of public concern. International classification societies played an important part in discussions on ship safety.

Already then DNV developed its purpose of "safeguarding life and property," which was later expanded to "safeguarding life, property and the environment." When I joined DNV, I was impressed how important the purpose was for the company and that every single employee of the 12,000 employees working in over 100 countries for DNV knows the purpose by heart.

DNV was well prepared in terms of competence and impact when commercial oil was discovered in the North Sea. The firm came to play an important role in this new industry as an advisor for both authorities and oil companies. Today DNV is a leading advisor to the maritime and broader energy sectors with a growing focus on the renewable energy sector including offshore wind and solar energy.

DNV's group president and CEO Remi Eriksen put *decarbonization* and *digitalization* at the center of DNV's strategy shortly after the Paris Agreement was signed in 2015.

While the purpose is something that will stay and is today more relevant than ever, we believe it is important to review and adjust the company's vision every 10 to 15 years. In 2019 we initiated a comprehensive "vision and values project" with the objective to capture input from internal and external stakeholders to develop a vision that was giving DNV a new direction. We traveled around the world and held workshops in many of our offices to engage our employees in the process of developing a new vision. We also talked to customers and other external stakeholders. The board of directors of the company approved our new vision of "Being a trusted voice to tackle global transformations" with a simplified set of values, "We care, we dare, we share," in 2020. In the following year a new five-year corporate strategy supporting the new vision was launched within the organization.

The world is entering a decade of transformation. A decade in which the pace of the energy transition will be set. A decade in which humanity will determine the speed and intensity of climate change, where we will see significant change in our food, health, ocean, and transport systems, and where digital technologies will mature from experimentation into large-scale application.

These global transformations bring immense challenges and opportunities. Companies will need confidence to make the right decisions about complex systems and solutions. In order to reach our individual and shared goals, the world needs an objective and clear voice it can trust.

The strategic plan for communications and public relations has a direct link to the company's corporate strategic plan, which is called an annual operational plan (AOP), and receives a lot of attention from our top management. This CPR plan should not be developed in isolation but must be linked to the corporate strategic plan. Each business area and functional area including PR and communications, HR, and finance need to develop their parts of the AOP for a joint comprehensive plan. Our PR function is at the heart of our group communications team. The chief communications officer is part of the company's executive committee and reports directly to the group president and CEO.

Communications and public relations' part of the corporate AOP includes planned activities and related budgets; for example, campaigns linked to product or report launches, activities linked to important external events like climate conferences and campaigns with a focus on thought leadership and positioning around specific topics. DNV has developed a strong position in the area of energy transition with annual publications of sought-after reports, such as *Annual Energy Transition Outlook* and *Pathway to Net Zero Emissions Report*.

ENERGY TRANSITION CASE STUDY

In 2017 DNV's Communications and PR team was asked to develop a strategy to position DNV on the important topic of *energy transition*, which covers incorporating more and more alternative, sustainable energy sources rather than fossil fuels in all applications. The company was not specifically known for its expertise in this area, but with a strong research team and industry expertise it was able to develop a model to predict what the energy mix would look like until 2050. This valuable insight matters for companies in most sectors and is a business development opportunity for DNV to expand its services to existing and new customers. For example, for a ship owner who is planning to order new vessels, it is important to know what type of vessels are needed in the coming years (e.g., should more oil tankers be built?), or whether the demand for LNG is growing, or whether there will be a real pick-up of the offshore wind sector and construction vessels for wind parks will be needed. Investors investing in energy technology also want to know which technologies they should invest in, such as traditional oil and gas technologies, transitionary technologies related to natural gas and hydrogen, or renewable energy.

Together with our research team we developed key messages for selected target audiences. We made a report launch plan, which included physical customer events in several countries, a media relations plan that included embargoed interviews ahead of the launch, a strategy for social media and customer-communication e-mail campaigns. We set ourselves key performance indicators (KPIs) with a focus on the high-level results (effects) that we wanted to achieve, measurable facts (goal) for a particular public or stakeholder group (audience) over a defined period of time (deadline). The overall effect is the strengthened brand in relation to the energy transition topic for our stakeholders that include existing and future customers, industry experts, journalists, and public sector stakeholders. We set ourselves one- year goals and measured different metrics including the number of media mentions, the number of report downloads from our corporate website, and views and engagement in social media. We reached our goal of 150,000 report downloads.

ACTIVITIES AND KEY PERFORMANCE INDICATORS FOR THE CAMPAIGN

Activities	Key performance indicators (KPIs)
• Report launch with physical events • Press release and media interviews • Social media plan • E-mail campaign • Webinars • Internal communication to DNV's employees	• Number of media mentions • Number of report downloads from website • Website visits and views • Social media views and engagement • Number of leads (people who download the report and who show interest will be contacted by the sales team)

We are now in our fifth year of positioning DNV on the topic of energy transition with an annual *Energy Transition Outlook* report and supplement reports that are provided to targeted stakeholder groups. We have reached annual download figures of 150,000, more than 10,000 participants attending the livestream launch events, a strong media presence with news outlets in several countries writing about DNV's findings, and regular interviews with CNBC News, national media, and leading business publications like the *Financial Times*. High-level speakers, including ministers and state secretaries, are now part of panel discussions on energy transition during the report launches. The participation last year, of Melanie Nakagawa, special assistant to the U.S. President and senior director for climate and energy, and an Energy Roundtable with the German President were part of recent successes that boosted DNV's position and brand.

To conclude I would like to mention that building a position and brand through a successful public relations and communications strategy doesn't happen overnight. It requires a strong link and integration with the corporate strategy and ongoing activities over several years. The result of a successful public relations and communications strategy is increased business and revenue for the company.

KEY WORDS

Strategic planning	**Tactics**
Organizational plans	**Objectives (four types)**
Operational plans	**EGAD**
Project plans	**Benchmark**
Contingency plans	**Strategies**
Management control	**PESO model**
Task control	**CSFs**
Performance measurement	**KPIs**
Performance management	**SWOT**
CPM system	**Culture**
Vision	**Business cycle**
Mission	**Value proposition**

Timeline	**Actuals**
Outputs, outtakes, outcomes, & outgrowths	**Bid**
	Invoice
Timesheet	**Mark up**
Budgets (two types)	**ROI**
Budget request	**Rate card**
Four core financial statements	**Three billing types**
Forecast	

REFERENCES

Anthony, R. N. (1988). *The management control function*. Harvard Business School.

Ariyachandra, T. R., & Frolick, M. N. (2008). Critical success factors in business performance management: Striving for success. *Information Systems Management*, 25(2), 113–120.

Berman, K., Knight, J., & Case, J. (2006). *Financial intelligence: A manager's guide to knowing what the numbers really mean*. Harvard Business Review Press.

Bourne, M., & Bourne, P. (Eds.) (2011). *Handbook of corporate performance management*. John Wiley & Sons.

Buytendijk, F., Wood, B., & Geishecker, L. (2004). *Mapping the road to corporate performance management* (Strategic Analysis Report R-22-0731). Gartner Inc.

Clampitt, P. G. (2010). *Communicating for managerial effectiveness* (4th ed.). Sage Publications.

Drucker, P. F. (1994, September/October). The theory of the business. *Harvard Business Review, 72*(5), 95–104.

Fields, E. (2016). *The essentials of finance and accounting for nonfinancial managers* (3rd. ed). AMACOM.

Freberg, K. (2021). *Discovering public relations: An introduction to creative and strategic practices*. Sage.

Hayes, D. C., Hendrix, J. A., & Kumar, P. D. (2013). *Public relations cases* (9th ed.). Wadsworth Cengage Learning.

Ittelson, T. R. (2009). *Reading financial statements: A step-by-step guide to understanding and creating financial reports*. Career Press.

Keyton, J. A. (2011). *Communication and organizational culture: A key to understanding work experiences* (2nd ed.). Sage.

Lindenmann, W. K. (2006). *Public relations research for planning and evaluation*. Institute for Public Relations. Available online at: www.instituteforpr.org/pr-research-for-planning-and-evaluation/.

Mintzberg, H. (2007). *Tracking strategies toward a general theory*. Oxford University Press.

Rich, J. S., Jones, J. P., Heitger, D. L., Mowen, M. M., & Hansen, D. R. (2010). *Cornerstones of financial and managerial accounting*. South-Western Cengage Learning.

Robert, M. (1997). *Strategy pure and simple II: How winning companies dominate their competitors*. McGraw-Hill.

Robert, M. (2006). *The new strategic thinking: Pure and simple*. McGraw-Hill.

Scheer, A-W., Jost, W., Heß, H., & Kronz, A. (Eds.) (2006). *Corporate performance management*. Springer Berlin.

Schoffner, H. G., Shelly, S., & Cooke, R. A. (2011). *The McGraw-Hill 36-hour course: Finance for nonfinancial managers* (3rd ed.). McGraw-Hill.

Siciliano, G. (2015). *Finance for non-financial managers* (2nd ed.). McGraw-Hill.

Smudde, P. M. (2011). *Public relations as dramatistic organizing: A case study bridging theory and practice*. Hampton Press.

Smudde, P. M., & Courtright, J. L. (2012). *Inspiring cooperation and celebrating organizations: Genres, message design and strategy in public relations*. Hampton Press.

RECOMMENDED READING

Austin, E. W., & Pinkleton, B. E. (2006). *Strategic public relations management: Planning and managing effective communication programs* (2nd ed.). Lawrence Erlbaum Associates.

Beard, M. (2001). *Running a public relations department* (2nd ed.). Kogan Page.

Berman, K., Knight, J., & Case, J. (2006). *Financial intelligence: A manager's guide to knowing what the numbers really mean*. Harvard Business School Press.

Botan, C. (2006). Grand strategy, strategy, and tactics in public relations. In C. H. Botan & V. Hazleton (Eds.), *Public relations theory II* (pp. 197–218). Lawrence Erlbaum Associates.

Croft, A. C. (2006). *Managing a public relations firm for growth and profit* (2nd ed.). Best Business Books.

Dozier, D. M., Grunig, L. A., & Grunig, J. E. (1995). *Manager's guide to excellence in public relations and communication management*. Lawrence Erlbaum Associates.

Ferguson, S. D. (1999). *Communication planning: An integrated approach*. Sage.

Hameroff, E. J. (1998). *The advertising agency business: The complete manual for management and operation* (3rd ed.). NTC Business Books.

Lordan, E. J. (2003). *Essentials of public relations management*. Burnham.

Mintzberg, H. (2007). *Tracking strategies … toward a general theory*. Oxford University Press.

Oliver, S. (2007). *Public relations strategy* (2nd ed.). Kogan Page.

Roetzer, P. (2012). *The marketing agency blueprint: The handbook for building hybrid PR, SEO, content, advertising, and web firms*. John Wiley & Sons.

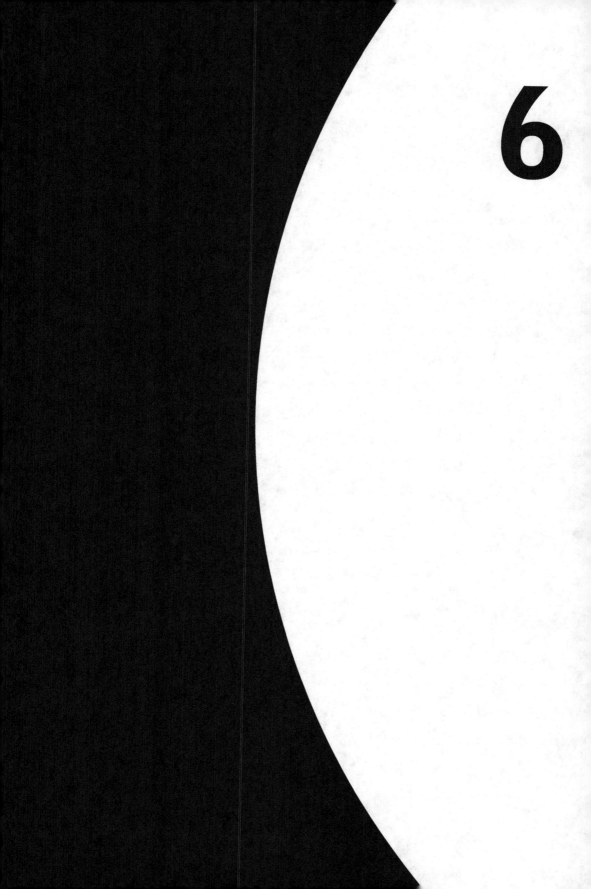

6

CHAPTER 6
OPERATIONS TOOLS II: PERFORMANCE MEASUREMENT, PERFORMANCE REVIEWS, AND HUMAN RESOURCES MANAGEMENT

CHAPTER OUTLINE

We are all in this together. That is, every operational area in an organization has the responsibility to demonstrate how it has contributed to the welfare of the whole. This demonstration is possible and necessary through the measurement of performance and, thereby, the management of performance through the allocation of resources stipulated in the strategic plan and budget. This chapter addresses generally the larger business perspective that public relations managers must know about—why and how to measure operational performance. The key topics, then, span the range from the whole public relations operation to the individual public relations professionals who make things happen. This chapter focuses on the important topics of performance measurement, employee performance reviews, and human resource management.

DOI: 10.4324/9781003208280-7

PERFORMANCE MEASUREMENT

A strategic plan includes performance measures in obvious places: objectives, key performance indicators, budget/resource allocations, timeline, and evaluation schemes. To determine value contributions, management controls are key, and performance measurements are the ways of tracking how well an organization and its operating units are getting the results needed to achieve objectives and realize the vision. (Chapter 7 will address the topic of value in more depth in relation to managerial decision-making.) Such measurements are based on data that are collected daily and reported on each day, week, month, and quarter—whichever periods are needed. These reports give management the information it needs to run the business, and the reports show employees how their work is paying off (or not). In general, accounting for value must minimally include regular and formal reporting (e.g., expenses, meetings, memos, progress reports) about the management of the public relations function and its constituent pursuits.

This work is part of a corporatewide system for management control, as we saw in Chapter 5. In that system, **performance measurements** are all quantitative and qualitative methods/tools used to evaluate progress toward or against defined objectives. Complementing the measuring of performance is **performance management**, which applies a combination of leadership skills and performance measurement tools to inspire people to attain or surpass objectives. Indeed, a corporate performance management (CPM) system, as we saw in Chapter 5, can be a software solution that undertakes the measuring of organizational performance and provides data to leaders so that they may monitor and understand the state and progress of the business in a variety of relevant and timely ways. For public relations, this system would naturally help to fulfill the PRSA's Code of Ethics provision for "enhancing the profession" by being a tool for making the business case for public relations, the role that it and its people play, and the value it contributes during dynamic times within and outside an organization. A performance-measurement system, as defined by Lawrence Maisel (2001) in a report from the American Institute of Certified Public Accountants (AICPA), is one that

> enables an enterprise to plan, measure, and control its performance and helps ensure that sales and marketing initiatives, operating practices, information technology resources, business decision[s], and people's activities are aligned with business strategies to achieve desired business results and create shareholder value.
>
> (Maisel, 2001, p. 12)

Simply put, a business measures what it must to make sure it achieves its objectives.

Indeed, for the public relations profession, concerted efforts have been made, especially over the last decade, to determine increasingly appropriate and accurate ways to account for public relations' value through well-defined methodologies (e.g., Horton,

2006; Paine et al., 2008; Watson & Noble, 2014; especially see the Institute for Public Relations). The purpose of this section is not to summarize any of those methods, which are amply explained and accessible in sources dedicated to them. This section is solely meant to present the big-picture business philosophy behind performance measurements and present one example of a dominant system used in performance management.

WHY *MEASURE* PERFORMANCE?

The point to measuring performance is to make sure that an organization and all its departments, employees, processes, teams, etc., work together in the best way possible to achieve the results called for in the strategic plan. The strategic plan, which was addressed in Chapter 5 and exhibited in Appendix A, is a detailed document developed by management that defines the direction of the business for a year or so by describing vision, objectives, and other matters vital to the company achieving success. The working together of all organizational members, systems, and processes means that everything is aligned and focused on meeting or exceeding corporate objectives.

From large, multinational organizations to small, local businesses, performance measurements are necessary to keep a company on track. Most important to having a system to measure performance, according to the definitive research by Franco-Santos et al. (2007), is to have a solid framework for what it will be and do for an organization. Two fundamental dimensions of that framework are the roles and structure of the business performance measurement (BPM) system. First, there are five roles that a BPM system should fill, many of which are obvious but are still vital to document. These roles are essential to knowing why performance must be measured so that a specific structure for measuring performance can be developed and employed. The following, then, are the essential roles for a BPM system:

1. "Measure performance"—This category encompasses the role of monitoring progress and measuring performance/evaluating performance.
2. "Strategy management"—This category comprises the roles of planning, strategy formulation, strategy implementation/execution, and focusing attention/providing alignment.
3. "Communication"—This comprises the roles of internal and external communication, benchmarking, and compliance with regulations.
4. "Influence behaviour"—This category encompasses the roles of rewarding or compensating behavior, managing relationships and control.
5. "Learning and improvement"—This comprises the roles of feedback, double-loop learning, and performance improvement (Franco-Santos et al., 2007, p. 797).

The second fundamental dimension of a BPM system that Franco-Santos et al. (2007) prescribe is its structure for measuring what matters. As you can tell from the roles, the measurements taken must represent those things that truly must be measured to show how well an organization is doing against its strategic objectives. In other words, the structure of a BPM system's measurements must provide data that can be used to reveal meaningful information about whether an organization is performing well or not, and that information must be usable and used to manage performance well. The following, then, are the essential categories of process structures for a BPM system that can be used at any level in an organization, from the whole business to individuals:

1. "Selection and design of measures"—This category comprises the processes of identifying stakeholders' needs and wants, planning, strategic objectives' specification, measures' design and selection, and target setting.
2. "Collection and manipulation of data"—This category includes the processes of data capture and data analysis.
3. "Information management"—This category encompasses the processes of information provision, interpretation, decision-making.
4. "Performance evaluation and rewards"—This category includes the processes of evaluating performance and linking it to rewards.
5. "System review"—This category includes the different review procedures (these procedures will ensure that there is a feedback loop within the system) (Franco-Santos et al., 2007, p. 798).

Any organization must be committed to applying these concepts so that everyone in the company knows where the company is headed and how it is going to get there.

WHY *MANAGE* PERFORMANCE?

Measuring the performance of a company, operating units, individuals, processes, programs, products and services, projects, and teams is critical to any organization's success. As the old saying goes, "You can't manage what you don't measure." Proof of the importance of measuring performance and then managing performance comes from a comparison of those companies that did measure their performance with those that did not. According to a study by Schiemann and Lingle (1999), companies that did measure their performance and manage their businesses accordingly substantially outperformed all companies that did not. Figure 6.1 breaks down the study's results.

Fundamentally, performance measurements are ways of tracking how well an organization is doing in getting the results it needs to achieve its objectives and realize its vision. Such measurements are based on data that are collected daily and reported on each day, week, month, and quarter—whichever periods are needed. These reports give management the information it needs to run the business (i.e., to manage performance), and the reports show employees how their work is paying off (or not). It is vitally important at this point to realize that performance measures focus on *both* financial and nonfinancial aspects of the business.

Measure of success	Measurement-managed organizations	Nonmeasurement-managed organizations
Perceived as an industry leader over past 3 years	74%	44%
Reported to be financially ranked in the top third of their industry	83%	52%
Three-year return on investment (ROI)	80%	45%
Last major cultural or operational change judged to be very or moderately successful	97%	55%

Figure 6.1 Comparison of measurement-managed and nonmeasurement-managed organizations

Source: Schiemann and Lingle (1999, p. 10)

If you think about it, financial measures alone only show you where the company has been and only in terms of its revenue, cash and equivalents, and debt and obligations. Financial measures are inherently lagging indicators about what happened in the past, not leading indicators for the future. Nonfinancial measures take into account things beyond finances that add value to the company and cause you to look to the future. Nonfinancial measures, like customer satisfaction, education, brand recognition, image, reputation, community efforts, etc., show key factors driving the business and indicate where a company is headed. The two kinds of measures together, then, make up a complete view of how well the business is doing in realizing its vision and fulfilling its strategic plan.

According to the American Productivity and Quality Center (APQC),

> performance measures allow employees to gain a greater sense of accountability, personal ownership, problem solving, and priorities based on stakeholder [e.g., employees, investors, suppliers, customers] needs. Organizations are likely to experience improvements in performance, fairness, objectivity, consistency, response time, and decision making. Performance measures also allow organizations to implement a common language and to be alerted to issues on the horizon.
>
> (APQC, 2002, para. 1)

Over the long term, the APQC says, performance measures have critical benefits to an organization. A performance-measurement system "can justify corporate support for [a] capital request, create an enduring focus, and justify capital allocation. Most importantly, performance measures are leading indicators of long-term health and consequently, [sic] represent a long-term planning asset" (2002, para. 2). We would look for similar benefits at any organization.

A company's own performance-measurement system can live up to these principles and, especially, accrue specific benefits that will help drive success. Measuring performance yields important and valuable information that, when used to manage performance, initiates and, ostensibly, sustains higher performance within an organization (Brudan, 2010). Some key benefits for a performance-measurement system lie in four areas:

1. Financial
   - Develop more accurate forecasts, based on customers in the pipeline, and produce these forecasts more quickly, which gives a clearer picture of demand that must be met.
   - Measure performance on a market-by-market basis to give a clearer picture of how well sales goals and company objectives are met.
   - Produce sales, financial, and performance reports faster with better data, which makes seeing and managing the company's competitive position easier overall and by market.
2. Internal business processes
   - Link an organization's mission and strategy, and then translate that strategy to operational objectives and measures—turning high-level strategy into action. Everyone works toward the same objectives in ways that pertain to their jobs, which means everyone knows what results are expected and how to achieve them.
   - Provide a link between lead generation and completed sales, which translates into knowledge about organizational performance.
   - Create a foundation for establishing daily, monthly, quarterly, and yearly goals for department, team, and personal performance, which means any measure can be viewed at any time to reveal performance in real time.
   - Make adjustments to or create new measurements as business needs dictate, which means an organization is well prepared to adapt to, measure, and capitalize on market changes.
3. Learning and growth
   - Identify opportunities and problems sooner, perhaps in real time, to meet sales performance goals, take advantage of strengths, and minimize weaknesses sooner.
   - Measure aspects of sales that tie back to the corporate strategic plan, which shows how work translates into the overall success of the organization.
   - Tie individual performance with team goals to recognize both, while emphasizing team contributions to the organization's growth, all of which means exemplary performance can be more easily identified and rewarded.
   - Encourage employees to enroll in education/training opportunities to expand their knowledge related to aspects of the business so that they develop professionally, personally, and intellectually in ways that also help the organization grow.

4. Customer focus
   - Track customer relationships and buying behaviors more effectively over time, which means anticipating customers' needs better and, consequently, building the business.
   - Know how customers feel about the organization and its products/services, as well as compare the organization to the competition, which means collecting and applying feedback from customers about organizational performance and its products and service.
   - Engage in effective communications within target markets to obtain new customers and inspire continued purchases from established customers.

These four areas of a business do not merely act alone (although each would be measured on its own) but, rather, work together (and the combination of all areas' measurements would yield a holistic view of organizational performance). The relationship among the financial, business, learning/growth, and customer perspectives of a business—as they support the organization's vision and strategy—is called a **"balanced scorecard" (BSC)**, and it is arguably the most-used performance measurement approach in the world. The BSC was developed by Robert Kaplan of Harvard Business School and David Norton of the Balanced Scorecard Collaborative (see Kaplan & Norton, 1996).

The four areas of the BSC have been visually organized in Figure 6.2 which puts the company vision and strategy at the center with the four key areas of any business

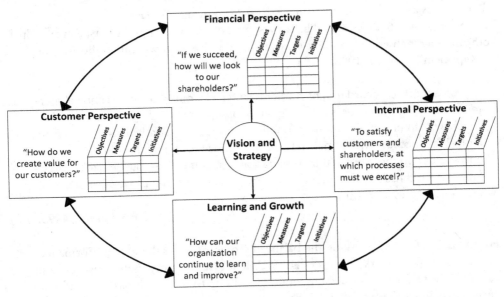

Figure 6.2 Balanced scorecard
Source: Kaplan (2001, p. 355)

radiating out from it. In the figure, given the approach to objectives presented in Chapter 5, "targets" would be the goals that would normally be stated in an EGAD-formed objective and associated benchmark. "Measures" are the specific metrics to be taken to measure goals/targets. "Initiatives" are a combination of strategies and tactics, leaning more on the latter, as means to fulfill the objectives.

A company's scorecard about its performance is said to be "balanced" when each of the four business perspectives support one another equitably, especially the financial perspective. More specifically, the balance that performance measurements should achieve is possible because they encompass essential dimensions that are financial and nonfinancial, leading and lagging, internal and external, quantitative and qualitative, and short-term and long-term.

There is an important distinction to note: the balanced scorecard is not only a system for measuring organizational performance, although it gives us a way to structure relevant measurements in each of the four business perspectives. The balanced scorecard is really a *management* system that helps an organization to clarify its vision and strategy so they can be translated into action by all employees in the work they do. In this way, the BSC is just the kind of application that would be integral to a CPM (corporate performance management) system as discussed in Chapter 5. The scorecard also establishes internal and external feedback mechanisms to ensure focus on both business outputs and outcomes through close examination of data from specific performance measurements and other sources. So this model is a useful way for a company to measure and manage performance on financial and nonfinancial dimensions.

All four areas are critical because they each help to manage discrete areas of the business in more effective ways. That is, when taken together, all four perspectives help a company stay focused on where it wants to go, not dwell on what it has been through. As Kaplan and Norton (1996) put it,

> The balanced scorecard retains traditional financial measures. But financial measures tell the story of past events, an adequate story for industrial age companies for which investments in long-term capabilities and customer relationships were not critical for success. These financial measures are inadequate, however, for guiding and evaluating the journey that information age companies must make to create future value through investment in customers, suppliers, employees, processes, technology, and innovation.
>
> (Kaplan & Norton, 1996, p. 7)

For the field of public relations, the balanced scorecard is not the only performance measurement framework; however, the BSC does give us a very useful way to capture data relevant to the operational function that rolls up to the organizational performance perspective. In particular, Vos and Schoemaker (2004) have explained a useful way

PR Quality Dimension	Financial	Internal Business Processes	Learning and Growth	Customers
Clarity	Clear positioning of the organization	Information to staff is clear	Communication vision is clearly defined	Clear positioning of brands
Environment Orientation	Maintain networks for the organization's reputation	Communication reinforces commitment and supports change management	Communication function is well embedded in the organization	Maintain networks for distribution and sales
Consistency	Coherence with other functions and with other communication domains	Coherent with HR and with other communication domains	Common starting points for communication besides room for organizational units and/or communication domains	Coherence marketing mix, with R&D and with other communication domains
Responsiveness	Monitoring and action based on issue management	Communication contributes to internal views on external changes and communication skills encourage internal responsiveness	Feedback is used for innovation of communication	Monitoring and action based on market research, consumer trends, and consumer complaints
Effectiveness and Efficiency	Assess corporate image, cost-efficient methods	Internal communication audits, cost-efficient methods	Assess communication quality, time management	Assess brand images, cost-efficient methods

Figure 6.3 Balanced scorecard for PR
Source: Vos & Schoemaker (2004, pp. 41, 44)

to apply the BSC for PR. Figure 6.3 shows how the parts of their approach fit with the BSC.

In their application of the BSC for PR, Vos and Schoemaker point to the most salient matters of quality in the practice of public relations that intersect with the BSC's four dimensions. The matters of quality are shown in the left-hand column. Each of these quality dimensions, then, is explained in terms of each of the four BSC dimensions. The result is a useful holistic view of how public relations value can be viewed and, most important, accounted for in particular performance measurements in a powerful performance-management system.

HOW ARE PERFORMANCE MEASUREMENTS APPLIED?

There are numerous financial and nonfinancial things a business can measure and report on. The trick is to select only the things that are critical drivers of performance under the strategic plan. So the availability of key information is essential in measuring performance and achieving success. And that key information comes from both internal and external sources that keep tabs on all aspects of the business important to management, employees, suppliers, investors, partners, etc. Most important, cause-and-effect relationships among the financial, customer, business processes, and innovation/learning domains help to determine which things are strategically important to measure and report on. Effective performance measures should fulfill the following basic conditions (Coveney et al., 2003, p. 71):

- Focus on key/strategic business factors.
- Be a mix of past, present, and future.
- Balance the needs of all stakeholders.
- Start at the top and flow down to the bottom.
- Have targets that are based on research and reality rather than being arbitrary.

A company will apply a performance-measurement system based directly on the company's strategic plan. The key parts of that plan are the company's vision, mission, objectives, strategies, and tactics, which were addressed in Chapter 5. Any performance-measurement system that tracks a company's results effectively will reflect the following characteristics, as described in Coveney et al. (2003, pp. 73–74):

- Align top-level strategic objectives and bottom-level initiatives.
- Identify opportunities and problems in a timely fashion.
- Determine priorities and allocate resources based on those priorities.
- Change measurements when the underlying processes and strategies change.
- Delineate responsibilities, understand actual performance relative to responsibilities, and reward and recognize accomplishments.
- Take action to improve processes and procedures when the data warrant it.
- Plan and forecast in a more reliable and timely fashion.

At a company level, several important financial and nonfinancial measurements will be taken regularly to manage an organization's business as effectively as possible. It is important for everyone to know that performance expectations are defined on an annual basis and applied periodically. This means that management begins a year with certain expectations, and each department works toward meeting or exceeding those expectations. The assumption is that performance expectations for the year will be met or exceeded as defined in the strategic plan. Only a major circumstance, like a severely faltering economy, a new and aggressive competitor, or unexpected heightened demand for a company's output, would significantly affect the company's ability to achieve its objectives and probably requires changes to the strategic plan and each department's work.

The company-level and individual performance measurements will be assembled into management reports that will be run twice a month (biweekly) so that everyone can see how well they are doing along the way, and not only at the end of the month when it is too late to address matters. Such reporting will present the best view of business performance (e.g., sales actuals and projections) over any period of time.

Monthly performance targets will be established and adjusted up or down so that they better reflect customer demand and projected sales. The specific targets for individual performance measurements will be defined together by each person and their management, based on projected sales performance and the strategic plan's objectives and goals.

The results of performance measurements, as published in the regular management reports, will help everyone see how well the organization is doing at any time. In this way, each operating unit—and each employee—can make adjustments to take advantage of new situations that come up or anticipate opportunities before they happen to make the most of them. The main idea is that we move closer to realizing the organization's vision and achieving its objectives.

PERFORMANCE REVIEWS

When someone joins an organization as a new employee, they learn about the many responsibilities and, especially, expectations for their position. So at an individual level, what each person does in a company has been distilled to the most important, measurable things that relate directly to the company's strategic plan and the individual activities that employees at all levels do. Other key performance measurements can be planned and tracked for particular team members based on their responsibilities, areas of accountability, and performance expectations.

These kinds of links among individual, operational, and organizational performance bring us to the topic of **performance reviews**. In any job you have ever had and will ever have, your performance in doing what is expected of you is key to determining whether you should continue to be employed and if you may be eligible for any rewards (e.g., pay raise, bonus, promotion, stock options, special recognition award) or for any punishments (e.g., pay cut, demotion, probation, firing). In every case, it is important to recognize that every organization has its own policies and procedures for conducting performance reviews for employees and others, including volunteers, outside firms, and so on. Indeed, in the big picture, performance reviews are meant to bring each employee and their manager's view into alignment over time. This idea is shown in Figure 6.4, which indicates how both internal and external matters of performance feedback have an influence on the process.

When it comes to employee reviews, there are common human resources practices and laws that must be followed. The leader of any operational function must work with the human resources (HR) department to ensure that all policies and procedures for performance reviews are followed. And those reviews require formal, periodic feedback at least once a year and probably at midyear or even quarterly as well. Other reviews would include informal, as-needed feedback while people are doing their work so they know immediately how well they are doing compared to expectations. Moreover, performance reviews are opportunities for dialogic communication between individual employees and their leaders, not monologic lectures from the leader to the employee.

Performance reviews depend on **four key sources** of information between an employee and their leader that facilitate a fair and principled judgment of how well someone has done, is doing, and can better do their job (Clampitt, 2017). The first

Figure 6.4 Bringing manager and employee views into alignment
Source: Clampitt (2017, p. 170)

source of performance information is **facts**, which are data about an employee's actual performance. The data concern chiefly the degree to which someone is either on track to or did achieve their personal performance objectives—simply put, what was done well, what was not, and what improvements can be made. As we covered in Chapter 1, a potent management approach for this source of information is management by objectives (MBO), which means that both an employee and their manager set the performance expectations for the employee's job—in tune with the strategic plan—and plot a path to success.

The second source of information is **standards**, which are written (and unwritten) statements about how to judge an employee's performance. These standards encompass general principles and precedents regarding their application to the facts about someone's performance. Everyone working in an organization is expected to know their jobs and expectations. Written standards are the most useful and include broad, organizational statements about employee performance as defined by organizational top leaders and managed by the HR department. A good example is Magna International's (2013) "Employee's Charter" (online at www.magna.com/company/for-employees/our-culture/employees-charter). Other written standards are most directly focused on any given employee and are documented in individual job descriptions and departmental plans. Unwritten standards are those that stem from an organization's culture and work environment, including such matters of "collegiality" and "professionalism." Indeed, the interpretation and application of all standards depend on precedents of how past cases of employee performance were judged as satisfactory or not plus whether conduct was tolerated or could be observed as acceptable.

The third source of information concerns **exceptions**. Factors beyond an employee's control (e.g., technology crash, internal reorganization) and factors unique to an employee's life situation (e.g., birth of a child, extended leave of absence because of health matters) can hinder or inhibit their ability to fulfill responsibilities and performance objectives. As a matter of fairness to both the employee and the employer, these factors should be taken into consideration and may, over time, become built into the standards when they make sense so that they may be applied to an employee's performance appropriately.

The fourth and final source of performance information is **judgment**. This source is the reasonable outcome of the previous three, and it rests well within the jurisdiction of the manager conducting the performance review to make a judgment. The judgment is not only based on the facts, standards, and exceptions the manager has collected and analyzed, but it is also made in response to the employee's perspective about the same matters. In this way, the performance review is a dialog about an employee's performance, with an eye toward continuous improvement in the future. The judgment also recommends rewards or punishments that are in line with organizational policies. Again, performance reviews given in either formal or informal ways must yield genuine and useful feedback whenever appropriate so that individual performance can be corrected or improved. A leader's role, as we saw in Chapter 1, is vital to ensuring success on personal and organizational grounds, and that means that all feedback must be actionable, not merely abstract.

As a matter of course for managing employee performance, leaders should keep good records about each of their employees' performance. The records can include any information from the four sources explained above. Moreover, leaders can help employees understand themselves and their contributions by using a SWOT analysis that focuses on their immediate jobs and their career objectives. Additionally, MBO can function as a useful and usable way to plot a personal plan based on the SWOT and include milestone checkpoints for progress. A relatively new approach to performance reviews is the "360-degree review," which fundamentally relies on the first three sources of information gathered anonymously from peers, superiors, and underlings (i.e., those who work all around you, like a circle). The information is then aggregated into a single report that an employee's manager shares and discusses with the employee during a formal performance review. These 360-degree reviews are typically done at all levels of an organization but may be especially reserved for people holding formal leadership positions.

Matters of performance at all levels can only be addressed through people doing what is expected of them, including finding ways to do their work better and going beyond expectations. Satisfactory—even great—performance begins with leading and managing the single largest, most expensive, and most important resource any organization has: its people. The next section about human resource management concisely addresses the matters of hiring, firing, managing, and developing communication professionals.

HUMAN RESOURCE MANAGEMENT

As we saw in the previous section, the human resources department is the key to all matters about employees. The **sequence of employment** is an interesting and useful way to concisely capture the "nuts and bolts" of hiring, firing, managing, and developing PR professionals. The sequence is based on a combination of Jablin's (2001) and Baird and Kram's (1983) work. The sequence progresses through five stages: anticipatory socialization, anticipatory organizational socialization, organizational entry, organizational assimilation, and organizational exit. Very important to remember is that the principles of effective leadership and followership from Chapter 1 must be applied instrumentally here. Figure 6.5 shows one way to visualize how someone goes through the sequence from initial interest to exit.

The convergence of the two lines of circles indicates the increasing degree of identification between an employee and an organization. The sequence begins with **anticipatory socialization**, which involves someone making broad career choices based on information gathered from many sources, ranging from personal to mass media, including family, school, peers, part-time jobs, internships, and other experiences. Next, **anticipatory organizational socialization** involves the specific targeting of one or more organizations that participate in the career or industry that was the substance of the prior stage. In this second stage, a useful metaphor is that of courtship between an employer and a prospective employee. The key in the courtship is organizational fit or identification. Realistic job previews through the interview process are instrumental in this stage. In some ways, culling through all the applications and resumes for a job can seem a lot like the playoff brackets for sports league championships, such as March Madness or the World Cup, at the very least because of the large quantity of applicants for any job and the meticulous process for evaluating applications fairly and efficiently.

Figure 6.5 Sequence of stages for organizational employment

Next in the sequence is **organizational entry**, which begins from the moment a job offer is accepted and extends into the first 6 to 18 months on the job, depending on the industry (public relations may be on the shorter side of this range). Instrumental in this stage is the "morale curve," when newly hired employees work through inflated expectations (even after the realistic job previews), culture shock, surprise at the full-time expectations, and ultimately the leveling out of expectations due to understanding, acceptance, and routine.

Forming a bridge from organizational entry is the next stage of **organizational assimilation**, which is the most prolonged stage in the employment sequence. This stage is sometimes referred to as "identification" or "metamorphosis" because there is a quantum change in the employee when the shared participation between the employee and the employer results in increasingly aligned perspectives. There also is an ever-improving fit between the expectations of the employee and their manager. In this stage, an employee's performance and record of accomplishment should soar, perhaps to also include opportunities to *mentor* new employees who seek the benefits of this kind of professional relationship. In the organizational assimilation stage, four dimensions emerge: (1) *establishment*, which is an employee demonstrating their commitment to the organization and vice versa, including any professional development opportunities (e.g., subject-specific education and experiences through coursework, seminars, and other training); (2) *advancement*, which is an employee's progress to increasing levels of authority, responsibility, and accountability through more exposure to others, challenging work, and other involvement opportunities; (3) *maintenance*, which is an employee's realization that they have reached the zenith of their career and will likely end their career at this level; and (4) *withdrawal*, which includes an employee playing more consultative roles within the organization and their operating unit and then, eventually, actively preparing for the final stage of organizational exit. In terms of mentoring, the ideal time to strike up a mentor– mentee relationship between an assimilated employee and a newer employee is in the dimension of maintenance because the other dimensions involve too much self-focus on the part of the would-be mentor.

That final stage in the sequence is **organizational exit**, which concerns employment termination, which can be the result of one of several circumstances— quitting, firing, laying off, dying, or retiring. What is very important to recognize about organizational exit—for those quitting, being laid off, or especially, retiring—is that exiting employees may hold a special affinity for their former organization. People who quit on good terms can still be interested in keeping abreast of what is going on, primarily through former coworkers who are also personal friends. Those who are laid off may harbor ill feelings toward the organization or they may be more accepting. It is paramount that an organization which lays off employees treats them respectfully and helpfully as they forcibly change their career trajectories. For people who die, their coworkers may experience feelings of loss and, perhaps, surprise at their comrade's passing, if the death was caused by an accident or another unexpected calamity. Most important, though, are retirees. These people have spent the bulk of their careers with an organization and have strong emotional and financial ties to it. In many ways, retirees are still insiders, or part of the "family," and they expect good treatment by the organization and its representatives—beyond the pension and benefits due to them—in return for the loyal service and important contributions they made during their years of formal employment.

Given this broad view of the employment sequence, we can focus next on particularly salient matters at the core stages that include hiring, firing, and developing employees.

HIRING

The hiring process spans the stages of anticipatory organizational socialization and organizational entry—from the job definition as advertised for the purpose of soliciting applications to the new employee's first day on the job. A critical point to the hiring process is to ensure that you follow the policies and procedures specified by your organization's HR department every step of the way, which must adhere to employment laws. Barring a lengthy narrative, the following outline summarizes the salient matters to conducting a sound hiring process.

- No clones of you! Look for people smarter than you and with skills needed in your group—*adding value.*
- Define the job.
  - o Obtain or create a definitive job description (used for screening candidates' worthiness).
  - o Decide on full-time, part-time, contract, or job sharing, based on personnel needs for the team.
  - o Define salary target, primarily based on industry comparisons and budget limits.
  - o The basis for the job definition is the "ideal" candidate for what is needed.
- Job posting and channels
  - o Usual channels: organization's website, job-search sites, social media, mainstream and professional/industry organizations' publications and websites
  - o Personal: professional search firms, especially for public relations, marketing, and corporate communication
  - o Outsourcing: freelancers, agency, consultants, vendors, temporary employment firm
- Collect and screen submissions—compare each applicant to the criteria of the job definition and expectations for qualifying, complete applications.
- Select and call candidates to interview.
  - o Carefully listen to and take note of the person and what is going on in the background during the phone conversation.
  - o Give information about what to prepare/bring, including a basic agenda for a candidate's visit.

- o Conduct background checks on and note any peculiarities about prime candidates' credit, social media presence, criminal record, search-engine hits, and other areas (see National Labor Relations Board, n.d.).
- Interview candidates individually (no group interviews).
- Check with HR for legal and organizational parameters for the whole process.
- Design and obtain HR's approval for interview questions and basic agenda.
- Pay attention to verbal and nonverbal dimensions of candidates.
- Probe their thinking, communication, and other things with questions and tests, including writing and personality tests.
- Look for personality and enthusiasm fits.
- Review and discuss competencies, credentials, and experiences.
- Don't cultivate confrontational situations.
- Realize that interviews primarily reveal how well someone interviews.
- Contact references and ask probing questions—within the law.
- Additional post-interview tasks for candidate (e.g., tests and problem-solving tasks)?
- Design offer with HR and boss based on:
  - o Salary range (operational budget)
  - o Candidate's salary history and credentials
  - o Competition (if possible)
  - o Human Resources Management Association database
  - o U.S. Department of Labor statistics on salaries and benefits
- Decide on the candidate with HR and boss.
- Offer position, pay, and benefits; engage in negotiation (presume success for both parties); determine starting date.
- Give introductions and begin orientation on starting day.
- Have workstation and all other things ready.

EQUITY, INCLUSION, DIVERSITY, AND ACCESS

At the most fundamental level, the common currency for what determines someone's eligibility to work and hold a particular job is their combination of knowledge, skills, abilities, and experience that make them stand out as well-qualified and highly promising. Other factors, like their character, attitude, reputation, personality, and others also can come into play as needed and allowed or protected by law. In the field of public relations, much study has shown disparities among employees at all levels, from men holding more top-level jobs than women, to the industry seeming to be one more for women than for men, to the industry being "too white" (e.g., Bardhan, 2021; Chitkara, 2018; Grunig et al., 2001; Khazan, 2014; Landis, 2019; Lehal, 2011; Mundy, 2016; Saunders & Monzón, 2021; Toth 2009). Table 6.1 shows statistics in the United States for people employed in communication professions, where public relations is tied with advertising and "related services" (U.S. Bureau of Labor Statistics, 2022). While these

Table 6.1 U.S. statistics for communication professions

Industry	2021					
	Total employed (in thousands)	Women	White	Black or African- American	Asian	Hispanic or Latino
Advertising, public relations, and related services	554	49.6	81.6	9.4	7.4	10.2

Source: U.S. Bureau of Labor Statistics (2022)

data are informational, they are not specific enough for the PR field; nevertheless, they are still revealing as they pertain to equity, inclusion, diversity, and access.

Equity is a function of fairness and justice for all. Equity encompasses two essential areas: (1) the treatment, access, opportunity, and advancement for people; and (2) identifying and eliminating barriers that inhibit or prevent people from participating, particularly people who have been historically excluded from participating. Fairness is joined, then, with justice to ensure that organizational or institutional systems of policy, processes, procedures, and resource allocations are enacted in ways that enable people to thrive (Wallace & Luttrell, 2021).

Inclusion concerns the creation and maintenance of environments where people can be and can feel genuinely welcome, respected, supported, and valued. Such an environment thrives on diversity that is not hampered by explicit (i.e., conscious/overt) or implicit (i.e., unconscious/covert) biases that inhibit inclusion. Respectful language, symbols, visuals, and behaviors are not only sensitively and upliftingly employed, but they also invite people to see themselves as engaged participants in the environment (Blow & Monzón, 2020; Wallace & Luttrell, 2021).

Diversity includes both similarities and differences among people, which subsumes (but is not limited to) dimensions of race, age, gender and gender identity, sexual orientation, religion/spirituality, marital status, language, culture, national origin, immigration status, class, socioeconomic status, mental or physical ability, education, or intellectual traditions (Saunders & Monzón, 2021; Wallace & Luttrell, 2021).

Access provides anyone, in tune with the concept of diversity and regardless of human ability or experience, with open avenues for participation that also provide resources to do what one needs to do as well as representation in published content about an organization or institution. All people are invited, encouraged, and supported by an organizational or institutional system so they may thrive in it through their participation to any degree.

Figure 6.6 Public relations role in equity, inclusion, diversity, and access
Source: Adapted from Mundy (2016)

Enacting equity, inclusion, diversity, and access for the public relations profession is something all PR professionals can and must do. Dean Mundy (2016) shows that the public relations literature and the organizational management literature about diversity synthesize into a coherent perspective for effectively and prudently enacting diversity, inclusion, equity, and access. Mundy explains that there are both structural and cultural dimensions to equity, inclusion, diversity, and access. At the same time, there are internal and external dimensions that intersect with the structural dimensions. Figure 6.6 shows what those intersecting dimensions include (adding the structural feature of policies) and how they interact so that public relations can exercise its expertise in applying them in and for an organization as well as for and with an organization's publics.

Public relations, as Mundy explains it, is uniquely qualified for what it is and does for people, organizations, and beyond to be a balancing and even a driving force for equity, inclusion, diversity, and access. In this way the model is just as much about enacting equity, inclusion, diversity, and access as it is about making sure that communication messages (verbal, nonverbal, and symbolic) uphold the principles of equity, inclusion, diversity, and access for all publics.

Very importantly for the public relations field, there are wonderful examples of diverse people and voices who have been outstanding PR professionals and leaders. Presently, the best single source showcasing them is Shelley and Barry Spector's (2018) book, *Diverse Voices: Profiles in Leadership*. The Museum of Public Relations (www.prmuseum. org/) also has rich resources for learning about the PR profession and, especially, the diversity of those who contributed so mightily to PR being the vital organizational and social function it is. In addition, the Public Relations Society of America's *D&I Toolkit*

(Saunders & Monzón, 2021) is a highly usable and comprehensive source about equity, inclusion, diversity, and access for PR professionals. The Institute for Public Relations likewise offers a wide-ranging body of research in its Center for Diversity, Equity, and Inclusion (https://instituteforpr.org/center-for-diversity-equity-and-inclusion/).

Three keys are useful here. The first is *self-awareness and self-improvement*, which necessarily go together as you become conscious about your beliefs, culture, biases, and privileges that influence your thoughts, feelings, and behaviors. A catalyst for this heightened self-awareness is expanding your knowledge of and sensibility about others, diverse cultures, and identity groups through credible and authoritative sources such as readings, documentaries, conversations with people, and other sources. The second key is *love*, which is willing the good of another as other (i.e., *agape*). As such, love would correct for human imperfections that allow for racism, agism, sexism, and other 'isms. So love is at the heart of antiracism as well as the principles that underlie equity, inclusion, diversity, and access. The third key is being an *accomplice*, which relies on the first two keys. Being an accomplice means you enter into someone's chaos and use your influence, position, privilege, and yourself to lift up others who have encountered systemic barriers; and then you accompany them to the best of your ability in their pursuit of the same dreams all people share for happiness, security, healthfulness, prosperity, dignity, respect, and so on.

Equity, inclusion, diversity, and access are matters that are very fundamentally the right things to do for everyone always. Having an organization or institutional system that includes barriers (intentional or not) to people anticipating entry to an organization, entering it, assimilating in it, and exiting it with dignity, pride, and a sense of accomplishment is morally and ethically wrong. Wherever and whenever barriers of any kind or scope exist, they must be removed and the system improved so everyone can thrive. You will need to wisely discern how you can enable such improvements.

TOXIC EMPLOYEES

The imperfection of humans is at the root of why we do not always get along with one another. But that imperfection doesn't excuse us for not "playing together nicely in the sandbox." In the workplace, whether that sandbox is as large as an organization or as small as a work team, personal relationships among people obviously are instrumental. So what is the deal when someone asserts persistent anger, resentment, bad attitudes, and any other way of kicking sand in the faces of others and what they are doing?

Employee relationships are the microcosm of internal communication challenges. For all the work that organizational leaders and employee-communication professionals may do, individuals are likely the single greatest variable in what can go right or wrong in an organizational environment. Employees span the continuum from exemplary to toxic, and both influence organizational performance at varying levels, depending on the spread of their elixir or venom, respectively, through their communication behaviors.

The degree to which those behaviors are supportive or not affects the reception, buy-in, and action on organizational messages. Very much of the time employee populations are largely skewed with more positive workers than negative, yet the negative ones can be so problematic.

The problems begin when you cannot know them when you see them—when you first interview them. Divisive personality traits, like deception, anger issues, grudge-holding, self-centeredness, vindictiveness, antagonism, negativity, and so on are not apparent so early on. Many organizations want and need to know about the characters of their prospective (and current) employees; accordingly, "tests" for personal integrity and ethics (PsychTests, 2016) may be used to identify toxic workers sooner rather than later. Even so, with the population of employees in an organization, knowing how positive or detrimental someone may be won't become apparent until they begin working with others and establishing a personal performance reputation.

Being aware of the phenomenon of **toxic employees** is a big step toward not hiring them (ideally) or (more likely) trying to help them reform, if possible. Robert Sutton (2007) identifies salient issues about these underminers of one's own and an organization's self-efficacy, and addresses ways to turn around the problem for the person and the organization. Michael Housman and Dylan Minor (2015) present valuable research on the affects and effects of toxic asshole bullies. Important to both of these examinations of the topic is that positive results can be obtained by either (a) converting the problem child to become at least an average performer or (b) avoiding or dismissing the person altogether after conversion efforts are applied but fail. The starting point is constructive interpersonal communication between a manager and the toxic person that, in turn, both helps them improve personally and begins that person's alignment with organizational messages and expectations.

Where conflict can and should be a positive thing that drives creativity because of the clash of perspectives and a unified desire among people to achieve success together (see Chapter 2), conflict can be negative when one or more people seize opportunities to assert control along the lines of a personal agenda. Especially insightful is Amy Gallo's (2016) counsel about managing toxic workers; she demonstrates how much toxic employees' venom infects the workplace and what behaviors may be behind the person's need to spread their venom. Discipline, listening, compassion, realism, and next steps about all dimensions of the toxicity are key. And as more than one study shows, forgiveness can and should be instrumental in a process of restoring harmony and rebuilding trust in the workplace (Worthington et al., 2010). *There is one caveat, however: sometimes people do not want to change.* In such instances, the manager/supervisor must be sure that there is a sound, documented case for the person's dismissal or other reasonable consequences.

Fundamentally, toxic employees can be found at any organizational level, and in this regard, all are followers as much as they are members of the same organization, whether they hold formal leadership/management positions or not. Toxic employees among organizational leaders tend to poison the culture from the top down, which at the very least undercuts corporate messaging and *esprit de corps* as a leader's words and actions are questionable. Toxic employees among "rank and file" personnel tend to create localized infections that subvert organizational and team messages, performance, and team spirit and could spread if sympathizers become allies.

Leaders have the special challenge to determine effective ways to involve followers (toxic and not) and enable critical-analytical thinking to achieve success. Recall from Chapter 1 Kellerman's (2008) five follower types in terms of their respective levels of engagement (i.e., from feeling/doing nothing to feeling/doing more than what's expected). Also recall from Chapter 2 the dynamics of teams and consider the importance of toxic people working on projects.

When we were much younger and playing with our siblings and peers, we learned how to play nicely together, and squabbles with others helped us learn how to deal with conflict. As we grew up, our interactions with others grew in complexity along with our understanding of who we are in relation to ourselves, others, and the world. Toxic people have been there with us all along. Effective organizational leaders look after their followers and other leaders, and effective followers look after each other and their leaders. In short, we're all in this together. So the point is to recognize toxic people early and fairly, and then the next step is to help them for their own good and the organization's good, even if that means firing them.

FIRING

The firing process is confined to the stage of organizational exit, and it spans activities from initial notification of a problem to formal dismissal. Organizations do not want to be accused of and party to a lawsuit claiming "**wrongful dismissal**," so it is imperative that the firing process follows the policies and procedures specified by your organization's HR department every step of the way, all of which uphold the law (see Orey, 2007). In short, you have to build a case for trying to help the employee redeem themself and the employee's successfulness in doing so. Again, instead of a lengthy narrative, the following outline summarizes the salient aspects of conducting a sound and basic firing process.

- Discuss with HR for procedure and policies.
- Document any and all problems and link them to the job definition and performance expectations, even if either or both of them have been revised.
  - Discuss problems and expectations with the employee privately, rationally, and earnestly.
    - Use the full personnel file and records about the employee.
    - The discussion serves as fair warning about the consequences of continued poor performance.

- Decide mutually on next steps to solve the performance problems:
  - Performance expectations
  - Timeline for completion (usually 90 days)
  - Documentation of performance.
- Document and monitor the employee's progress on expectations *within the specified timeframe.*
- Give feedback promptly (positive and negative).
- If the employee is still not cutting it, follow firing organization's firing procedures.

A special case of firing is **layoffs**. Remember that employees represent the single largest expense to organizations. Layoffs are imposed on many employees at once in multiple areas of an organization in which employment costs are the most effective means for cutting operating costs. Decisions for laying off employees are never taken lightly, and many in management literally lose sleep for days before and after layoff announcements because they care about people. The plan behind layoffs is to reduce the organization's costs and have funds to rebuild the business. In PR agencies, when accounts are lost, entire account teams (leaders and followers) may be laid off because the work they used to do is gone and there may be nowhere in the agency to absorb anyone from the team. In corporations, it is likely that individuals would be laid off in a PR department, and perhaps that department is reorganized with another, like advertising.

A major result of layoffs includes job consolidations, so those who are not laid off will be picking up what those laid off used to do. Great care is taken in deciding in which areas of an organization any layoffs should be made so that losses in productivity and, most important, in performance can be minimized with fewer people on hand. Layoffs are not necessarily about people's performance, but that concern can play a role when having to choose whom to lay off and whom to keep. Another result in layoffs is fear and remorse among those who are still employed because they, too, feel badly for their former colleagues and are fretful for the future of the organization. If you are laid off, you would be entitled to certain benefits for having been laid off, such as severance pay and job-search help. Chapter 11 covers matters about seeking employment that also apply in a layoff situation.

In the case of layoffs and quitting, organizations may ask these employees leaving the organization to participate in an **exit interview**. Exit interviews are important and nonconfrontational opportunities for an organization to learn what employees think about their organization's strengths, weaknesses, and opportunities for improvement. Exit interviews would be held on an employee's final day of work, led by either the employee's manager or a human resources representative, and use a prepared questionnaire through which information, ideas, and comments are gathered. Exit interviews are not normally conducted with employees who are fired for poor performance, breaking organizational policies, or other relevant grounds for discontinuing employment. For anyone leaving an organization, whether or not they go through an exit interview, any personal identification cards, keys, cell phones, computers, and other company property provided to them to do their jobs will be taken. Immediately after an employee leaves, all points of online and other access the employee had to the organization will be terminated, as will the former employee's pay and benefits.

DEVELOPING EMPLOYEES

Developing employees belongs to the organizational assimilation stage of the employment sequence, and the material in Chapter 1 is most applicable. Check with your organization's HR department about any rules and restrictions on professional development for employees. The principal idea in developing employees is to help them become better and better at what they do, how they do it, and who they are while at work. Also, in an effort to avoid a lengthy narrative and get to the point, the following outline summarizes the salient issues when conducting a sound **employee development** process.

- Help establish a sense of ownership of the business by
  - o   connecting the dots between the organization's objectives and performance and employees' role in them
  - o   applying and excelling in knowledge, skills, and experiences
  - o   involving them in goal-setting and other appropriate matters
  - o   establishing ways to measure/document their performance.
- Conduct effective formal and informal performance reviews.
- Seek and recommend educational opportunities for employees based on job and/or career objectives.
- Entertain suggestions from employees for educational/professional development opportunities (e.g., degree or certificate programs, classes, conferences, workshops, seminars).
- Have educated/developed employees share/summarize what they learned and how it would be helpful to others and the group.

Major corporations and many other organizations of every type already recognize public relations' value by including it as a stand-alone, executive management function. But the vast majority of organizations do not. Public relations professionals must understand their organizations' basic business issues, management theory, performance measurement, and the work of their peers in other organizational functions. The bottom line: public relations' value can only be known and appreciated when it can be clearly demonstrated as directly linked to an organization's business strategy and performance. The operations management tools of this chapter and Chapter 5 subsume many of the salient features of successful public relations management and, most important, show how to connect the dots between the operating area and an organization's larger business. In the next chapter we examine the framework for applying these tools for managerial decision-making.

EXECUTIVE VIEWPOINT

A Case of How Communicators Can Help Solve Enterprise-wide Issues with Data and Metrics

Tina McCorkindale, PhD, APR, President and CEO of the Institute for Public Relations

Measurement in the public relations industry is one of those puzzles that the field has been trying to solve for some time, but we still are not there yet. The number of industry professionals who really understand how to best measure and apply insights from data is disappointingly small. But those who have the knowledge base are extremely powerful allies who can have a positive impact on the organization and its performance with their expertise, especially if they are able to work cross- functionally. They become indispensable experts.

The organization I lead, the Institute for Public Relations (IPR), is a nonprofit industry research foundation founded in 1956. In 1997, the IPR Measurement Commission was created to "promote standards and best practices for research, measurement, and analytics that contribute to ethical, strategic, and effective public relations" (IPR, n.d., n.p.). The Commission comprises leaders in academia, nonprofits, corporations, and research firms who contribute thought leadership to the industry. One of the Measurement Commission's signature studies, *The Communicator's Guide to Research, Analysis, and Evaluation* (IPR, 2021), offers theory and research-based processes for finding effective, outcome-based metrics based on strategic goals and objectives. The report also features guides and best practices to help people through all stages of their measurement journey. I think it's the best resource for understanding the strategy behind research and measurement.

This report highlights the importance of research and measurement in guiding strategies and helping leaders speak the language of data that is common in business leadership. The report states, "By translating PR results to everyone's benefit, communicators minimize emotional decision-making, mitigate risk, gain efficiencies, and optimize business outcomes" (IPR, 2021, p. 4).

Communication leaders who work across the enterprise and effectively cross functional boundaries help make decisions that improve the overall business and the growth of the organization. One excellent case and one of my favorites that demonstrates the full potential of the influence of the communication function on the overall business is the Southwest Airlines "Start Strong" campaign.

SOUTHWEST AIRLINES "START STRONG" CAMPAIGN

Airline delays have long been a challenge for the airline industry. In 2020, Airlines for America predicted that airline delays cost passenger airlines several billions of dollars in additional expenses (Airlines for America, 2020). There is also the impact on the customer, who experiences losses of both their time and money. The airline's reputation can also be affected, and they may run the risk of losing future business because of disappointed customers.

In 2013, Southwest Airlines, which had historically strong numbers of on-time performance (OTP), saw their OTP ranking among other carriers fall to the bottom as they were trying to integrate the schedules of their newly acquired airline, AirTran Airways. Faced with this challenge, Southwest embarked on an enterprise-wide effort to improve its OTP using data from communication and other functions to drive a "Start Strong" campaign that was featured in an Institute for Public Relations (2016) White paper, *Irreversible: The Big Data Revolution*.

Prior to this initiative, the communications team shared data with the operations recovery team to give an overall view of how metrics across the enterprise influenced other variables, such as OTP. Finance, operations, and customer relations were other functions that supplied data to give a holistic picture. The cross-functional team then analyzed and correlated the data to understand the trends and variables (i.e., complaints, customer service calls, refunds, etc.) that influenced factors such as net sentiment and net promoter scores.

The data indicated that, not surprisingly, OTP correlated strongly with customer satisfaction. If customers were late, they were unhappy and took to social media to air their grievances. The data from operations also revealed that one of the biggest predictors of OTP was whether the first flight of the day left on time. If it did not, it impacted operations throughout the rest of the day and subsequently affected the net promoter score and sentiment driven by customer complaints. Southwest tracked these numbers daily.

Using this information, Southwest Airlines knew they had to create an initiative focused on getting that first flight out as early as possible. In early 2014, Southwest created the "Start Strong" campaign to encourage the first flight of the day to leave exactly on time and not within the 14 minutes of schedule that the government defines as an on-time flight. They also added more time between flights to allow the airline to better manage any unexpected issues and encouraged customers to board sooner. Gary Kelly, who was the Southwest CEO at the time, said in an interview published in *The Arizona Republic* (Gilbertson, 2014, para. 5) that the campaign was "probably the best coordination we've ever had amongst all workgroups."

The Southwest Airlines campaign demonstrates the need for public relations to serve as a key integrator across functions. Not having a complete picture is akin to the parable of the blind men and the elephant. Without coordination and discussion of the different components of the animal, the men would never be able to understand what an elephant is. Data are the language of business, and communicators can play an integral role in improving business strategy and outcomes through their contributions and knowledge. This demonstrates the power of how measurement should be used to predict, anticipate, and solve.

REFERENCES

Airlines for America. (2020). U.S. passenger carrier delay costs. Retrieved from: www.airlines.org/dataset/u-s-passenger-carrier-delay-costs/#:~:text=Assuming%20%2447%20per%20hour*%20as,2018%20to%20be%20%2428%20billion.

Gilbertson, Dawn. (2014, February). Southwest does the hustle to improve its arrival times. The Arizona Republic. Retrieved from: https://eu.azcentral.com/story/travel/2014/02/22/southwest-does-the-hustle-to-improve-its-arrival-times/5725329/.

Institute for Public Relations (IPR). (n.d.). IPR Measurement Commission. Retrieved from: https://instituteforpr.org/ipr-measurement-commission/about/.

Institute for Public Relations (IPR). (2016). Irreversible: The big data revolution. Retrieved from: https://instituteforpr.org/irreversible-public-relations-big-data-revolution/.

Institute for Public Relations (IPR). (2021). *Communicator's guide to research, analysis, and evaluation*. Retrieved from: https://instituteforpr.org/communicators-guide-research-2021/.

KEY WORDS

Performance measurement

Performance management

BSC

Performance reviews

Four sources of employee
performance information

Five stages of the employment
sequence

Equity

Inclusion

Diversity

Access

Three keys to EIDA

Toxic employees

Wrongful dismissal

Layoff

Exit interviews

Employee development

REFERENCES

American Productivity and Quality Center (APQC). (2002). *Performance measurement benefits*. Author. Retrieved July 30 2002 from: www.apqc.org/ pm/pmbenefits.cfm.

Baird, L., & Kram, K. (1983, Spring). Career dynamics: Managing the superior/ subordinate relationship. *Organizational Dynamics*, 46–64.

Bardhan, N. (2021, June 16). The way PR leaders communicate about diversity, equity, and inclusion matters. Institute for Public Relations. Available online: https:// instituteforpr.org/the-way-pr-leaders-communicate-about-diversity-equity-and-inclusion-matters/.

Blow, F., & Monzón, A. G. (2020, October 16). How communicators can lead the way on diversity and inclusion. *PR News*. Available online: www.prnewsonline.com/ diversity-inclusion-PRSA.

Brudan, A. (2010). Rediscovering performance management: Systems, learning, and integration. *Measuring Business Excellence, 14*(1), 109–123.

Chitkara, A. (2018, April 12). PR agencies need to be more diverse and inclusive. Here's how to start. *Harvard Business Review*. Available online: https://hbr.org/2018/04/ pr-agencies-need-to-be-more-diverse-and-inclusive-heres-how-to-start.

Clampitt, P. G. (2017). *Communicating for managerial effectiveness* (6th ed.). Sage Publications.

Coveney, M., Ganster, D., Hartlen, B., & King, D. (2003). *The strategy gap: Leveraging technology to execute winning strategies*. John Wiley & Sons.

Franco-Santos, M., Kennerley, M., Micheli, P., Martinez, V., Mason, S., Marr, B., … Neely, A. (2007). Towards a definition of a business performance measurement system. *International Journal of Operations & Production Management, 27*(8), 784–801.

Gallo, A. (2016, October 3). How to manage a toxic employee. *Harvard Business Review*. Available online: https://hbr.org/2016/10/how-to-manage-a-toxic-employee.

Grunig, L. A., Toth, E. L., & Hon, L. C. (2001). *Women in public relations: How gender influences practice*. Guilford Press.

Horton, J. (2006). *What's it worth? Publicity metrics reconsidered* (revised). Retrieved June 28 2008 from: www.online-pr.com/Holding/Pub- licity_Metrics_Reconsidered__REVISED.pdf.

Housman, M., & Minor, D. (2015). *Toxic workers*. Harvard Business School. Available online: www.hbs.edu/ris/Publication%20Files/16-057_d45c0b4f-fa19-49de-8f1b-4b12fe054fea.pdf.

Jablin, F. (2001). Organizational entry, assimilation, and disengagement/exit. In F. M. Jablin & L. L. Putnam (Eds.), *The new handbook of organizational communication* (pp. 732–818). Sage Publications.

Kaplan, R. S. (2001). Strategic performance measurement and management in nonprofit organizations. *Nonprofit Management and Leadership*, 11(3), 353–370.

Kaplan, R. S., & Norton, D. P. (1996). *The balanced scorecard: Translating strategy into action*. Harvard Business School Press.

Kellerman, B. (2008). *Followership: How followers are creating change and changing leaders*. Harvard Business School Press.

Khazan, O. (2014, August). Why are there so many women in public relations? *The Atlantic*. Available online: www.theatlantic.com/business/print/2014/08/why-are-there-so-many-women-in-pr/375693/.

Landis, K. (2019, April). The public relations industry is too white and the solution starts with higher education. *INSIGHT into Diversity*. Available online: www.insightinto diversity.com/the-public-relations-industry-is-too-white-and-the-solution-starts-with-higher-education/#:~:text=The%20problem%20is%20that%20public,5.7%20percent%20Hispanic%20or%20Latinx.

Lehal, J. (Ed.) (2011). *Maximising opportunities: Broadening access to the PR industry*. Public Relations Consultancy Association. Available online: www.prmoment.com/images/cms/files/Broadening%20access%20to%20the%20PR%20industry.pdf.

Magna International Inc. (2013). Employee's charter. Available online: www.magna.com/company/for-employees/our-culture/employees-charter .

Maisel, L. S. (2001). *Performance measurement practices survey results*. American Institute of Certified Public Accountants.

Mundy, D. E. (2016). Bridging the divide: A multidisciplinary analysis of diversity research and the implications for public relations. *Research Journal of the Institute for Public Relations*, 3(1). Available online: https://instituteforpr.org/wp-content/uploads/Dean-Mundy-1.pdf.

National Labor Relations Board. (n.d.). *The NLRB and social media*. Available online: www.nlrb.gov/node/5078.

Orey, M. (2007, April 23). Fear of firing: How the threat of litigation is making companies skittish about axing problem workers. *BusinessWeek*, 52–62.

Paine, K. D., Draper, P., & Jeffrey, A. (2008). *Using public relations research to drive business results*. Institute for Public Relations. Retrieved June 24 2008 from: www.instituteforpr.org/files/uploads/UsingResearch_ DriveBusiness.pdf.

PsychTests. (2016, December 23). Office pollution: New study looks into the core traits of toxic employees. The Courier. Retrieved from: https://wcfcourier.com/office-pollution-new-study-looks-into-the-core-traits-of/article_ab5f722f-7bef-5a75-816f-bd0031e1eb16.html

Saunders, A. F., & Monzón, A. G. (2021). *D&I toolkit*. Public Relations Society of America. Available online: www.prsa.org/docs/default-source/about/diversity/prsa-2021-toolkit---6-3-21.pdf?sfvrsn=26ff3dfd_0.

Schiemann, W. A., & Lingle, J. H. (1999). *Bullseye! Hitting your strategic targets through high-impact measurement*. The Free Press.

Spector, S., & Spector, B. (2018). *Diverse voices: Profiles in leadership*. PR Museum Press.

Sutton, R. I. (2007). *The no asshole rule: Building a civilized workplace and surviving one that isn't*. Business Plus.

Toth, E. L. (2009, April 9). Diversity and public relations practice. Institute for Public Relations. Available online: https://instituteforpr.org/diversity-and-pr-practice/.

U.S. Bureau of Labor Statistics. (2022, January 20). *Labor force statistics from the current population survey*. Available online: www.bls.gov/cps/cpsaat18.htm

Vos, M., & Schoemaker, H. (2004). *Accountability of communication management: A balanced scorecard for communication quality*. LEMMA Publishers.

Wallace, A. A., & Luttrell, R. (2021, December 28). 4 steps for adopting a "diversity first" practice in PR. *PR Daily*. Available online: www.prdaily.com/4-steps-for-adopting-a-diversity-first-practice-in-pr/.

Watson, T., & Noble. P. (2014). *Evaluating public relations: A guide to planning, research, and measurement* (3rd ed.). Kogan Page.

Worthington Jr., E. L., Greer, C. L., Hook, J. N., Davis, D. E., Gartner, A. L., Jennings II, D. J. et al. (2010). Forgiveness and spirituality in organizational life: Theory, status of research, and new ideas for discovery. *Journal of Management, Spirituality & Religion, 7*(2), 119–134. DOI: 10.1080/14766081003765273

RECOMMENDED READING

Collins, J. (2001). *Good to great: Why some companies make the leap and others don't*. Harper Business.

Davenport, T. H., Harris, J. G., & Morison, R. (2010). *Analytics at work: Smarter decisions, better results*. Harvard Business School Press.

DeNisi, A. S., & Griffin, R. W. (2008). *Human resource management* (3rd ed.). Houghton Mifflin.

Eckerson, W. (2011). *Performance dashboards: Measuring, monitoring, and managing your business* (2nd ed.). John Wiley and Sons.

Epstein, M. J., & Birchard, B. (2000). *Counting what counts: Turning corporate accountability to competitive advantage*. Perseus Books.

Harbour, J. L. (1997). *The basics of performance measurement*. Productivity Press.

Howard, P. J., & Howard, J. M. (2001). *The owner's manual for personality at work*. Bard Press.

Kaushik, A. (2010). *Web analytics 2.0: The art of online accountability and science of customer centricity*. Sybex/Wiley Publishing.

Muller, M. (2009). *The manager's guide to HR: Hiring, firing, performance evaluations, documentation, benefits, and everything else you need to know*. AMACOM.

Pfeffer, J., & Sutton, R. I. (2000). *The knowing-doing gap: How smart companies turn knowledge into action*. Harvard Business School Press.

7

CHAPTER 7
DECISION-MAKING IN TUNE WITH THE STRATEGIC PLAN

CHAPTER OUTLINE

Choices define us and our futures. With all the work done to set up the "business" of a public relations operation in any organization, as the previous chapters have explained, choices and decisions must be made and defended. Leaders and managers are paid for getting results—the results they said they and their teams could get through the plans they devised and resources they applied. The presumption behind any organizational operation is that it is valued, valuable, and adds value to the whole organization.

The strategic plan and the overall operating environment make up the context of what can and must be done to obtain (even exceed) desired results. In turn, these things also are the focus of effective decision-making, which establishes and demonstrates the value contributions the PR function gives to the larger organization. In this chapter we, accordingly, begin with an examination of value and how PR delivers it before we explore the dynamics of managerial decision-making that advance and substantiate that value to internal and external organizational publics and stakeholders. This chapter ends with a brief return to the concept of resource management but strictly in terms of communication media as resource concerns.

DELIVERING VALUE

Like the vast majority of professionals in all other fields, public relations people work hard and are proud of their work. Their bosses (and *their* bosses) expect public relations actions to add value to the organization. That value is something beyond the planning,

DOI: 10.4324/9781003208280-8

execution, and measurement of public relations campaigns and tactics. The concept of value can mean many things and has been the focus of numerous books and articles in the trade press. Very basically and in the context of business, **value** means not only that something has inherent worth (however defined), but also—and very importantly—something has been made better than before or enables something to become better than it was. It is not necessarily tied to strictly financial measures of price, cost, asset worth, and so on. Nonfinancial measures, like reputation and image, can and should be linked to it (see Epstein & Birchard, 2000).

Adding value is the primary concern of all business functions. To do so means, on the one hand, that a functional area's contributions have simultaneously bolstered the organization's mission and moved the business closer to realizing its vision. On the other hand, adding value means pragmatically that a functional area has helped to enhance (or at least not hurt, especially in a challenging economy) a company's financial position through its allocation of resources and budget versus actual expenditures. Not that every organizational function must be cash-positive, because even a function that tends to depend heavily on expenses (as public relations can do) can spur income-making opportunities that drive things like sales, donations, grants, supportive sentiment, and so on. Public relations has the added benefit of sparking crucial attitude- and behavior-changing opportunities that enhance image, reputation, perception, brand equity, and so on that also affect the financial picture. The link between the two—public relations actions and corporate income/gross receipts—is a tenuous thing at best to measure directly and has been the focus of numerous studies, especially through the Institute for Public Relations.

Delivering value is key to public relations' success. Value is demonstrated through measurements of performance, which are orchestrated through the single system of strategic planning, management-control, and task-control processes addressed in Chapter 5 and Chapter 6. For public relations, value is added constantly, but the traditional measurements for it have been problematic (e.g., advertising value equivalency [AVE], clip counts). These measurements are at least useful, however, as initial data points to indicate where to further measure campaign initiatives against business objectives (Oates, 2006, p. 12). Most important in this regard are the **Barcelona Principles**, which were adopted globally by numerous professional communication associations (originally in 2010) and have been updated twice, so that they are now in their third version: *Barcelona Principles 3.0* (AMEC, 2020). This document is meant to provide PR professionals worldwide with a definitive statement of standards and practices that would guide any measurement and evaluation of public relations. Those principles, directly concerned with measuring PR's value, in brief are these:

1. *Setting goals [objectives] is an absolute prerequisite to communications planning, measurement, and evaluation*—Objectives must be specific, measurable, actionable, relevant, and time-bound on things that directly matter to what will define success (or failure) for a given public relations effort of any size and scope.
2. *Measurement and evaluation should identify outputs, outcomes, and potential*

impact—The most effective measurements are those things that not only account for the production of individual PR discourses, but also result in measurable changes in awareness, attitudes, and actions that came about because of those discourses.

3. *Outcomes and impact should be identified for stakeholders, society, and the organization*—What public relations achieves is part of the larger organizational, business, and social picture, plus it needs to be able to fit the wide variety of organizations and communication opportunities that are enacted.

4. *Communication measurement and evaluation should include both qualitative and quantitative analysis*—These measurements must focus on the content and the impact of PR efforts on stakeholders in terms of variables like tone, source credibility, medium appropriateness, testimonials from outside spokespeople, sensual prominence (visual or auditory), and degree of positiveness, negativeness, or neutrality/passivity.

5. *AVEs are not the value of communication*—AVEs never have and never will be proper or effective measures of PR's value because AVEs equate PR efforts with only the cost of media space and not the other dimensions that matter (i.e., awareness/ knowledge, attitudes/opinions, and actions/behaviors). Moreover, multipliers of AVEs based on any medium's reported user data (circulation, viewers, listeners, etc.) are also irrelevant and improper because they are merely inflations of the media-space cost calculations based on user data.

6. *Holistic communication measurement and evaluation includes all relevant online and offline channels*—Measuring online and offline channels, whether they are paid, earned, shared, or owned, is vital to tie results to specific, well-wrought objectives.

7. *Communication measurement and evaluation are rooted in integrity and transparency to drive learning and insights*—All measurements should be valid (i.e., measure precisely what they are supposed to measure), reliable (i.e., measure that effect accurately every time if and when the method is repeated), and transparent (i.e., easy to identify and understand so that the links between PR and organizational performance are clear). Assessment of communication in context and with attention to any biases that may exist in the research methods, calculations, and interpretations is essential to be aware of them and correct for them whenever possible, including future communication programs.

Spanning across these principles are the integral matters (i.e., "validated metrics") for measurement; namely, awareness, knowledge, interest, intent and support, and action. As we saw in Chapter 5 about the construction of proper objectives, the things that inspire people to think with their *heads*, feel in their *hearts*, and act with their *hands* (and feet) make up a holistic way to determine value, not just any one of these matters alone. Too many campaigns are solely focused on raising awareness, but do not focus on changing attitudes and/or, especially, inspiring behavior. In these cases, the move from awareness to attitude formation and/or action is assumed, but it must not be. The Barcelona Principles will prove instrumental in ensuring that the matters of the **head, heart, and**

hands (see the topic of objectives in Chapter 5) are all properly addressed and measured to demonstrate public relations' value.

Of particular importance is Fraser Likely's (2013) framework for reporting usable, useful, and used information about the public relations function to an organization's CEO and other top leaders. His framework is shown in Table 7.1, and it applies Drucker's (1995) **five dimensions of information** that executives truly need:

- *Foundational information*—concerns basic financial data, from cash flow and liquidity projections to key ratios between certain financial measures, like inventory versus sales, receivables versus sales.
- *Productivity information*—concerns how much value is added to the organization over all costs associated with its productivity, relying on benchmarks against best performers in a market or industry.
- *Competence information*—concerns the effectiveness with which an organization can muster its resources for its core business to meet customer demand.
- *Resource-allocation information*—concerns managing organizational performance so that wealth is created through the wise use of capital and people, which focuses on the planning and budgeting process.
- *Environment information*—concerns data about markets; customers (present and potential); stakeholders; technology; industry; local, national, and worldwide economics and politics; global financial markets; and other areas that play primarily in the realm of strategy execution.

These dimensions of information act individually and, especially, together as diagnostic tools to determine the strength and viability of an organization. These dimensions also complement Drucker's (2006 [1967]) eight practices of effective executives covered in Table 1.3 in Chapter 1. Most important, the information from these five dimensions is valuable to management because it is the basis on which appropriate action can and must be taken. Although Drucker's five information dimensions above are meant for the broader organization, they, just like an organizational plan, can and must be tailored for operational units; namely, public relations. Likely's (2013, pp. 471–473) framework for management information in Table 7.1, then, gives us a way to think about and capture the kind of performance information from inside and outside a PR unit that matters to top organizational leaders and prove PR's value in the larger organizational picture. Very important also is to recognize that the combination of Table 7.1 and Figure 6.3 can guide managerial decision-making very potently, as the content of each not only complements the other, but they can serve to build a stronger case for what to do, why, and for what value to an organization.

In terms of any organization's "business," public relations is part of the **value chain** that brings a finished product, service, or other economic output to a market or target public or customer. Any organizational function exists within a defined value chain of all other functions (see Figure 7.1), and each function—each link in the

Table 7.1 Likely's framework of public relations department information reporting

Executive level	Foundational information	Productivity information	Competence information	Resource allocation information	Environmental information
Organization Head/CEO	Information on historic budget allocation Information from benchmarking budgets allocated to the function (FTEs; salaries; total budget; agency costs; etc.)	Information on process efficiencies (tasking; production; delivery; approval) Information on legacy program requirements	Information on PR/C core competencies vs. non-core competencies Information on PR/C team and individual executive performance and organizational relationships and networks Information on use of the challenge and coaching functions with senior executives Information on corporate result indicators: corporate trust/reputation; stakeholder relations; employee engagement	Information on the allocation of resources (capital and people) within the PR/C function (on programs; on campaigns; on channels/media; on product production; etc.) Information on the allocation of resources against organizational priorities/objectives Information on the benefit-cost ratio for proposed new investments	Information on stakeholders and publics (and risks inherent in their positions) for input into the organization's future, intended strategy formulation process Information on the state of current strategy execution across the organization and any communicative obstacles Information from internal silo boundary spanning about strategy execution discontinuities as input into the organization's emergent strategy formation process

(continued)

Table 7.1 Cont.

Executive level	Foundational information	Productivity information	Competence information	Resource allocation information	Environmental information
Business Line or Staff Function Head/CFO/ CMO/ CHRO	Information on the previous and proposed spends	Information on legacy program requirements Information on value vs. cost for programs/ campaigns Information on in-house vs. outsourcing or contracting out (make vs. buy)	Information on Account Executive and support unit performance Information on innovative performance based on best practice core competency Information on business result indicators for programs/ campaigns	Information on the allocation of resources (capital and people) to the business line or staff function (on programs; on campaigns; on channels/ media; on product production; etc.) Information on the allocation of resources against business line or staff function priorities/ objectives Information on the benefit-cost ratio for proposed new investments	Information on markets/customers, stakeholders, and publics for input into business strategies and campaign plans Information on competitor PR/C program and campaign investments, priorities and positioning

Source: Likely (2013, pp. 471–473)

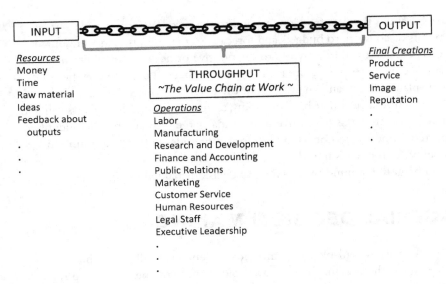

Figure 7.1 Value chain

chain—contributes to the organization's success or failure. The value chain begins with **inputs** of various resources needed to produce an organization's **outputs**. What happens in between is **throughput**, which is the work that all the operational areas of an organization employ using the resources that apply to them to create the outputs required of them. Throughput also involves all of an organization's systems, processes, policies, and procedures that enable the organization to turn inputs into outputs. In this way, public relations is as important as research and development, human resources, sales, finance and accounting, manufacturing, customer service, and so on. The value that each function contributes is just different, but it must be significant and, therefore, measured. As long as each organizational function is utilized, each one is expected to add value in specific ways—financial and nonfinancial. Additionally, feedback about outputs comes back as inputs, which serve as a means for evaluating performance and making any improvements. Consistent with what we covered in the preceding chapters, organizational functions that contribute significant value are retained and, perhaps, augmented, if it makes strategic sense. Those functions that add little or no value or take away value could well see their resources reallocated or eliminated. The value chain is as strong as its weakest link. A value chain, then, can be made stronger by making links stronger and/or eliminating weak links.

So value is determined by performance measurements, and performance is something that must be managed. As we saw in Chapter 6, performance management combines the rigor of measurement methodologies with the incisiveness of leadership and management practices. Instrumental in performance management is the regular reporting of performance measures, and a framework like that shown in Table 7.1 can be valuable in making performance data meaningful and actionable. Those reports ideally should be formal and written so that there is consistency in the presentation of the data and the messages about the data from one period to the next. Performance data, then, are critical points to compare to budgets and forecasts so that adjustments in resource allocations can be made to address swings to the positive or negative. In addition to these performance measures, which are really internally focused because they tie back to the strategic plan, research and analysis about the external world's state and trends of the market, competition, customer base, economy, technology, and other factors can and must be applied. Any problems (definitive or potential, large to small) that are identified must be reported immediately, not covered up or swept aside under the assumption they will go away. All problems must be remedied fast and early, not in "good time" and when they can be gotten around to. An effective decision-making process is key.

MANAGERIAL DECISION-MAKING

Given all the information available to organizational members at all levels, there are many pressures to use the best information available to make the best choices possible from one situation to another. These pressures point to the common behavior of judging what is going on for what can and should be done. This behavior is the substance of decision-making, and it has a particular nature for those who lead and manage the operational areas of any organization. Three topics are key in this subject: the centrality of perceptions, the process view of decision-making, and the fact that good leaders can make bad decisions.

PERCEPTION IS CENTRAL

Everyone makes thousands of decisions every day, spanning the full range of inconsequential to potentially monumental matters in one's life or other people's lives. People have a powerful cognitive capacity for taking in, making sense of, and acting on immense amounts of data gathered through their senses. But people cannot possibly perceive and process all stimuli. So the human brain has ways to handle any stimuli that matter very efficiently and pretty effectively (but not perfectly) most of the time, resulting in **perceptions** that arise from a process of sensing, selecting, organizing, and interpreting information so that all of it is meaningful, memorable, and retrievable or reusable at another time (DeVito, 2009). Perception is a function of attention: to what do we devote any amount of attention (or not) at any time in any situation, and what do we perceive and what do we miss? The fact that we have certain patterns of perception also plays into the potential for us to experience **deception**, because we think we perceive something that truly is not present or vice versa. Perception can be understood as a **five-step process**, as shown in Figure 7.2. First, people purposefully *sense and select* which data (e.g., information, experiences, messages, people) they want or need, depending on certain criteria. This step encompasses not only the taking in of data, but also the avoidance of other data because of certain personal criteria for what is interesting, important, urgent, or for another reason. This step alone, then, can be pivotal in determining after a decision is implemented why it was good or bad.

Sense and
Select

Organize

Interpret
and Evaluate

Memorize

Recall

Figure 7.2 Perception process

When sufficient data are collected about something, people take the second step
in the perception process to *organize* things, using "**cognitive shortcuts**" because
people are imperfect—they cannot process absolutely every sensory input. Simply
put, cognitive shortcuts allow people to make sense of all the data that bombard them
about anything. These shortcuts can also enable deception. They are natural and highly
efficient operations of the human brain that virtually instantaneously assess something
based on one or more of three kinds of structure. One shortcut structure is *rules*, which
sorts data based on proximity (i.e., closeness in space and/or time), similarity (i.e.,
resemblance to prior experience and present knowledge), and contrast (i.e., differences
among things keep them from being grouped together). The second shortcut structure
is *schemata* (singular, *schema*), which are mental templates or "cookie cutters" that
help sort out patterns in data about, for example, one's self, others, and social roles,
based largely on personal experiences. A stereotype is an example of a schema. The
last cognitive shortcut structure is *scripts*, which are a kind of schema that outlines
a general sequence or basic series of expectations about events, such as a date, a job
interview, or a negotiation. Gladwell (2005) explains the very pragmatic dimensions to
cognitive shortcuts (although he does not refer to it in this way or to the theoretical
foundations in cognitive science—namely, schema theory; see McVee et al. [2005] for a
useful summary) as he argues that people engage in the "thin slicing" of experiences to
unconsciously and "fast and frugal[ly]" find patterns in situations and behavior based on
very small samples ("slices") of all the data that surround an experience.

With the data selected and organized, the next steps of the perception process make
the data usable for the future. The third step in the process is to *interpret and evaluate*,

which is the point where the organized data are given meaning subjectively, based on the cognitive shortcuts themselves and the parameters on which they operate. This step would also be an important one to identify possible deception. The fourth step is to *memorize* for later, based on certain key factors that stand out so they can be easily retrieved. In this step, the cognitive shortcuts help immensely as filters for what goes with what and whether any shortcut needs revision based on new data. The final step in the perception process is to *retrieve or recall*, which relies on any cognitive shortcut's ability to be used to make sense of new data. Data that are consistent with cognitive shortcuts are easy to recall, but data that are inconsistent with a cognitive shortcut would be difficult to recall. Moreover, data that are dramatically different from cognitive shortcuts would likely require revision to the applicable shortcut.

The most important point about the perception process is one key limitation: its reliance on cognitive shortcuts is, on the one hand, helpful in gaining quick understanding, building memory, and aiding recall; but on the other hand, these same shortcuts—because of their very nature as efficient but not wholly complete structures—can mislead people (i.e., deceptions) or cause recall of impertinent factors if they are not careful to select, organize, interpret, store, and apply truly sufficient data accurately and thoroughly. Trusting your gut is okay to a point, but that gut feeling must also be tested and verified as true or false.

DECISION-MAKING AS A PROCESS

Peter Drucker, as we saw in Chapter 1, provides us with a very usable and useful means (his eight practices shown in Table 1.3) for leveraging our perceptions to effectively manage what is going on in an organization. With ever-increasing knowledge, experience, and foresight, people (the vast majority of the time) become increasingly better at making decisions. That is great news because experience and knowledge, combined with measurable results (successes and failures), contribute to wisdom and efficiency. Often there may be an abundance of information but not everything you want, and a decision still must be—and can be—made and made well in the face of any risks and limitations. Bazerman and Moore (2009) address the **decision-making process** of organizational leaders. They explain that managerial decision-making is a process that is driven by perceptions and is threatened by a range of biases (personal to organizational) that can undermine effectiveness. Indeed, they explain that decision-making relies on **five "bounds"** for that process:

- *Bounded rationality*, which subsumes the logical expectations that would result from a decision reached based on an accurately assessed situation.
- *Bounded willpower*, which concerns the greater weight given to short-term factors over long-term ones.

- *Bounded self-interest*, which tempers one's own interests with concern for the welfare of others.
- *Bounded awareness*, which addresses the emphasis of failures over successes and the overlooking of obvious, important, and abundant information.
- *Bounded ethicality*, which concerns parameters that drive people to be concerned about and pursue what is considered fair and ethical, especially situations where someone acts in opposition to his or her own principles of fairness and ethics.

Because people have an inherent self-interest and a tendency to rely on intuition, they also have, according to Bazerman and Moore (2009), an inability to interpret information without bias. The key to resolving this problem is adopting a more conscious and systematic approach to decision-making that is most appropriate and necessary for sound personal and organizational performance. Gladwell (2005) parallels this point as he proposes that, even though decisions can be made very quickly (i.e., in the blink of an eye) and be as good as decisions made methodically, the limitations of quick decision-making must be recognized because snap judgments, first impressions, and so on can be wrong precisely because of the imperfections of humans. Those imperfections are in line with the explanation of the cognitive shortcuts given above and can be used to determine why a decision was bad. For managerial decision-making, Bazerman and Moore propose a six-step process, a visual of which is given in Figure 7.3.

Key to applying the decision-making process in organizations is recognizing the kind of "judgmental heuristic" by which one is operating to reach a decision (Bazerman & Moore, 2009). There are **three judgmental heuristics**. The first is the *availability heuristic*, which seeks data about the frequency, probability, and so on of something, based on how much of it is in stored experiences (personally and organizationally). The second is the *representativeness heuristic*, which relies on the presence of data that are consistent with or correspond to previously formed expectations (i.e., schemata). The final one is the *affect heuristic*, which concerns the importance of emotional factors (e.g., personal feelings, extenuating circumstances, environmental conditions) associated with something or someone that can adversely displace other factors needed for sound reasoning about that thing or person.

The objective for effective managerial decision-making is not to make perfectly good decisions all the time. Although that objective is attractive, it is not realistic given human imperfection. Strategies that simplify the assessment of situations (i.e., cognitive shortcuts, thin slices, judgmental heuristics) should be used to produce correct or nearly correct judgments, with the understanding that there are inherent limitations that may well require correction for bias and incompleteness.

Figure 7.3 Decision-making process
Source: Based on Bazerman and Moore (2009)

GOOD LEADERS BUT BAD DECISIONS

There is an important difference between poor outcomes and poor decisions, both of which can be experienced by good leaders. In spite of fastidious attention to detail about a situation and its expected results, poor outcomes can occur because of the influence of many variables, many of which were likely beyond one's control and/or unforeseen. In contrast, poor decisions are recognized retrospectively as poor, "if the knowledge gained would lead to a different decision if a similar situation arose" (Klein, 1998, p. 271). Indeed, there is a difference between people who see things as black or white ("unequivocal" decision-makers) and people who see shades of grey ("ambivalent" decision-makers). Table 7.2 summarizes the differences based on Wang's (2010) summary of a research study on the subject. Very important, however, as Wang explains, is that influential factors of personality and culture appear to play roles in forming the two kinds of decision-makers. Additionally, individual characteristics given in the table may not always be present, and one's unequivocalness and ambivalence can be determined through psychological testing. Combining Wang's findings about decision-makers with Bazerman and Moore's five "bounds" for decision-making, we can begin to see in Table 7.2 how the making of decisions can be effective or not, particularly when irrelevant or inappropriate inputs are considered and applied.

A focused study of leaders making bad decisions by Campbell et al. (2009; also see Finkelstein, 2004) reveals such decision-making to be a **two-part**, "hardwired" **process**. The first part is *pattern recognition* that is similar to schemata. As we saw earlier in

Table 7.2 Comparing basic traits of two decision-maker types

Unequivocal decision-makers	Ambivalent decision-makers
• Speak their minds or make quick decisions	• Procrastinate or avoid making decisions
• Are more predictable in decision-making	• Feel more regret after making decisions
• Are less anxious about making wrong choices	• Are thoughtful about making the right choice
• Have relationship conflicts that are less drawn out	• Stay longer in unhappy relationships
• Are less likely to consider others' points of view	• Appreciate multiple points of view

Source: Based on Wang (2010)

this section, the problem is that our brains can fool us into thinking we understand situations because they somehow fit familiar experiences when they do not. The second part is *emotional tagging*, which involves making associations about paying attention or not and taking action. Aligned with the explanation of perception and decision-making, the problem occurs unconsciously and makes it hard to check the data and logic for good decision-making. Campbell et al. (2009) explain that when good leaders make bad decisions, three **red-flag conditions** emerge: (1) the presence of inappropriate self-interest, (2) the presence of distorting emotional attachments, and (3) the presence of misleading memories. These red-flag conditions link back to Bazerman and Moore's (2009) recognition of the role of bias in decision-making and to Wang's (2010) accounting for inappropriately influential factors. Discovering the red flags is key, and Figure 7.4 shows the process for identifying those conditions (Campbell et al., 2009). Beyond identifying the red-flag conditions for good leaders on the verge of making bad decisions, Campbell et al. (2009) prescribe three safeguards that can and should be applied: (1) inject fresh experience or analysis, (2) introduce further debate and challenge, and (3) impose stronger governance.

Add to this view the concept of **groupthink** (Janis, 1972), which is defined as "a premature striving by group members for unanimous agreement on a course of action," and it "cuts off necessary consideration of the pros and cons of the various decision options" (Ahlfinger & Esser, 2001, p. 32). Groupthink includes "high group cohesiveness, a stressful situation, and a variety of structural or administrative factors such as insulation of the group, promotional leadership, lack of methodical decision-making procedures, and lack of variety among members' values and perspectives" (Ahlfinger & Esser, 2001, p. 32). The presence of groupthink marks fundamentally flawed decision-making; Figure 7.5 shows the three types of groupthink and their symptoms, of which Type III

Figure 7.4 Process for identifying red flags for poor decision-making

Figure 7.5 Groupthink types and their symptoms
Source: Ahlfinger and Esser (2001)

is the most scary. No matter what type, groupthink leads to seven symptoms of defective decision-making (Janis, 1972):

1. Incomplete survey of alternatives
2. Incomplete survey of objectives
3. Failure to examine risks of the preferred choice
4. Failure to reappraise initially rejected alternatives
5. Poor information search
6. Selective bias in processing available information
7. Failure to develop contingency plans.

These symptoms actually flow from one to the next, and the result is a greater likelihood that poor decisions will be made. A good way to protect against groupthink is to take the seven symptoms of defective decision-making and reverse them into their positive forms (e.g., prepare a thorough survey of alternatives, conduct a substantial survey of objectives, examine the risks and benefits of the preferred choice). This approach, especially when joined with the other approaches for sound decision-making in this section and Drucker's eight practices shown in Chapter 1's Table 1.3, can mitigate against many or all of the problems of ineffective or flawed managerial decision-making.

COMMUNICATION RESOURCE MANAGEMENT

So much of managerial decision-making involves the allocation of resources, and for a public relations function in any organization, agency or nonagency, there are many matters that must be addressed, and personnel matters are among the most vital, as we saw in Chapter 6. Likely's (2013) framework for reporting operational performance information (see Table 7.1) can be instrumental in the management of resources. In this final section of the chapter, we will address three particular resource-management matters for communication because of their special prominence in the profession: the strategic role of tactics, the false dichotomy of controlled and uncontrolled media, and traditional and new media.

STRATEGIC ROLE OF TACTICS

One key to understanding the force of history on people's views of public relations is tactics, as we saw in Chapter 1 and in Chapter 5. After all, publics experience what PR professionals do, not the thinking and the process behind it. Yet public relations as a field has done a poor job of promoting itself. As Budd (2003) finds, "Public relations is too short-sighted, too fragmented … to mount any true industry offensive. World class PR demands world class political skills, attributes in short supply" (p. 380). Remember, too, Budd continues, that public opinion has been long on mistrust toward business, but it can best be overcome by deeds, not words alone. The field, then, still faces a difficult task to better inform the public, inspire a cooperative attitude, and result in supportive actions toward the profession. According to the PRSA's ethics code, practitioners are called on to "enhance the profession," which means to do so for anyone—especially those outside the field.

The **tactical bias** that runs through public relations is especially evident in what it teaches. Chapter 5 argues against a bias toward tactics and argues for a bias toward strategy. But a tendency in industry to seek **recipes** (i.e., privilege tactics) for effective corporate communications dominates, as professionals are increasingly asked to "do more with less," "work smarter," and adhere to other slogans meant to inspire excellence in work, but, as Deming (1986) tells us, slogans "generate frustration and resentment" (p. 67). Public relations discourse is the sum of many people's enactments shared, selected, and retained, according to organizing recipes, during the process through which they make sense of what is going on and what must be done. As Weick (1979) says, recipes are "the means to generate structures that have the characteristics you want. Adapted to organizing, the question becomes: given our need for a sensible enacted environment, how do we produce it?" (pp. 46–47).

This quest for recipes is promulgated through multiple resources. Numerous textbooks and trade books are available about how to write specific forms of public relations discourse. In comparison, far less work has been published about strategy and strategic planning specifically for public relations, but examples like Ferguson (1999), Moffitt (1999), Oliver (2007), and Potter (2006) are available, even though they cover the topic in isolation from the larger organizational picture as this book covers it. Additionally, a great variety of "how-to" seminars are offered annually by stalwart organizations (e.g., the PRSA, the IABC, Regan Communications, Melcrum Publishing, the Word of Mouth Marketing Association), as well as luncheon or dinner meetings in PRSA and IABC chapters that address everything professional communicators might need to enhance their tactical skills, and scholarly and practice-based journal articles that place much emphasis on the tactics of public relations efforts through case examples or lived experiences.

There is immediate satisfaction from tactics—a rush from seeing work come to life. That is why tactics are so attractive and easy to focus on. It also explains why, on the one hand, there is much celebration of especially successful work; and, on the other hand, much confusion about why public relations should be involved as a strategic function. *A tactics bias, then, must be meticulously shifted to a strategies bias.* If we think of attention as an economic commodity (Davenport & Beck, 2002), like that of iron ore in making steel, silicon in making microchips, and so on, the means *and* the ends for getting and maintaining attention are both integral. Tactics are the ends of public relations, but much more important, the means that makes them possible and successful is the intense strategic planning that must be done in advance and enacted effectively, as we saw in Chapter 5. Put in concise terms,

> strictly tactical thinking is focused on just "getting the word out." But truly effective and successful communications depends on strategic thinking that focuses on the bigger picture, making tactics subservient to larger objectives that tie directly to an organizational mission and vision. Strategy is necessary in the full range of strategic communication efforts, from the simplest announcement to the most complicated crisis.
>
> (Courtright & Smudde, 2010, p. 69)

THE SPECTRUM OF MEDIA

In the field of public relations there are at least 41 types of discourse that practitioners may use, as shown in Figure 5.7 in Chapter 5. Those discourse genres are made all the more publicly usable, useful, and used because of the Internet and organizations' application of it to manage much of their communications in addition to traditional mass media. So all that discourse, whether digital or not, makes up a wide spectrum of media available for tactical purposes. Which begs the question, "Who has control over any communication effort and the messages?" Smudde and Courtright (2012) demonstrate that sometimes companies have complete control over what, how, and when audiences get any discourse. At other times, companies choose to give up that control and rely on the mass media to convey messages to audiences. (This point recalls the PESO approach to selecting media.) Somewhere in between, however, companies can collaborate with mass media in their strategic communication, which calls into question the traditional (but flawed) dichotomy of controlled and uncontrolled media.

Controlled media involve a company's target audiences getting exactly the communication it created for them and in the way it wanted them to get the communication (e.g., mobile phone apps, annual reports, brochures, websites). *Uncontrolled media* involve a company's target audiences not getting exactly what it would like them to get because a third party—the mass media—makes the choices as to what, how, and if any messages would be sent from any discourse that a company provided to the media (e.g., news releases, press conferences, interviews). For example, when we think of product recalls within the broadest context of all strategic communication efforts, audiences rely largely on uncontrolled media. This reliance makes sense because the best interests of the general public are of the utmost importance. Once we examine other kinds of corporate communication efforts, however, the dichotomy breaks down and becomes a continuum.

Most practitioners know there can be a certain amount of cooperation between them/ their companies and media outlets so they both get something of what they want. An easy example is a feature story pitched and ghostwritten for an executive by a communication professional and acquired, edited, and illustrated through an editor at a top trade publication that meets readers' needs while highlighting a company's viewpoint and offerings. Video news releases also exhibit a fair degree of give and take, as companies provide a finished piece and extra footage ("B-roll") that news organizations may use, or they even might add their own footage. Such co-creation of discourse for a company's ultimate audiences results in a middle ground of what Courtright and Smudde (2010) call *semi-controlled/semi-uncontrolled media*, depending on how far toward one end of the continuum one goes with the creation and dissemination of organizational messages.

This **PR tactics continuum** (see Figure 7.6), then, becomes much more strategically valuable as practitioners consider what discourse forms may best convey the messages and best fit the occasions they face on behalf of their organizations and audiences. Discourse competence in any or all genres is vital and involves an acute sensibility about the use, benefits, and risks of controlled, uncontrolled, and semi-controlled/ semi-uncontrolled media (see Smudde & Courtright, 2012). Being mindful of and implementing an organization's overall strategic plan is the responsibility of all organizational members, especially its leaders and, in particular, its communication professionals.

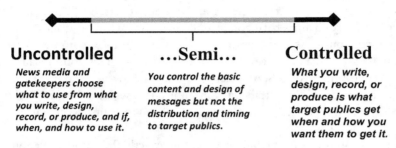

Uncontrolled
News media and gatekeepers choose what to use from what you write, design, record, or produce, and if, when, and how to use it.

...Semi...
You control the basic content and design of messages but not the distribution and timing to target publics.

Controlled
What you write, design, record, or produce is what target publics get when and how you want them to get it.

Figure 7.6 Continuum for PR tactics

TRADITIONAL AND "NEW" MEDIA

The developments of movable type printing, telegraph, radio, television, the Internet, and mobile computing have much in common because of the revolutions in communication that each caused. The diffusion of technologies is at the heart of these revolutions, and the cries were loud that the existing, "traditional" communication technology would be supplanted by the innovative, "new" technology. A new technology has benefits of its own but also needs to bridge the benefits of the traditional technology. This is why the Internet is made up of "sites," "pages," and other metaphorical references to printed discourse. In fact, the design and usability standards that have developed for the Internet, social media, and mobile technology owe their existence to the rules that govern printed texts and served as the basis for what works and what does not in electronic discourse.

Although the cries about the demise of traditional media are hastily proffered, they are very often greatly exaggerated. The reason is simple: both traditional and new digital and social media have great utility for and attractiveness to many sectors of the population. Only when there is truly little to no use for a technology (as when the telegraph faded from use after radio and the telephone, but is still used as a back-up system) will people cease using a technology. Indeed, Richard Edelman et al. (2012) explain well (and fairly consistent with the PESO model) the scope and, especially, the intersection of the four realms of the "**media ecosystem**":

1. *Mainstream*—the traditional mass media channels of newspapers, television, radio, and magazines, which are still the largest contributors of revenue to their organizations' revenue
2. *Tra-digital*—the hybrid channels that have arisen from the combination of traditional mass media channels and new, Web-based/digital media, such as newspapers' websites, Huffington Post, and Politico

3. *Social*—the individual online communities built by dedicated companies, such as Facebook, Mastodon, TikTok, and the rest
4. *Owned*—the particular websites, smartphone apps, and digital content created and maintained for organizations that want them, including the content on organization-specific YouTube and other Web-based channels.

Public relations professionals, then, use the full range of traditional media, and many of those media have been adapted to the electronic realm: personal journals (i.e., blogs), news releases (i.e., social news releases), short personal comments (i.e., toots), and any document that can be turned into a Portable Document Format (PDF) file or hybrid form, like a website, can be an electronic brochure. Additionally, of course, public relations professionals use any social medium to their strategic advantage, provided that they post content that fulfills specific purposes, fits the technological parameters (including data fields) of the medium, and, especially, complements the interests, attitudes, and expectations of users. The PESO approach to identifying and selecting strategically appropriate media can help to make sense of what may be the best thing to do to achieve strategic objectives. Overall, employing strategic use of digital, analog, and experiential tactics must be done wisely and based on research, as Chapter 5 explained.

One distinction that has been made elsewhere in this book is important to reemphasize: social media do not make up one medium, as is so often mistakenly thought. Social media are comprised of many, separate, Web-based and mobile technologies and digital media channels that facilitate interpersonal interaction, collaboration, and community development among Internet users who create and share their own content. In this way, social media are much more idiosyncratic in their facilitation of discourse because of the combination of technological constraints and user/community norms about what is allowed and acceptable content. That content is shared over channels that include blogs, podcasts, wikis, virtual worlds, Internet forums, networking sites, and so on. To this end there are numerous "new" media channels along with traditional media to fulfill specific, measurable objectives. .

Social media, like other channels for PR discourse, are tactics that are chosen in light of a thorough strategic planning process (see Chapter 5). In particular, social media and all tactics are resources that require meticulous management, as this chapter shows. As Duhé (2007) argues, the complexity of decision-making for public relations leaders is especially intense as publics and stakeholders of all kinds seek ways to interact with organizations. Indeed, Duhé argues that not engaging with publics and stakeholders is far more risky than doing so, especially (although not necessarily exclusively) through digital media, when organizations face situations that need great public/stakeholder support.

What is very important to acknowledge at this point is the paradox of social media's controllability. On the one hand, users can employ social media as they wish, which makes that content controlled; but on the other hand, other users can respond any way they wish, which makes the use of the initial socially mediated message uncontrolled. For example, while organizations focus on defined publics and stakeholders, there are people who are predisposed to insert themselves into the fray of public opinion. These people are often on the fringes of an organization's known publics and stakeholders, and they do not have the same kind of vested interest in an organization as stakeholders do. These people are called **stakeseekers**, and they are "groups that seek to put new issues on the corporate agenda" (Holzer, 2008, p. 51) and, thereby, claim argumentatively to be stakeholders. Stakeseekers include, for example, protest groups and activists for a social movement. They have a great willingness to assert their opinions publicly (and to do so aggressively) over online communication channels and social media, and they can damage (or bolster) an organization's image, reputation, and brand (Coombs & Holladay, 2012). Making supportive stakeholders out of stakeseekers is the objective, and social media can be one especially potent approach.

Organizations, then, must adopt a strategic approach to using social media as they would for any strategy and related tactics. Breakenridge (2012) prescribes a common-sense approach to taking advantage of social media for PR that can aid critical analysis and decision-making for effective and successful communication that inspires cooperation between an organization and its publics/stakeholders:

1. Monitor social media on a regular basis (sometimes with a dedicated person) for messages on the macro level (i.e., overall outcomes and reputation impact) and on the micro level (i.e., specific programs, buzz/word-of-mouth communication, digital sharing of information, etc.), then share this intelligence with the relevant areas of the organization that need and can act on it.
2. Provide content within a definitive context that will (a) repurpose existing messages in any medium for social media (e.g., turning video news releases into Vimeo sites; revising brochure text for focused Facebook posts), and (b) search for new content ideas that grab publics' attention and entice them to use it (e.g., trending topics; crowdsourcing).

Social media, again, are means to the end of strategic, ethical, and successful communication between organizations and their publics. Integrating social media and any other medium into strategic plans for public relations takes us back to Chapter 5 and calls to mind the wisdom of Edward L. Bernays that is vital to decision-making.

Public relations pioneer and "father" of the field Edward L. Bernays is known for his social-scientific approach to his work (see Grunig & Hunt, 1984). Key to his approach to public relations was strategic planning within the context of a big picture—knowing well what had to be done by any means or medium necessary, whether his clients understood or embraced it or not, and doing it well (see Bernays, 1965). Bernays recognized the problems with jumping to tactics, saying in his book, *Public Relations* (1952):

Do not think of tactics in terms of segmental approaches. The problem is not to get articles into a newspaper or obtain radio time or arrange for a motion-picture newsreel; it is, rather, to set in motion a broad activity, the success of which depends on interlocking all phases and elements of the proposed strategy, implemented by tactics that are timed to the moment of maximum effectiveness.

(Bernays, 1952, p. 167)

Strategic thinking and clear, focused, and rational decision-making that leads to real value contributions is at the heart of any public relations operation. Our next chapter focuses on the work needed to build the business of a public relations operation whether it is an agency or not.

EXECUTIVE VIEWPOINT

Planning Leads to Decision-making for Successful Implementation

Elliot S. Schreiber, PhD, Consultant and Author

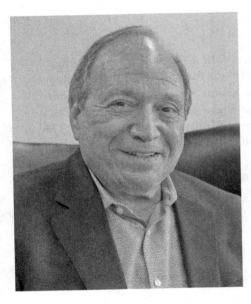

Public relations operates at a senior level of most organizations, reporting either to the CEO or to a member of the executive committee of the company. This puts the head of PR in a position to have a seat at the table when decisions are made, and to have a prominent role in both the development and execution of the strategic plan.

IMPLEMENTATION OF STRATEGY

Chapter 5 covered the role of public relations in strategic planning, and this chapter focuses on making decisions based on strategic planning. While strategy is important, there is a saying in business that success is 5% planning and 95% implementation. The best laid plans are worthless if the organization cannot execute them.

The board holds the CEO responsible for the development, communication, and execution of the strategic plan. Public relations is a key player in both the communication and execution of the plan.

Strategic plans are not set in stone; they must adapt to rapidly changing situations. A key role for public relations is to continually monitor both internal and external environments and advise the CEO and business leaders if there are situations that call for a change to the strategy. Your role should be to assure that the "voice of stakeholders" is heard. Everyone in the organization must be adaptive and flexible, and it is the job of public relations to help employees and external stakeholders understand if and when there are changes in strategy.

DECISION-MAKER VERSUS ADVISOR

PR certainly has a major role to play in support of the CEO, with speech writing, messaging, media relations, and monitoring of factors that might impact the company and its strategy. The goal of the senior communication person should be to become a "trusted advisor" to the CEO and board. The ultimate acknowledgement that PR is adding value is when executives want PR to be at the decision-making "table." This is not easy to achieve, but when it is, it establishes PR as one of the most important functions in the company, helping the CEO to not only make important decisions, but also to communicate those decisions both formally and informally to senior executives and throughout the organization. At times, PR must challenge potential decisions because of their impact on key stakeholders. One must establish credibility to be in such a position. The best PR people see themselves as strategic advisors and consultants using their specialized skills to enhance the value proposition of the organization.

THE BEST ADVICE I EVER RECEIVED

I was fortunate to work in the office of the chairman, serving the legendary chairman of the DuPont Company, Irving Shapiro. Irv had been the general counsel of DuPont previously and was the first non-chemical engineer to be elected chair. Irv's advice was to always be a businessperson first and never let anyone define what I did, other than me.

> If you think primarily as a lawyer, PR, or HR, person, you will only be invited to meetings when others believe you are needed. But if you think and act like a businessperson and use your particular expertise to help them achieve their objectives, you will always be wanted in meetings because you add value.

NOT ALL COMPANIES ARE THE SAME

I worked in three large global corporations during my career, and have been a consultant to a number of international corporations, nonprofits, universities, and trade associations. Each made decisions differently. The thing that all had in common was that those involved in the decision-[making] were judged to be "worthy" of being there. The title or function was less important than one's individual credibility and influence in the organization.

At DuPont, the decision-making was formalized. Presentations were developed, and formal presentations were presented in meetings. Most large conservative companies at that time operated similarly. Bayer had fewer formal presentations. Individual influence mattered and much of the decision-making occurred informally—in the hallway, over coffee or lunch, or while traveling together. It was important to "have someone's ear" so that one could persuade them. At Nortel Networks, we had perhaps 20 people who were considered to be "worth listening to." They were known by the first names only. Everyone knew who they were. When they spoke, they influenced decisions.

Decision-making is changing as companies become less formal and seek to get input from a more diverse group of people. Strategic decisions are becoming more "open," [with leaders] seeking advice from employees instead of restricting decisions to only the top executives. Some companies have even rejected PowerPoint presentations, in favor of discussion and debate.

ARE YOU A "PR PURIST"?

One situation in particular sticks out in my memory as illustrating the importance of adhering to the advice of Irv Shapiro. One of my direct reports was a seasoned professional in charge of our annual report, an important report to shareholders and financial analysts. I went with my colleague to review the design with our CEO and, hopefully, get approval for the design. Review of the text would come later. We got approval, but the CEO wanted us to change a few colors used in the design.

After the meeting, my colleague became quite angry with me that we had allowed "our recommended design" to be changed by the CEO, who he felt was not expert in communication. I asked him to recognize that while we produced the report, it would reflect more on the CEO than on us once published.

He expressed a "purist" view that was contrary to the advice from Irv Shapiro at DuPont.

The role of public relations is "commercial." It is not designed to hang in a gallery or win design awards, but rather to help the company achieve its objectives.

RECOMMENDATIONS

1. When you join a company, pay close attention and understand how decisions are made. Don't assume that what you learned in school or at another company will apply in the new situation.
2. Don't assume PR is defined similarly everywhere. There is, of course, a job description, but the head of PR typically defines how the function is viewed in the company. The fact that many business executives do not know what PR is, does, or can do, can be seen as a problem or an opportunity. One can accept the definition that they have, or one can define the role. Prove your value by showing how communication can help achieve business objectives.
3. Not everyone needs to become a decision-maker to have a rewarding career. Every organization needs more people who can execute decisions flawlessly than they need decision-makers.
4. Remember the advice I was given by Irv Shapiro at DuPont, and avoid becoming a "PR purist." Provide your advice in terms of the business benefit. Your advice may not always be accepted. If it is not, you will be expected to execute the decision. Everyone, even the CEO, has a boss (the CEO reports to the board). You must have a loyalty and obedience to the final decisions, even those you disagree with.
5. A good PR person must be willing to speak up when a potential decision could result in a loss of reputation or risk to the organization. You may not always win the argument, but you should provide your best advice. Always have the "courage of your convictions," but always remember that your personal interests must take a back seat to the best interests of the organization you serve.

KEY WORDS

Value	**Deception**
Value chain and its components	**Decision-making process**
Barcelona Principles	**Five bounds for decision-making**
Head, heart, and hands	**Three judgmental heuristics**
Drucker's five information dimensions	**Two parts to bad decision-making**
Perception process (5 steps)	**Red-flag conditions**
Cognitive short cuts	**Groupthink**

Tactics bias

Recipes

Media ecosystem

PR tactics continuum

Stakeseekers

REFERENCES

Ahlfinger, N. R., & Esser, J. K. (2001). Testing the groupthink model: Effects on promotional leadership and conformity predisposition. *Social Behavior and Personality, 29*(1), 31–42.

Bazerman, M. H., & Moore, D. A. (2009). *Judgment in managerial decision-making* (7th ed.). John Wiley & Sons.

Bernays, E. L. (1952). *Public relations.* University of Oklahoma Press.

Bernays, E. L. (1965). *Biography of an idea: Memoirs of public relations counsel Edward L. Bernays.* Simon & Schuster.

Breakenridge, D. (2012). *Social media and public relations: Eight new practices for the PR professional.* Financial Times Press.

Budd Jr., J. F. (2003). Public relations is the architect of its future: Counsel or courtier? Pros offer opinions. *Public Relations Review, 29,* 375–383.

Campbell, A., Whitehead, J., & Finkelstein, S. (2009, February). Why good leaders make bad decisions. *Harvard Business Review,* 60–66.

Coombs, W. T., & Holladay, S. J. (2012). Internet contagion theory 2.0: How Internet communication channels empower stakeholders. In S. C. Duhé (Ed.), *The new media and public relations* (2nd ed., pp. 21–30). Peter Lang.

Courtright, J. L., & Smudde, P. M. (2010). Recall communications: Discourse genres, symbolic charging, and message design. *International Journal of Strategic Communication, 4*(1), 58–74.

Davenport, T. H., & Beck, J. C. (2002). *The attention economy: Understanding the new currency of business.* Harvard University Press.

Deming, W. E. (1986). *Out of the crisis.* Massachusetts Institute of Technology Center for Advanced Engineering Study.

DeVito, J. A. (2009). *Human communication: The basic course* (11th ed.). Pearson Education.

Drucker, P. F. (1995, January–February). The information executives truly need. *Harvard Business Review,* 54–62.

Drucker, P. F. (2006). *The effective executive.* HarperCollins. (Original work published 1967.)

Duhé, S. C. (2007). Public relations and complexity thinking in the age of transparency. In S. C. Duhé (Ed.), *The new media and public relations* (pp. 57–76). Peter Lang.

Edelman, R., Holdheim, R., Hass, M., Gomes, P., & Rubel, C. (2012). Digital communities: Social media in action. In C. L. Caywood (Ed.), *The handbook of strategic public relations and integrated marketing communication* (2nd ed., pp. 257–253). McGraw-Hill.

Epstein, M. J., & Birchard, B. (2000). *Counting what counts: Turning corporate accountability to competitive advantage.* Perseus.

Ferguson, S. D. (1999). *Communication planning: An integrated approach*. Sage.

Finkelstein, S. (2004). *Why smart executives fail and what you can learn from their mistakes*. Portfolio Trade/Penguin.

Gladwell, M. (2005). *Blink: The power of thinking without thinking*. Back Bay Books.

Grunig, J. E., & Hunt, T. (1984). *Managing public relations*. Harcourt Brace Jovanovich.

Holzer, B. (2008). Turning stakeseekers into stakeholders: A political coalition perspective on the politics of stakeholder influence. *Business & Society, 47*(1), 50–67.

International Association for Measurement and Evaluation of Communication (AMEC). (2020). *Barcelona Principles 3.0*. Available online: https://amecorg.com/barcelona-principles-3-0-translations/.

Janis, I. L. (1972). *Victims of groupthink*. Houghton-Mifflin.

Klein, G. (1998). *Sources of power: How people make decisions*. The MIT Press.

Likely, F. (2013, March 6–10). Public relations/communication department CCO reporting: What information do CEOs truly need? In Y. G. Ji & Z. C. Li (Eds.), *16th International Public Relations Research Conference: Exploring the strategic use of new media's impact on change management and risk in theory and practice* (pp. 453–479). Available online: http://iprrc.org/docs/IPRRC_16_ Proceedings.pdf.

McVee, M. B., Dunsmore, K., & Gavelek, J. R. (2005). Schema theory revisited. *Review of Educational Research, 75*, 531–566.

Moffitt, M. A. (1999). *Campaign strategies and message design: A practitioner's guide from start to finish*. Praeger.

Oates, D. B. (2006, October). Measuring the value of public relations: Tying efforts to business goals. *Public Relations Tactics, 12*.

Oliver, S. (2007). *Public relations strategy* (2nd ed.). Kogan Page.

Potter, L. R. (2006). Strategic planning: Timeless wisdom still shapes successful communication programs. In T. L. Gillis (Ed.), *The IABC handbook of organizational communication: A guide to internal communication, public relations, marketing, and leadership* (pp. 80–92). Jossey-Bass.

Smudde, P. M., & Courtright, J. L. (2012). *Inspiring cooperation and celebrating organizations: Genres, message design and strategy in public relations*. Hampton Press.

Wang, S. S. (2010, September 28). Why so many people can't make decisions. *Wall Street Journal*, D1–D2.

Weick, K. E. (1979). *The social psychology of organizing* (2nd ed.). McGraw-Hill.

RECOMMENDED READING

Argenti, P. A., & Barnes, C. M. (2009). *Digital strategies for powerful corporate communications*. McGraw-Hill.

Breakenridge, D. (2008). *PR 2.0: New media, new tools, new audiences*. Pearson.

Garten, J. E. (2000). *The mind of the CEO*. Perseus Publishing.

Howard, C. M., & Mathews, W. K. (2013). *On deadline: Managing media relations* (5th ed.). Waveland.

Li, C., & Bernoff, J. (2009). *Marketing in the ground-swell*. Harvard Business School Press.

Lipman-Blumen, J. (2006). *The allure of toxic leaders: Why we follow destructive bosses and corrupt politicians—and how we can survive them.* Oxford University Press.

Moffitt, M. A. (1999). *Campaign strategies and message design.* Praeger.

Rice, R. E., & Atkin, C. K. (2013). *Public communication campaigns* (4th ed.). Sage.

Scott, D. M. (2009). *The new rules of marketing and PR: How to use news releases, blogs, pod-casting, viral marketing, and online media to reach buyers directly.* John Wiley & Sons.

8

CHAPTER 8
CLIENT-CENTERED COMMUNICATION

CHAPTER OUTLINE

You are always working for someone. That someone—a "**client**"—has expectations of you and you of them. Mindreading is not a possibility, and even if it were, it might scarcely make sense to another person. Therefore, good communication with your clients is essential. When public relations professionals are employed by a nonagency company, their "clients" are people in other operational units for or with which PR work is being done. When public relations professionals are employed by an agency, consultancy, or vendor, or if PR professionals are freelancers, their clients are the organizations for which they are contractually obligated to complete certain work. When public relations professionals are employed by companies, nonprofits, nongovernmental organizations, or other institutions, their clients are not only the other operating units within their organizations, but also their organizations' constituents, which include donors, benefactors, employees, members, volunteers, community leaders, and others. In every case, clients need and want to know what is going on and why. Also, in every case, public relations professionals are serving in the best interests of others, which, as we saw in Chapter 3, has major moral, ethical, and legal responsibilities.

Client-centered communication, very broadly speaking, concerns the reinforcement of gratification about what has been and will be done for a client and its constituents. A related purpose may include reducing buyer remorse in a client who is having second thoughts in the face of a well-laid plan. Obvious dimensions to good communication—openness, honesty, candor, respectfulness, dialog, timeliness, professionalism, accuracy, and so on—are necessarily parts of client-centered communication. So is keeping promises. In this chapter we look at two pivotal topics of client communication: knowing the audience and using certain frameworks for good communication.

KNOW YOUR AUDIENCE

People have many things going on in their lives that demand their attention. People have varying degrees of control over things that happen or that may happen. And

DOI: 10.4324/9781003208280-9

people respond to messages and media differently. Taking just these factors together is enough to suggest how important it is to know what someone needs and wants when communication about something is required. In short, know your audience. This is a maxim that is true of all forms of communication, and it is something we all learned all along in our education, beginning with writing. An effective way to enact this maxim is to apply a "**you-attitude**," which places the emphasis on the audience through a combination of particular language choices and pertinent themes or topics essential in a communication act (Shelby & Reinsch, 1995).

Remember, too, that you-attitudes go both ways—PR expert to client and vice versa. From the client's point of view, as Croft (2006) explains, the relationship with PR experts requires strategy-based solutions; quick responses with enthusiasm, energy, and creativity; solutions before clients think of them; relentless attention to detail; being part of the client's team; unexpected added value; wise budget management; daring to be different; commitment to client success; expertise the client does not have or cannot afford in-house; the objectivity and courage to ask tough questions; good listening; no surprises; making the client a hero; proactive environmental scanning for emerging issues, business opportunities, or threats; exuding a genuine can-do attitude; delivering more than expected results; and thinking innovatively.

From the PR expert's point of view, according to Lukaszewski (2003), the relationship requires the information necessary to do the job, methods for enacting planned communications (strategies and tactics), enough time to complete the job, support of the expert to others in the client's organization, problem-solving attitude, courage to raise sticky issues and push the client, and willingness to tell the client when they do something puzzling or irritating. Additionally, the client should share responsibility for success or failure fairly equally with the expert, accept responsibility for their own ideas and feelings, and share those ideas and feelings with the expert.

In Lukaszewski's (2003) view of client-centered communication, a PR expert (internal and external) must:

- Not **overpromise** and **underdeliver** (or vice versa, as either way it looks like something was not thought through correctly)
- Pay attention to their own internal alarm ("gut feelings") because there may be something to it
- Make their own values and philosophy clear
- Avoid accepting the client's definition of the problem or opportunity
- Look for patterns in what has and what could go on
- State their own goals and expectations clearly
- Define what will be done and how by both client and expert
- Know the "real client."

Effective listening is vital to working with clients, especially if there are times when they resist you and your ideas. Handling client resistance, as Lukaszewski (2003) advises, begins with being able to recognize that it is happening and it has a certain pattern. What is that pattern? The client may use language reflecting that they may be avoiding responsibility, flooding you with detail, responding to your questions with one-word answers, attacking you angrily, merely complying with whatever you say without expressing real feelings, changing the subject, maintaining silence, nit-picking at minute details, or asking too early and continuously for a solution. It is important to calmly seek clarification based on the communication behaviors and statements, not on any judgments about what may be behind those behaviors and statements. Then continue to listen carefully for verbal and nonverbal, intended and unintended messages. What are they, and what do they indicate? Make sure you remain engaged with the conversation and, especially, support the client's underlying concerns and recognize any vulnerabilities.

Realize, too, that the way in which something is said matters, and the medium and the message work together. In client (or any) communication, there are pros and cons to any chosen channel (Lengel & Daft, 1988). Theories and research about **media richness** (i.e., the degree to which information can be conveyed over a medium; the more information that helps a task and reduces uncertainty, the richer the medium) and **media synchronicity** (i.e., the degree to which channels enable communication flow and communication combinations across media that pertain to task decision-making) explore and explain how and why it is that communication channels provide varying levels of utility and effectiveness, including in the workplace and among work teams (see Dennis et al., 2008; Kahai & Cooper, 2003; Thatcher & Brown, 2010; Turner et al., 2010).

People vary in their ability to handle different channels, but more to the point about knowing an audience, people also have **channel preferences** in obtaining and sharing information over different media (Gu et al., 2011). So communication channels have certain, basic characteristics to be considered:

- *Face-to-face*—usually the best, richest channel as people are physically in the same place at the same time; much richness of the channel; can gage commitment and engagement; direct feedback; expensive and time-consuming if people must travel to be together; no automatic record
- *Video virtual meetings*—mimics face-to-face communication; limits channel richness by technology (e.g., audio quality, video quality, video frame, talking heads, bandwidth, same or compatible technology at both ends); saves on travel expenses; sessions can be recorded; document/file sharing is possible
- *Telephone*—avoids face-to-face contact; usually not good for complex matters, unless you have arranged an appointment to call; relies on astute perceptions and handling of paralinguistic features of conversation

- *E-mail, text messages, and voice mail*—avoids face-to-face contact; poor for complex, personal matters; good for quick matters; texting can wreak havoc on spelling and grammar, and cause other language problems; e-mail can include attachments to support main messages; provides a record of messages
- *Formal presentations*—focuses attention of group and efficiently conveys an argument in one setting; answers doubts and objections; possible for emerging support to be apparent; may require extra time for people to assess and respond to content
- *Group meetings*—useful for getting status updates and making decisions and assignments; not ideal for conveying information, but good for establishing rationales
- *Memos*—use relies on particular organizational rules for their formatting and composition; conciseness is key; provides a written record; can be considered at the convenience of persons addressed; effective writing in all respects is essential
- *Corporate publications*—good as internal records of organizational policies, news, and other purposes; unreliable as to how much they may be read and at what levels in an organization; effective writing and layout in all respects are essential.

Across these and other channels of business communication with clients, the important thing to remember is to know people's preferred communication media and use them well. More ambiguous messages (e.g., those that convey information whose content may be guarded or is still being worked out but it is important to say something) require rich media, such as face-to-face channels. Conversely, very plain messages (e.g., those that convey concrete information and data) require lean media, such as publications or memos (see Downs & Adrian, 2004). Convenience in your sending any messages does not necessarily equate to effectiveness in either the client's receiving or knowing the message content. To ensure that communication content is strong in any channel, a few simple and useful frameworks offer ways to develop messages.

FRAMEWORKS FOR CLIENT COMMUNICATION

Client-focused communication may take one of many forms, but the purpose for it very likely will be either informative or persuasive. Informative messages seek to establish a level of knowledge and familiarity with a subject so that it connects with what people already understand and/or are coming to understand. Informative communication, then, is often educational in nature, as in giving background and details about something. Persuasive messages seek to inspire someone to assent to or "buy into" one's thesis (see Perelman & Olbrechts-Tyteca, 1991). That assent to a thesis or argument is made possible by the combination of (1) the PR expert's text and (2) the client's own knowledge and reasoning—**self-persuasion** (Burks, 1970), which can involve various acts. Self-persuasion can be viewed as a sequence of stages like that of Rogers' (2003) diffusion theory, which is fairly predictable and can feature different communication channels at different times:

- A matter gains one's attention,
- becomes a legitimate concern,
- is tried out,
- is implemented,
- then is evaluated.

As we saw in Chapters 1 and 6, deception is something you must be on guard against in your own communication and that of others. Language choice in communication is, of course, vital. One of the most useful frameworks for ensuring effective messages in business communication is the **7 Cs of effective communication** (Murphy et al., 1997), and the PRSA endorses a very similar breakdown in its study guide for its accreditation exam for PR professionals. The 7 Cs (see boxed text) should be used for all client-focused and other professional communication efforts. Capturing and communicating concisely and compellingly what is necessary to make a decision is possible through Lukaszewski's (2003) **five steps for recommendations**: (1) explain in 40 words why a situation, problem, or opportunity is important to the client; (2) analyze in 60 words the impact of or risk concerning the matter; (3) provide options, costs, and benefits of doing nothing, doing something, doing something more, and doing something else; (4) recommend one of the options for what must be done; and (5) provide a rationale about why that option must be used by differentiating it from the other options, examining potential unintended consequences, and defending anticipated outcomes. Figure 8.1 shows a worksheet that can be used to capture the relevant information to facilitate the kind of client communication needed.

This worksheet is a guide for your discussion with a client, not necessarily a document to give to the client. It is something you use to formulate how you (and your team) see a situation and what could be done. Overpreparing is far better than underpreparing! The starting point for using this worksheet is to succinctly define the situation and its importance, including what is at risk or what impact (positive or negative) it will have for the organization. Consistent with Lukaszewski's five-step approach, at least four options must be specified and then explored in terms of their strengths, weaknesses, messages that could be conveyed, and audiences who would receive those messages. Notice that each column of the table in the worksheet yields something important for a strategic plan, as indicated by the small black row at the bottom of the columns (see Chapter 5 and Appendix A).

As you work through each cell for the intersecting rows and columns of the worksheet's table, more details about what can be done and how to do it point to dimensions of communication action that may be better than others, thereby resulting in your ultimate decision about which option to recommend and why. Note at this point what your criteria are for choosing any option over the others, applying the decision-making process from Chapter 7. State your recommendation as to which option to adopt, give the rationale for why it is best, and list what tactics you would use to enact that recommendation.

DEFINE THE SITUATION: _____

SITUATION'S IMPORTANCE (IMPACT/RISK): _____

OPTIONS	STRENGTHS	WEAKNESSES	MESSAGES	AUDIENCES
1. DO NOTHING				
2. DO SOMETHING:				
3. DO SOMETHING MORE:				
4. DO SOMETHING ELSE:				
(OBJECTIVES REVEALED)	(CRITERIA REVEALED)		(DISCURSIVE ACTION REVEALED)	

RECOMMENDATION (CRITERIA-BASED): _____

RATIONALE (CRITERIA-BASED): _____

TACTICS (DISCOURSE-BASED): _____

EVALUATION (OBJECTIVE-BASED): _____

  OUTPUTS: _____

  OUTTAKES: _____

Projected { OUTCOMES: _____

          { OUTGROWTHS: _____

Figure 8.1 Client communication worksheet

From this laying out and weighing of options, the recommending of one of the four options, and the listing of tactical approaches to make it happen that would fold into a proper strategic plan (see Appendix A), the final formal component of this worksheet is showing initial ideas as to how the recommended option would be evaluated in terms of "**the four outs**" (Lindenmann, 2006; also see Chapter 5 and Appendix A):

- *Outputs* (measurements of what tactics were created and how well they were deployed, and the level of exposure for an organization)
- *Outtakes* (measurements of the audience's immediate or short-term responses to communication)
- *Outcomes* (measurements of the audience's medium-term response to communication)
- *Outgrowths* (measurements of the audience's long-term and cumulative response to communication as it affects an organization's reputation and image).

Consistent with Chapter 5, audience responses for outtakes, outcomes, and outgrowths are measured against stated objectives over defined periods of time, which would target people's heads (awareness and knowledge), hearts (attitudes and emotions), and hands (actions and behaviors). Make sure you also mention what research method(s) you would use to measure against the objectives, so you would know what results you would expect. Additional notes may be added to this form at the bottom as needed to explain or draw attention to anything necessary.

Even after attending to so many matters of effective communication based on your client's expectations, there is still every reason to formally measure whether your communication with the client has been effective and to what degree. You may, of course, talk about it and, thereby, obtain personal statements about what has worked and what has not. You may also send an e-mail or memo with the question, "What do you think about how we have communicated with and served you?" But that question is too open-ended and would not be considerate of the client's time and effort to answer it. A better way to obtain the feedback you need that can also serve as documentation of your effectiveness is to prepare and send a brief questionnaire about multiple aspects of customer service. The content of the questionnaire, an example of which is shown in Figure 8.2, should touch on the salient matters about the business relationship between the client and the PR expert, including communication. It is important that the questionnaire is focused and simple to complete. The questionnaire may be prepared in any medium you wish, print or electronic—as long as your client can complete it easily and in a short amount of time, and as long as you can collect the data and use it meaningfully for the business.

An important matter for a satisfaction survey is to make sure you get any feedback, so follow up with your client to make sure they complete the form and return it. Once you get the completed form, read it, analyze it, and discuss it with your team. Do a SWOT analysis based on the feedback and other data you have from the client that pertains to your perceptions of their satisfaction with your work. Summarize the

Your feedback is important to us!

Thank you for choosing Bill & Ted's Public Relations. We are committed to providing all our customers with complete customer satisfaction, so please complete this brief questionnaire and send it back to us. On behalf of the entire Bill & Ted's Public Relations team, thank you for your business!

About You

Your Name_____

Company_____

Street Address_____

City_____ State_____ Zip_____

Phone_____ Fax_____

E-mail_____

Type of Project/Program We Worked on for You

____Media Relations   ____Product Launch   ____Other: _____

____Investor Relations   ____Integrated Communications

____Employee Communications   ____Reputation Management   _____

____Event Planning   ____Crisis/Issue Management   _____

Notable project details:_____

_____

Personal Service

	Bad	Poor	Good	Very Good	Excellent

Was the project estimate accurate?   ___Yes   ___No   ___Not Applicable

Was our account staff helpful?   ___Yes   ___No   ___Not Applicable

Did our project manager address your project's needs promptly?   ___Yes   ___No

	Bad	Poor	Good	Very Good	Excellent
How effective was our account team's communication with you?	1	2	3	4	5

Comments:_____

_____

_____

Work Quality

Was the project done on budget?   ___Yes   ___No

Was the project done on time?   ___Yes   ___No

Were our team members on site with you on time?   ___Yes   ___No

Were our people easy to work with?   ___Yes   ___No

	Bad	Poor	Good	Very Good	Excellent
How would you rate the overall quality of our work?	1	2	3	4	5

Comments:_____

_____

_____

Figure 8.2 Customer satisfaction questionnaire

Overall Experience

		Not at All	Somewhat Satisfied	Satisfied	Very Satisfied	Completely Satisfied
Overall, based on all aspects of our work on your project, how satisfied are you with us?		1	2	3	4	5

		Not at All	Maybe	Possibly	Probably	Definitely
How likely would you be to want us to work with you again?		1	2	3	4	5

How You Heard About Us

___Referral from someone   ___Website
___Prior project with you   ___News/Magazine article
___Phone call   ___Advertisement
___Literature   ___Other:_____

Marketing Information

Would you be willing to give a testimonial?   ___Yes   ___No

What trade shows do you attend?_____

_____

What trade publications do you read?_____

_____

What news or business publications do you read?_____

_____

Additional Comments

What are our strengths when working with you?_____

_____

_____

_____

_____

How can we do better when working with you?_____

_____

_____

_____

_____

Thank You!

Please mail your completed questionnaire in the enclosed, postage-paid envelope.

Figure 8.2 (Continued)

findings, prepare some recommendations for improvement, and outline steps to be taken in the short and long terms. Then, finally, discuss this report with the client so that the relationship you share becomes better and stronger.

Unfortunately, on rare occasions, an agency may have a client that is difficult to work with because of any number of factors (e.g., unreasonable, aggressive, in default of paying invoices, etc.). In such a situation, an agency may be better off firing the client. Doing so is possible because, presumably, the contract allows for either party to terminate the business relationship (without financial penalty) at any time for any reason (probably in writing). Similar to firing an employee, the agency will have to at least (1) make a case for why the firing is necessary; and (2) propose a means for completing any unfinished work, if any exists, and getting paid for it. Again, like firing an employee, it is best to do it at a face-to-face meeting and to have the required and proper documentation to terminate the business relationship. The client may have a lot of questions and, maybe, feel personally hurt. Focus on the business factors and refrain from using judgmental language. In other words, "take the high road" to firing the client and leave on as amicable grounds as possible. After all, your agency's handling of this situation must be as professional and fair as any other.

Like any relationship between people, communication must be effective. It will not always be perfect, but it must be effective so that people view things, expectations, and each other as similarly as possible. All the principles and practices of good, effective leadership and management in public relations are as important in small matters as they are in big matters. The character of an organization and the character of PR professionals is a supremely valuable asset to protect at all times.

THE SEVEN Cs OF EFFECTIVE COMMUNICATION

COMPLETENESS

- Provide all necessary information—who, what, where, when, why, how
- Answer all questions asked—stated and implied
- Give something extra, when desirable

Example: Please e-mail me in return the departures from Singapore to Hong Kong on the 8th. [Your response should give more details about the times of day, airlines flying that route, costs, and departure/arrival times.]

CONCISENESS

- Eliminate wordy expressions—use one word in place of phrases; one sentence instead of two; read aloud to listen for wordiness
- Include only relevant material—omit trite expressions; ask what information is truly relevant for the reader and your message
- Avoid unnecessary repetition—see if the same word or idea appears too often

Example: Will you ship us sometime, anytime during the month of October would be fine, or even November if you are rushed (November would suit us just as well, in fact a little bit better) 300 of the regular 3 by 5-inch blue felt armbands with white sewn letters in the center?

Thank you in advance for sending these along to use by parcel post, and not express, as express is too expensive.

Revised: Please ship parcel post, before the end of November, 300 regular 3 by 5-inch blue felt armbands with white sewn letters in the center.

CONSIDERATION

- Focus on "you" instead of "I" or "we"—see your material from your reader's (listener's) point of view; "you" is generally more desirable than "I" or "we"
- Show audience benefit or interest in the receiver—readers (and listeners) like to know benefits and should be a prominent part of the message
- Emphasize positive, pleasant facts—positive words elicit favorable reactions from readers (and listeners); remember to balance the good and the bad

Example: We don't refund, if the returned item is soiled or unusable.

Revised: We refund when the returned item is clean and resalable.

CONCRETENESS

- Use specific facts and figures—be precise when using factual data.

Example:

(1) Eastern Europe is making progress in obtaining investments. [vague, general, indefinite]
(1a) In 1990 investments in Eastern Europe were about $30 million (U.S.). Today that figure has increased 12 percent. [concrete, precise]
   - Put action in your verbs—people prefer reading active voice rather than passive voice; use action in verbs rather than in nouns and infinitives

Examples:

(2)   The tests were administered by the professors. [subject receives action]
(2a) Professors administered the tests. [subject performs action]
(3)   Vice President Smith will give consideration to the report. [action hiding in a "quiet" noun; "deadly" verbs: be, give, have, hold, make, put, and take]
(3a) Vice President Smith will consider the report. [action in the verb]

(4)   The duty of a secretary is <u>to check</u> all incoming mail and <u>to record</u> it. In
       addition, it is his or her responsibility <u>to keep</u> the assignment book up to
       date. [action hiding in infinitive]
(4a)   A secretary <u>checks</u> and <u>records</u> all incoming mail and <u>keeps</u> the assignment
       book up to date. [action in the verbs]

- Choose vivid, image-building words—use these words strategically

Example:

(5)   Some women were stopped in their promotions. [literal, dull]
(5a)   Many women faced the "glass ceiling" in their companies. [more vivid,
       figurative]

CLARITY

- Choose precise, concrete and familiar words—readers (and listeners) prefer
  words they know; avoid Latin terms when possible

Example: After our perusal of pertinent data, the conclusion is that a lucrative
market exists for the subject property.

Revised: The data we studied show that your property is profitable and in high
demand.

- Construct effective sentences and paragraphs—(length) use short sentences
  of 17–20 words; (unity) develop one idea for each sentence; (coherence)
  arrange words in sentences so ideas clearly express your intended meaning
  and place modifiers close to the words they are modifying

Example: Her report was about managers, broken down by age and gender.

Revised: Her report focused on age and gender of managers.

Revised: Her report about managers focused on age and gender.

COURTESY

- Be sincerely tactful, thoughtful and appreciative—reflect a sincere, genuine
  you attitude; get someone else's opinion if you have doubts

Example: Clearly, you did not read my latest e-mail.

Revised: Sometimes my wording is not precise. Let me try again.

- Use expressions that show respect—avoid language that may offend your reader; use humor cautiously; ask someone's opinion if you have doubts

Examples of discourteous phrases:

(1) Contrary to your inference...
(2) I'm sure you must realize...
(3) Obviously you overlooked...
(4) We find it difficult to believe that...
(5) Why have you ignored...
(6) You are probably ignorant of the fact that...
(7) You should know...
(8) You surely don't expect...
    - Choose nondiscriminatory expressions—be aware of gender, race, age, color, creed, sexual preference, and ethnic origins

Examples of neutral terminology:

(1)   freshman → first-year student
(2)   manpower → workers; employees; workforce; personnel; people
(3)   Anyone who comes late to class will get his/her grade reduced.
(3a) Anyone who comes late to class will have their grade reduced.

CORRECTNESS

- Use the right level of language—formal (unconversational, impersonal, complex style usually for scholarly work, legal documents, governmental assignments); informal (conversational, personal, simpler style typical of business writing); and substandard (colloquial, incorrect/improper words, grammar, etc.)
- Check accuracy of figures, facts and words/names—verify statistical data; double check your totals; avoid guessing at laws that affect you and your reader; have someone read your work; determine if any facts have changed over time
- Maintain acceptable writing mechanics—apply rules of grammar, syntax and usage and discourse conventions for any type of document you prepare

Source: Derived from Murphy et al. (1997, pp. 31–65)

EXECUTIVE VIEWPOINT

Focus on Others and Authenticity in Client Communication

Tiara M. Tucker, Entrepreneur & Communication Consultant

For nearly two decades, I have had the opportunity to professionally work in the fascinating field of communication. If I date back to when I won my first communication-related award in kindergarten, when I wrote a letter to Santa Claus that landed me a plush seat on an Amtrak train to have breakfast with him, then it is fair to say that I have been in love with the power of communication and creating communications my entire life.

What I have enjoyed most about my journey in PR and communication is the diversity of experiences and opportunities I have been afforded over the years. From being a corporate communicator for a well-known and respected Fortune 50 company; to becoming an entrepreneur owning and running my own award-winning boutique PR and communications firm, Tiara PR Network, LLC; to creating and leading my nonprofit organization, Speak That! Movement, Inc., that is making noteworthy strides in the women's empowerment, mental health, and social justice spaces, I have learned that the most critical key to success (or lack thereof) is my ability to impactfully communicate with my various clients and audiences to help them reach their desired goals and dreams.

In the next few paragraphs, I will share some of my takeaways as a PR practitioner and communicator focused on client-centered communication working as a Corporate America employee, an entrepreneur, and a nonprofit leader.

CLIENT-CENTERED COMMUNICATION AS A CORPORATE AMERICA EMPLOYEE

I believe there is so much to be gained from working in Corporate America. Granted, not all PR and communication teams are the same—some may be very small where communicators are expected to be the "jack of all trades," while others may be large with communicators having more specialized roles that are dependent on others. Whether your clients are your internal business partners or external groups, your communication with your audience is typically on behalf of the organization for which you are working. The ultimate goal is a consistent client experience, which may involve creating and adhering to communication processes, guidelines, strategies, and approval processes.

CLIENT-CENTERED COMMUNICATION AS AN ENTREPRENEUR

While working in Corporate America, I found great joy doing unique and passion-filled PR and communications work outside of my day job. Working as an entrepreneur certainly has its highs and lows. Once you get over the hurdle of deciding to be an entrepreneur, there is the uncertainty of whether you will ever have paying clients (do not underestimate what you can learn from having non-paying clients as you start out), and then the complexities of it being your responsibility to have the processes and structures in place to keep your clients satisfied. At the center of it all is being able to keep your clients in the forefront of *how* and *why* you started your business in the first place.

As the founder and owner of Tiara PR Network, I have provided PR and communications services for all types of clients, individuals, and organizations, including: the nation's leading civil rights attorneys, justice-seeking families impacted by police who wrongfully murdered their loved one, a celebrity who murdered someone, speakers, authors, nonprofit leaders/organizations, professional athletes, entertainers, small business owners, etc. My greatest strengths have been my desire to work long hours, learn as I go, understand my clients and their needs on a deeper level, empathetically communicate with them, and do everything I can to be one of their biggest assets.

CLIENT-CENTERED COMMUNICATION AS A NONPROFIT LEADER

The most successful nonprofit leaders operate and communicate from a place of purpose and passion. Clients can range from the individual and organizations in the community who benefit from an organization's efforts and services; generous donors and supporters who are relied on to help the organization fulfil its mission; and volunteers who graciously donate their time. As the founder and leader of my 501(c)(3) charitable organization, Speak That! Movement, communication drives everything that my organization does.

We frequently communicate to educate, equip, empower, inspire, and connect people in the communities we serve. We have to communicate regularly and creatively via social media, e-mails, text messages, phone calls, and through our events to gain and maintain financial and nonfinancial supporters to help us with our efforts. We take pride in communicating with intention, sincerity, and gratitude.

CLIENT-CENTERED COMMUNICATION NUGGETS FOR STUDENTS

Since my award-winning letter to Santa, I have earned many more awards, accolades, honors, and much fancier trips in airplanes versus trains. I will humbly attribute this to hard work, dedication, continuous learning, maintaining the best work–life balance I can, my faith, and most importantly, keeping my clients and various audiences at the top of my mind. I would encourage you to do the same; however, if you need a few more client-centered communication nuggets to guide you along your journey with your current and future clients, remember my C.L.I.E.N.T. acronym based on all of my above-mentioned experiences:

C—**Communicate Regularly:** Maintain a habit of regularly communicating with your clients so they know what to expect from you, what you should expect from them, when, and how. This also includes being considerate in *when* you communicate because some clients may prefer communicating with you very early in the morning before they start their day, while others may prefer communicating at the wee hours of the night, and everything in between. Set expectations early on so that you don't feel the pressure of waking up from your sleep because your client just had a bright idea after a late night out with friends. On the other hand, some communications may require a sense of urgency, so be clear on what is expected of you. Also, be flexible in *how* you communicate, recognizing that some clients may prefer to communicate with you via text messages, phone calls, e-mails, video chats, face-to-face visits, or by utilizing communication platforms, such as GroupMe, Slack, Google Drive, etc.

L—Listen Attentively: There is truth in knowing that we have one mouth and two ears for a reason. The best way to understand your clients' needs is to ask good questions (sometimes the same question in multiple ways) and listen attentively. Although not every client may be able to clearly articulate their needs (hence, why they may be depending on you), it is still very important to listen to what they are saying and not saying. Learn to be agile, ask for feedback regularly, and adjust accordingly.

I— Invest in Your Craft: Being a sought-after and talented PR practitioner and communicator does not happen overnight. It takes thousands of hours and multiple decades of continuous learning, evolving, and adapting. It will entail overcoming fears and doubts, screwing up, feeling lost and confused, dealing with the anxiety of working with new clients, and the infamous Imposter Syndrome making you feel like you are in the wrong profession. Trust me, I know. However, as a college student or current professional in communication reading (or skimming) this book right now, you are investing in your craft more than you may realize. Don't stop!

E—Educate Yourself and Your Clients: One of my favorite communicators, Oprah Winfrey, is quoted for saying, "I think education is power. I think that being able to communicate with people is power. One of my min goals on the planet is to encourage people to empower others." Read that again and let it sink in! As professionals in the communication industry, remaining educated and informed about what matters in our industry and in the world of your clients is powerful. I would suggest you make time to read relevant online articles, social media posts, books, and newsletters from time to time. Also, attend in-person or virtual webinars and conferences, or join organizations, such as your local Public Relations Society of America chapter, to continuously learn new ideas and concepts from a variety of people with different experiences. Make LinkedIn your friend! There are tons of communicators and communication groups on LinkedIn. You may just find your next client or career move there. Additionally, being able to communicate with your clients—in impactful ways—is powerful. As you continue to learn and work on new projects, you will feel more confident in your ability to encourage and empower your clients to reach their goals and dreams. And that, my friends, is power!

N—Never Give Up: Along your PR and communication journey, never give up! Nothing more needs to be stated here. You get it!

T—Thank Others Often: Two words that should be said more often in our field are: *Thank You!* Never lose sight of the importance of thanking your clients for choosing you to provide them a service. Remember to thank the people on your team who helped you crank out your work or who have your back. Show gratitude to your loved ones who believe in you. Thank your mentors, leaders, and professors who pour into you. Lastly, be sure to thank yourself for not giving up on your goals and dreams of being the best PR practitioner and communicator you can be!

KEY WORDS

Client

You-attitude

Over-/Underpromising

Over-/Underdelivering

Self-persuasion and process

Media richness

Media synchronicity

Channel preferences

Seven Cs of communication

Five steps for recommendations

"The four outs" (outputs, outtakes, outcomes, and outgrowths)

REFERENCES

Burks, D. M. (1970). Persuasion, self-persuasion, and rhetorical discourse. *Philosophy & Rhetoric, 3*(2), 109–119.

Croft, A. C. (2006). *Managing a public relations firm for growth and profit* (2nd ed.). Best Business Books.

Dennis, A. R., Fuller, R. M., & Valacich, J. S. (2008, September). Media, tasks, and communication processes: A theory of media synchronicity. *Management Information Systems Quarterly, 32*(3), 575–600.

Downs, C. W., & Adrian, A. D. (2004). *Assessing organizational communication: Strategic communication audits.* Guilford Press.

Gu, R., Higa, K., & Moodie, D. R. (2011). A study on communication media selection: Comparing the effectiveness of the media richness, social influence, and media fitness. *Journal of Service Science and Management, 4*, 291–299.

Kahai, S. S., & Cooper, R. B. (2003). Exploring the core concepts of media richness theory: The impact of cue multiplicity and feedback immediacy on decision quality. *Journal of Management Information Systems, 20*(1), 263–299.

Lengel, R. H., & Daft, R. L. (1988). The selection of communication media as an executive skill. *Academy of Management Executive, 2*, 225–232.

Lindenmann, W. K. (2006). *Public relations research for planning and evaluation.* Institute for Public Relations. Available online: www.instituteforpr.org/topics/pr-research-for-planning-and-evaluation/.

Lukaszewski, J. (2003, March 19). Effective consulting: Getting those you advise to listen to and act on your advice. Presentation at the PRSA Southeastern Wisconsin Professional Development Conference, Milwaukee, WI.

Murphy, H. A., Hildebrandt, H. W., & Thomas, J. P. (1997). *Effective business communications* (7th ed.). McGraw Hill.

Perelman, C., & Olbrechts-Tyteca, L. (1991). *The new rhetoric: A treatise on argumentation.* University of Notre Dame Press.

Rogers, E. (2003). *The diffusion of innovations* (5th ed.). Free Press.

Shelby, A. N, & Reinsch Jr., N. L. (1995). Positive emphasis and you-attitude: An empirical study. *Journal of Business Communication, 32,* 303–328.

Thatcher, S. M. B., & Brown, S. A. (2010). Individual creativity in teams: The importance of communication media mix. *Decision Support Systems, 49,* 290–300. DOI:10.1016/j.dss.2010.03.004

Turner, T., Qvarfordt, P., Biehl, J. T., Golovchinsky, G., & Back, M. (2010, August 10–15). Exploring the workplace communication ecology. In *CHI '10: Proceedings of the SIGCHI Conference on Human Factors in Computing Systems* (pp. 841–850). Association for Computing Machinery.

RECOMMENDED READING

Beard, M. (2001). *Running a public relations department* (2nd ed.). Kogan Page.

Croft, A. C. (2006). *Managing a public relations firm for growth and profit* (2nd ed.). Best Business Books.

Dickinson, D. (2003). *The new account manager.* The Copy Shop.

Hameroff, E. J. (1998). *The advertising agency business: The complete manual for management and operation* (3rd ed.). NTC Business Books.

Lordan, E. J. (2003). *Essentials of public relations management.* Burnham.

Maister, D. H. (1993). *Managing the professional service firm.* Free Press.

Roetzer, P. (2012). *The marketing agency blueprint: The handbook for building hybrid PR, SEO, content, advertising, and web firms.* John Wiley & Sons.

9

CHAPTER 9
BUSINESS-DEVELOPMENT PRINCIPLES

CHAPTER OUTLINE

Organizations do not and cannot just open for business and assume people will be inspired to transact with them. "If you build it, they will come" is an idea that only works in the movies. Building business with present, past, and potential customers is an important matter, because it concerns how the organization can obtain more market share from competitors, especially by leaning on its value proposition. Public relations is naturally concerned with matters of business development because much of the work PR people do is used by people who are making buying, investing, donating, and other decisions.

For this reason, public relations managers must know what it takes to develop new business from present, past, and potential customers. Indeed, a corporate public relations department must be known for and always produce great work that gets desired or better results for other operating areas of the company. An agency also must be known for and always produce excellent work that gets expected or better-than-expected results for many clients in multiple industries with wide ranges of products and services. In this way, corporate public relations operations and agencies are very similar: they each serve customers—the former's are internal, the latter's are external, and all are vital to growing the business and value for public relations.

DOI: 10.4324/9781003208280-10

This chapter focuses on three interrelated arenas for business development. First is the arena of promoting the public relations function. PR people are so busy inspiring cooperation between organizations and their publics that they rarely focus on doing the same for their own operations and the profession. And this PR about PR is sorely needed. Second is the arena of market positioning. PR is instrumental in communication that affects people's knowledge, attitudes, and behaviors toward an organization and what it offers. Having an idea about how market positions are determined and how they are central to communication efforts is essential to managing public relations resources. The third and final arena for this chapter is cold, warm, and hot calls. Again, organizations must make a concerted effort to specifically obtain sales that build their businesses. "Sales" concerns transactions between people, and the kinds of "sales" public relations people do (e.g., to sell a story to journalists) are very similar to the sales made by sales representatives. Understanding that there are different degrees of calls and ways to strategically engage in sales contacts can help build business—especially public relations business—as greater and greater success is attained.

PROMOTING THE PUBLIC RELATIONS FUNCTION

Because public relations naturally deals with communication and every human can communicate (of course, many are better than others), PR is seen as easy. At the same time, it is very interesting to discover how bad organizational leaders can be at writing, public speaking, and interpersonal communication, even though they still "rise through the ranks." Still, when public relations is viewed as easy, it is because it is seen as the organizational mouthpiece and its practitioners are merely the vocal chords for what the management brain wants to say. Of course, this view is very unfair and unrealistic. It is grounded in the negative stereotypes for the profession that persist and fly in the face of the ethical, strategic, and challenging work of PR professionals that is vital to inspiring cooperation between organizations and their publics. If organizational leaders do not understand what public relations is and what value it offers in business terms, public relations will not be included in the strategic management for the organization. As always, any public relations practitioner has the duty and responsibility to educate people—no matter who they are—about the very real value and power of public relations.

In addition to the added value that public relations offers organizations, as covered in Chapter 7, the exercising of **power** is an important matter for successful public relations management. The notion of power is a tricky one because the concept mixes negative, positive, and neutral meanings. Negative connotations often coincide with the sense and reference of words like "domination" or "oppression." Positive to neutral connotations can often parallel senses and references of words like "control" or "authority" or "influence." But, depending on one's attitude, the negative connotations could be viewed positively and the positive connotations viewed negatively.

Power is more complicated than positive, negative, or neutral attitudes suggest. Also, power is not a thing to be possessed but, rather, is a direct function of personal relationships. That is, "power is a community-based phenomenon that people confer on each other through their [system of] relationships with one another" (Smudde & Courtright, 2010, p. 184). Organizations are communities of people, all of whom are involved in the *top-down and bottom-up* conferring and, thereby, exercising of power among leaders and followers, executives, and staffers. To this end, power in public relations is not just a matter of one dimension but, instead, a matter of exercising power in three dimensions that coexist and comingle simultaneously. The **three dimensions of power** for public relations are:

1. *Hierarchical*—Organizations have particular structures, usually defined in **organization charts** (see Figure 9.1) that show who relates to whom in terms of rank/title, authority, and sphere of control. Such charts can be larger or smaller (also called "flatter"), depending on an organization's complexity. One alternative organization chart is "circular," as it shows management flow among leaders and followers. Every type of chart depicts a hierarchy, and all are entwined with the political issues (for better and for worse) that naturally emerge among people

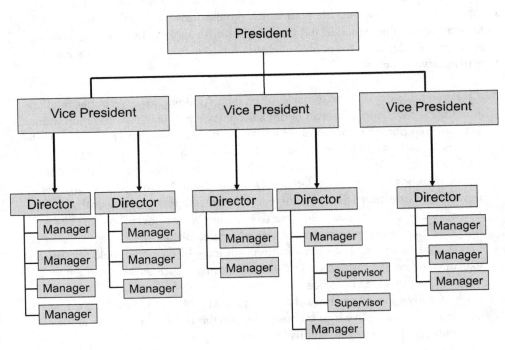

Figure 9.1 Organization chart

who work together, and those issues play out in the personal relationships people have with one another as they seek to get their work done. So-called "dominant coalitions" are a function of hierarchy and will be addressed shortly.

2. *Rhetorical*—People are unique among other living species in that they are creators, users, and misusers of language and symbols (Burke, 1970, 1989). To this end the effectiveness and effects of human communication are always at play in all human activity. So the ways in which people use language, symbols, knowledge, and discourse make up this dimension of how power is exercised.

3. *Social*—The combination of individuals and the organization of them in a single, cohesive unit (e.g., business, nonprofit, NGO) is focused on achieving certain shared objectives according to certain rules, practices, traditions, and so on. This dimension subsumes matters of ethics and professionalism, which affect perceptions of the profession because of PR professionals' work, attitudes, behaviors, and so on. This interaction among people at the macro and micro levels within a social framework intersects with the two other dimensions.

Power has been problematic for people to understand and use. People tend to think about power in only one of these three ways when they should pay attention to all three simultaneously. Additional factors that cloud people's understanding of power include whether they are approaching it through selfless or selfish motives, which reinforce positive or negative views of power, respectively. Economic, regulatory, cultural, technological, and other factors can also affect the corporate context in which power is exercised and understood. Rather than thinking about power as merely a necessary component of organizational life with which professionals must deal, it can be embraced as something enabling. Smudde and Courtright (2010, pp. 181–182) present a way to exercise power effectively for public relations professionals, and the approach hinges on **five proactive practices**:

1. *Coalition building:* At an external level, coalition building involves public relations practitioners working on behalf of one's organization to establish common ground with another person or group on which they can collaborate and achieve mutually beneficial ends. At an internal level, coalition building involves public relations professionals working well with others within their own organizations so that the public relations function is valued and valuable. Central here is recognizing the upward and downward flow plus the micro and macro levels of power that are at play. Especially important, Bowen's (2009) study shows how PR professionals gain membership in an organization's **dominant coalition**, which is comprised of "positions of authority in an organization's structure or hierarchy, including the chief executive officer (CEO), and other C-level executives, such as the Chief Finance Officer, Chief Operations Officer, and Chief Marketing Officer" (p. 419). Bowen's study identifies five routes toward "getting a seat at the table" with the dominant coalition, each route of which is consistent with this book and revolves around answering particular key questions (in order of importance):

a. *Crisis situation*—How much do I know about crisis management, and am I ready to act decisively when the crisis comes? Answer it primarily by reading about crisis communication theory and cases.

b. *Ethical dilemma*—Do I feel prepared and knowledgeable enough to counsel and advise on ethical dilemmas? Answer it primarily by reading about ethics plus the building and keeping of trust for organizations.

c. *Credibility gained over time through correct analyses*—Have I voiced an opinion on important issues and gained credibility for offering correct analyses over time? Answer it primarily by reading about the management of public relations and general business operations and practices.

d. *Issues ranked highly on mass media's agenda*—Am I prepared to counsel top management on the best ways to manage an issue of high media interest? Answer it primarily by reading about strategic issues management or organizational rhetoric.

e. *Leadership*—Do I know what characteristics make a great leader, and am I displaying those traits consistently? Answer it primarily by reading about leadership and motivational research.

2. *Strategy development:* Public relations professionals must participate in the process and provide counsel for the organization to manage its strategic plans for success in its business and operations. It is the province of public relations to act as a seer of future opportunities and threats to an organization's image, business, and legacy and to address them proactively whenever possible. Strategy development, together with the ancillary practices of message design and genre choices, is the unseen element to public relations that publics and stakeholders do not readily recognize.

3. *Message design:* Taking publics' knowledge, attitudes, and actions into account is the essence of effective message design. Through message design, public relations professionals focus on the relationships among their organizations and the publics/stakeholders that they depend on. (See especially Smudde & Courtright [2012 and 2013] for this practice.)

4. *Genre choices:* The actual outputs of public relations professionals' work (i.e., the tactics) must also balance an organization's needs and wants for communication with the publics' needs and wants in communication. In this way, the discourse genres chosen to present any messages must fulfill expectations on multiple levels. (Also see Smudde & Courtright [2012] for this practice.)

5. *Program execution and evaluation:* The final production and dissemination of public relations work to target publics are what most people recognize as public relations but are, in reality, only the result of much hard planning and preparation. Public relations practitioners must also evaluate how well the program worked for both the target publics and the organization through systematic and appropriate measurement methods (see Stacks & Michaelson, 2010). With attention to ethics and professionalism in this and the previous points, public relations may serve as the management of power relations between organizations and the publics on whom their success depends.

Promoting the public relations function, then, is naturally a matter of internal selling about the value and power of PR as much as it is an external one. That selling encompasses both the features of public relations (i.e., what it is and can do) and, most important, the benefits of public relations (i.e., the value contributions and power). Competence, integrity, enthusiasm, and savviness are just a few of the characteristics that PR professionals must genuinely demonstrate in who they are, what they do, and how they do it at all times. Representing the entire profession is an important responsibility, and it goes hand-in-hand with representing your organization. After all, you are being paid to be an expert communicator and the expert in public relations.

Whether a public relations operation is an internal department or an external agency, relationships matter as much as they do in and for any other operational unit. For public relations, however, the importance is all the more pronounced because relationships are part of its name and its core business for an organization. Public relations for an agency or a nonagency organization still can be viewed as a client-centered operation. To this end, public relations managers and their staffs have the responsibility to look out for the greater good for their clients, whether these are their own organizations or organizations with whom they have contractual agreements to do PR work. Understanding how one's organization/client is positioned in the market is of crucial concern to representing that organization and building business effectively, ethically, and successfully.

MARKET POSITIONING

One of the more useful and parsimonious definitions of **positioning** is as follows: it is "what you do to the mind of the prospect" (Ries & Trout, 2001 [1976], p. 2). Key to this view is imprinting or affixing a brand or product indelibly in the mind of customers, especially in positive ways at the first experience with it. Positioning is central to an organization being able to create and build its business (for-profit, nonprofit, NGO, or other). Companies seek increased sales from strategic market positions and, if desired, increased investment from investors. Nonprofits seek increased donations, grant funding, material resources, and volunteers/members. Nongovernmental organizations seek increased support for social change, including anything from people, to money, to material.

No matter what kind of organization it is, there are two basic dimensions to market positioning. The first is **brand positioning**, which very basically focuses on the ways in which an organization's brand name is clearly unique among all the others in a market, especially in terms of value. The second is **product/service positioning**, which basically focuses on direct or indirect comparisons of an organization's product (or service) with those offered in the marketplace, especially in terms of features and, primarily, benefits. Fundamental to both dimensions of market positioning is **differentiation**, which concerns the one thing that makes a brand, product, or service unique from anything else similar to it (Trout & Rivkin, 2000). Differentiation is a natural fit for public relations, and we will shortly explore it further as part of the larger process for determining market positions.

Understanding what positions may exist in a market is important to communicating the right messages in the right ways to the right people. To find a singular way to capture market positioning and the importance of differentiation is not an easy task because of the numerous models and methods available online and in print. Ries and Trout's (2001 [1976]) main metaphor for positioning is **"ladders" of the mind**, where each market is defined by its own ladder and brands in each market occupy different rungs, with the leader at the top. Moving up a ladder is harder than moving down. And introducing a new product or service means providing customers with a new ladder. The key to effective positioning is precise language use. More specifically, positioning is largely a function of word choices about one's product or service. As Silbiger (2012) summarizes it, ten rules for positioning revolve around words:

1. Own a word that uniquely ties to your product/service in customers' minds.
2. Begin positioning with the product's/service's name.
3. Use a unique name for a unique product/service.
4. Own a word by being the first to use it.
5. Stay on message about the product/service every time.
6. Introduce a new brand to respond to a new competitor, and do not dilute the original brand.
7. Create a new market category a leader cannot occupy but a challenger will.
8. Find a niche in customers' minds the leader does not fill but a challenger will.
9. Reposition the competition in a market or undercut the leader's messages.
10. Maintain consistency in the positioning choice for the long term.

For our purposes, Ries and Trout's (2001 [1976], 1993) work provides us with a very useful heuristic between their two highly influential volumes about marketing and positioning. The **positioning heuristic** (see Figure 9.2) is a way to conceptualize the various ways an organization may *position itself and its products/services* in the markets it serves. Ries and Trout also address positioning for followers in a market and how to reposition competitors with your organization's own communication, as Rule 9 above suggests. For our purposes in PR, what is most beneficial about this heuristic is its utility for either brand or product/service positioning.

For example, the overall brand of Coke is the leader in the soft drink market, so much so that in parts of the southeastern United States, any soft drink is referred to as a Coke (e.g., orange coke) even though the drink may have its own name (e.g., Orange Crush). Market positions are fluid and take a lot of work to attain and, especially, to maintain. (It is easier to attain market leadership than to maintain it.) An organization can occupy one position, and then move from it to another on its own or by being forced to do so by competitor(s), holding one market position at a time. An exception would be "first

Leader
- The perceived or recognized leader in a market.
- Examples: Coke, Nike, Google

Challenger
- The perceived next-best option in a market, right behind the dominator.
- Examples: Pepsi, Adidas, Bing

Niche Occupier
- A specialty option that targets a narrow band or particular interest in a market.
- Examples: Snapple, L'Oréal ("Because I'm worth it."), Ask.com

First Mover
- An organization creates a new market category with a product or service no one else has.
- Examples: Chrysler's minivans, Amazon.com, Zipcar

Repositioner
- An organization chooses to remake itself and, thereby, its place in the market.
  - Example: Boston Chicken changed to Boston Market.
- An organization repositions a competitor and, thereby, redefines its own position.
  - Example: Wrangler Jeans urging customers to check its U-shaped crotch design as more comfortable than jeans made with a V-shaped design.

Figure 9.2 Heuristic of market positions
Source: Based on Ries and Trout (2001 [1976], 1993)

mover," as that position would always be true no matter what other market position an organization held. For example, a first mover may be able to create a new market (see Rule 7 above), as Chrysler did with its first minivans, and then for a period of time command a market niche (see Rule 8) as other companies begin to break into that new market. In this way, a company may, as Chrysler was able to do, be a leader for a market niche in which it was the first mover.

To understand an organization's positioning, many questions must be answered that span several categories of needed information. In public relations, you must be able to help position an organization (including its brands, products, and services) through effective, strategic communication, whether that organization is the one that employs you or is one that you represent through a contractual arrangement. Again, our focus here is proactive positioning from an organization about itself and its own offerings. For our purposes, seven crucial questions must be answered to establish a firm grasp of an organization's market position so that it can, in turn, be realized through communication and other actions.

1. *What are your organization's differentiators?* An answer to this question relies on three things. First, a **unique selling proposition** (**USP**) (see Trout & Rivkin, 2000) defines simply the specific benefit that can be had from a product or service that (1) is truly different from all others and (2) can be "diffused" through the marketplace (see Rogers, 2003). Second, the **compelling competitive advantages**

(**CCAs**) of a product or service give evidential support for, or proof of, the USP. Third, the *image and reputation* for an organization prevails and even precedes people's ideas about what it is, stands for, and has done. The combination of these three things also produces a highly useful statement that is essential in a strategic plan: the **value proposition**. The value proposition (see Appendix A), in turn, can and should function as the key message platform because it captures the very essence of an organization (on a macro basis) or an organization's product/service (on a micro basis). The example strategic plan in Appendix A shows an example of how this matter of differentiation is played out and rendered into a value proposition.

2. *What are your organization's strengths and weaknesses?* An answer to this question can be prepared through a SWOT analysis (see Chapter 5) or another environmental-scanning method or situation analysis. Three other methods can be valuable. One method, a **gap analysis**, very simply put, seeks data of any kind about why there is a gap between where the organization is now (its current state) and where it wants to be (its ideal or future state). Then the analysis of these data determines whether the ideal state is reasonable on applicable grounds/criteria, what is keeping the organization from moving from the current state to the ideal state, if there are alternative states the organization should seek, and how the chosen ideal state could be attained.

Another environmental-scanning method is a **force field analysis** (Lewin, 1997). Simply explained, this method examines the forces that can enable change for the better (i.e., driving forces) and forces that can inhibit change (i.e., restraining forces). This method, modeled in Figure 9.3, is useful when working with social, political, or economic forces because of their broad range of sources and levels of strength.

Figure 9.3 Force field analysis

PHASE 1: Order	**PHASE 2: Pollution and Assignment of Guilt**	**PHASE 3: Purification**	**PHASE 4: Redemption**
The state of things about and for an organization, what it stands for, and what it offers is stable.	Something from within, without, or both upsets or significantly changes the stability of things, and blame or responsibility must be assigned for it on the public stage.	Efforts to make things right gradually secure the public's approval, where the success of one side over the other(s) becomes increasingly apparent, especially as an organization may accept responsibility of its own accord or is saddled with responsibility by others.	• For an organization that secures the public's favor, final vindication of it is given and a new order is created, which would bolster its image and credibility. • For an organization that does not secure the public's favor, it must cope with the new order, which (adversely) affects the organization's reputation and credibility.

Figure 9.4 Order restoration model
Source: Smudde (2011, p. 158)

Central to a force field analysis is recognizing that not all forces are equal; they can counter or balance one another because they have a certain *valance*, or strength, which can be rated on a numerical scale (see Figure 9.3). Force field analysis focuses on things that influence people's behaviors, assuming that behavior is influenced by a mix of forces. This form of analysis can also be used to determine critical success factors (see Chapter 5 and Appendix A). The objective, then, is to identify which forces must be increased *and* decreased to obtain the kind and degree of change needed. When forces are in balance (not necessarily a perfect but, possibly, a favorable balance), they create homeostasis. By communicating effectively and ethically about these factors, we can alter the balance of forces and affect behavior.

Another model for scanning the environment is the **order restoration model** shown in Figure 9.4 (Smudde, 2011). The model helps us to understand the progression of things in context from the way they are now ("order") to the way things need to be ("redemption") through some change that is initiated in such a way that it "pollutes" the order. From there, one understands who or what may have been "guilty" of causing the change (whether internal, external, or a mix of both), their level of responsibility for it, and how order can be restored or "redeemed" for the organization and its publics through a process of "purification" that makes things better. In this way, the context for what is going on for an organization (whole or in part) is as much retrospective as it is prospective. Organizational officers, of which PR professionals are a part, can not only make sense of how the order of things changed, but they can also plan to ethically "pollute" the order of things to achieve strategic objectives, like those related to the launch of a unique product into a market or the introduction of a new public policy to remedy a social situation.

3. *How is your organization perceived today?* An answer to this question is contingent on answers to several interrelated matters of perception in the overall market, by current and prospective customers, in the community, by current and potential investors, by industry and market analysts and key publication editors, and by relevant organizations and institutions like professional or trade organizations, research groups, and universities. This information would be valuable as the foundation for what people think about your organization on its own and as it compares to others.

4. *Who are your target customers?* An answer to this question requires the gathering and analysis of valid and reliable data about the details of target customers (people or organizations). Such data may be gathered through primary or secondary research, and it often should reflect customers' demographic makeup (e.g., age, gender, race, education, location) plus their psychographic profile (e.g., attitudes, behavior inclinations, values, lifestyle). This information will be instrumental in realizing the common ground of needs and wants people have based on key factors of their lives as a group.

5. *What are the results of your organization's most recent competition/market analysis?* Answers to this question require reasonably detailed information about the other players in the market(s) in which your organization participates. This point, like the others, works well for for-profit, nonprofit/institutional, NGO, and other types of organization because people need to know who is "out there" and how they "stack up." The salient matters for data collection are identifying any other organizations competing with yours to any degree, things your organization does differently from competitors, unique messages and actions of competitors, recognition for the market positions competitors hold, and ways to overcome these and other pressures and perceptions.

6. *How do you want to be positioned in the market?* The answer to this question defines what an organization wants to be. The answer, then, is the conclusion derived from the answers to all the previous questions and results in a final view of what market position the organization will seek to establish, along the lines of that shown in Figure 9.2 and, perhaps, in tune with the model in Figure 9.4.

7. *Do you have all the necessary resources to successfully achieve the market position you want?* The answer to this final question could be the one that says, "Go!" or "No go." A thorough and, most important, honest analysis of an organization's wherewithal (e.g., money, people, material, systems) will reveal the degree to which the desired market positioning strategy can be carried out or not within the duration of time truly necessary to do it right and do it well.

Public relations' role in positioning is a potent one and represents "the strategic attempt to stake out and occupy a site of intentional representation in the contested space where meanings are constructed, contested, and reconstructed" (James, 2011, p. 98). Public relations attends to positioning, as James (2011) argues, through the interplay of three factors: an organization's ideal state, the story to support that ideal state, and the particular discourse used to convey that story. Additionally, forces from within and without affect the degree to which positioning can be attained. The challenge is to obtain and maintain customers' attention with a product or service. Organizational messages become important in undergirding an organization's claim to hold any market position. C. Heath and D. Heath's (2008) SUCCES model for message design is especially helpful to make messages "sticky" and stay in people's minds. The more of these six characteristics that are used, the better:

- *Simplicity*—Messages are core and compact.
- *Unexpectedness*—Messages are surprising and interesting, plus they evoke curiosity.
- *Concreteness*—Messages demonstrate human actions and appeal to the senses.
- *Credibility*—Messages' ideas have an internal authority and testability.
- *Emotions*—Messages appeal to people's feelings, self-interest, needs.
- *Stories*—Messages convey real/realistic situations as simulators.

Once it is clear what an organization wants to be, based on what it is and from where it has come, communication and other core operations can engage in their work to make it happen. In tune with the strategic plan, market positioning establishes the claim an organization has to do its business for those whom it is targeting. Instrumental in the work of developing new business is making contacts with all kinds of customers.

COLD, WARM, AND HOT CALLS

There are basically **three types of customers** you may encounter in sales situations, including those for raising money, signing up volunteers, soliciting material support, and so on. Those three customer types are: (1) those who plan to buy from you, (2) those who would never buy from you, and (3) those in between who need help making up their minds. That third group is the key to increasing sales, because if you do little else, the first group will come to you anyway, and you might as well forget about the second group.

Cold calling is a highly concentrated persuasive activity. Cold calling focuses on Type 3 customers, who have never done business with you or do not even know your business exists. You must use a small number of words to say a lot in a compelling way to achieve your ultimate goal for any call. Cold calls are instrumental to penetrating the thinking of the people who would benefit from your company's work but have not thought about it. *More than anything, your goal with cold calls is to get a meeting with these potential customers—nothing more.* In a sense, this is the first sale that may lead to the ultimate payoff—a closed deal between your firm and the customer's.

Now before we go further, what does cold calling have to do with public relations management? *The principles and practices given here about contacting customers to build business are precisely the same kinds of things you need to do to promote your clients or your organization.* Such promotion would naturally involve media relations, for example, and you should apply the process for calling journalists and other parties as you might for calling on *Type 1, Type 2, or Type 3 customers.* After all, depending on your relationships (and your clients' or your organization's relationships), calls to journalists, analysts, donors, and so on could likewise be hot, warm, or cold. So when we refer to "sales" in this section, think about the broad range of things that can be "sold," from products and services to news stories and client expertise.

If you have done any follow-up on news releases, you have an idea about what cold calling is. If you are wary of cold calling, you are not alone. Some people loathe it, yet some love it. In reality most people fall in the middle of these two extremes. Whatever your feelings are about cold calling, remember that all you are really doing is having an impromptu conversation with someone you would like to meet anyway. And you do not spend all day doing it, as you will see later. An important thing to know and remember is that, although cold calling may be nerve-racking to do, it is truly something you can master. *And attitude is everything.* If it helps, think of cold calling as a challenge to take in the competitive arena of sales. You should find it valuable to you personally and professionally as you gain experience, build your network, and grow in success.

This section is meant to (1) help you grow in your comfort in placing cold calls, so you can get closer to having more closed sales; and (2) inform you about *how* to do cold calls and *why* what you will do will work for you personally and the company generally. There is much more to this subject, and this section has distilled selected key aspects of it for you to use right away. So this section should serve you well as a kind of tutorial that can get you started. And later on, if you are inclined to learn more, you can seek out resources online, information in print, or training through sales seminars.

PREPARATION

There is much to do before you make any cold calls. After all, you cannot call just anybody. The "shotgun approach" to cold calling is very ineffective and a grossly inefficient use of your talents and time. You must have a plan and know exactly whom to call and why.

Cold calling differs from what I call "hot" and "warm" calling. **Hot calling** involves talking to Type 1 customers who are already very interested in doing business with you and your company, and they may already have done or are doing business with you and are satisfied or enthusiastic. Hot calls can be thought of as the most "organic" way to build business because you are proposing that an existing client take advantage of other products and services. **Warm calling** involves contacting Type 3 customers who may have done business with your company some time ago but have not recently, and they have favorable feelings about your company and would be willing to work with your firm again. Warm calling also can involve certain Type 3 customers who have never done business with your company but are willing to check out your firm because of good word-of-mouth referrals. Cold calls to Type 3 customers dominate because you are truly prospecting for new business from those you have not served before and would like to serve. Both hot and warm calls are easier to do than cold calls because of preexisting relationships or favorable preconceived notions about your company. Remember, however, we are talking about cold calling.

No matter whom you call and why, you *must* do a certain amount of research to understand what you want, what your target customers want, who your competition is, and how your work fits into the big picture of your company's business development. Typical products of such research are contact lists of prospective customers who meet most or all of the criteria for a viable customer. (Another similar and familiar list is a media list of journalists to whom you would pitch news.) You may already know much of this, and it is important to document that knowledge so you can make the best use of it at any time. Let's explore each of the dimensions of your preparation.

KNOW YOUR COMPANY

Why is your employer such a great company to hire for advertising and/or public relations? This is a critical, fundamental question you must be able to answer for yourself and, especially, for any customer.

If you think about it, there are several very good reasons for hiring you. All of these reasons are **key messages** that customers should come to know, and your work enables that. So you must be able to talk about these things competently and naturally, and that may mean gathering any necessary backup data to support your claims. (These data will be important for your meetings, as described below.) Some specific kinds of information you may need might include:

- Core areas of the business
- Current projects (customers, requirements, challenges, cost [if permitted to give these out])
- Most recently completed projects (customers, requirements, challenges, results/ successes, cost [if permitted to give these out])
- Notable past projects (customers, requirements, challenges, results/successes, cost [if permitted to give these out])
- List of customers who'd be willing to give references
- Pricing guidelines (for reference only; do not share with customers or give quotes over the phone—information gained at a meeting will be needed to prepare an accurate quote)
- Any news about the company and its people

- Regulatory pressures
- Website address (give this out rarely so people do not use it as an excuse to not meet with you; save it for the meeting and give the person a tour of the site)

With this intimate knowledge about your company, you can apply it more accurately to what your target customers want and need.

KNOW YOUR TARGET CUSTOMERS

Remember the three basic customer types. It is not easy to identify them, but you can and you must. In many ways, you already have an idea of who your target customers are, whether they are predisposed to buy from you, or are in need of information about who you are and why they should buy from you. This is where a little research and savvy thinking pay off. *The objective here is to use your research to create a "screen" through which you sift out the best opportunities to schedule meetings with new customers that may turn into sales.*

Knowing your customers will help you focus on their needs and wants when you talk with them at any time. Get to know their businesses. (Know journalists' news organizations inside and out, as well as knowing individual journalists' areas of coverage ["beats"], preferences in being contacted, and needs for developing stories.) Learn all you can about your target customers, because the more knowledgeable you are about them, the more impressive you are as someone who cares enough to learn as much as you can. That is a large component of trust, which is foundational in your relationship.

Most importantly, the more you know about your target customers, the more you understand what value they are probably looking for and how you and your company can provide them with that value or more. Find out what "pain" target customers (including consumers of journalists' work) have and figure out how you can cure that pain and head off other potential pains that may come along. *It is all about the benefits and value added to the customer's business for the investment in having your company do any project.*

Who are your target customers? You must identify and understand the broad categories of customers important to your company. In each of these categories think about who the ideal customer would be, which amounts to the basic substance of your screen for each category. (See the section "Track Your Progress" for a detailed list of data points that can reflect on your screen as well.) Refine your screens with information about what your target customers need and want by reviewing the projects the company has completed over its history, especially over the past couple of years. You will find information about projects' specifications, successes, challenges, etc.

Take note of any current or established customers that show up on your cold-call list (and make sure they are not among your cold-call targets). Because they are already customers, they really should not be approached like an absolutely new business lead. Do note what business your company is doing with them, because that information may be useful in your calls.

You should also read trade publications that pertain to those customers, so you get a sense of what issues are important, how they talk about them, and what kinds of approaches are employed for any given project. This last item is important because you can stay on top of technology and systems people want to install and know what kinds of approaches may be applied to install them.

Visit target customers' websites, if they have them, and learn all you can. Look for key messages the company wants people to know. Figure out what its strategic direction seems to be. Read any literature on the website that describes the company's performance, operating divisions, markets, etc. Also obtain copies of any printed company literature and analyze them too.

You should also search the Internet and library for news articles about your target customers. You may learn about issues that are helping or hurting the company. You may discover how a particular strategic decision may require new facilities and therefore represent a new business opportunity for you. You may also find out which people you may want to speak to when you call.

Attend conferences or trade shows that your target customers attend. You will be able to sit in on seminars about topics important to them, which will give you vital information about how problems or projects are being addressed. And naturally you will be able to meet many new people and gather leads, set up or have on-site meetings, and follow up on any contacts.

You can use published data about companies in directories like those published by Dun & Bradstreet, local business periodicals, and Gale Research. If a company has stock that is publicly traded, you can look up information on the Internet at the websites for the New York Stock Exchange, NASDAQ, any number of financial news websites (e.g., Yahoo! Finance, TheStreet.com), and the U.S. Securities and Exchange Commission. There are other ways, too, to learn about your target customers, and you've probably used them on other occasions. Use those tools also to your advantage to learn all you can and impress your customers with your knowledge of them, especially during your meetings.

In an important way, the work you do to learn about your customers also serves as a way to identify new business leads—trade shows, for example. This area of **lead generation** is part of the research involved in discovering opportunities for cold calls. There is much information available on the Internet, in books, and in articles about effective lead-generation strategies. Although this topic is an important one, it is uniquely separate from the subject of cold calling. If you are interested in understanding it further, seek resources online (search term: "lead generation") that can give you the details you need.

KNOW YOUR COMPETITION

What is the difference between what your company can do and any other organization like it? How you answer this question matters greatly, because *what you do not know* becomes at least as important (if not more so) as what you do know. The trick here is to find out what you do not know by researching your competition and add that to what you do know. The good news is that once you do this research, and do it to a reasonable level of detail, you can use the information in myriad ways and only need to update it once or twice a year, depending on market dynamics.

To manage this task for the benefit of each person and the company, apply the simple idea that many hands make light work. Assign each person one competitor to research, then collect all information about all competitors and share it with everyone either in print or electronically by e-mailing the file(s) or accessing the file(s) securely on a company database.

How do you conduct this research? You do it pretty much the same way you did for researching your target customers. Websites are a great place to start. You can also collect and analyze any literature you can find from the companies.

What things do you have to know? There are many dimensions to research, but some key ones include:

- Region served
- Markets served
- Services offered
- Pricing and pricing strategies
- Value proposition
- Market positioning
- Awards and other industry recognition
- Quality philosophy
- Customer service
- Customer relationships (direct/indirect; long-term/short-term)
- Showcase customers
- Company mission
- Union work/relationships
- Employee/staff expertise
- History/years in business
- Regulatory environment
- Reputation
- Financial viability/Strength of business
- Aggressiveness in marketing
- Known/preferred communication channels to reach customers
- Key messages
- Rumors/hearsay (date them)
- News items (date them with sources)

You may think of other dimensions that should be researched. If you do, add them to your task and share them with others.

The bottom line is: the more complete your research is about your competition, the better you can know what competitive advantages you have over them (or they over you), and the better you can persuade target customers about why your company should do a project instead of anyone else. So you (and your colleagues) must decide to what level of detail you need to go in your research.

In addition, you should discover ways in which your company complements the work of other firms, because if a customer has already signed a firm to do work, perhaps there is something it cannot do and you can. Knowing what gaps there may be to fill in on a project that is being handled by any other firm can get you additional business by persuading the customer that you can meet that unmet need. (Note: These kinds of issues are best handled at the first meeting you schedule and thereafter.)

UNDERSTAND THE BIG PICTURE

All this preparation is important because the more you know, the better you can screen out opportunities who, in all likelihood, would not buy from you, and you can focus on those that would. The role of cold calling in the sales process is pretty straightforward. It is the spark that starts the flame of a potentially strong customer relationship. *The equation is simple: no calls = no prospects = no sales = no job.* And you do not want to be solely at the mercy of the market, where you are always waiting for people to call you. If people do not know about you, why would they call? So, think of cold calling's place in the big picture of the sales process in Figure 9.5.

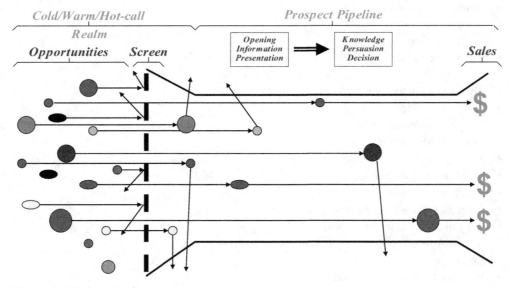

Figure 9.5 Sales pipeline

The sales process is broken down into discrete parts. The two most basic are the **calling realm** and the **pipeline**.

The calling realm (which includes hot, warm, and cold calls) is concerned with identifying from the field of all opportunities, which come in many different sizes and kinds, the best ones that are worth pursuing. Having the in-depth knowledge about yourself and your customers, you can accurately assess which opportunities

you want to invite into the pipeline through a cold call. That knowledge amounts to a "screen" that you use to sift out the best candidates. Many do not make it through, and some never get a second glance because they do not ever plan to buy from you for any number of reasons. Only a select few get your call, because you believe strongly that these are well worth your time and effort to try to schedule a first meeting.

The second basic part of the sales process model is the prospect pipeline. Notice that any target customer is not called a "prospect" until they fully enter the pipeline because you scheduled a meeting. Until this point, any target customer is merely an "opportunity." It is possible that opportunities will not turn into prospects after your cold call, and that is when they exit the process early. When an opportunity becomes a prospect, there is some length of time between your first meeting and the decision to buy or not, which is represented by the arrows of varying length into the pipeline. Once a prospect decides to buy, they move on to a closed sale and are considered an established customer. A prospect may, however, decide to not buy, and thereby exit the pipeline; whereas, they may represent another opportunity in the future.

In the prospect pipeline you will notice that the sales communication you engage in— the opening, the information you share, the presentation at the first and subsequent meetings—serves the prospect as knowledge, persuasive reasons to buy, and a decision to buy (or not). This communication is instrumental and dynamic throughout the pipeline, and you have primary responsibility for making it work. Remember that you are both establishing and maintaining a relationship, and your language, behavior, and other factors all affect how your customer responds to everything about the deal that is taking shape. And that deal only came into being because you recognized a viable opportunity, made a simple call, and followed through on it.

Complacency is the enemy of sales. When times are good it is not the time to relax. What will you do when times are not so good or even downright bad? Placing cold calls is an effective and efficient way to manage market cycles. When business is strong, you are making calls to shore up business when times are not so good. And when sales are down, you are working just as hard to bring in prospects. Cold calling, then, helps smooth out and control much of the ebb and flow of market cycles. And that is critical for maintaining the business and jobs.

SCRIPTS

Know what you will say before you say it—know it well and be genuine, truthful, friendly, confident, trustworthy, and natural. This principle is key to success in your calls. Believe it or not, the person you call will pick up on what kind of person you are based on how well you present yourself over the phone. Your vocal qualities, from intonation to pronunciation, all affect what impressions someone creates about you—research has shown this repeatedly. Who wants to listen to someone who mechanistically recites a text or sounds like their heart is not in it? The caller will not seem worthy of trust, does not appear confident, sounds unnatural in their speech, and other factors. This kind of call would be offensive to a listener and a waste of time. It would also undermine the caller's credibility. Appendix B gives you sample scripts to review and use.

It is important, therefore, to practice, practice, practice. And you may want to practice for a couple of hours and even involve someone to role-play with you so you get it down before you make your first call. Athletes do not go into an event without proper conditioning and preparation, and neither should you.

Fundamentally, your call is an interruption, and anyone you call is not expecting or prepared to talk with you. So you must make sure the person you call understands who you are, what you have to offer, and especially what is in it for them. And you must do this simply, directly, yet vividly, with no fancy or gimmicky ploys for attention. Scripts are given in Appendix B that will help you do this.

When is the best time to make any cold call? There is really no right or wrong answer, but there does seem to be some wisdom in the idea that by calling earlier in the day, even if you leave a message, you have a better chance of getting through than later on when people are deep in the throes of their work. There also seems to be some wisdom in the idea that you can get results if you call late in the day, after 5:00 p.m. or so (even on Fridays), because people are winding down, major work for the day is done, and they have some time to think more clearly about other things. You need to try times that seem to work best for both you and your target customers. Again, some understanding about your customers can pay off here, too.

The more comfortable and familiar you are with what you want to say, the easier it is for you to have a conversation on the phone with someone you have not yet met. That is why your preparation and scripts are so vital. Add to that the fact that the more calls you make, the more experience you get, and the more effective you become. But make sure you truly know your stuff before you even begin.

Remember that your goal is to *get a meeting*. (A meeting with a journalist would be included here too.) Bridge back to this issue gracefully if the person takes you off track. You should answer the person's questions, but not in too much detail, because you want to meet with that person to do that. Examples of how to bridge back to your goal are given in Appendix B in the context of "negative" responses. ("Positive" responses are those that result in a meeting straightaway.)

In case you must answer some specific questions during your calls, based on what you plan to say, have basic information ready. For example, you may need the total number of customers/projects your company has had over time, the names of clients who will be glad to be references for your company, and various project examples with relevant summary data about them. Remember that you do not want to give out a lot of detail during the call—give just enough information to maintain interest so that you can schedule a meeting to go into greater depth.

AT THE MEETING

You have done your homework. You have made your calls. You have scheduled some appointments. What will you do at your first meetings? Now is the time for all your preparation to really pay off. And the objective of this first meeting is to get another one or a signed deal, depending on how the prospect wants to proceed. (Play it conservatively and shoot for another meeting or even a quote you send.)

Remember that cold calls are, in general, concentrated persuasive endeavors to get a meeting. During your call you made some important claims that you now have the opportunity to prove with evidence. That evidence will come in the form of your presentation, printed material, and any other documentation as well as oral arguments you make in response to the prospect's questions and statements.

To this end, your presence in person must reaffirm the confidence, enthusiasm, friendliness, and naturalness that you exhibited on the phone. Now you can really bring your research to bear on whatever the prospect says. You should come across as knowledgeable and credible without appearing aloof, pompous, or aggressive. Relax, be yourself, and genuinely reflect interest in the prospect and their business.

It is all about the benefits and value added to the prospect's business for the investment in having your company do any project. With this principle in mind, what should you plan to say, and what should you bring? Based on your research, you should prepare an agenda about key points that are of interest to the customer. Those points should relate to the pain that needs curing and the value that your company will add to the prospect's business. It is up to you to organize the points in a logical way that makes sense to the prospect. Leave time for open discussion at the end. It is also up to you to decide what you will say about each item on the agenda.

If you think about what you plan to say in terms of a formal argument, each claim you make requires you to have evidence to back it up and clear reasoning about why that evidence helps you arrive at that claim. This simple pattern suggests that you need to collect only enough printed material and other documentation that you feel will sufficiently back up your claims and are directly relevant to the prospect. (More on that in a minute.) You are doing a certain amount of educated guesswork here, but if you have come to know the prospect well enough through your research, you should be prepared for almost anything. It is, after all, a first meeting, and your objective is to get to the next step: either a meeting to discuss a quote, or another meeting that will result in a request for a quote, or even a signed deal, depending on how the prospect does business.

The basic agenda might be as follows. Note that it begins with a focus on the prospect, which symbolically says that your interest in the prospect is primary and that you've done some homework on them.

- Thank you for this meeting
- Review of the prospect and opportunities
- Value that your company can add
- Examples of projects relevant to the prospect
- Proposal for working on one or more of the prospect's opportunities
- *Ask for the business*
- Open discussion and next steps

This agenda sets up a simple persuasive progression: identifying needs, showing how the needs can be met through your company's added value, visualizing that value through real success stories, and proposing that a business relationship be started. Also notice that you must formally ask for the business to make it absolutely clear what you're after and how the prospect stands to gain. Remember, your objective is to get to the next step—a closed deal or a new meeting that would lead to a sale.

In your presentation, try to work in the key messages about your company. Also, emphasize the company's reputation for accurate and timely quotes, dedication to safety, and on-time completion record. As a rule of thumb, plan no more than 15 to 20 minutes for one presentation. The whole meeting may last from 30 minutes to an hour. Go with whatever the prospect has time for. And make no mistake: your presentation skills (i.e., your communication skills) must be good. You are not putting on a show, but you are showcasing your company and representing the company. Practice any presentation a few times before you give it. Read up on effective presentations or attend a training session. Again, at this meeting it is important to be yourself, natural, and flexible so that the prospect is comfortable talking with you—*continuing the conversation you started with your cold call.*

In general, some of the best kinds of material to bring to a meeting include printed matter that backs up points you make in your presentation. (At least that means another contact with the prospect.) More specifically, at least bring the following items (use a single binder with the company logo for easy reference and use):

- Letter of introduction from senior executive, president, or CEO
- Current brochure or summary sheet on your company's work
- Individual case studies of the success stories you show
- Biographies on yourself and management
- Full contact information, including website address

If the prospect asks about something that you are not prepared to answer, admit that fact and say that you will send it right away when you get back to your office. Use your follow-up letter (see below) to do two things: thank the prospect for the meeting and highlight the information they asked for that you are sending with the letter. By the way, giving little gifts at a first meeting may be nice, but they really are not deal-makers. Unless it is common practice or you know a prospect really likes to receive trinkets from salespeople (almost as if they are tolls to pay on the highway to a sale), save them as more meaningful tokens of appreciation rather than simple giveaways. Many companies today have rules about gifts, including not allowing employees to accept gifts at all or placing dollar limits on the value of any gifts received. Try to find out these rules for each prospect; if you do not know them, err on the side of caution and do not give gifts.

FOLLOW-UP LETTERS

Once your first meeting is done, your work becomes increasingly important, because you have only just begun to establish a relationship with a customer. You must maintain that relationship and ensure that any customer feels they matter to you uniquely by following up effectively now and in the future. Follow-ups are generally simple and elegant in character, and they say a lot about how you and your company value any relationship with customers. The best way to show your appreciation for a meeting with any customer and the value that person has to you and your company is to send a letter.

Letter writing has long been an art, tracing back at least to the Renaissance and the art of *belles lettres*. Letters stand as the most powerful and personal way to reach someone after you have met with them for the first time. But you do not have to be a gifted writer to prepare and send an effective thank-you letter. You just need to be genuinely appreciative of the customer's consideration and sensitive to what may be the best way to let the person know you listened.

The letters that are most impressive are those that are handwritten. Handwritten notes are much more personal and, therefore, symbolize a higher level of involvement and caring than a typed letter. Realize, though, that this means your notes should not be long-winded. Like your call scripts, you must be both engaging and to-the-point. Thank the person for meeting with you, then address a pivotal issue that came up during the meeting and mention how well your company can respond to it. Think about how to reflect a key message about the company. If you must prepare a long response, with ample detail and attachments, you may want to type a letter anyway. In either case, make sure you use company stationery.

As in any writing, correct grammar and spelling count! You may wish to write a couple of drafts of any letter before you prepare the final version for sending. Have someone proofread your letter, both drafts and final form, to make sure everything is just right. Triple-check the spelling of company names and people's names.

When you mail your letter, use regular mail. Unless time is of the essence, there is no need to overnight your letter—such an act could suggest carelessness and frivolity. However, overnight mail may be best if you have to send information that you didn't have at the meeting.

E-mail may be an appropriate option *only when time is critical and you know the person accepts or prefers e-mail.* Like a typewritten letter on stationery, an e-mail note does not have the same level of personal symbolism that a handwritten note does. You also run the risk of your e-mail being deleted (possibly by a secretary who has access to and screens your contact's e-mail) or, worse, never seen because it was automatically removed by spam-blocking software before it reached your contact's e-mail inbox. You can, however, use this time-critical channel to do the same things you would in a handwritten note. *And remember not to send attached files unless they are completely free of viruses.* So use e-mail sparingly and wisely.

As long as your prospect maintains the relationship, you should follow up with him or her as often as required. At this level phone calls and e-mail are effective channels of communication to check in or report on progress. You must find out what any prospect's preferred channels of communication are, even optimum times for using them.

TRACK YOUR PROGRESS

Record keeping is vital, because you must know how well you are doing in ways that help you become more successful. You should know at least the following things through your cold-calling efforts:

- The total number of cold calls you make over an extended period (e.g., ten weeks, quarter, half year, year)
- The total number of people spoken to over that period
- The total number of first meetings set up over that period
- The total number of sales visits, including first meetings
- The total number of sales over that period.

Based on the data gathered from these dimensions, you can set reasonable and challenging goals. Once you understand how effective you are from these numbers, you can find out what your strengths and weaknesses are and address them. More specifically, you can calculate averages, measure your performance, and set goals as follows:

- The average number of cold calls you must make each day
- The average number of people you must speak to each day to get an appointment
- The ratio of cold calls to first meetings
- The average number of first meetings needed to be scheduled per day or week
- The average number of subsequent sales visits each week
- The ratio of appointments to each sale

There are other statistics you could calculate, like the average number of cold calls you must make each week or the average number of sales visits each week. *The point is that by breaking down the whole data set to meaningful statistics, especially daily or weekly averages, you can see how easy it is for you to manage your calls and overall sales efforts.* This kind of performance measurement is key to knowing how effective and successful you are and where you can improve. As the old saying goes, you cannot manage what you do not measure.

This individual level of performance measurement is critical to your success and satisfaction on another level. That is, you want to avoid having peaks and valleys in the sales cycle. You need to make sure there are always opportunities you are turning into prospects in the pipeline. As you saw earlier in this section, if there is ever a time with no prospects in the pipeline, that means no work was done early enough to get them in there. *And no calls = no prospects = no sales.*

New-business leads and sales are vital to building your company's business beyond those customers who would plan to buy anyway, and your cold calls and sales efforts are critical to this success. On a company level, a separate report on performance measurements has been prepared and covers the broader need and implications for ensuring the company is always on track.

The range of data you could track is extensive. You need to select the data that are the most meaningful to you *and* management. The range of data points include the following:

- Company name
- Contact person(s) and title
- Complete contact information for contact person(s)
- Company type (independent, division/subsidiary/operation)
- Company affiliation (individual, franchise)
- Preferred media (by title; traditional and new media)
- Market type (per core business segments)
- Organization affiliation(s) (professional/trade societies)
- Product(s) purchased (project order details, including end date)

- Service(s) purchased (project order details, including end date)
- Date of purchase(s)
- Purchase frequency
- Future purchase plans
- Amount of last purchase (if applicable)
- Amount of all purchases by date
- Promotion or discount used
- Satisfaction score (your company establishes this; score from survey's five-point scale)
- Loyalty score (your company establishes this; score on a ten-point scale based on total sales revenue, number of purchases over time, probability of future purchases, length of relationship, number of referrals, satisfaction score, testimonials/references)
- Lead source and date (i.e., customer information channels)
- Follow-up service request type
- Willingness to do testimonial
- Third-party source demographics (e.g., Dun & Bradstreet)
- Support sales performance measurements
- Additional important notes that do not fit these categories

It may be impractical to track all these dimensions, and you and management must decide on what data to collect and how to measure and report them. You can create a simple spreadsheet with columns for these dimensions and rows for each cold call you make. You could also use a database program, like ACT! or the similar capability in Microsoft Excel, to manage your cold-call data. Whatever method you use, it must be flexible, easy to use, and powerful enough to make you as effective as possible.

With the volume of data that you and others may collect, it is possible that your company may need to implement a dedicated system to handle it all. Such a system is called a "customer relationship management" or **CRM system**. Fundamentally, CRM is a management approach used collaboratively across an enterprise to learn more about customers' needs and behaviors, develop stronger relationships with them (especially to retain the "right" customers), and get more new ones.

CRM systems include processes, facilitated by specialized computer software, that help bring together a lot of information about customers, sales, marketing effectiveness, responsiveness, and market trends that affects the many operations of a company, from sales and planning to manufacturing and R&D. When used analytically, a CRM system

> applies a variety of data analysis and modeling techniques to discover patterns and trends in customer data. It predicts potential variations so organizations can react to changes before it is too late. Decision makers and front-line employees use these deep insights to understand what their customers want and predict what they will do next.
>
> (Phalen, 2001, para. 8)

CRM systems can be and should be used to determine how and what media can be targeted to diffuse messages in the most effective ways among target publics.

FINAL THOUGHTS ABOUT CALLS AND BUSINESS DEVELOPMENT

Cold calling is a dynamic part of building the business for your company. Your cold calls get meetings where you can showcase your company to qualified customers and start the sales process. To some extent, some customers will always come to your business because they know you well or have had a good impression of your business because of its strong reputation. You will likely meet with them too. Even though some customers may never come to your business, you know that there are many customers that need to know your business and what it has to offer—in terms of value, expertise, safety, and responsiveness.

The work you do to make the cold-calling process successful is valuable in many ways, as you have seen. The payoff is in establishing a continuous rhythm of prospects that can become final sales. Managing the business cycle in this way means a more dependable flow of future projects, more stable business planning, and greater satisfaction for everyone in your company.

From here the next step is formal responses to specific requests for help in realizing public relations objectives. The next chapter examines RFPs (requests for proposals) and situations for pitching new business to customers of any sort, internal or external.

EXECUTIVE VIEWPOINT

The Business of Building New Business

Jillian Collins Bohr, Director of U.S. Growth at Golin

New business culminates in the highest of highs (when we win) and lowest of lows (when we lose). Pitching is like final exams: it's high stakes, a lot of work, and hopefully a high reward. It brings the best of the agency together to find creative solutions for some of the most exciting brands and organizations in the world facing big challenges—to increase awareness, retain employees, or handle an issue. We have the chance to be part of the change and grow our own business while doing so.

In large public relations agencies, the growth function is a central part of its operating model. This is inclusive of our marketing and our new-business team, whose job is to essentially do PR for the PR firm.

The new-business team is focused on overall growth for the firm. We can grow in three ways:

1. *Organic*: Growing existing client remits. This is an important focus for our account team leaders to continuously evolve our relationship with the clients in which we have already earned their trust. A strong account lead is keeping a pulse on the business needs and identifying additional solutions we can provide, in turn growing the business.
2. *Proactive*: Prospecting includes identifying brands and organizations we can service. When identifying a prime prospect, we consider:
   a. *Industry*: Do we have expertise in the industry? We need to be able to provide strong counsel backed with relevant experience. We also need to ensure we're clear of conflict in that industry. For example, if we work for McDonald's, we cannot work for another quick-service restaurant as that would be in violation of our contract terms with that brand.
   b. *Relationship*: Do we know someone at the brand that can provide an introduction? Gaining the trust of a brand means gaining the trust of an individual. If we have a warm relationship, the likelihood of conversion is higher.
   c. *Potential budget*: We need to ensure we are speaking with prospects that not only fit from a category perspective, but that also make financial sense—doing the due diligence of understanding the financial resources the brand can commit to a public relations initiative. It's important to have this understanding with your leadership team as it will protect time and precious resources in the long run.
3. *Reactive*: This is the most traditional way to think of growth, when a brand or organization identifies a need to bring in an agency and issues a request for information (RFI) or request for proposal (RFP). When receiving these inbound requests, it's imperative for the team to ensure the agency is well positioned to convert the business. Much like the proactive type, we look at industry expertise, relationships, and potential budget. In addition to these, we also need to look at resources and ability to service the account should we win.

Building a response for an RFI or RFP is much like a group project in school—team collaboration and having a clear path is crucial to success. There are steps in the process that are common across many RFIs and RFPs that we need to work against, including:

1. *Vetting calls*: Once we receive the RFI/RFP, we hop on the phone to ask initial questions and ensure we are in a solid position to convert ahead of committing to participating in the search.
2. *Briefing and Q&A calls*: The client will offer time to walk through the brief with the agencies. This is a time to further interrogate the brief and ensure we are clear on the remit.
3. *Chemistry/capabilities meetings*: Choosing an agency partner is much like any other relationship; you need to ensure there is chemistry between the teams to encourage a positive partnership. We typically use this time to walk through relevant experience and get a deeper understanding of what a successful partnership looks like.
4. *Issue session*: When responding to a creative brief, a issue session is typically offered to share our work-in-progress strategy and creative territories. This meeting is incredibly valuable—not only are we getting feedback, but we're also continuing to build chemistry and beginning to sell-in our idea.
5. *Pitch*: This is the big day. It's a live meeting with the key decision-makers, in which we walk through our proposed idea, which typically includes a creative campaign, channel plan, and measurement approach.

This entire process can be condensed to two weeks or expanded to three-plus months. Typically, companies meet between three and six potential agencies, making it a highly competitive process. After the pitch, we enter into negotiations with procurement and align on a mutually beneficial scope of work.

Pitching a new account can be complicated to navigate while also servicing current clients. A way to alleviate the pain points in this aggressive process is to ensure we're all working from the same frame of reference. Having a repeatable model to creating winning proposals and impactful campaigns could be the difference between a stellar win rate and a losing one. Each step should include clear roles, responsibilities, and outcomes—all welldefined and easily understood across specialties and levels.

Having this guide will make the process bearable, and even fun! New business pitches provide you with the opportunity to stretch beyond your day-to-day client grind. It can be career-defining and exhilarating if you embrace it.

KEY WORDS

Power	Value proposition
Three dimensions of power	Gap analysis
Organization charts	Force field analysis
Dominant coalition	Order restoration model
Five proactive practices for power	Three types of customers
Positioning	Three types of calls
Two dimensions to positioning	Key messages
Differentiation	Screen
Ladders of the mind	Lead generation
Positioning heuristic	Calling realm
USP	Pipeline
CCAs	CRM system

REFERENCES

Bowen, S. A. (2009). What communication professionals tell us regarding dominant coalition access and gaining membership. *Journal of Applied Communication Research, 37*, 418–443.

Burke, K. (1970). *The rhetoric of religion: Studies in logology.* University of California Press.

Burke, K. (1989). Poem. In H. W. Simons & T. Melia (Eds.), *The legacy of Kenneth Burke* (p. 263). University of Wisconsin Press.

Heath, C., & Heath, D. (2008). *Made to stick: Why some ideas survive and others die.* Random House.

James, M. (2011). A provisional conceptual framework for intentional positioning in public relations. *Journal of Public Relations Research, 23*(1), 93–118.

Lewin, K. (1997). *Resolving social conflicts and field theory in social science.* American Psychological Association.

Phalen, S. (2001, June 15). *Increasing customer value: Harness the power of predictive CRM.* Montgomery Research Inc. Available online: http://mthink.com/ article/ increasing-customer-value-harnesspower-predictive-crm/.

Ries, A., & Trout, J. (1993). *The 22 immutable laws of marketing: Violate them at your own risk*. HarperBusiness.

Ries, A., & Trout, J. (2001). *Positioning: The battle for your mind*. McGraw-Hill. (Original work published 1976.)

Rogers, E. M. (2003). *Diffusion of innovations* (5th ed.). Free Press.

Silbiger, S. (2012). *The ten day MBA: A step-by-step guide to mastering the skills taught in America's top business schools* (4th ed.). Harper Business.

Smudde, P. M. (2011). *Public relations as dramatistic organizing: A case study bridging theory and practice*. Hampton Press.

Smudde, P. M., & Courtright, J. L. (2010). Public relations and power. In R. L. Heath (Ed.), *Handbook of public relations* (2nd ed., pp. 177–189). Sage.

Smudde, P. M., & Courtright, J. L. (2012). *Inspiring cooperation and celebrating organizations: Genres, message design and strategy in public relations*. Hampton Press.

Smudde, P. M., & Courtright, J. L. (2013). Form following function: Message design for managing corporate reputations. In C. E. Carroll (Ed.), *Handbook of communication and corporate reputation* (pp. 404–417). Wiley-Blackwell.

Stacks, D., & Michaelson, D. (2010). *A practitioner's guide to public relations research, measurement, and evaluation*. Business Expert Press.

Trout, J., & Rivkin, S. (2000). *Differentiate or die: Survival in our era of killer competition*. John Wiley & Sons.

RECOMMENDED READING

Cialdini, R. B. (2001). *Influence: Science and practice* (4th ed.). Allyn & Bacon.

Garten, J. E. (2001). *The mind of the CEO*. Basic Books.

Inside the minds.com. (2002). *The art of public relations: Industry visionaries reveal the secrets to successful public relations*. Aspatore Books.

Moore, G. A. (1999). *Crossing the chasm: Marketing and selling high-tech products to mainstream customers* (revised ed.). Harper Business.

Ries, A., & Ries, L. (2009). *War in the boardroom: Why left-brain management and right-brain marketing don't see eye-to-eye—and what to do about it*. Collins Business.

CHAPTER 10
REQUESTS FOR PROPOSALS AND NEW-BUSINESS PITCHES

CHAPTER OUTLINE

If cold, warm, and hot calls are a proactive way to build business for a public relations organization, "**requests for proposals**" (**RFPs**) are a reactive way to build business. Calls involve contacting customers, but RFPs represent customers specifically inviting expert help. (An alternative name is "request for quote" [RFQ]. We will use RFP.) In this way, RFPs are tools that corporate, nonagency organizations use to solicit the help of qualified external firms. RFPs are not something used within a corporate, nonprofit, NGO, or other organization to obtain help from existing operating units. (The closest thing would be a formal written request for a meeting between one department, say R&D, and another, say public relations, regarding innovations the organization is creating.) Notice, however, that with a RFP, there are two sides—the inviting organization and the responding organization.

The process for the two to eventually come together is an important one to examine and understand so that it can be managed effectively. It is also the substance of **new-business pitches** (**NBPs**) in which both an agency and a potential client engage to determine if there is a good fit between them so that each can help the other meet its needs. This chapter focuses on these two main topics: RFPs and NBPs. Viewing them from both sides of the table—the inviting organization (potential client) and the responding organization (potential agency)—reveals important similarities and differences that play out in the dance which may result in a contractual arrangement for the agency to work for the client.

DOI: 10.4324/9781003208280-11

WHAT IS A RFP?

Requests for proposals are formal documents that specify what an organization needs and wants from external providers/suppliers to solve a particular problem within certain parameters, including time, money, performance objectives, and material. A related but subordinate way to build business is a "**request for information**" (**RFI**), which an organization may use to find out more details about an agency's capabilities, client successes, and so on in order to decide if it should be sent a formal request for a proposal. RFPs typically target singular projects, and if a project is large enough, parts of it may be divided into separate RFPs either at the start of the RFP process or as part of the negotiation with eligible providers. The **RFP process**, simply put, typically proceeds this way:

1. An organization writes and then releases a RFP with a hard deadline for responses (i.e., day, hour, and minute). Any responses submitted late—to the minute—are immediately rejected because it is a reflection of (right or wrong) the responding provider's lack of commitment to timeliness, respect for deadlines, and perception of the project as proposed. Providers must plan for complications in submitting their responses, such as lost or delayed packages during delivery.
2. Providers interested in responding to a RFP must send them to the requesting organization by or before the deadline. The provider must follow the RFP's instructions in every way. RFPs are structured in ways to make comparisons across multiple vendors as directly and as fairly as possible, so the submitted material must be presented in as nearly the same form and format from one agency to the next. Although the ideas can and should be innovative and impactful, save the extra "flash" for the presentation, if you are invited to give one. The response to a RFP is more about substance than style.
3. Organizational stakeholders in the requesting organization review the responses against the criteria for selection spelled out in the RFP. The result of the reviews is a short list of providers who best fit the criteria.
4. The requesting organization invites the providers on the short list to give individual, private presentations to a small group of selected organizational stakeholders. The providers' presentations focus on themselves and their proposals, going beyond what was stated and, for example, explaining what value they will have added in specific terms during the period of the proposed project. Substance and style merge best here.
5. The requesting organization's stakeholders review the presentations with the proposals and rank order them from most preferred to least preferred. Depending on the scope of the RFP, the requesting organization would offer the project to one or more of the responding providers. If, during the negotiation, a provider refuses the offer or the offer is rescinded, the requesting organization goes to the next provider in the rankings.

As step 1 says, the whole process begins when a RFP is needed and must be written. The writing process for a RFP can be lengthy and involve multiple internal parties. For most public relations RFPs, the scope of work would encompass only the PR function and, as needed, involve other organizational units during the course of the project. To write an effective RFP, an organization must know well what **problem/ opportunity** it wants addressed, what objectives must be met, by when, and within what budget. In other words, the problem/opportunity is thoroughly researched and defended in business terms. This analysis defines the nature and scope of the problem/ opportunity. Any problem/opportunity will have conditions that unequivocally must be met ("needs") and other things that it would be great to have but are not absolutely necessary ("wants"). The people preparing the RFP must distinguish between needs and wants, with a bias toward making sure the needs are top priorities. Language in the RFP, then, must reflect what is a need and what is a want. Include an attorney during the process to ensure legal protections, like matters of any party defaulting on agreements or canceling the agreement before it is fulfilled.

During the writing process for the RFP, those responsible for it must have a clear idea about what an ideal provider(s) would be. That ideal will guide statements about the capabilities and expertise **requirements** a provider must have to be considered, and the criteria for selecting the best providers from among those who respond and, ultimately, offering the job to the most-referred provider(s), depending on the scope of the project. Disclosures about the RFP process are included and give specific dates, times, and contact information for those who choose to submit a proposal. Figure 10.1 presents a basic outline of the contents of typical RFPs for public relations work. The **content** may be expanded or contracted, depending on an organization's requirements. Some RFPs require far more content, such as those for government organizations. So, again, it is very important to know the requirements for RFPs as a writer of them *and* as a responder to them. Note that a RFP is *not* a contract for work but, rather, an invitation for interested and qualified parties to "bid" on the work. Only after a thorough review of providers and their proposals will an offer be tendered to the one that is most preferred and, subsequently, a contract be negotiated and consummated between the parties. Again, legal representation is critical to have during the process, especially during contract negotiation.

From a prospective provider's perspective, a RFP can be relatively simple to very complex, depending on certain requirements from the requesting organization and, if applicable, requirements under the law. Searching the Internet for RFPs can show the wide range of content that different organizations use. Figure 10.2 shows an example of the requirements (also called a "**scope of work statement**") for PR agencies responding to a RFP. Meticulous review of any RFP is essential if an agency thinks it should respond to a RFP. What is said between the lines throughout the RFP is as important as what the lines of the RFP's text say. Realize, too, that second-guessing the requesting organization's desires or motives could be a big mistake. If you have questions about what is said or implied in a RFP, call the contact person and ask appropriate,

- **Background**
  - Organization (offerings, market position, target customers, and differentiators)
  - Key message platform
  - Need/situation summary
  - Objectives
- **Scope of Work**
  - Work to be performed
  - Output specifications
  - Contractor's performance expectations
- **Program Management**
  - Management (names, titles, and contact information)
  - Schedule (full project, excluding RFP process)
  - Budget and resource stipulations
- **RFP Process and Schedule**
  - RFP invitations
  - Response deadline (date and time)
  - Proposal reviews and short-list decision
  - Invitation for next step (e.g., interview; problem-solution presentation)
  - Final decision
  - Contract negotiation and consummation
- **RFP Evaluation Criteria**
  - Qualifications (firm and team members)
  - Track record (results show successfulness)
  - Quality (proposal's correctness, accuracy, design/layout, service, etc.)
  - Reasonableness (cost, time, and resource estimates)
- **Proposal Content Requirements**
  - Letter of transmittal
  - Statement of understanding about the scope of work
  - Proposed plan, expected results, and schedule
  - Estimated complete budget
  - Project team and backgrounds of members
  - Capabilities (relevant to RFP and beyond)
  - Business relationship management and daily account management habits
  - Resources needs/access
  - Relevant experiences and references
  - Licensing, bonding, and insurance (if applicable)
- **Limitations**
  - Freedom in reviewing and choosing proposals in organization's own best interests
  - Contacting references and acquiring any needed information is granted by submitting proposal
  - No representations, warrantees, or guarantees are expressed or implied in RFP, including obligations or liabilities between the organization and proposer
- **Confidentiality and Public Records**
  - Safeguard proposals and discussions in confidence under applicable law until final decision or process termination
  - Applicable law may enable/require sharing of proposals upon request as a matter of "public record"
- **Attachments**

Figure 10.1 Basic RFP outline

well-formed questions that get at what you want to know, and do not "beat around the bush" by asking questions that are vague or off-topic from the RFP.

A good, solid, formal submission to a RFP will follow the rules for what prospective providers must provide, while also giving a strong case for a provider's expertise, capabilities, and personality. This last aspect of personality is really a matter of

PR Agency Requirements:

⊙ Media and industry-analyst relations: Open influencers' doors to create and take advantage of opportunities for published articles and reports from publications and analysts.

⊙ Help build top-of-mind awareness about our company among influencers (see Appendix A).

⊙ Secure media placements for editorial coverage in Tier 1 and Tier 2 publications.

⊙ Help keep analysts updated and gain coverage in published reports by Tier 1 and Tier 2 analysts.

⊙ Set up two press/analyst tours and follow up on them.

⊙ Perform other activities as needed to help meet or exceed the PR objectives and goals.

⊙ Speakers bureau: Find, secure and publicize speaking opportunities for our company's executives (and customers) at appropriate events, including trade shows, conferences, local executive briefings, etc.

⊙ Communications counsel and support: Propose and help implement the more effective ways to promote our company and to fulfill its external communications goals. Also provide counsel and support for investor relations, internal communications, crisis communications, and issues management.

⊙ Fulfill requirements specified in the evaluation criteria given below.

Figure 10.2 Sample requirements for PR agency

"chemistry" between the two parties, and if the prospective provider is called upon to give a presentation about its proposal, then is the time to demonstrate good chemistry. This objective requires detailed research and observation about who the people are at the requesting organization and their organization's culture. So an agency's response to a RFP can be as creative as possible, and there are four basic **possibilities for response**:

- "Yes" (respond to a RFP exactly for what it seeks, no more or no less)
- "Yes and …" (respond to a RFP for what it seeks and add more ideas beyond the scope of work)
- "No but …" (respond to a RFP to present a vastly different approach to meet the prospective client's needs as defined)
- "No" (respond to a RFP by saying that it simply cannot be addressed for certain business reasons, such as too big, too small, no resources to dedicate to it)

One important note here about these possible responses: a potential client can respond to an agency's proposal in one of these ways too. The idea in this case—particularly for the middle two options—is that the potential client sees (or doesn't see) something in the agency's proposal, informs the agency about that, and possibly, asks for some kind of additional response. Such a request could be a good sign to an agency that a potential client wants to find out more because of a good-quality proposal.

In any case, a reasonably conservative approach to the presentation may be best, as you can loosen up to the degree that works as you learn about the requesting organization's people. Again, know the audience! Some RFPs may be so strict that the requesting organization will only review responses that present exactly what is sought exactly as it wants it. Sometimes multiple meetings or presentations may be required, and if this happens, it is very likely that the requesting organization places an especially high value on chemistry between the two groups that will work together and has a favorable opinion of your group.

Use the evaluation criteria for both needs and wants to ensure that your proposal is as strong as it can be. Figure 10.3 shows an example of criteria for a RFP used to secure the help of a public relations agency. Those who write a RFP and will evaluate the

Evaluation Criteria ("Needs")
Public relations agencies that respond to this RFP will be evaluated on the following criteria:
⊙ Core competency in media and analyst relations in high-tech/software sector, especially for enterprise software and/or ERP (enterprise resource planning) systems.
⊙ Demonstrable connections and good relationships with mainstream business writers and publications, plus finance and IT writers and publications. Relationships with key freelance writers are also important.
⊙ Evidence of solid experience and success in investor relations, internal communications, crisis communications, issue management, organizational change communications, and other areas.
⊙ Excellent references from strong client list.
⊙ Partnership with client. Evidence of long-term clients that are referenceable.
⊙ Proven track record with moving clients to and maintaining thought-leader status.
⊙ Bias toward proactive measurable work. Measurement includes content analyses of editorial coverage, media audits, performance measurement, ROI for client.
⊙ A performance measurement program in place for clients and open to adding client-specific metrics.
⊙ A view of PR/corporate communications that fits our company.
⊙ Agency location facilitates easy communication with our company in the USA and possibly with UK links to support our UK operation.

Additional Areas of Interest ("Wants")
We are also interested in knowing details about how you manage the day-to-day business of our account with you. Here are the areas of our relationship that we'd like you to address with clear and concise statements or attachments for each of them:
⊙ Reporting and visit/calls on program/project status, wins, issues, opportunities, etc.
⊙ Access to agency principals.
⊙ Client and staff turnover
⊙ Relationship structure between the agency and our company.
⊙ Method/approach for daily account activity and overall management.
⊙ Time allowed for account administration.
⊙ Prescribed budget allotment for unforeseen events and project/miscellaneous expenses.
⊙ Competitive and market research and analysis capabilities.
⊙ Identifying and scheduling speaking opportunities and related PR.
⊙ Biographies of agency principals and those on our company's account.
⊙ Turnover of clients and agency staff.

Figure 10.3 Example RFP criteria

submissions to it put themselves partially in the position of the responding organization so that the content will be understandable and usable by prospective providers. By the same token, prospective provider organizations must put themselves in the position of the requesting organization so that those agencies can best address the knowledge, attitudes, and actions expected of them.

Back on the requesting organization's side of the process, the key question that must be answered compellingly is this: where is the agency's plan taking the client? The evaluation criteria would be applied fastidiously against the proposal and presentation(s) of the final candidates to answer that question and select the winner to do the work stipulated in the RFP. People in the decision process should evaluate each agency individually and then, later, come together to compare their evaluations and establish a definitive, group-based evaluation.

An effective way to apply the criteria to each response to a RFP is to create a score sheet. List the criteria (needs and wants) like those shown in Figure 10.3 from most important to least important. Assign a numerical value of importance (say 1 to 5, with 5 being the highest) to give the appropriate weight to each criterion. This value for importance helps mitigate the possibility of ties in the final calculation of a provider's final score, if there were no weighting factor for importance. Next apply a small scale of values (say 1 to 5, with 5 being the best) to each criterion to determine how well a provider appears to meet a criterion. Then multiply a criterion's value by its importance value to get the final rating for the provider on that criterion. A spreadsheet can be an effective way to format and handle the scoring. The provider with the highest total score across all criteria would be the winner. No completed evaluations would be shared with the prospective provider, as the evaluations are the proprietary property of the client. If it is necessary, explaining why a provider did not make the short list can be done by explaining orally the criteria that were and, especially, were not sufficiently met.

One final and important note about the RFP process and any NBP—under U.S. copyright law, summarized in Chapter 3, the material presented in the RFP responses and the NBP presentations is the property of the respective firms and cannot be used by the client. Thus, it is illegal to use the ideas of an agency that bid on your job through your RFP (or other NBP; e.g., if it was shared by e-mail or in an informational meeting like that covered in Chapter 9) but did not win. Such use is also unethical under the codes of ethics for the Public Relations Society of America, the International Association for Business Communicators, and other professional organizations focused on communication. If you wish to use one or more of an unsuccessful bidder's ideas, it would be best to negotiate a fee for their use; otherwise, simply file away the unsuccessful proposals because you were not going to go with those firms anyway.

NEW-BUSINESS PITCHES FROM BOTH SIDES OF THE TABLE

With the RFP submitted, accepted, and reviewed, a prospective provider waits to find out if it will be called for a presentation. This meeting is a big deal for those on both sides of the table—the requesting organization (client) and the potential provider (agency). Everyone knows what is at stake and what grounds will be used to make all decisions about which firm wins. The **three principal factors** of the business relationship—**quality** of imagination, products, and service is high, **service** of the client and account is strong, and **price** for all work to be done is competitive—are scrutinized throughout the process (see Figure 10.4). Indeed, the RFP process seeks information about all three, and meetings and negotiations seek agreement about what will be done, by when, and at what cost. The written documentation has shown what each side is, but that same material leaves out the personal side of who makes up the organizations. The question on everyone's minds on both sides of the table is: "Who would we be working with?" The meeting is the opportunity to answer that question to a reasonable extent. Then, if the meeting is successful for one agency, it enters contract negotiation with the client.

THE MEETING

Both parties prepare for the meeting. The substance of the meeting is a new-business pitch, which is the agency making its case interpersonally with the selected internal stakeholders for the client. The client, when inviting the agency for the meeting, would have explained to the agency what the expectations would be for the meeting. If the agency accepted the invitation, it would have to follow the client's instructions to prepare appropriately. For example, a client may give the agency a hypothetical situation to address within the scope of the RFP to see how it responds. That response would reflect many dimensions simultaneously, such as creativity, knowledge of the client, knowledge of the client's market and environmental pressures, problem-solving abilities, resource allocations, client service, communication philosophy, business philosophy

Figure 10.4 Three-legged stool of business relationships

and priorities, operations organization, project management capabilities, and so on. Of particular interest to the client would be sensitivity to any organizational-political dynamics, potential roadblocks, and other matters that may bear on the project's success or failure.

Most important, the response as given by agency representatives in a meeting with the client's people highlights the personalities of everyone present. The people in the room may all end up working together in some ways, some more than others. So everyone is being evaluated: do we like this agency? Do we like this client? However, those from the agency are in much more of a fishbowl for observation because it is they who are seeking the work, and the client has its pick from among those who have submitted proposals. A prospective agency is well advised to get anything clarified in advance that it feels needs clarification, but to do so without being too bothersome and demanding.

Again, the invitation to meet has some ambiguity built in to find out how an agency thinks and can best demonstrate (1) its genuine enthusiasm for the job and (2) its superiority above others to understand what is at stake and to get results. (At this point, the great value of the work covered in Chapter 9 pays off.) Those from the agency should have worked well together to prepare the presentation and be the people who would be assigned to the client if the agency wins the job. Everyone from the agency team should have something to contribute to the presentation and be ready to answer any questions. Beyond development meetings for the new-business pitch, two or more rehearsals of the pitch should be done as well to make sure bases have been covered from the client's perspective. Experienced veterans would play the role of client representatives as the agency team gives its pitch and takes questions. Any ideas for improvement should be noted and revisions made as a result of these rehearsals.

From the client side of the table, the **evaluation criteria** in the RFP still rule the day. New-business pitches, then, can be evaluated on those criteria by taking notes on which criteria are addressed well or not. However, a client could choose to develop a new set of criteria that complements the RFP's criteria to evaluate the agency's pitch. In this way, the team who developed the RFP and evaluated responses to it may outline how they will know not just a strong presentation, but more importantly, a strong agency that follows directions, builds upon its proposal, and demonstrates a solid case for its selection as the most-preferred provider—the winner of the RFP process.

Basic matters of public speaking are obvious choices for the criteria of agencies' new-business pitches, and those criteria should be included. More specific criteria should be included about the agency team's level of creativity, interpersonal behaviors among agency team members, interpersonal behaviors of the agency members with client people, perceived genuineness in wanting to work on the project and with the client, perceived enthusiasm about working in the agency, clarity in communicating, sense of humor, sense of confidence, and sense of humility, including case examples as evidence of competence and success. The evaluation sheet for the pitches from the finalists can be structured as a kind of score sheet (based on Figure 10.3) with room for notes and comments as a presentation is given. A new score sheet would be used by each client person for each agency pitch. A blank score sheet may be shared with the agency after the meeting, but no completed score sheets or personal notes would be shared, as they are proprietary and the property of the client. If necessary, an oral explanation of the criteria that were and, especially, were not sufficiently met could be given if an agency wants to know why it did not win. For the winner of the job, the next step is negotiating a contract.

THE NEGOTIATION

During the negotiation process, the nature and scope of the work have been disclosed from the beginning, so there will not be any surprises. The negotiation process proceeds along a line of several steps: planning and preparation (doing the homework to negotiation well), defining ground rules (the who, what, where, and when of the actual negotiations), clarifying and justifying matters (asking and answering questions), bargaining and problem solving (the give-and-take between parties), and closing and implementing (signing the final agreement and starting work on it) (Robbins & Judge, 2008). Given the client's RFP and additional communication plus what the winning agency presented, however, there may be some alterations because there were some great ideas that may require changes in the nature and scope of work that will, in turn, be transferred to a contract that all parties will sign. Chapter 3 addressed contracts briefly, and involving an attorney at this phase is essential. The content of a contract can vary as much as the work asked for in a RFP can vary. Because of this variance, a basic understanding of key negotiation concepts is important for a public relations leader to have.

Much has been prepared over the years in many media about negotiation and being an effective negotiator, and a PR leader ought to acquire knowledge and skills for good negotiating. For our purposes, there are three concepts that are important to know because of their prominence in the negotiation process: origin of negotiation, situation rules, and process. Greater detail and skillfulness in negotiating can be gained through additional study and, especially, practice.

ORIGIN OF NEGOTIATION

As long as two or more sides on an issue exist, there is conflict. That conflict may be simple or complex to understand and resolve, if it is resolvable at all. In a RFP process, in spite of there being substantial documentation about what each party thinks, needs, and would like to do, one agreement must be reached about what precisely will be done, how, and under what parameters. Conflict, then, is the source of negotiation, and it can be approached in one of two ways. One way is, "I win, you lose." This is the kind of negotiation that children often use when playing together with the same toys or in the same game. This approach is simple and easy to understand. It reflects a self-centered, take-it-or-leave-it attitude that, depending on the conflict situation and the people involved, may work or may not. If all sides of a conflict have this attitude, a negotiation can break down quickly, and everyone is frustrated.

The other approach to **negotiation conflict** is: "We win." This kind of negotiation is by its nature more complicated, but it has the benefits of greater engagement among the parties as they come to know each other and their interlocked interests better. Realize that a "we win" approach does not guarantee that any agreement may be reached, but it does increase the probability. The reason for the "we win" approach's greater usefulness is that its nature is to emphasize the importance of knowing both one's own and the other party's positions. In the end, a "we win" agreement would give all parties much of what they want but without some of the other things they wanted. How such agreements are reached is contingent on fulfilling certain rules for the negotiation.

SITUATION RULES

Within a negotiation the parties involved share a particular situation. In the case of a RFP, that situation, of course, is bounded by the RFP and other discourse (written and oral) shared by all parties during the process. That situation also encompasses the implied or understood factors in the business environment each party faces that may or may not be known by all parties. Having an attorney for your organization involved during the whole negotiation is essential.

The parties who will participate in a negotiation need to follow three basic **situation rules** to complete the "homework" necessary for an effective and fruitful negotiation. First, define each party's objective for the negotiation. For a RFP process, this rule is relatively easy to follow. The client wants an agency to be and to do specific things within certain limits, including budget, performance expectations, and time. The agency wants the client to provide resources, information, and guidance in usable ways and when needed during the course of the contract, including being paid on time and evaluated fairly for work done.

The second rule is to complete sufficient and accurate research about the other party. The point here is to understand as much as possible the other party's perspectives, interests, and constraints while negotiating. For example, the following questions can be helpful to investigate both the other parties to a negotiation and one's own position for the negotiation:

- How do we/does the other party truly view us and our project?
- What other interests might we/the other party have in entering into an agreement?
- What pressures may we/the other party be facing to enter into any agreement?

- What minimal agreement might we/the other party accept?
- What would keep us/the other party from reaching an agreement?

This rule for research is very similar to conducting a thorough audience analysis before writing an article for a publication or planning a particular communication project. The research does not end after gathering and analyzing data about the other party. The process continues with astute listening to what the other party says and does not say, what the party does or does not do. Listen to and watch what you say, and not say, do, and not do as well for the same reasons. All these things convey some meaning and should be considered as relevant as possible.

The third rule is to know the limits for yourself and the other parties. Because of the work you do to fulfill the second rule, you have a sufficient and, presumably, accurate database about what limits likely exist for the whole negotiation. These limits must be understood for your own organization and each party to the negotiation. Additional limits arise in two new categories: assumptions and estimates. For assumptions, the best information available indicates at least the reasons, attitudes, and motives for other parties (and your own organization) to enter into a negotiation. Documenting and understanding them can reveal much about how each party may behave during the negotiation and suggest what they may ask for in the process. The second category of limits is estimates, and it concerns matters about the amounts of financial, material, and temporal resources that may be needed and wanted. Financial resources would encompass the amount paid for the work proposed, including mark-ups for subcontractors, out-of-pocket expenses, and other costs related to completing the work asked for in the RFP. Material resources encompass produced communications, personnel, equipment, facilities, and other things needed to do the work specified. Temporal resources focus on time needed to complete the work plus the length of time produced work should prove valuable during the contract period so that a return on the investment is secured.

KNOW THE BATNAs

The combination of the information and analysis about objectives, rules, and limits among all parties in a negotiation can now result in a singular view of the point at which negotiation may stop. That point is called the "best alternative to a negotiated agreement," or **BATNA** (Fisher et al., 2011; Leverich, 2006; Robbins & Judge, 2008; Yemm, 2005). Most people think of the point just before a negotiation stops/fails for a party as "the bottom line," which typically focuses on one dimension and primarily price. BATNAs actually are the culmination of the three situation rules. One's BATNA is similar to a "bottom line," but it is better because of all the work that goes into arriving at it. A BATNA is "the lowest value acceptable to you for a negotiated agreement" (Robbins & Judge, 2008, p. 500). Value here is the key because it involves price, of course, but it also involves all the things that go into substantiating it. This approach opens up more avenues for creativity in negotiation when one dimension, like price, cannot change but other factors can. So, in addition to having done all the homework in preparation for the negotiation, knowing your own BATNA plus the other party's BATNA will serve everyone well during the negotiation process.

PROCESS-BROADENING OPTIONS

If all people did in negotiations was to demand the same thing over and over without consideration of other **options**, negotiations would rarely be fruitful and all the more confrontational. Instrumental to any negotiation is creativity because many things are at stake and, thereby, open for consideration. In this way, negotiation is much more about problem solving than merely finding a mutually agreeable position. Viewing negotiation in terms of problem solving naturally invites an attitude of creativity, ingenuity, invention, and innovation. Remember from the negotiation process that what is not said or done can be as important as what is said or done. Add to this the dynamics of interpersonal communication, and the result is many minds working together—with their own best interests at heart, to be sure—to figure out a win–win approach to a problem. So what may not have been said or done in a negotiation may end up being a key to moving the negotiation along, to solving the problem more effectively than if only what was documented was all that could be used. Figure 10.5 summarizes an effective way to broaden options during a negotiation through creative attention to both theory and practice about what is wrong and what could be done.

In this process, there is a balance between what is wrong and what could work in theory and what is wrong and what would work in practice. It begins in Step I with a clear understanding of the problem and moves through three more steps until ideas that make the most sense and can provide the greatest benefits are realized. Key to the process is defining criteria for an effective solution that would be used to test a proposed solution. The process allows for movement from specific ideas to general ones, accepts alternative perspectives from other fields, relies on different arguments with different strengths, and permits changes in the scope of the proposed solution until a final agreement is reached.

In addition to the problem-solving aspects of broadening options there are others. One aspect is time and space. If a negotiation takes a long time to complete, it may be best to rely on distance from the problem by getting away from it for some time. Factors of an organizational or ethnic culture may dictate how negotiations proceed from beginning to end, and those factors must be well understood when working through the three situation rules. Another important aspect is separating people from the problem or opportunity. Although people ultimately will be involved in the implementation of an agreement, all parties in a negotiation must realize that the focus is the problem/opportunity, and people involved can be adjusted. With the focus squarely on solving a problem or seizing an opportunity through a rational and fair negotiation, matters like personalities *during a negotiation* have little to nothing to do with reaching an agreement, and their influence on the process is minimized drastically. If those matters arise as

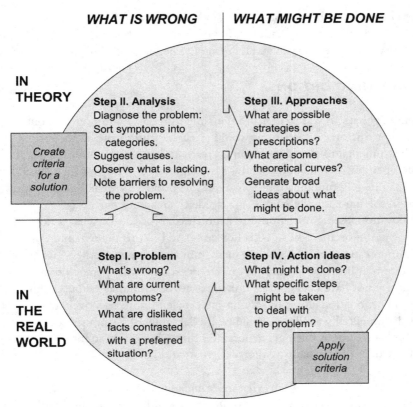

WHAT IS WRONG | **WHAT MIGHT BE DONE**

IN THEORY

Create criteria for a solution

Step II. Analysis
Diagnose the problem:
Sort symptoms into
  categories.
Suggest causes.
Observe what is lacking.
Note barriers to resolving
  the problem.

Step III. Approaches
What are possible
  strategies or
  prescriptions?
What are some
  theoretical curves?
Generate broad
  ideas about what
  might be done.

Step I. Problem
What's wrong?
What are current
  symptoms?
What are disliked
  facts contrasted
  with a preferred
  situation?

Step IV. Action ideas
What might be done?
What specific steps
  might be taken
  to deal with
  the problem?

IN THE REAL WORLD

Apply solution criteria

Figure 10.5 Process model for inventing options in negotiation
Source: Adapted from Fisher et al. (2011, p. 69)

problems, they can be addressed separately, but the big picture of success in problem solving through the negotiation is the key.

Finally, negotiations can achieve one of **three possible outcomes**. One is a definite yes, and all parties are happy, ready to go, and enter into a legally binding agreement to fulfill particular promises documented in a contract and other supporting discourse. Another outcome is no but with contingencies. This outcome means that there is still hope that an agreement can be reached, provided that certain things are addressed. The last outcome is a flat-out no. In this outcome, no one's BATNA was accepted, the negotiation is finished, and it may never be broached again. But maybe not. Perhaps the problem/opportunity can be addressed differently at a different time.

EXECUTIVE VIEWPOINT

Managing RFPs and NBPs: A Dozen Things to Know and Do

Gary Myers, Cofounder and Former President, MorganMyers

I spent 39 years in the agency business, 23 of them running my own firm. What follows are some insights I wish every potential client knew about agencies, our pursuit of new business, and our view of the RFP process.

First, prospective clients should know they are being evaluated, too. Here's a short list of questions we asked ourselves when deciding to pitch a client prospect or to take a pass:

1. Can we do the work well? Are we well positioned and highly qualified? Why pitch an account where we don't have expertise or experience; especially when we're going up against other firms that are a better client match? Why waste the energy? Instead, stay focused on what we do best.
2. Does the client prospect have growth potential beyond the initial engagement? Are there other divisions or product groups our firm can serve in the future? If the initial engagement is for marketing/publicity, is there upside potential for picking up other disciplines such as employee relations, corporate affairs, website management, investor relations, or more? Can the client prospect turn into a long-term "agency of record" account?
3. Does the client prospect want to be an industry leader? Does their business plan reflect an aggressive attitude? Are they properly resourced to achieve their goals?
4. Who will be our counterparts on the client side? Are they experienced pros? Will they be strong and effective advocates for communication within the client organization? Do they understand agencies and are they able to properly represent

the agency to the client and the client to the agency? (Will they partner well with the firm's account manager counterparts?)

5. Will the prospective account bring meaningful new experiences and relationships to the firm?

6. Can we make a fair buck on the business? It isn't all about money, but we look for clients who value insights, strategy, creativity, and loyalty. We run away from pure price shoppers who don't appreciate good work and will frustrate every staff member who touches the account.

If the answers to the above questions are satisfactory, then we'll go for it with an unrelenting passion to win.

Now, here is some time- and aggravation-saving advice for any organization sending out RFPs in search of an agency partner:

1. Do your homework. Research and pre-screen the list of agencies and make sure they all show potential. Avoid "cattle calls" with ten or more agencies invited to pitch. An ideal list includes about five or six agencies for RFPs. Then narrow it down to three finalists for oral presentations.

2. Let the agencies know what you're really after. Give them the score card on which they will be evaluated in advance of the RFP response and the presentation.

3. Avoid hidden agendas. For example, if you're looking for a new firm because the former agency was always over budget and missing deadlines, then don't keep that secret. Instead, ask about agency cost-control and traffic systems in the RFP/pitch. Address all concerns head-on.

4. Make sure the decision-makers are on the selection committee from the start. A committee of four to six is very workable. But keep everyone on the same page and make sure you have key personnel involved. While it never happened to us, I've heard horror stories from other agency owners who "won the business" in the RFP and pitch, but the company president (who had not been on the selection committee) awarded the account to a golfing buddy's firm or his wife's nephew.

5. Don't be afraid to talk about money. Do it up front. Talk to the agency about rates, billing practices, budget control, and terms. Unresolved financial issues will ruin agency–client trust and ultimately the relationship. Remember, it is in the client's best interest if the agency makes a fair profit. (Our firm has a policy that clients can audit their account's financial records at any time. We stress that point in our RFP responses and pitches.)

6. Realize what you're asking. A RFP that requests agency credentials and case histories is fairly simple to create from preexisting agency files. On the other hand, elaborate proposals that entail speculative (spec) creative work can be very time consuming and expensive for the responding agency. The goal of an agency search and the RFP/pitch process should be to identify the firm best suited to serve the client. Ask for enough spec creative work to get good insights into how the agency

thinks, but don't ask for a full-blown campaign. The RFP/pitch process can take months to complete, especially if the account is large and multiple presentations are involved. New business is costly in both nonbillable agency time and out-of-pocket expenses. It is not uncommon for an agency pitching a large account to invest a significant percentage of the first year's profits in pursuit of the new business. That's especially true if one includes the nonbillable time agencies invest in initial planning and getting "up to speed" during the first year of building the new agency–client relationship.

Taking all of this together, know that agencies view new-business pitches as a competitive sport on a highly professional level. We are motivated. We put together strong pitch teams and deliberately strategize the game plan. Our opponents are the other agencies in the contest. This is serious business. We know that our agency's fortunes rise and fall on how well we play the new-business game. Agency leaders look at prospective clients as officials in the game. The client writes the rules and also assumes the role of referee. True agency competitors want and deserve a level playing field.

Press ahead.

KEY WORDS

RFP

RFI

NBP

RFP process

RFP response possibilities

Problem/opportunity

RFP content

Scope of work statement

Three legs of business relationship stool

Requirements

Evaluation criteria

Negotiation

Situation rules

BATNA

Options

Three possible outcomes

REFERENCES

Fisher, R., Ury, W., & Patton B. (2011). *Getting to yes: Negotiating agreement without giving in* (updated & revised ed.). Penguin.

Leverich, J. (2006, December 25–31). Negotiate and win. *Enterprise/Salt Lake City, 36*(25), 9.

Robbins, S. P., & Judge, T. A. (2008). Conflict and negotiation. In S. P. Robbins & T. A. Judge, Organizational behavior (13th ed., pp. 482–515). Pearson Education.

Yemm, G. (2005, Winter). Ask for more—you may get more!! *Management Services*, 36–37.

RECOMMENDED READING

Browne, M. N., & Keeley, S. M. (2011). *Asking the right questions with readings: A guide to critical thinking.* Prentice Hall.

Engel, S. M. (2000). *With good reason: An introduction to informal fallacies.* Bedford/St. Martin's.

Ries, A., & Ries, L. (2002). *The fall of advertising and the rise of PR.* Harper Collins.

Schultz, D., & Schultz, H. (2004). *IMC: The next generation.* McGraw-Hill.

Yemm, G. (2005, Winter). Ask for more—you may get more!! *Management Services*, 36–37.

11

CHAPTER 11
PERSONAL CAREER-PLANNING APPROACHES

CHAPTER OUTLINE

The focus of this book has been, from the beginning, on the ways of thinking in which public relations leaders engage on a daily basis. This approach has at least two important benefits: (1) it shows you much of what commands management's attention every day, so you can prepare yourself for a leadership position at some point later in your career; and, perhaps most immediately important, (2) it shows you how you will be led and managed as you start in your career, so you can perform better than you would have without this knowledge because you know what your bosses face. This book concludes, then, with this final chapter on ways you can best represent yourself to potential employers and to fellow professionals in the public relations field at the start of and throughout your full-time PR career.

As you think about and plan for your career in public relations, you must remember two simple realities, which this chapter explores. *First, your career is all about you.* The sum of your knowledge, skills, experiences, and personal character makes you who you are, and you will fit well in some organizations but not in others. Your quest in your career is really to demonstrate to others that you are competent in all ways that matter. In other words, you will be paid to be one of the best communicators and communication counselors in the organizations for which you work. Always make sure you prove that maxim every day in every way.

The second reality is that only you own your career. No one else is responsible for your career, although some people may be more influential than others as you make certain choices in life. So much of what you do in your career is choice-driven. As you begin

DOI: 10.4324/9781003208280-12

your career in public relations, you have the responsibility to successfully run one of the most important communication campaigns in your life—a campaign about your own value, which will run into your retirement. If you cannot promote yourself well and honestly, why should anyone hire you to promote their organization? Always make sure that your campaign about yourself is ethical, accurate, and compelling.

IT'S ALL ABOUT YOU

Remember in your childhood being asked, "What do you want to be when you grow up?" Your immediate answer then was likely different than it is now. Probably no one would have answered, "I want to be a PR person!" But we grow older and wiser, and public relations has become a career of choice and importance for organizations and society. The question itself, however, reveals a profound truth about planning for the future. Indeed, planning for the future requires one to be a bit visionary—to see the possibilities about one's self. But it does not end there. Just like strategic planning for an organization, you should do something similar for yourself. As Figure 11.1 shows, the future you see for yourself can be realized if you figure out the things you need to get there from where you are today. In other words, think backwards—from your ultimate future job to today, and consider the path to get there from here. The path between today and your future is your **career path**. Along that path you will reach certain **milestone** achievements, such as promotions, new jobs at different organizations (but not necessarily at higher levels of authority), awards, and so on, that all show you are advancing in your career. Setbacks in your career may also happen (e.g., a poorly executed project or a bad boss), and over time they will help you grow as a more competent professional and, perhaps, reveal certain opportunities that can evolve into career advances.

Going down that path you have the greatest control of your career. You need to be *diligent, flexible*, and *opportunistic*, but also *strategic*. Be diligent so that you work hard and do so ethically, enthusiastically, and intelligently, all of which reflect your personal character as a genuinely good professional and good person. Be flexible so you can obtain experiences that make the most of your knowledge, skills, experience, and interests. Be opportunistic so you can take advantage of promising circumstances and events that you find for yourself or that arise for you. Not every opportunity should be followed, however. ("No" is a good thing to say to some opportunities.)

Figure 11.1 Career path

So be strategic—no matter what opportunities, diversions, or detours you may take on your career path, remain focused on realizing the vision for yourself and your career. By the way, you may change your path toward your vision, just as you may change a route on a trip so you can see sights you did not originally plan for, and still get to your final destination. Alternatively, you may change your vision because of any variety of factors in your life that influence you to make such a change. In this event you embark on a whole new career–life path, and that is okay.

As you embark on your journey down your career–life path, two areas of knowledge are very important. The first is knowledge about yourself, and the second is knowledge about the field.

KNOW YOURSELF

Socrates professed the maxim, "Know thyself," because, simply put, for one to excel in life, one must first know who one is and in what ways one is moved to action or inaction. In terms of career management, you need to know what drives you to do what you do and to become what you want to become. This drive encompasses all aspects of your life, not just work. After all, as the old saying goes, "No one ever died wishing they had spent more time at work." Balance between work and the rest of your life matters greatly, and much research and advice have been published over the last two decades showing this point to be true. (More about this topic will be given at this chapter's end.) Companies listed on the 100 Best Places to Work are ample evidence of the increasing attention to and models for effective *work–life balance* that employers can enact.

Realize, too, that often in life you will work to live, and other times you will live to work. Priorities change, and in the public relations profession, you are frequently needed to work beyond the stereotypical 9:00 a.m. to 5:00 p.m. workday, extending into weekends. The reason is simple: organizations need to reach out to or serve constituents at various times and days that suit their schedules, and that means you work on those schedules for your organization. By the same token, organizations recognize that healthy, energetic, and thoughtful employees add the most value when they are fully engaged and enthusiastic because there is concern for them on many levels (see Gebauer et al., 2008; Shaffer, 2000).

So how do you know yourself? The best way is through honest self-reflection. That is, think deeply and candidly about who you are, what is important to you, and what you want to achieve in life. Questions like these are instrumental in self-reflection:

- What are your values (personal and professional)?
- What inspires you to want to work in public relations *and why*?
- How may you best continue to grow in professional expertise?
- How may you best improve as a person for yourself and others?
- How do you prefer to work *and why*?

- What work would you like most to do *and why?*
- Where would you like most to work *and why?*
- What would you like most in an employer *and why?*
- What kinds of people would you like to work with *and why?*
- What dislikes about a job would you want to avoid *and why?*
- What dislikes about an employer would you want to avoid *and why?*
- What dislikes about a work environment would you want to avoid *and why?*

Answers to these and other questions you may have will be valuable to you as you come to know yourself better and, especially, plan for your career as realistically as you can at any time in your life. The "why" parts of the questions are most important because they reveal the reasons for your preferences that, in turn, reflect your **personal values**. Values are the foundation of each person and the nexus for understanding who someone is. Check to see if your stated values are consistent with your stated and, especially, unstated values in your answers to the other questions.

Your values are instrumental in how you take advantage of the time you have any day. So be mindful of your commitments on and off the job. Plot out all the regular commitments you have each day of the week, including sleep, church, job, family, friends, and so on. Then examine the open time slots you have to see how balanced your life is. Make adjustments where needed. This work will show you how well you seem to use any day to do what you need to do.

Being always organized and mindful is a matter of self-discipline and essential to being successful in what you do. Projects, commitments, tasks, and so on vary in their levels of importance and urgency. Sort them in a daily to-do list so that you do the most important *and* most urgent ones first, then work your way down to those that are less important and less urgent. Categorize importance using numbers (i.e., 1, 2, 3, where 1 is supremely important). Likewise, determine urgency using letters (i.e., A, B, C, where A is supremely urgent). In this way you can classify your responsibilities and get them done within the daily timeframe you have.

A modified SWOT analysis can be a very useful way to engage in a **self-analysis**; Figure 11.2 shows an example of how you can address the salient matters in this process. The form in Figure 11.2 breaks up the SWOT items into two tables so that proper focus can be directed to career-life matters. The first half of the form is for brainstorming about your values, strengths, and weaknesses. These three factors, along with your answers to the questions above, are essential for completing the second half of the form, which concerns how you may act on your values, play to your strengths, and reduce or eliminate your weaknesses. The second half of the form focuses you on what you can do to realize your objectives, especially as you consider opportunities and threats/obstacles within a defined timeframe. Answers to the above questions will be most valuable here. Notice how the first objective is in the distant future and works back to the present. You may set objectives as far out into the future as you wish. This

SWOT Analysis for Your Career Path

Values (Personal and Professional)	Strengths		Weaknesses

Objectives	Opportunities and Action Steps	Completion Date	Potential Threats (Obstacles)
10 years:			
5 years:			
3 years:			
2 years:			
1 year:			
6 months:			

Figure 11.2 A SWOT self-analysis tool

form reflects the career path–planning process shown in Figure 11.1. The work you do for Figure 11.2 is the basis for other work you do for your self-analysis, and it will be refined and revised by additional information, as you will see.

At this point the principles of professionalism and ethics covered in Chapter 3 combine more obviously with who you are. You know well what the public relations field's expectations are, and you can now plot the ways in which you meet or need to meet those expectations. Sources like the online career resources for the Public Relations Society of America and the PR Council or a broader source like *PR Week*'s annual *Career Guide* can be helpful here too. Use this understanding to fine-tune your SWOT analysis from Figure 11.2. As you engage in anticipatory organizational socialization with different employers with whom you would like to work, you will discover ways in which your perspectives on work and public relations may (or may not) mesh with those organizations. These points of intersection become grounds on which you can and should make decisions to continue to seek employment with an organization or, if given a job offer, whether you want to truly work for that organization.

If you have had one or more internships, they have revealed much to you about the "real world" of working in public relations. But those jobs did not reveal everything because of the nature of your position as an intern and, most important, the limitations organizations can have for involving interns in certain things. For example, full-fledged, full-time employees will be most often invited to participate in pivotal policy or other decisions because that is part of their jobs. As an intern you are not expected to participate in many decisions, but you would likely be involved in developing some aspects of them as management sees fit.

Your first full-time job as a public relations professional, then, plays a new role in your career—as your formal entry into the field. You are more involved in more of the technical aspects of the work of PR professionals and called upon more in implementing decisions and actions you were not qualified to carry out as an intern. Any potential employer may ask you what salary you want, and you must have a good answer. A good answer is one that is based on data about very similar jobs, and you can get that data through credible online sources that use valid and reliable research for the profession and can sort the data on salaries based on zip code and city. Searching the Internet for "salary calculators" can reveal numerous providers you should use to determine what the probable salary would be for the kind of job for which you will interview. Also know that you are eligible for benefits as an employee that you would not get as an intern, including, for example, health, dental, and life insurance coverage; retirement savings; and perhaps employee stock purchases. You should become familiar with these things so you know what choices you should make based on your personal financial situation. In addition to conducting your own research, seeking the advice of a certified financial planner and/or a human resources/labor attorney can be helpful.

KNOW THE FIELD

Having established who you are and what you have to offer through a self-SWOT, you can go deeper. You should understand how well you fulfill the expected **competencies** of public relations professionals. You should be familiar with these competency areas through your study of and, perhaps, internships in public relations. To crystallize the range of competencies into a usable and useful framework for career planning purposes, Sha (2011, pp. 189–190) shows there are **12 categories of work** performed by (not practice areas of) public relations professionals:

- *Account/client management*—Key work activities include "establishing client relationships, coaching and counseling clients, managing expectations, etc."
- *Strategic planning*—Key work activities include "conducting research, setting goals, engaging customers and key stakeholders, developing messages for specific audiences, etc."
- *Public relations program planning*—Key work activities include "conducting research, identifying key audiences, producing a detailed PR plan, managing marketing communications, creating measurements of effectiveness, leveraging interactive elements of the campaign, etc."
- *Project management*—Key work activities include "creating and managing the budget, assessing resource allocation needs, planning logistics, managing the team, working with vendors, etc."

- *Media relations*—Key work activities include "identifying audiences, training organizational spokespersons to work with media, pitching stories, writing and distributing press releases in traditional and online ways, monitoring media coverage, coordinating publicity, measuring media engagement efforts, etc."
- *Social media relations*—Key work activities include "utilizing Web-based social networks, developing social media strategies for communications efforts, producing in-house or client blogs, apprising clients on how to use social media channels for communications efforts, SEO [search engine optimization], blogger relations, etc."
- *Stakeholder relations*—Key work activities include "developing strategies and key messages, arranging tours and conferences, forging strategic partnerships, etc." for defined stakeholder groups.
- *Issues management*—Key work activities include "assessing and developing strategies around long-term and business-impacting issues, writing crisis [and issue] management plans, providing strategic counsel to clients or stakeholders, resolving conflicts, etc."
- *Crisis management*—Key work activities include "executing crisis management plans, coordinating release of information via traditional and social media, understanding the varied and different crisis situations that may erupt, training spokespersons, monitoring and analyzing media coverage of company crises, etc."
- *Internal relations and employee communications*—Key work activities include "developing action plans, assessing in-house communication needs, developing and producing in-house publications in print and online, developing Web content, managing organizational change, etc."
- *Special events, conferences, and meetings*—Key work activities include "developing themes, promoting products and planning roll-outs, coordinating logistics and external promotions, etc."
- *Community relations*—Key work activities include "sponsoring community events, developing corporate giving plans, communicating with different audiences building alliances, community outreach using social media, etc."

Across these 12 work categories, public relations professionals are expected to possess certain **knowledge, skills, and abilities (KSAs)** in six broad categories that make up the grounds on which professionals are considered competent or not. A formal and rigorous approach to certifying that a professional possesses these competencies is the process for a PR professional to earn the Public Relations Society of America's (PRSA) Accreditation in Public Relations (APR). This professional credential, which is very similar in importance to credentials required of professionals in other professions, is based on specific KSAs that are organized as follows (PRSA, 2021a and 2021b; see the website for the details for each):

1. Researching, planning, implementing, and evaluating programs
   a. Research: concepts, applications, and analysis
   b. Planning: strategic thinking, programming, identifying publics, and diversity

   c. Implementation: budgets, timelines, and execution
   d. Evaluation of programs
2. Applying ethics and law
   a. Ethics: professional integrity and behavior
   b. Law: First Amendment issues, privacy issues, and other legal issues
3. Managing issues and crisis communications
   a. Issue and risk management: identify matters, analyze matters' probability and potential impact, and plan and enact response
   b. Crisis management
   c. Counsel to management
4. Understanding theories, models, and concepts of public relations
   a. Communication/public relations theories and models
   b. Barriers to communication
   c. Knowledge of the field
5. Leading the public relations function
   a. Business literacy
   b. Organizational structure and resources
   c. Problem solving, decision-making, and resource management
   d. Leadership skills
   e. Organizational skills
6. Managing relationships
   a. Relationship building
   b. Reputation management
   c. Internal stakeholders
   d. Media relations
   e. Networks

You may assess your level of competence in the 12 work categories and the six KSA categories by rating yourself on a five-point scale, with 5 being the highest level of competence. Figure 11.3 shows a way you may arrange the work categories and KSAs so that you may perform a self-assessment of your level of competence in each area. Notice that the KSAs are shown according to the broad categories, and you will need to refer to the specifics for each category as given above and on the PRSA website.

For the self-assessment, understand that a rating of 5 would equate to that of a highly seasoned professional with many years of experience. The analysis of the PR field in this book would give you background on how to employ the rating scale. And be honest with yourself! If you have only held a couple of internships and have been studying public relations in a PR program, you will likely have many more areas that rate low (say 1 or 2) than other areas that rate higher, and that is okay. Such ratings show you where you need to focus or perhaps point more to your career path planning, where you would rather focus to realize your career vision. As you go down your career path, you must look for opportunities to acquire the experience, knowledge, skills, and

Work Categories	Personal Rating					SWOT Relationships
	No/Little Background..............................Much Background					
Account/client management	1	2	3	4	5	
Strategic planning	1	2	3	4	5	
Public relations program planning	1	2	3	4	5	
Project management	1	2	3	4	5	
Media relations	1	2	3	4	5	
Social media relations	1	2	3	4	5	
Stakeholder relations	1	2	3	4	5	
Issues management	1	2	3	4	5	
Crisis management	1	2	3	4	5	
Internal relations and employee communications	1	2	3	4	5	
Special events, conferences, and meetings	1	2	3	4	5	
Community relations	1	2	3	4	5	
KSAs						
Research, planning, implementation, and evaluation of PR programs	1	2	3	4	5	
Applying ethics and law	1	2	3	4	5	
Managing issues and crisis communications	1	2	3	4	5	
Understanding theories, models, and concepts of public relations	1	2	3	4	5	
Leading the public relations function	1	2	3	4	5	
Managing relationships	1	2	3	4	5	

Figure 11.3 Self-assessment tool for rating one's competence in PR work categories and KSAs

Source: Based on PRSA (2021a, 2021b) and Sha (2011, pp. 189–190)

abilities that will make you a better and better PR professional. Use this self-assessment tool periodically in your career to find out how you have grown, and perhaps have your bosses and mentors fill it out for you, and discuss your professionalism and competence in PR. Notice also that it is not enough to merely rate yourself, but you must make the ratings meaningful by translating your present level of competence into actionable items for self-improvement in your SWOT analysis.

During your journey down your career-life path, you will need to keep track of what you did, when, and how. You will always be in the position of having to prove your value to your current and future employers. Keep track of the *value* you have given every employer in the roles you held, not just the duties you fulfilled in every job. This approach goes beyond a mere list of things you did on typical resumes. You must track your *results* for your work. For example, you may have written press releases, but what were the outcomes in terms of media coverage, knowledge growth, attitude change, or behaviors sought among target publics? Your **resume** is the primary document you will need to chronicle your work and other relevant experiences and, especially, results during your career. You also must have good, clean examples of the work you produced during your career. These examples go into your **portfolio**. Creating printed and electronic versions of your resume and portfolio can be very helpful, as you may then share your stuff with people in the best ways to meet their needs. Also be ready to prepare **cover letters** in either printed or electronic form.

Frame your employment record (on paper and in person) like a case study. Show your results as evidence about why you are the best and worth hiring above anyone else because of the high value you provide for companies. At every step of the way, you are advancing an argument that follows this pattern:

- *Claim:* I have the "right stuff" for this job and should be interviewed. Ultimately you should hire me.
- *Evidence:* Relevant prior experience, strong results from all work done, appropriate education, awards and other applicable recognition, and strong references.
- *Reasoning:* I fulfill the requirements stated in the job posting and known in field-specific expectations for public relations professionals for this type of job.

This approach is based on Toulmin's (1958) model of argument. Most important, this approach should guide you well throughout your campaign (yes, like a good PR campaign) to obtain not only your first full-time job, but also all other jobs that come your way to advance you in your career. The sophistication of your argument will necessarily change over the years as the kinds of jobs and levels of responsibility and authority change/enlarge. In addition to your resume, you should also collect work samples, especially programs (all steps), to show what you have worked on and be able to tell the stories behind the work you did and the overall programs. Throughout your written and oral discourse during your job hunt, focus on the key message platform about your career accomplishments and aspirations—based on your vision and career strategy. (This key message platform is very useful in cover letters and job interviews, too.) In a very real way you are, in tune with the concept of positioning in Chapter 9, establishing and promoting yourself as a brand—"brand YOU" (see Kaputa, 2012). At any time, you are the only person who controls your career trajectory, even in the face of people who may influence your career (for better and for worse). So you must own your career and manage it and yourself well.

Think about your job search like a cold-calling effort. Your overall objective in applying for a job is, of course, to get the job; however, that result will not happen solely from someone seeing your resume and cover letter. So the immediate objective in applying for a job is to get an interview. The immediate objective of an interview is to get a job offer or, at least, another interview. In your cover letter and resume, you must present yourself on paper (or on screen for online applications) as effectively, accurately, and completely as possible, given page-length and other constraints that may be stated in a job posting. In an interview, you must present yourself similarly but now in person. The "tangibles" of a strong background that fits the job are expected, but the "intangibles" of who you are are highly scrutinized. From a hiring manager's perspective, they will scrutinize you for your attitude, drive, enthusiasm, trainability, fit with the organization's culture, politeness/courteousness, ways of thinking, and ways of expressing yourself. Your manner of communication and personal demeanor with anyone you meet will be noted. The quality of the questions you ask will matter greatly also. To come up with good questions, assume you were hired and ask what would be expected in certain circumstances. Remember, too, that at the same time you are being interviewed, you are interviewing the organization on similar grounds for yourself.

As you search for your first full-time job in public relations, you will be assessed for your competency in the many factors covered in this section. One area that very likely will be assessed through some form of examination is your writing. *The reason is that public relations is a writing-intensive profession, and you are expected to be an excellent writer.* Writing is about process and product. You can only obtain a good product through a sound process. The writing process involves a lot of problem solving about a particular assignment. Each writing session results in more and more insight and understanding about a problem and what you must do to be successful in solving it. A very important part of all this is mastering the rules for grammar and Associated Press (AP) style plus demonstrating competence in organization and discourse expectations. The writing product is the outcome of thinking and researching. Product is the thing you create, improve, and produce so others can understand and follow your argument. Products of writing are generated in multiple sessions as drafts and, finally, created in a final form that is shared with others. So a writing exam may be given to assess your abilities and competence as a writer and problem solver. After examining agencies' and nonagencies' writing exams over the years, I have found certain patterns among them that point to ways in which people can prepare and perform well on writing exams.

Appendix C shows you those patterns and, most important, should help you prepare for taking one of these exams. Remember that exams' content will be different from one organization to another, as each organization tests for competence in its own way. Also, an organization will revise or update its exams, so what one person takes when going through the hiring process likely will be different from what another person takes during a later hiring cycle. The big point, then, is being prepared for whatever questions there are on an exam, and Appendix C ought to prove helpful to you.

OWN YOUR CAREER

Only you can truly make the career you want. Other people and circumstances (some of which you can control and many you cannot) will have various levels of influence (positive, negative, and neutral) on your **career trajectory** toward your vision of what you want to be and achieve. You should make or find opportunities for career growth. Keep your eyes and ears open for opportunities to get the experience, knowledge, skills, and abilities you need to grow and succeed. New and different job assignments can do that. Additional education and training in new and different areas can help as well. In all these ways you will meet more people in the public relations profession who may be able and willing to help you. Building your network of people in and connected with the public relations industry can serve you well in developing yourself and moving along your career path as you want to. As you rise into the management ranks, part of your network may eventually include recruiters, especially people who work in executive search firms. These folks can be very helpful in refining your argument for your employability and expertise at higher levels of leadership and in different industries, such as consumer goods, transportation, health and medical, and any other industry.

One particularly valuable component of your network is **mentors**. As we covered in Chapter 6, mentors are at a unique place in their careers where they enjoy helping up-and-coming professionals to advance in their careers. Mentors can provide the kind of highly valuable insight about professionalism, career management, and organizational idiosyncrasies that few others can. Most important, a trusted mentor can provide you with a level of candor and advice about and for you that can make you a better person and professional. This kind of relationship assumes there is a great deal of mutual respect and openness between mentor and **mentee**. Such a relationship does not occur immediately and must be cultivated genuinely and honestly between people. Phoniness and selfishness are easy to spot and big turnoffs to would-be mentors. You may find your own mentor or ask for one to be recommended to you. A mentor need not be someone with whom you work but, rather, may be someone who works in another organization and is willing and available to help you at different times. Once you find someone whom you believe is a good mentor for you, genuinely get to know that person and let that person get to know you on personal and professional terms. Meeting for lunch once in a while, chatting after work, asking for advice on a challenging project, working together in a chapter of a professional organization, or going to a conference or seminar together are easy examples of ways to build a mentor–mentee relationship.

Something that you will experience and may want a mentor's advice about is career change. Whether you feel the need to quit a job for another job, have been offered a new job in the same or another organization, are laid off, or have new life pressures that require you to completely rethink your career vision, it is important to recognize when it is time for a change. In every case, the intellectual and the emotional sides of career change matter, and one of these—usually the emotions— will appear to rule your thinking. A knee-jerk response is all too often *not* the best response. Instead, take stock of your feelings and your reasons for change. Examine the pros and the cons for change as honestly and as completely as possible. Share your findings, thoughts, and conclusions with a mentor and other important people in your life, especially family and trusted friends or peers.

CAREER CHANGE CAUTIONS

Once you have a job, whether you love it and your employer or not (or somewhere in between), there is never anything wrong with periodically looking at the job market for what is going on there. Let's face it: we are curious creatures, and it is somehow comforting to find out that our careers are on the right tracks for us. And if our careers are not on track, we can seek new paths with new employers or other (perhaps entrepreneurial) opportunities.

Remember, though, your employer may not share this enlightened attitude. Your employer made an investment in hiring you and expects you to perform well in every way for the organization. There are many stories of people (and one friend of mine) who lost a job because companies monitor employees' communications. And companies may use that information to dismiss employees for seeking—not necessarily accepting—another job with another employer. The seeking of other jobs includes making phone calls, meeting with people, and sending e-mail. The basic logic is, "You are looking for a job, and that must mean you do not like it here, so you can be on your way right now to do the job searching you seem you would rather like to do." (Looking for jobs within your employer's organization is an exception.)

Is this monitoring of employees' communications legal? Yes. You are working on "company time" with company resources, and your employer has every right to make sure you are doing your job effectively and properly with the resources it gives you to do that job. Your personal privacy is not a company concern when you are "on the clock" and using company resources. You probably signed a contract or other employment agreement that touches on your conduct. And remember that the personnel handbook for your company is loaded with policies you are expected to know and live by.

Because you work for an organization, your behavior "off the clock" also matters to your employer (and your career). People know for whom you work. Just think of Michael Vick and how his direct involvement in dog fighting got him in trouble with his employer, the Philadelphia Eagles, and the National Football League. His is an extreme case to be sure, but it is illustrative nonetheless. Your conduct outside of the office also should be addressed in the personnel handbook. Even if you do not have an employment contract/agreement, there is ample case law that could be used to back up your employer's arguments about its decision to dismiss any employee for misconduct on/off the clock (including searching for other jobs) according to company policies and expectations for employees. Your behavior at events that are directly pertinent to your job, such as dinners, award ceremonies, parties, etc., all require you to behave well as a person and, especially, as a professional representing an organization.

If there is no stated policy or expectation about your making contacts for other employment, you could ask someone in HR to clarify this matter. But that approach could be risky because it may suggest that you are already on the hunt, even if you are just curious about the job market. It would be prudent, too, for you to seek advice from seasoned professionals in your local PR industry who also have intimate knowledge about personnel rules and expectations. And remember, the network among PR professionals is wide, and news of job openings and job seekers can travel fast, which can be good or bad, depending on who learns about your ambitions.

It is important to remember that you have the right to seek a better living and career to enable you to have the life you want. Your employer cannot take that away. (A kind of exception is employment with direct competitors, which may be covered in an employment contract/agreement, especially for high-ranking employees. Case law can be applied here too.) But your employer can say that certain activities, such as job searching, are out of bounds when you are on the job. (Again, seeking a new job within your employer's organization is an exception.) Remember that the importance of company policies and expectations presented in the employee handbook is very high.

Based on this knowledge, here are five basic, vital, and ethical steps for you to take to manage your conduct as an employee and a person looking around the corner for your next big gig.

1. Make sure you know, understand, and have on your desk/bookshelf a complete and updated copy of your employer's personnel policies or employee handbook.
2. Review your employment contract/agreement, if you signed one, to relearn what you agreed to. See an attorney if you have questions. (Ideally, you could see an attorney before you sign such a contract/agreement.)
3. Never use your employer's computing system to do any kind of job searching on the Internet or by e-mail. Your employer can still trace your activity— especially your e-mail activity on your noncompany e-mail accounts because you are using your employer's server to access it.
4. Never place phone calls from your desk phone at work to inquire about jobs. And if you have a company-issued cell phone, never take or place calls or text messages about job possibilities. Phone bills show all calls and are a record of your phone activity. Using a company-issued smartphone to do any job-searching tasks also can be tracked, so do not do that either.
5. Always do your job searching off company time and off company resources, including your company's wireless network (if equipped). Make phone calls on your personal cell phone off your employer's campus or on your home phone. Access the Internet and your e-mail at home or somewhere else, like the public library or a friend's home. (Lunch time *technically* does not count, because your company is legally obliged to allow you that period and, therefore, you are still on company time. But it still may be a useful time for you to use your personal cell phone to make calls away from the office campus.)

Remember that it is important to sustain your employment and be successful at any employing organization for a "significant and reasonable" amount of time. I say it this way because there is no precise amount of employment time that is standard. But it is important to show future employers that you have staying power, get solid results, and do not skip around from job to job over short periods of time with little or no reason. So before you take any job, make sure any company that offered you a job meets all your criteria for a good, strong, and valuable employer that suits your career vision.

LEAVING AN EMPLOYER

If and when you leave any employer for another one, make sure you do not "burn any bridges." Stay on good terms as much as possible because you want your last impressions to be amicable. Be professional and courteous during an exit interview, if you have one (see Chapter 6). Also, you will likely need your previous employer to confirm your employment there, and, if permissible under corporate policy, people there may be willing to be references for you. Always be honest, sensible, and diplomatic with anyone about your experiences and your feelings about previous and present employers. If you "bad-mouth" any previous employer, people wonder what you will say about your current one.

If you decide to quit a job for any reason, including personal reasons like being a stay-at-home parent or wanting to become a sole practitioner (e.g., freelancer or consultant), you may do so at any time. Organizations generally have an "**employment at will**" agreement with their employees, which means that either the employer or the employee may terminate employment at any time with sufficient cause and notice. If you are caught in a moral, ethical, or legal dilemma you believe to be problematic, have tried to remedy it, and have been unsuccessful, your only recourse may be to quit. If you have found a new career opportunity at another organization, you should make sure you give your present employer suitable notice of your decision to quit and move to another organization. Joining a competitor may get you moved out of the company the same day (even the same moment) you announce your decision, and you must also be aware of and abide by certain legal obligations you have to your employer that may prohibit you from getting a job at a competitor. If you are laid off, as explained in Chapter 6, you have more freedom to work where you wish, even for competitors, because your employer made the decision about your employment, not you. You would also be entitled to certain **benefits** for having been laid off, such as severance pay and job-search help.

Because any of these circumstances (and others) that lead to a career change are possible, you should always make sure your resume and portfolio are up to date. An updated resume and portfolio will serve you well if you take on any work as a sole practitioner so that you can showcase yourself and your expertise. You can examine the job market for fun or for profit—just make sure it is in line with your career vision and *not* in conflict with any employer's policies and expectations.

FINAL POINTS

As you look upon yourself for who you are now and who you want to be and what you want to achieve over time, you should realize it is a dynamic process. You are always involved in making sure you are doing the right things in the right ways at the right times for the right reasons for yourself and others. Embedded in this dynamism are two final topics you must not take for granted: impression management and leisure.

IMPRESSION MANAGEMENT

First impressions are very important, and they can be difficult to change in people's minds. Remember that how you present yourself in any way—in person, in writing, on the phone, online—all contributes to people's impressions of you. People can spot phony people immediately, so genuine interest, energy, friendliness, curiosity, and so on are vital and expected. Be a good person doing well in everything you do (see Chapter 3). Be mindful of how you present yourself in any way at any time. As Chapter 6 indicated, hiring decisions include background searches on people who are strong candidates for a job. The Internet (especially Google) has made conducting such searches easy and economical.

From traffic tickets to credit scores and from Facebook pages to Mastodon toots, how you say who you are and how you portray yourself can help you or hurt you. As Conlin (2006) shows most dramatically, "You are what you post." He explains:

> Google is an end run around discrimination laws, inasmuch as employers can find out all manner of information—some of it for a nominal fee—that is legally off limits in interviews: your age, your marital status, the value of your house (along with an aerial photograph of it), the average new worth of your neighborhood, fraternity pranks, stuff you wrote in college, liens, bankruptcies, political affiliations, and the names and ages of your children.
>
> (Conlin, 2006, pp. 52–53)

Conlin's report is indeed sobering. In addition, recent studies reported by Johnson (2012) show the increasing frequency with which organizations screen social media before and after employing people. At the very least, as Johnson (2012) reports, organizations should screen job applicants' social media only after getting their permission to do so, should not create fake accounts on social media sites to gain access to users' posts, and should allow applicants to explain or defend problematic information about them on social media sites.

In the bigger picture of this topic, the U.S. National Labor Relations Board (NLRB) has issued three reports (2011, 2012a, 2012b) about multiple cases of employer use of social media in employment matters. The NLRB is focused on protecting employees' rights, whether they are unionized or not. In all cases about social media use, the matters revolve around issues of protected/unprotected speech under the First Amendment. In these reports, the NLRB found some employer policies about employees' social media use unlawful, but found others lawful. In two particular rulings about firing employees for their social media use, the NLRB found the employers' dismissals (one at a car dealership and the other at a nonprofit) unlawful because the employees' use of social media qualified as protected speech (NLRB, n.d.). One important point to take away about social media use is that both employers and employees have rights; however, the evolution of law to protect those rights has been slow to keep up with the frenetic pace of technology advances and people's use of those technologies.

On balance, because of poor impression management of yourself online, given the climate of what is legally permissible, you can put your personal and professional reputation at risk as long as you post words and images that undermine yourself or others, including your employer or client. Remember that the First Amendment does not mean that anything goes, because there are protections for some forms of speech and no protections for others—know the limitations. Also, just because you can say something does not mean you should say anything. If you frequently post negative messages on social media about anything, you effectively portray yourself as a negative person. Also remember, your friends (and their friends) may be posting stuff about you (accurate or not) without your knowledge and consent, and that may work against you as well. The example of Olympic gold medalist Michael Phelps shows the damage to one's personal reputation that can result from poor choices, after a video of him smoking marijuana ran rampant through social media and the news media covered it. In short, guard your reputation at all times. New tools for monitoring your online image can help.

Although it is understood that you personally cannot police and correct all content about you that appears on the Internet (data placed on the Internet is there forever and findable with search technologies), it is also understood that you and only you have responsibility for yourself. In tune with the material in Chapter 3, always be the best person you can be anywhere at any time, have fun when you can, and be mindful of the fact that what you say or do reveals who you are and what your values are. The deep self-reflection about yourself through Figure 11.2 can help keep you focused. Know yourself!

LEISURE

An important topic that is often overlooked is **leisure**. The value of leisure is very high, and that is why people look so fondly toward the weekend. But realize, too, that weekends alone are not usually enough. Bender and Farvolden's (2008) psychiatric study chronicles the great prevalence of depressive disorders among people in the workplace, which the authors argue has been largely unmitigated due to various reasons but can be addressed in various ways. Even so, too often people think that *only* large blocks of time off from work are what is needed to recharge and revitalize. To be sure, any number of days off from work does wonders for the mind, heart, and soul. But let us not forget about integrating a bit of leisure during the course of a busy day.

A medical study by Biswas et al. (2015) showed that sitting for long hours undermines health and shortens life. During any day at work, you need to relax and release your mind and body from the stresses you have endured, no matter how great or small the stresses have been. Short, frequent breaks that divert your attention to other things, especially restful things, give your mind and body the opportunity to refresh.

Truly, how often have you gotten up to get a drink or go to the washroom or take a short walk and been struck by a new idea? It has very probably been a lot more often than you may want or are able to remember. The simple change in focus has released your mind to think differently and freely and, thereby, released a kind of creativity you needed.

As the old saying goes, "Do what you love. Love what you do." At the same time, we must seek a favorable balance between our professional and our personal lives, a concept often referred to **work–life balance**. For public relations professionals, Jin et al. (2014) explain that a healthy work–life balance is possible and essential, as practitioners combine both "proactive cognitive and passive coping" (p. 77) approaches that work for them.

People who are highly effective in their lives and careers have certain common habits, and Steven Covey (1989, 2004) is well known for explaining those eight habits: be proactive, begin with the end in mind, put first things first, think win/win, seek first to understand then to be understood, synergize, sharpen the saw, and find your voice and inspire others to find theirs. This book about public relations management has addressed these habits in various ways, although not systematically. Of Covey's eight habits, sharpening the saw is especially potent and important to the journey along your career-life path, especially if it's toward a position of leadership and management in public relations.

You need to continuously improve yourself in ways that matter, and that includes taking time to recharge, revitalize, and renew yourself in mind, body, and spirit. Yes, matters of work–life balance are included, but so are matters of education, skills, and motivation to be and to do the best you can, as well as being and doing better than you ever have before. The better you become as a person and as a professional, the more you help to make public relations the valuable and valued organizational function that can truly inspire cooperation between organizations and their publics.

EXECUTIVE VIEWPOINT

Personal Qualities for Career Success in Communications

Jessamyn Katz, President of Heyman Associates

As you build a communications career, there are two keys to success. First and foremost is to be a perpetual learner—being open to the constant flow of information and determining how to process it both to the benefit of your client or business partner (be that from an agency or in-house perspective) and for how it makes you a better communicator. The other key to success is being someone others want to be around—someone they trust, someone they can depend on, someone they know will give them advice based on the situation and what future impact any action might have. People want to hire and promote qualified people they respect, trust, and enjoy working with. Your ability to relate well with others will help your job prospects and professional growth for years to come. While your technical expertise will get you an interview, your personal qualities and reputation will land you the job.

As a professional communicator, you will need to manage the constant volume, velocity, and variety of information in all its forms. To become a communications "leader," you will need to connect your communications programs to the overall business strategy of your organization. Know how what you do impacts the company's goals, bottom line, and purpose.

What will set you apart from other qualified candidates and your colleagues are intangible qualities. These "soft" skills are the unique, intangible ways you handle yourself and relate to others that create a positive impact on a hiring manager and other stakeholders. Intangibles are your people skills, presentation ability, reliability, honesty, and professional courage. Intangibles are what make you you. You can't fake them, and you shouldn't try. The goal is not to be perfect; the goal is to be authentic. Real is likable.

Connect your job search and career path to your passions; you will feel freer to be yourself. Find environments, industries, companies, and roles that match your interests. Show your enthusiasm for the position you want. Volunteer within your organization for projects that interest you, regardless of your role. Take on challenging work. Even though you cannot feign interpersonal skills, you can improve them. Take a public speaking or business writing course. Read as much as possible to become knowledgeable about and well-spoken in current events and other topics of relevance to your career. Expand your perspective outside of your comfort zone. Take on leadership positions whenever possible. Network all the time, not just when you need a job. In networking you will not only develop your interpersonal skills, you also will make and maintain connections for your own career and help others who may one day return the favor.

As you get ready for an interview, do your homework. Preparation will enable you to comfortably demonstrate your professionalism, enthusiasm, and authentic self. Anticipate as best you can the interviewer's questions and practice your answers. The interviewer might ask about your strengths and weaknesses, so do a self-assessment before the interview and have examples ready. The interviewer might ask what you know about the company, so study the organization's website and look up news about the company. The interviewer might ask how you stay current on what is happening in business, politics, and the world at large or what was the last book you read, so plan your response. Prepare at least one question for the interviewer to show your interest in the job. You might ask why the position is available, what the interviewer likes most about the company, or what a typical day is for your potential role. Do a mock interview with a friend—in person and on screen. Also be aware of your body language because poor eye contact or a weak handshake (in an in-person meeting) can end an interview before it starts.

Remember that the interview process is not necessarily over when it's over. Follow-up is important, thank yous (written and spoken) are important, and being kind and appreciative to those who schedule meetings is important. That all demonstrates who you are and what you'd be like as a colleague. If you feel strongly about your fit for the position, say so. In a group of equally qualified candidates, the person who receives the offer is often the only one who said, "I want the job." If the potential employer needs more time to interview other candidates and/or make a decision, follow up politely. If the company offers you an entry-level position you want, accept graciously without too much concern over the salary. Get started on your career and prove yourself for promotions in the future. Compensation will follow.

As a reminder, have your personal online brand match your professional one as much as possible. Maintain responsible and professional social media accounts. Assume a potential or current employer will see everything you post.

In your communications career, qualify yourself with your technical skills, but differentiate yourself with your approach. Be a lifelong learner and good listener. Constantly improve upon your interpersonal skills to let your passion come through in a genuine, professional, and likable way.

For further reading, I recommend Susan Cain's book, *Quiet: The Power of Introverts in a World That Can't Stop Talking* and Malcolm Gladwell's books, *The Tipping Point*, *Talking to Strangers*, and *Outliers* (among others). There are many others as well as podcasts to help you stay up to date in business and career trends.

KEY WORDS

Career path	**Competencies**
Milestones	**12 PR work categories**
Personal values	**KSAs for PR**
Career self-analysis	**Cover letter**

Resume	**Employment at will**
Portfolio	**Benefits**
Career trajectory	**Leisure**
Mentor	**Work–life balance**
Mentee	

REFERENCES

Bender, A., & Farvolden, P. (2008). Depression and the workplace: A progress report. *Current Psychiatry Reports, 10,* 73–79. https://doi.org/10.1007/s11920-008-0013-6.

Biswas, A., Oh, P. I., Faulker, G. E., Bajaj, R. R., Silver, M. A., Mitchell, M. S., & Alter, D. A. (2015, January 20). Sedentary time and its association with risk for disease incidence, mortality, and hospitalization in adults. *Annals of Internal Medicine, 162*(2), 123–143. https://doi.org/10.7326/M14-1651.

Conlin, M. (2006, March 27). You are what you post: Bosses are using Google to peer into places job interviews can't take them. *BusinessWeek,* 52–53.

Covey, S. (1989). *The 7 habits of highly effective people: Powerful lessons in personal change.* Fireside/Simon & Schuster.

Covey, S. (2004). *The 8th habit: From effectiveness to greatness.* Fireside/Simon & Schuster.

Gebauer, J., Lowman, D., & Gordon, J. (2008). *Closing the engagement gap: How great companies unlock employee potential for superior results.* Portfolio/Penguin Group.

Jin, Y., Sha, B-L., Shen, H., & Jiang, H. (2014). Tuning in to the rhythm: The role of coping in strategic management of work-life conflicts in the public relations profession. *Public Relations Review, 40*(1), 69–78. https://doi.org/10.1016/j.pubrev.2013.11.007.

Johnson, S. (2012, January 22). Those Facebook posts could cost you a job. *The Pantagraph,* C1, C2.

Kaputa, C. (2012). *You are a brand! In person and online, how smart people brand themselves for business success.* Nicholas Brealey Publishing.

National Labor Relations Board. (2011). *Employees' Facebook postings about job performance and staffing were protected concerted activity* (Memorandum OM 11–74). Author.

National Labor Relations Board. (2012a). *Discharge for Facebook comments and for violation of nondisparagement rule was unlawful* (Memorandum OM 12–31). Author.

National Labor Relations Board. (2012b). *Rules on using social media technology and on communicating confidential information are overbroad* (Memorandum OM 12–59). Author.

National Labor Relations Board (n.d.). The NLRB and social media. Retrieved from www.nlrb.gov/node/5078.

Public Relations Society of America (PRSA). (2021a). *Detailed knowledge, skills and abilities tested on the computer-based examination for accreditation in public relations.* Author. Available online: https://accreditation.prsa.org/MyAPR/Content/ Apply/APR/APR.aspx.

Public Relations Society of America (PRSA). (2021b). *Study guide for the examination for accreditation in public relations.* Author. Available online: https://accreditation. prsa.org/MyAPR/Content/Apply/APR/APR.aspx.

Sha, B-L. (2011). 2010 practice analysis: Professional competencies and work categories in public relations today. *Public Relations Review, 37,* pp. 187–196.

Shaffer, J. C. (2000). *The leadership solution.* McGraw-Hill.

Toulmin, S. E. (1958). *The uses of argument.* Cambridge University Press.

RECOMMENDED READING

Berger, B. K., & Reber, B. H. (2006). *Gaining influence in public relations: The role of resistance in practice.* Lawrence Erlbaum Associates.

Boldt., L. G. (1996). *How to find the work you love.* Penguin.

Boldt, L. G. (1999). *Zen and the art of making a living* (expanded and updated). Penguin.

Bridges, W. (1994). *Job shift: How to prosper in a workplace without jobs.* Perseus Books.

Bridges, W. (1997). *Creating you and co.: Learning to think like the CEO of your own career.* Perseus Books.

Coombs, W. T., & Holladay, S. J. (2013). *It's not just PR: Public relations in society* (2nd ed.). Blackwell Publishing.

Edwards, L., & Hodges, C. E. M. (2011). *Public relations, society and culture: Theoretical and empirical explorations.* Routledge.

Hansen-Horn, T. L., & Neff, B. D. (Eds.). (2008). *Public relations: From theory to practice.* Pearson.

Moss, D., & DeSanto, B. (2011). *Public relations: A managerial perspective.* Sage.

Public Relations Society of America. (2013). Find a job. Available online: www.prsa.org/ jobcenter/career_resources/.

Tymorek, S. (2010). *Ferguson career launcher: Advertising and public relations.* Checkmark Books.

A

APPENDIX A
TEMPLATE FOR STRATEGIC PLANS WITH DEFINITIONS AND EXAMPLES

This appendix, which largely supplements Chapter 5, is structured to reflect the organization of an actual strategic plan. You may use the organization of this appendix (i.e., its headings and subheadings plus its tables and graphics) for your own strategic plan, making sure you (1) read the explanations and examples in each section; and then (2) use those explanations to guide you in *writing in your own words* what works specifically for your purposes. Note that while developing a strategic plan you may need to go back to sections that you already prepared to improve them so they work with later sections, plus early sections will foreshadow and apply to content in later sections and will need concomitant text to work with them. These matters are essential to effective cohesion in the document and must be fastidiously accomplished. Also create a nice cover page that names the client (use its logo), labels the document as a strategic plan for a defined period of time, and discreetly state who worked on the document and the date it was completed.

TABLE OF CONTENTS

EXECUTIVE SUMMARY

This section places the entire plan in context and, most important, very concisely summarizes the plan's content by focusing on the problem, the recommended solution, and anticipated results within a specific timeframe. Write it only after the final revisions to the rest of the document are made.

1.0 ORGANIZATION BACKGROUND

This first major section covers necessary and fundamental information about what an organization is, why it exists, how long it has been in operation, where it operates, and so on. In this broad introduction to this second major section of the document, explain what it is about, why it is important to the document, and what content will be covered in the order it will be covered.

1.1 BUSINESS DEFINITION

This subsection concisely and concretely states what the business is for your organization. The content in this section essentially states the obvious about what an organization does or offers to customers, and it provides the basic context for the following sections that go into greater detail that are necessary to understanding your organization.

1.2 VISION

In this subsection, concisely state the long-term, ideal, *future* state for the organization. This statement must reflect what the organization wants to be and achieve in a reasonably distant and attainable future. If your organization does not have a vision, propose one and explain why it fits.

1.3 MISSION

In this subsection, concisely state the immediate reason why an organization exists *today* and how it does its business on a daily basis. If your organization does not have a mission statement, propose one and explain why it fits.

1.4 VALUE PROPOSITION

This subsection presents a definitive statement about the unique value an organization offers to customers. This statement, based on clear thinking about everything that surrounds sections 1.1, 1.2, and 1.3 (and later sections), is called a "value proposition." It is a concise outline about what truly differentiates an organization from any other with which it may compete. Additionally, the value proposition is key to an organization's market positioning, which is addressed in section 2.5. A value proposition can be constructed simply as a two-part statement composed of content developed according to sections 1.4.1 and 1.4.2.

1.4.1 SLOGAN/THESIS/THEME

This statement is the one supremely important idea, written in a simple statement, that makes an organization uniquely different from all others with which it competes and, therefore, valuable for others to know and remember. This statement asserts (at least implicitly) why people should rely on an organization over anyone else or risk failure.

- A *slogan* is a very short, highly compelling, relevant, and very memorable phrase or simple sentence. Examples abound in advertising and can be useful in PR.
- A *thesis* is the opposite of a slogan, as it is a fairly complex and detailed statement that captures a situation well, being similar to a thesis used in a research paper.
- A *theme* is a middle-ground statement between a slogan and a thesis, as it asserts in a short sentence the all-encompassing nature of the idea in largely (but not exclusively) emotional terms.

1.4.2 PROOF POINTS

These points are a handful of individual statements of evidence that directly and concisely support why the slogan/thesis/theme is true and compelling. These proof points can include statements of advantages or benefits to people from having experienced the organization in any way through products, services, or other opportunities. Proof points also can include statements of accolades, awards, achievements, and other recognitions of an organization's superiority in what it does of any kind or degree that would matter to publics.

1.4.3 VALUE PROPOSITION AS A KEY MESSAGE PLATFORM (KMP)

A value proposition (VP) functions also as a universal "key message platform" (KMP) for any and all communication an organization may create and share. The purpose of a VP/KMP is to focus the core message on the intellectual, emotional, *and/or* behavioral needs publics have about the idea so they, ultimately, identify with it (i.e., see themselves in the messages). For individual programs and projects, done in accordance with the organizational or operational strategic plan, individual KMPs would be developed, but they must be able to reflect back on the points in the value proposition in the larger plan as a matter of message consistency. The idea is that such a platform helps corporate officials "stay on message" and helps audiences remember the key "takeaways" even if they forget everything else.

- How can the messages best be crafted to establish identification between target audiences and the organization?
- Will the messages work to achieve the plan's objectives in tactics that are used?
- Are the messages designed to inform, change attitudes, and/or inspire behaviors?
- Are the organization's expectations realistic?

The KMP or VP should ethically and sufficiently enact the drama about the scene, act, actors involved, means for doing the acts, and reasons for doing them within its situational context. A successful key message platform is one that inspires publics to cooperate with the organization because they identify with (see themselves in) the drama the organization enacts in its discourse.

1.5 ORGANIZATION STRUCTURE

This section explains how your organization is organized between upper management and lower-level members. This section should also show how your organization is structured along hierarchical lines by using an organizational chart of some kind. Additionally, job titles and basic descriptions for management-level positions should be given so that readers know at a glance who does what and for whom in the organization. More detailed information about all positions on the chart may be included in an appendix, such as the section of a bylaws document that defines roles and responsibilities of officers.

1.6 HISTORY AND CULTURE

This section summarizes how the organization came into being and what important milestone achievements or events matter to understanding why the organization remains and will remain in operation over the foreseeable future. It also addresses the things that define organizational culture (i.e., beliefs, attitudes, values, and ways of thinking/seeing the world). Note that organizational leaders have responsibility for the maintenance of organizational culture.

2.0 SITUATION ANALYSIS

This second major section of the plan covers what is presently going on for the organization that matters to the vision and mission. It is a thorough description of the state of the environment the organization faces, internally and/or externally. In this broad introduction to this second major section of the document, explain what it is about, why it is important to the document, and what content will be covered in the order it will be covered.

2.1 DEFINITION AND SCOPE OF SITUATION

This subsection is simply a narrative that explains in sufficient detail what the situation is that your organization faces and how extensive it is. Any relevant factors about the situation can and should be addressed. What is the state of the business that needs changing? What change is needed? Why? What is the company in danger of losing, what has it already lost, or what could it stand to gain but cannot? What internal and external forces are acting on the organization's ability to achieve success in any way?

This section may need to be lengthy or not, as it depends on many variables that are necessary to be documented in order to create an effective plan. A problem-solving process for business cases is useful here. Depending on the quantity of topics and the depth of content required, this subsection may need to be organized into subsections to make using the content as easy as possible when referencing particular points about the situation. This section is instrumental in identifying data for the SWOT analysis or other approach used in section 2.4.

2.2 STAKEHOLDERS AFFECTED

Stakeholders are people on whom an organization's success or failure depends. *Publics* are people with any amount of reasonable interest but not necessarily a vested interest in the organization. If it helps, think of external and internal publics or audiences that *truly* matter to your client's success/failure, not just anybody. In this section you must explain why each stakeholder matters to the client. Information and analysis here should be considered for the SWOT or other analysis. Two basic categories of stakeholders are internal and external, and specific groups in them must be identified and sufficiently defined.

Additionally, you may want to account for groups that are not stakeholders but, for whatever reasons they respectively hold, want to become stakeholders. In this way, these groups are called "stakeseekers," and they can be important as one or more publics to monitor in the event that they escalate their interactions with your organization in ways that make them new stakeholders, or show they joined any existing stakeholder group. Publics and stakeseekers benefit incidentally from communication with stakeholders.

2.3 COMPETITION

This subsection not only lists competitors, but it also explains how each competitor challenges your organization—which ones are very strong, which are strong, and which weak (or some kind of rating)—and what this all means. Organizations can compete on varying levels and in various ways, such as product-to-product, service-to-service, customers/clients/benefactors sought, needs or wants met, and others. Going through this simple analysis reveals great insights about the position your organization has against all others with which it competes, thereby affirming your value proposition and market position. In all these ways, this section also suggests additional material that is important in the SWOT analysis.

2.4 SWOT ANALYSIS (OR OTHER ENVIRONMENTAL-SCANNING METHOD)

This part of this situation analysis section employs one environmental-scanning method (SWOT) of those discussed in Chapters 5 and 9. Any such method is introspective because it is the place where you candidly, concisely, and concretely present your organization's strengths, weaknesses, opportunities, and threats to success. All the previous work in this and the first major section of the plan would have revealed what your organization is good at, what your organization must rectify, how your organization can capitalize on its strengths and minimize or eliminate its weaknesses, and what barriers may emerge that are either within or beyond its control that can adversely affect success.

Using a SWOT analysis, a table format like the one below is an effective way to document and present your findings. Working across each row, (1) identify all the strengths, weaknesses, opportunities, and threats you can ("aspects" column); (2) define what each item in each SWOT row means to the organization ("implications" column), and (3) identify possible ways to play to a strength, mitigate/eliminate a weakness, leverage an opportunity, or defuse a threat ("possible actions" column). Note that strengths and weaknesses are exclusively about the organization itself internally in any way. Opportunities and threats come from outside an organization by forces, circumstances, or anything that can open avenues for success (opportunities) or produce blockades for success (threats).

	Aspects	Implications	Possible actions
Strengths	•	•	•
Weaknesses	•	•	•
Opportunities	•	•	•
Threats	•	•	•

2.5 MARKET POSITION

This subsection, relying on guidance about the topic from Chapter 9, synthesizes the material in all the preceding content of the document to assert what place your organization possesses in the market in which it operates and explains why, using the market position model in Chapter 9 (see Figure A.1 below) of five general market categories. It is crucial to present and analyze matters about market positioning in sufficient (not exhaustive) detail. Key to market positioning is differentiation, which concerns the one thing that makes a brand, product, or service unique from anything else similar to it (see Chapter 9).

Leader
- The perceived or recognized leader in a market.
- Examples: Coke, Nike, Google

Challenger
- The perceived next-best option in a market, right behind the dominator.
- Examples: Pepsi, Adidas, Bing

Niche Occupier
- A specialty option that targets a narrow band or particular interest in a market.
- Examples: Snapple, L'Oréal ("Because I'm worth it."), Ask.com

First Mover
- An organization creates a new market category with a product or service no one else has.
- Examples: Chrysler's minivans, Amazon.com, Zipcar

Repositioner
- An organization chooses to remake itself and, thereby, its place in the market.
  - Example: Boston Chicken changed to Boston Market.
- An organization repositions a competitor and, thereby, redefines its own position.
  - Example: Wrangler Jeans urging customers to check its U-shaped crotch design as more comfortable than jeans made with a V-shaped design.

Figure A.1 Market position model

3.0 PLAN

This introduction should explain that this section is the culmination of the document, because this section provides the guidance about how to make the organization better. The specific things that the organization must do during a one-year (or multi-year) period to get it closer to realizing its vision are specified and defined in this section. In this broad introduction to this third major section of the document, explain what it is about, why it is important to the document, and what content will be covered in the order it will be covered.

3.1 OBJECTIVES, STRATEGIES, AND TACTICS

This subsection presents the core of the strategic plan, which is composed of objectives, strategies, and tactics (see Chapter 5) presented in Figure A.2 below, and all are necessary for evaluating the ultimate success of the plan. *Objectives* focus on particular outcomes by stating a desired effect, a measurable goal, a defined target audience, and an established deadline. Objectives must address matters that will, indeed, help move an organization closer to realizing its vision while simultaneously contributing to the mission. Objectives are accompanied by rationales and benchmarks. *Benchmarks* give a point of comparison for the goal, and the *rationales* state support for why the specified goal is appropriate. *Strategies* are categorizations of discourse and actions that will be utilized to realize a given objective. These specific activities and discourse are the *tactics* of the strategic plan that, when executed, will ultimately achieve the related objectives by applying the value proposition. Taken together, the contents of Figure A.2 ensure that objectives can be fulfilled cohesively and efficiently.

Objectives (EGAD)	Strategies	Tactics
1. Gain employee understanding of new safety procedures by 30% of employees within six months. (*Benchmark*: Employees' understanding of safety procedures is 73% per last employee survey.) (*Rationale*: All or at least nearly all employees must know what the safety procedures are to ensure they do not get hurt on the job and the organization maintains its "good standing" with OSHA.)	Provide *salient information* about the new safety procedures for employees in selected internal publications. Engage employees on new safety procedures with *interpersonal communication*.	Publish printed material that is portable and easy to understand and apply. • Brochure • Workstation summary sign • Breakroom posters Hold meetings with employees about the new procedures: • All-employee • Teams • Supervisor one-on-ones • Performance reviews

Figure A.2 Example table showing objectives, strategies, and tactics

3.2 CRITICAL SUCCESS FACTORS (CSFs)

CSFs are things, events, or circumstances that could help or hurt success, so knowing these matters is critical to managing them if/when they arise. CSFs should reflect things you document in the "implications" column of the SWOT analysis, as they could help or hinder your achieving the goals in the previous section. The whole of the CSF table (below), then, is more forward-looking, as the SWOT (or other approach) is mostly backward-looking. Using the explanation in Chapter 5, Table A.3 below can simply and compellingly account for the CSFs that affect each objective in your plan. Additionally, an explanation may be needed to point to the big "takeaways" from the overall collection of CSFs and what they mean for the plan's enactment.

Table A.3 CSFs tied to the objectives

Objective	Opportunities	Barriers	Environment	Resources
1.	•	•	•	•
2.	•	•	•	•
3.	•	•	•	•
n.	•	•	•	•

3.3 KEY PERFORMANCE INDICATORS (KPIs)

KPIs are milestone measurements taken along the way to track progress toward fulfilling the objectives. This subsection, then, presents why knowing these things is valuable by measuring how well things are going in your quest to achieve your objectives. KPIs use "leading indicators," which simply are the actual effects sought in any objective you must measure in a specific and direct way so you can regularly monitor your progress toward achieving that objective over the timeframe of the plan.

Note that, for each objective, a *direct* measurement of only the effect sought matters. For example, if you want to measure a public's awareness of something, you *do not* measure the amount of news coverage—you must measure how much the public's awareness changed from before the announcement to after it. You must check your leading indicators at predetermined intervals (e.g., weekly, monthly, quarterly) so you can make any adjustments. For each leading indicator, calculate the amount of the goal stated in an objective that should be achieved based on the frequency you will monitor progress according to the deadline. For example, if an objective is to obtain in the first two months after a new product roll-out eight news stories in selected prominent media outlets, your leading indicator is four stories per month or one story per week. An easy way to show KPIs is in Table A.4.

Table A.4 KPIs tied to the objectives

Objective	Leading indicator	Measurement frequency
1.		
2.		
3.		
n.		

3.4 BUDGET AND RESOURCE ALLOCATIONS

This subsection outlines and explains what will be needed for and what assumptions apply to each aspect of the plan—particularly to implement section 3.1—and how much each aspect will cost during the sequence of events. It also summarizes total costs and, if appropriate, makes any comparisons to similar or related programs in the past. Include items like postage, mileage, labor, overhead, and 10% for unforeseen expenses. Identify major supporters and financial resources. In a budget you must give data as specifically as possible, explain what's needed and why, what the return on investment (ROI) should be, and the value-added amount for the organization. Bottom line: the benefits of the plan justify the costs for doing the work. A separate budget spreadsheet as an attachment will be needed to show items line by line, including any notes to give context or needed information to understanding any item and its cost.

3.5 TIMELINE (BEGINNING WITH THE PROPOSAL'S ACCEPTANCE/ APPROVAL)

A timetable, either outlined in text or presented in a chart (e.g., a Gantt chart), shows the start and finish of all events within the context of section 3.1. A timeline presented in a Gantt chart ought to be in an appendix because of its size and horizontal orientation. In any form, a timeline helps to ensure that all tactics and leading indicators are met when planned and relate back to their respective objectives and KPIs.

3.6 EVALUATION METHOD AND ANTICIPATED RESULTS

This subsection shows how the plan will be evaluated based on specific measurements against the objectives and then compared to the benchmarks given in section 3.1. This step typically relies on quantitative research methods, like amounts of outputs, network analysis of reach and spread of messages on digital media, written or phone surveys, and content analyses about media coverage. This section can also apply qualitative research methods, like focus groups, one-on-one interviews, and anecdotal statements about what happened.

All final evaluation measurements must be linked to the objectives given in section 3.1 and essentially cumulative measurements of the KPIs in section 3.3. This section, building on section 3.3, adds detail about the method to be used to measure *each* objective. The measurements given in this section would be used to create a summative analysis of the plan—they define overall success/failure for the whole plan—against the objectives and compared to the benchmarks. Compile the data about performance, analyze the results, and report on the findings, including conclusions, lessons learned, and recommendations for doing better next time.

APPENDICES

Appendices are not required, but it is very likely you will have some additional material (e.g., visuals, data, documents) that should be included for easy reference when your plan calls for that extra information. Make sure you refer to each appendix in the order you use them, from the start to the end of your plan. The first appendix you refer to is

Appendix A, the second is Appendix B, and so on. Make sure that each appendix starts on a new page and is clearly labeled for what appendix it is and what it contains.

A. Appendix title
B. Appendix title
C. Appendix title

REFERENCES

If any primary or secondary sources are used to provide evidence in any way in the plan, those sources must be listed separately in this section. Any style (e.g., APA, MLA, Chicago) for documenting sources in the text and in this list will do—make sure they are used consistently and accurately throughout. Material directly from your client does not need source citations, but you should explain/state what client source you used.

B

APPENDIX B
SCRIPTS FOR DIFFERENT TYPES OF NEW-BUSINESS CALLS

Customizing scripts	Cold-calling scripts have been formulated to help you right now, and they are presented below (based on Schiffman, 1999). If the language is not exactly "your style," that is okay. You may customize these scripts for your use, and it may be best to do so for special target customers based on the pitch you want to make to them. The variables that you have to fill in the scripts will also help you to customize your calls.

Realize, however, that whatever script you use, it must be as concise and to-the-point as these are. *The point: to get a meeting.* The directness and specificity in these scripts is there by design, because a no-nonsense approach has been proven to be more effective with customers than any gimmicky approach.

One last point: Although the context for this Appendix is trying to obtain new business, it can also be used for pitching news stories to people in various media channels. Think about how much the person knows your organization and what it does and offers, then tailor your script accordingly.

Sample script with a positive response	Here is the core example cold-calling script. It assumes everything works well and you get the response you want. Make sure you fill in the blanks and practice a lot with it before you use it.

Again, it is important to recognize the directness of the scripts. For example, you do not (and should never) begin by saying, "How are you?" That is way too vague and a real turn off. You can get the person's attention best by saying their name with your greeting. You will see other aspects of directness in the script. (For a journalist, always ask, "Are you on deadline?" before you go into your pitch.) So here goes:

"Good morning, Mr./Ms._____. This is <YOUR NAME> from <COMPANY NAME>. We're a <STATE YOUR COMPANY'S CLAIM TO FAME>. The reason I'm calling you today specifically is to set an appointment, so I can stop by and talk with you about our <CONCISELY GIVE SPECIFIC SERVICE(S), EVEN IF IT IS PROJECT-SPECIFIC> that will < CONCISELY STATE TANGIBLE BENEFITS/VALUE OF STATED SERVICE(S)>. Mr./Ms. _____, I'm sure that you, like <GIVE SPECIFIC NAME OF AN ACTUAL, REFERENCEABLE CLIENT THAT USED STATED SERVICE>, are interested in <REPHRASE BENEFITS OF STATED SERVICE IN SIMPLE TERMS>."

With an affirmative answer, set an appointment with specific date,
time, and location, using the following script:
"That's great Mr./Ms. _____, then we should get together. How's
<TIME> <DATE> at your office? ... Thank you! I'll see you then."

Sample scripts to negative responses	Many cold calls are not as immediately positive as the situation for the core script implies. Turning a negative response to your opening statement (above) into a positive conversation is not necessarily easy, but it truly is doable. The trick is to use the negative response (or the person's question to you, as the case may be) as an opportunity to *bridge* the conversation back to your goal and make it a positive call.

The following scripts can be used to turn a negative call into a positive
one. The scripts do not cover every situation, but you get the idea
about how to handle others that may come your way. You may find
you need to use more than one of these scripts during a call. And
you may come up with your own scripts to handle other situations
not covered here. If you are successful, ask for an appointment at a
specific time, date, and location. If you are not successful, finish the
call in a genuinely friendly way, which is also given below.

There's one caveat: try not to turn around more than three negative
responses in a row. (You do not want to come off as pushy.) *Also
realize that all statements in these scripts must be true and potentially
verifiable.*

SAYS "HAPPY WITH PRESENT PROVIDER"

"I think it is great, Mr./Ms. _____, that you're using <PRESENT PROVIDER>
for <STATED SERVICE>. Many other firms <STATE ACTUAL, REFERENCEABLE
CLIENTS> have said the same thing before learning about how we work,
especially for <STATED SERVICE> and how it complements what <PRESENT
PROVIDER> is doing. You know, we should get together. How about
<TIME> <DATE> at your office?"

SAYS "NOT INTERESTED"

"Well, Mr./Ms. _____, many people, like <STATE ACTUAL, REFERENCEABLE
CLIENTS>, had the same reaction you did when I first called—before
they had a chance to see how we work and what value our approach
to <STATED SERVICE> gives them. Let's get together to explore this. How
about <TIME> <DATE> at your office?"

~ OR ~

"I'm just curious, how do you handle <PROBLEM OR STATED SERVICE>? ...
{PERSON RESPONDS} ... Very interesting. Based on what you've told me,
we really should get together, because we've helped other firms on
very similar projects. How about <TIME> <DATE> at your office?"

SAYS "I'M THE WRONG PERSON"

"I'm curious, what is it that you do? … {PERSON RESPONDS} … Then you know what, we absolutely should get together, because <STATE REASON BASED ON RESPONSE>. May we meet <TIME> <DATE> at your office?"

If after all this, the person absolutely is not the right person:

"Oh, whom should I talk with? … {PERSON RESPONDS} … [Take data and use for next call—see below.] Thank you!"

Your next call, then, would go like this (there is no need to go through a full explanation, because you're working off from a referral):

"Hello, Mr./Ms. _____, I'm <YOUR NAME> from <COMPANY NAME>. We're a <STATE COMPANY'S CLAIM TO FAME>. The reason I'm calling you today specifically is that I just spoke to <NAME OF PREVIOUS PERSON>. They suggested that I give you a call to set up an appointment. I wanted to know if <TIME> <DATE> at your office would be okay."

If the referred person asks why you were told to call them, you could respond like this:

"I originally called <NAME OF PREVIOUS PERSON> because I had just worked with <NAME OF RELATED COMPANY>. We have an excellent reputation for reliability, customer service, and competitive prices. When I told them that, they said I should talk with you to set up an appointment. … {PERSON RESPONDS}… Then we definitely should get together. How about <TIME> <DATE> at your office?"

Note: This approach can be used in the event someone refers you to someone else, and this referral amounts to a new-business lead.

SAYS "I'M TOO BUSY"

"Well, Mr./Ms. _____, the only reason I was calling was to set an appointment. Would <TIME> <DATE> at your office be okay?"

REQUESTS LITERATURE

"There's more I can show you about the success customers have had in similar projects we worked on for them. Can we just get together? How about <TIME> <DATE> at your office? I'll bring information you can keep."

THE ANSWER IS STILL NO

"Thank you for your consideration, Mr./Ms. _____. Have a great day."

Sample scripts for messages

When leaving messages, you must say something meaningful in an even shorter text that will elicit a positive response in the form of a returned call. There are a couple of situations in which you may need to leave messages (e.g., secretary or voice mail).

LEAVING A MESSAGE (SECRETARY OR VOICE MAIL)

"I'm <YOUR NAME> from <COMPANY NAME>. My phone number is <YOUR PHONE/CELL NUMBER>. I'm calling about <STATE PROJECT OR SERVICE TYPE FROM REFERENCEABLE CUSTOMER>."

Your response when the person calls back should be:

"Thanks for calling me back. The reason I called you is that we recently did a project with <REFERENCEABLE CUSTOMER>. The project's success may be of interest to you. ... {PERSON RESPONDS} ... Let's get together to discuss your project. How about <TIME> <DATE> at your office?"

LEAVING A MESSAGE BASED ON A REFERRAL

"I'm <YOUR NAME> from <COMPANY NAME>. My phone number is <YOUR PHONE/CELL NUMBER>. Please call me in reference to <STATE REFERRING PERSON'S NAME>."

Your response when the person calls back should be:

"Thanks for calling me back. The reason I called you is that I recently talked with <STATE REFERRING PERSON'S NAME>. They recommended that I call you about <STATE TOPIC>. ... {PERSON RESPONDS} ... Then we really should meet, because we've worked on similar projects very successfully for other firms. How about <TIME> <DATE> at your office?"

Sample script for call backs

Sometimes when you get through to a person and things seem to be going well, something happens and the person you called asks you to call back so you can finish the conversation. This is a good sign, because the person still has interest and may want to pursue things further with a meeting. You have likely reached this point because you have done well with your pitch so far, and the person you called sees something worthwhile. You now have time to prepare for a "call back" conversation—one that should result in the scheduling of a meeting.

Make sure you get an idea about when to call back, whether it is the same day, next week, in 30 days, in 90 days, or whatever. This way you will know they are committed to talking with you again. And if you call a little early, that may be all the better, especially if you are to call back months from now. The person may just need some time to work out something but does not know exactly how much, so you can at least give that person some "space" to do that.

Here's a sample script for such a call. After identifying yourself and reconnecting to the previous conversation, say:

"You know, I was just thinking about you as I <GIVE ACTUAL CIRCUMSTANCE>. I'll be in your area on <DATE>, and I thought we could get together...."

REFERENCE

Schiffman, S. (1999). *Cold calling techniques (that really work!)* (4th ed.). Adams Media Corp.

C

APPENDIX C
OBSERVATIONS ABOUT AGENCY AND NONAGENCY WRITING EXAMS

BASICS

- All exams complement an interview for a job.
- All exams measure your writing skills—content, reasoning, interest, accuracy, organization, style, grammar, spelling, formatting, etc.
- All exams measure your PR skills and thinking (cases and genres).
- All exams are timed to some extent.
- All exams are open book for AP style (*make sure you have yours!*)
- All exams require detailed knowledge about the firm.
- Some exams may restrict you from using the Internet.
- Some exams may ask about current events/news and their effects on clients/the company.
- Exams may include analytics problems.
- Exams may be done by e-mail or on site.

GENERAL TOPICS

- Company/organization (agency or nonagency)
  - History
  - Business (brands, markets, customers, industry[ies], competitors)
  - News and current events (prominent; possibly connect with organization and its stakeholders)
  - Areas of company that interest you and why

- Research
  - Secondary sources that could be used and why (based on a scenario)
  - Methodologies that could be used and why (based on a scenario)

- Writing
  - Creative and concise language used in tune with conventional purposes (persuasion, education, celebration, information, commiseration, etc.)

- Technical language use (editing, conciseness, reasoning, organization, accuracy, interest, vocabulary, tone, audience appropriateness, grammar, punctuation, AP style, spelling, formatting, proofreading, etc.)
- Focuses on both content creation and content improvement
- Correctness and effectiveness sought (includes use of PR discourse genres)
- Media savviness
  - Traditional media (organizations, key personnel, content areas, audiences targeted)
  - Digital media (organizations, key personnel, content areas, audiences targeted)
  - Trends across all media and implications for PR strategy and practice (PESO: paid, earned, shared, and owned media)
  - Research sources for media and choosing best media for situations/purposes
  - Pitching stories to journalists working in any medium (e-mail, letter, or phone script)
- Problem solving and decision-making
  - Scenario-based examples of realistic situations
  - Strategic planning (research, situation analysis, message design, objectives, execution, and evaluation)
  - Strong, sound answers and articulate defense sought
- Data analysis and presentation
  - Quantitative data in a scenario's context
  - Identification and presentation of salient patterns and explanation of their importance
- You
  - Personal communication habits (analog and digital media created, used, followed)
  - Brands, apps, and trends that matter to you and why
  - Experiences related to career and company that reveal who you are professionally
  - Interests that you have that reveal who you are personally
  - Self-definition/-description

INDEX

Note: Entries in *italics* refer to figures.